THE POLITICAL ECONOMY OF NEW
AND OLD INDUSTRIAL COUNTRIES

Butterworths Studies in International Political Economy will present new work, from a multinational stable of authors, on major issues, theoretical and practical, in the international political economy.

General Editor

Susan Strange, Professor of International Relations, London School of Economics and Political Science, England

Consulting Editors

Ladd Hollist, Director, Program for International Political Economy Research, University of Southern California, USA

Karl Kaiser, Director, Research Institute of the German Society for Foreign Affairs, Bonn, and Professor of Political Science, University of Cologne, West Germany

William Leohr, Graduate School of International Studies, University of Denver, USA

Joseph Nye, Professor of Government, Harvard University, USA

Forthcoming Titles

The East European Economies in the 1970s
France in the Troubled World Economy
War, Trade and Regime Formation
Japan and Western Europe: Conflict and Cooperation
Defence, Technology and International Integration
International Political Economy – A Text
Economic Issues and Political Conflict: US – Latin American Relations

The Political Economy of New and Old Industrial Countries

Edited by
Christopher Saunders

Sussex European Research Centre
University of Sussex

Butterworths

London   Boston   Durban   Sydney   Toronto   Wellington

First published 1981

© Butterworth & Co (Publishers) Ltd 1981

British Library Cataloguing in Publication Data

The political economy of new and old industrial
   countries.
   1. Economic policy – Congresses
   I. Saunders, Christopher
   330.9   HD82   80-41938

   ISBN 0-408-10774-X

Photoset by Butterworths Litho Preparation Department
Printed in England by Redwood Burn Ltd.

Acknowledgements

The Sussex European Research Centre is grateful to the United States Mission to the European Economic Community for substantial assistance in financing the preparation of this book and the organizing of an international conference (as described in the Appendix) to discuss the chapters in draft.

Acknowledgements

Contents

Abbreviations

CPE   Centrally planned economies
DAC   Development Assistance Committee (of OECD)
EEC   European Economic Community
GSP   Generalized System of Preferences
MFA   Multi Fibre Arrangement
MTN   Multilateral Tariff Negotiations
NICs   New(ly) Industrial(izing) Countries
OECD   Organization for Economic Cooperation and Development
OPEC   Organization of Petroleum Exporting Countries
SITC   Standard International Trade Classification (of United Nations)
UNIDO United Nations Industrial Development Organization

Statistical conventions

–	nil or negligible
. .	not available
billion	thousand million
ton (or tonne)	metric ton

Introduction and selective summary

Christopher Saunders*

This book brings together a series of authoritative studies of the problems posed by the recent, and continuing, spread of industrial power in the world economy, from its historical centres in Europe, North America and, later, Japan, to a number of nations in the rest of the world. The focus of attention is thus the economic, social and political influence of what have come to be known as the 'new industrial countries' – a concept which, even if ill-defined (as shown below) is familiar enough for the book to use throughout, for brevity, the convenient acronym 'the NICs'.

The geographical spread of industry – the (so to speak) 'continuous creation' of new industrial competitors to the old centres of production and trade – is, of course, nothing new. Thus authors have drawn upon economic history for their analyses of the recent past and their forecasts of expectations and recommendations for the 1980s and early 1990s. It is hoped that the book will serve to cast new light on the following topics:

(1) how the international system is changing and how the NICs fit into the system;
(2) comparisons of the development strategies (so far as conscious 'strategies' can be said to exist) of the new with the old industrial countries;
(3) the appropriate national, regional and international policies to meet the continuously evolving economic situation in the world; and
(4) common assumptions about the emergence of the NICs and the need for new directions of enquiry.

It should be made clear that the book is essentially about the NICs and about the present and future interaction between their economic progress and the economic progress of the older industrial economies. Most authors touch only rather incidentally on other aspects of the world-wide problems of economic development. This does not necessarily mean that progressive industrialization on the historical pattern is the *only* path for economic and social development.

Further, most of the analyses are concerned essentially with the interaction between the market economy NICs and the industrial (or 'Western')

* Sussex European Research Centre, University of Sussex

1

market economies. It is recognized at the same time that the European socialist countries are playing, and may play in future, an increasing role on the world's industrial stage; so may other socialist countries, including China, which have so far exercised only a peripheral influence on the economies of most of the rest of the world.

Who are the NICs?

The NICs do not, as yet, constitute an officially recognized, statistical category of economies and it will be found that different authors in this book, as elsewhere, use different groupings.

Probably it is the OECD which has done most to publicize the concept. In its important report, *The Impact of the Newly Industrializing Countries*[1], the OECD selects from what it describes as the 'dynamic continuum' of developing economies, 10 countries for its tentative and admittedly arbitrary analysis:

> In *Southern Europe*: Greece, Portugal, Spain and Yugoslavia
> In *Latin America*: Brazil and Mexico
> In *East Asia*: Hong Kong, South Korea, Singapore and Taiwan

As **Plessz** points out (ch. 10, section 10.2), in a critical discussion of what countries might qualify, the OECD has adopted the criteria that to become a NIC 'a country needs, at least, a large urban labour force, a class of local entrepreneurs, political stability and, most important, outward-looking or export-oriented growth policies'. And the OECD report says that 'apart from a rapid penetration of world markets for manufactures, the NICs tend to have two features in common: a rising share of industrial employment and an increase in real GDP per capita relative to the more advanced industrial countries'[2]. The 10 countries listed above are the countries obviously qualifying as NICs and, from the vital point of view of involvement in international trade in manufactures, account for about 80 per cent of manufactured exports from all developing countries (however developing countries, in their turn, may be defined). Of this 80 per cent, the four East Asian NICs–the redoubtable 'Gang of Four' – account for over half[3]. But others could claim entry. In particular, there is India, to which ch. 8 **(Balasubramanyan)** is devoted. As this author points out, India's industrialization began a long time ago. What is new is India's emergence with a diversified industrial structure and as an exporter not only of textiles but of engineering goods, despite rather moderate growth of GNP by comparison with other NICs and despite hesitations in embarking upon export-oriented growth in general. Nevertheless, India's exports of manufactures to OECD countries are not very different, in dollar value, from those of Brazil. In ch. 1, **Stecher** also includes some detailed analysis of India's comparative export performance.

Other possible candidates might include, for example, Argentina, Malaysia, Pakistan, Philippines and Israel, all with exports of manufactures of over half a billion dollars (in 1976). And the classification could be stretched further: as pointed out by **Hughes** (ch. 5, section 5.2) more than 30 developing countries were exporting over $100 million of manufactures in the early 1970s, and others – such as Malta and Mauritius – are rapidly becoming significant exporters. Moreover, as is noted above, some of the European socialist countries – notably Bulgaria, Romania, Poland and Hungary – share many characteristics with the southern European market economies in rates of industrial growth and increasing foreign trade dependence. However, this is not the place to design or apply a new definition of NICs. The purpose is only to point out that any definition must be arbitrary and, as the world moves forward, shifting.

By way of background, *Tables I.1* and *I.2* provide a summary record of export performance in major groups of manufactures, and economic growth, for the OECD Ten and six other countries which might qualify as NICs. The tables illustrate the considerable diversity among the NICs.

- While textiles, clothing and footwear still comprise a large proportion of NIC exports of manufactures nearly everywhere, these 'traditional' exports by no means dominate the export patterns of 1977. The three product groups nowhere comprise much more than 40 per cent of total manufactured exports (except in Pakistan); the median proportion is 21 per cent.

- On the other hand, exports of machinery and transport equipment (mainly machinery) have come to take a leading place – approaching 40 per cent or more of total manufactured exports in a few NICs (Brazil, Singapore, Yugoslavia, Spain, Argentina) – although only beginning to make an appearance in others (Greece, India, Pakistan, Malaysia). The median proportion is 22 per cent – slightly greater than the percentage of the three 'traditional' export groups.

- The growth rates of manufactured exports from the NICs in the 1970s (*Table 5.2*) mostly appear very fast – up to 46 per cent a year for South Korea with a median rate for all 16 countries of about 25 per cent a year. The figures are in current dollar values and thus embody a considerable inflationary element. The price element no doubt varies considerably between products and countries. But, as a rough guide, it may be observed that the UN index of dollar unit values for total manufactured exports from the principal OECD exporters, although a very doubtful indicator of 'world prices', about doubled in 1971–1977 – an increase of 12 per cent a year; and the current dollar value of total OECD exports of manufactures rose over the same period by about 19 per cent a year. These figures give some perspective to the observed rates of export expansion in the NICs.

Table I.1 New industrial countries: exports of total and selected manufactures, 1977 ($ million)

SITC category	Total manufactures 5–8	Textile yarns and fabrics 65	of which				
			Clothing 841	Footwear 851	Chemicals 5	Iron and steel 67	Machinery and transport equipment 7
OECD Ten							
Brazil	3077	383	101	174	184	263	1390
Mexico[a]	1156	126	33	11	252	56	249
Hong Kong	8950	825	2986	85	338	11	1558
Singapore	3543	192	211	..	294	108	2017[c]
South Korea	8534	1082	2062	488	226	392	1741
Taiwan	7951	922	1322	616	216	102	2108
Greece	1505	283	217	54	159	125	145
Portugal	1389	311	223	48	103	40	299
Spain	7357	357	209	480	654	718	2616
Yugoslavia[a]	3766	227	235	221	353	219	1363
Others							
Argentina[a]	975	32	38	6	140	89	406
Israel[a]	1872	54	121	..	261	10	274
India[a]	3018	743	334	38	119	367	315
Pakistan[b]	571	378	31	10	12	..	15
Malaysia[a]	1166	52	57	15	32	..	53
Philippines[a]	525	29	80	..	26	8	22

[a] 1976
[b] 1975
[c] n.b. includes substantial re-exports, and transit trade to and from Malaysia.

Note: Data relate to 'special exports' (i.e. excluding re-exports) except for Brazil ('national exports'), India, Malaysia, Mexico, Pakistan, Philippines and Singapore (all recording general exports).

Sources: UN Yearbook of International Trade Statistics, 1977, except for Taiwan (whose trade and other statistics are excluded from UN statistical publications since the admission of the People's Republic of China to the UN).

Table I.2 *New industrial countries: growth rates of total and selected exports and gross domestic product in the 1970s*

	Annual growth rate of exports (%) 1971–1977 in dollar values							Gross domestic product		
	Total manu-factures	Textile yarns and fabrics	Clothing (not fur)	Footwear	Chemicals	Iron and steel	Machinery and transport equipment	Per head (1977 $)	Annual growth rate (%) in volume (1970–1977) Total	Per head
SITC category	5–8	65	841	851	5	67	7			
OECD Ten										
Brazil	37.9	41.3	51.2	34.6	23.9	31.5	47.8	1360	9.8	6.7
Mexico[a]	14.4	26.4	23.6	24.8	18.9	0.7	7.4	1120	5.0	1.6
Hong Kong	22.3	17.8	22.2	6.0	19.2	11.8	28.6	2590	8.2	6.1
Singapore	34.9	18.0	29.2	..	30.1	31.0	42.4	2880	8.6	7.0
South Korea	46.1	41.0	37.6	53.4	57.4	58.9	64.6	820	10.4	8.2
Taiwan	29.5	24.3	21.8	50.6	33.3	13.1	34.0	1170	7.8	5.8
Greece	34.7	34.7	63.4	33.3	21.9	34.0	50.9	2810	5.0	4.3
Portugal	12.1	9.3	13.9	22.8	5.4	24.0	19.6	1890	5.3	4.5
Spain	26.4	21.8	21.7	18.5	29.1	35.0	27.1	3190	4.8	3.8
Yugoslavia[a]	23.0	23.1	18.7	26.9	22.0	29.3	24.8	1960	7.1	6.1
Others										
Argentina[a]	29.8	66.1	48.3	38.3	18.7	20.3	37.5	1730	2.9	1.6
Israel[a]	21.9	2.7	12.2	..	26.4	22.1	36.7	2850	5.9[c]	3.0[c]
India[a]	22.2	7.0	50.2	19.2	21.3	39.9	25.2	150	3.0	0.9
Pakistan[b]	11.5	7.7	42.1	9.0	31.3	..	15.6	190	3.6	0.5
Malaysia[a]	22.7	39.3	57.4	40.8	20.6	..	14.3	930	7.8	5.0
Philippines[a]	44.5	33.2	157.6	..	32.6	-1.0	55.3	450	6.4	3.6

[a] Exports 1971–1976
[b] Exports 1971–1975
[c] 1970–1976

Sources: For exports, as in Table I.1. For GDP, World Bank, *World Development Report*, 1979, Annex Tables

- Finally, can any clear association be found among the 16 countries between the rates of growth of manufactured exports and of gross domestic product? From *Table I.2*, a certain, but weak, positive correlation can be calculated (a Spearman rank correlation coefficient of 0.5, significant at 95 per cent probability). However, the big differences in rank orders are few: Greece, Argentina and the Philippines show high rates of growth in manufactured exports, although rather low rates of GDP growth: Hong Kong experienced rather slow export growth compared with its fast GDP growth. For the remaining 12 countries, the correlation is good (rank correlation 0.8), which may give a little support, although not of course conclusive in itself, to the proposition, discussed in several chapters, that export expansion is intimately linked with successful economic performance – whichever way the chain of causation runs.

Structure of the discussion

The book has a fivefold structure:

Part I   Four chapters (1–4) deal with the nature of the new industrial countries; and particularly with the differing emphasis in theories of economic development on 'diffusion' and 'dependency' as explanations of growth (**Stecher, Aujac, Campos/Valentino** and **Kreye**).

Part II   Two chapters (5 and 6) concentrate on the place of the NICs, and of their relations with the old industrial countries, in the world economy. (**Hughes** takes a global outlook on trends in production, trade, finance and economic policies; and **Shepherd** analyses developments in two industrial sectors – textiles/clothing and motor cars – where the interaction between old and new producers is of particular importance for the future.)

Part III   Three chapters (7–9) written by nationals of the countries concerned are intended as case studies of progress and policies in three NICs – South Korea, India and Brazil (**Kim, Balasubramanyan** and **Campos/ Valentino**).

Part IV   Three chapters (10–12) deal with the responses to the emergence of the NICs made in three major established centres of world industry – Western Europe, North America and Japan (**Plessz, Baldwin/Bale** and **Okumura**).

Part V   A final chapter (13) takes a general view of the interactions between the old and new industrial economies, leading to a consideration of the prospects for more hopeful ways of 'managing' the international system (**Hager**).

The following pages cannot claim to be anything like a summary of the rich material in the rest of the book. It is only a selective guide to some of the issues with which the authors deal. It reflects the impressions of the editor who hopes it may not do excessive violence to the authors' presentations. The reader should bear in mind that the papers were written in late 1979 or early 1980; by the time of publication, some expectations and forecasts may inevitably have been overtaken by events.

Part I   The nature of the new industrial countries: dependency or diffusion?

The central theme is the nature of the conditions which determine the emergence of societies into the world's industrial economy. The argument can hinge on two broad (and not, as will become clear, mutually exclusive) interpretations of the development process, applicable both to the historical experience of the older industrial countries and to more recent experience in the Third World.

What is described as the 'diffusionist' viewpoint puts most emphasis on the ability of governments and of the leading forces within the economy and society to use the opportunities presented by the international environment to pursue appropriate economic policies. In a sense, the diffusionist interpretation comes close to a 'self-generating' concept of development, although one element in it must be the successful absorption of what can be learnt from more fully developed societies. This in turn is related to the cultural, political and social structure of the society. Thus it can be suggested that the successful economic performance of the Sinic societies of East Asia, as compared with that of many parts of Latin America, or Africa, or some other parts of Asia, is to be explained by the great differences – extending over centuries – in cultural, political and social development.

The 'dependence' interpretation, by contrast, stresses the spreading internationalization of the production patterns, technologies and financial resources built up in the already established industrial societies of the West. On this view, economic development – and in particular industrialization – in the Third World depends upon the injection of Western systems into Third World societies whether by investment or by the operations of transnational enterprises or by the opening-up, mainly on Western initiative, of trading channels. The essence of dependence is that the new systems not only derive from the advanced societies, but are instilled with the primary objectives of serving the interests of those societies. Historically, this dependence has often been reinforced by the exercise of political authority, or at least of political influence, by the dominant nations of the West. It is clear enough that the two forms, so far as they can be distinguished, must affect both the patterns of development in the newly emerging societies and the pattern of their economic relationships with the older industrial nations.

Three of the chapters contributing to this discussion can be regarded as stressing various strands in the 'diffusionist' interpretation, although probably none of them would claim whole-hearted allegiance to this viewpoint.

Thus **Stecher** (Chapter 1) is concerned chiefly with the development of economic policies within the NICs during the last 30 years. He emphasizes the transition in the more successful performers from import-substituting strategies in the 1950s, to the subsequent export-oriented strategies, expressed in government measures of assistance to export industries. He notes also the distinction between rather sporadic and unselective export aids on the one hand, and the more systematic industrial strategies, pursued particularly in South Korea and Taiwan, with a view to make use, by specialization, of a country's existing, and, also, potential, comparative advantages. This author, like many others, comments strongly on the disadvantageous side-effects of import-substitution, despite the growing protectionism in the NIC markets.

A statistical analysis of the factors associated with expanding manufactured exports differentiates between two groups of the NICs surveyed. In some countries (South Korea, Singapore and Taiwan) the main factor appears to have been increasing competitiveness, expressed as rising shares of world markets – which could be regarded as supporting the diffusionist interpretation. By contrast, in other countries (Brazil, Hong Kong, India, Mexico) the expansion of exports is to a much greater extent associated with the general trend of world import demand – a finding which might come closer to one aspect of the 'dependency' viewpoint – as it suggests that the 'pull' of the market plays a larger role than the 'push' from within the exporting country.

The nature of the development process – in fact the question whether development, and particularly industrialization, occurs at all – depends on the whole historical background of the country concerned. **Aujac** (ch. 2), taking us back into history, stresses the profound importance of long-standing cultural, social and political structures in creating favourable (or unfavourable) conditions for industrialization and the form and pace which industrialization takes. He uses the examples of industrial development in France and Japan – in some ways analogous, in others contrasting – to show the influence of what he describes as the 'general social order' inherited from historical experience and, in his view, remarkably persistent. In Japan, the social order was mobilized to absorb and encourage the transformation of Japan into a leading industrial power; in France, the persistence of important elements of the old social order – even of that of pre-Revolutionary days – acted as a brake, at least until recently, on the pressures for industrial progress. This interpretation, which concentrates on internal factors in development, has significant implications, in Aujac's view, for economic progress in Third World countries – implications which he illustrates by the examples of Brazil, where the transformation of several divergent social groups into an organized whole is occurring, but only slowly; and of the Ivory Coast, where the problems of integrating a nascent industrialization into a traditional social order without destroying the established living society are being met by a state power anxious for modernization.

In a rather different approach to the spread of industrialization, **Campos** and **Valentino** (ch. 3) stress the variety of valid interpretations of the process of industrialization. They suggest that the contrast between dependent and independent development has resulted in a conceptual blurring of the real issues of development and fails to 'explain why some dependent countries are rich and others poor'. They support the view that development is not a single path but 'a complex network of routes' – an eclectic view confirmed by the same authors' account of Brazilian development (ch. 9). Moreover, in discussing the dependency interpretation, **Campos** and **Valentino** point to the 'reverse dependency' of the other industrial economies on the rest of the world.

By contrast with these diffusionist, or eclectic, approaches **Kreye** (ch. 4) insists strongly on the dependency aspect. He holds that industrialization of developing countries, when it has occurred, is the result of the 'transnational organization of production in an integrated economic system which remains dominantly a capitalist one'; and that both import-substitution and export production in the NICs are predominantly the result of the profit-seeking activities of the transnational enterprises based in the advanced industrial countries. He points out that it is enterprises and not 'countries' which initiate and control economic activities, and it cannot be expected that the interests of enterprises – especially of those controlled from abroad – should coincide either with the building up of an integrated and complex industrial structure in a developing country or with the reduction of poverty, malnutrition and the necessary amelioration of social conditions. Hence he takes a fairly gloomy view of the prospects for continued industrial development and growth of industrial employment in the majority of Third World countries, especially as capital-intensive technological progress in modern industries is likely to reduce the incentives to international enterprises to locate production in low-wage countries.

Part II   *The NICs in the world economy*

Hughes (ch. 5) looks broadly at the entire subject: she reviews the major trends of production and trade during the last 20 years in the major country groups of the world economy and of the economic relations between the groups. The conventional groupings of countries are, as she points out, essential for summary analysis but, more importantly, reflect political convenience rather than a real homogeneity. Development is a continuum in geographical and in temporal terms. The gaps in standard of living and in economic performance between a country 'just emerging from primitive agricultural production and a "new" industrial country such as Spain or Singapore are much greater than those between the latter and the "old" industrial countries'.

This world-wide review leads into a discussion of prospects for the 1980s based on the implications of two alternative scenarios, symbolized as the '2 per cent future' and the '4 per cent plus future' (the first relates roughly to the growth rates of GNP in the industrial market economies during the pre-World War II period; the second to the growth rates required in the same economies for something like full employment and comparable with performance in the 1950s and 1960s). Current pessimism among the prognosticators, in the author's view, appears to be causing them to move towards favouring the '2 per cent' scenario, rationalized in some cases by visions of a leisure-oriented and non-materialistic society, or justified, in other cases, by the impossibility of sustaining faster growth without intolerable inflation, because of the prospect of continuously rising oil prices. This pessimistic outcome for growth would be accompanied, in her view, not only by increasing difficulties of economic and social management in the industral West but also by swelling pressures for protectionist policies. On the other hand, return to a '4 per cent plus' growth, although the prospects for it remain dim, appears highly attractive. The obstacles to its realization are principally 'ideological and political rather than economic', and particularly the difficulty of 'persuading vested interests to accept short-term sacrifices for long-term gains'.

What are the implications of these alternative scenarios for the developing countries – and particularly for the NICs? **Hughes** suggests that experience in the 1970s indicates, encouragingly, a diminishing dependence of the developing countries as a group, and especially of the larger economies, on rates of economic growth in the industrialized world; the fact that GNP in the developing countries as a whole grew during the 1970s at much the same rates as during the 1960s while growth rates in the industrial West slowed down may be quoted as evidence[4]. She further suggests that slow growth in the industrial countries could increase the pressure on developing countries to improve their own growth strategies. The moral is that although maintenance of satisfactory growth rates in the developing countries cannot be completely 'de-linked' from the performance of the industrial economies, the ways in which the developing countries can improve their performance by adapting their own domestic policies, even in the absence of much growth in the international economy, should be stressed. The further implication seems to be that fast growth in the older industrial countries is not a completely *necessary* condition for the progress of the developing world.

The more generalized discussion of strategies and prospects is developed in more detail by **Shepherd** (ch. 6) for two industrial groups that play a major role in the internationalization of manufacturing production and in the evolution of the structure of world trade: textiles and clothing and motor cars.

Textiles and clothing, particularly textiles, are the classic and long-standing case of the adjustment process – and of the difficulties caused by adjustment. The author describes the substantial degree of adjustment which has already occurred; between 1973 and 1978 alone employment declined by 10–25 per cent in each of the leading Western industrial countries including Japan (the decline representing around 1–3 per cent of total employment in manufacturing in the countries concerned). It is, however, significant that the greater part of these losses of employment have resulted from increases in labour productivity in the industries where growth of domestic demand in the Western countries is normally slow. Rising imports from NICs have played a comparatively small part – though a larger one in clothing than in textiles – and this is largely because of the restrictions applied under the Multi Fibre Arrangement and other protectionist measures. The strategies adopted in the industrial countries by governments and by firms are classified by **Shepherd** into the 'defensive' (essentially protectionist) and the 'offensive'; the latter include both rationalization of the organization and products of the industries and a measure of internationalization of production by investment, sub-contracting and outward-processing especially in Southern Europe, Eastern Europe and the other NICs. (It is significant that sub-contracting is generally concentrated on neighbouring countries, thus tending to reinforce *regional* integration.) However, strategies in the industrial countries, in these as in other 'sensitive' industries, are mostly a mixture of the defensive and offensive.

The motor car industry presents a somewhat different picture. The growing international organization and specialization of production has only recently begun to extend beyond the industrial countries, but may in time present increasingly substantial problems for the management of economic relations between the old and the new industrial centres. The industry is characterized – far more than textiles and clothing – by very substantial economies of scale; hence its increasingly oligopolistic structure into which Japan is the only major new entrant, as an important exporter, since World War II. The motor industry is also as clear a case as any of the dependence of production in the NICs on the strategy of the multinational producers and of the interaction between them and the host countries (the latter being able to insist on stipulations such as increasing proportions of use of locally manufactured components and thus to introduce a limited element of control over relations with the multinationals). Although small assembly plants have been set up in at least 100 developing countries – generally in some form of cooperation with foreign firms – South Korea is the only NIC in which an independent car industry has been established and thus to have embarked on the high-risk strategy of entering the world market.

Taking both industry groups together, **Shepherd** very tentatively classes the leading industrial countries according to the mix of defensive and offensive policies applied. At one end of the scale, Germany (in textiles and cars) and Japan (but only in textiles) have opted most clearly for positive adjustment and some liberalization of imports. At the other end, the UK has become more protectionist in both groups. In the middle, the US, France and Italy have protected textiles and clothing, but their car industries are undergoing competitive adaptation.

Part III   Prospects for the NICs: three country studies

We pass to case studies of three industrializing countries – South Korea, India and Brazil. Although not intended as a representative sample, these countries in fact illustrate different modes of development in varying economic, social and political circumstances, with diverse historical backgrounds and, in **Aujac's** terms, contrasting 'social orders'. They illustrate, too, differing mixtures of import-substituting and export-promoting strategies: Korea represents a classic case of very recent, rapid and export-oriented industrialization; India and Brazil – particularly India – are examples of the building of diversified industrial structures, mainly by various protective strategies, on old-established but originally somewhat narrow industrial foundations. Korea's recent success in penetrating world markets has been based on a firm outward-looking set of policies; in both Brazil, with its rapid economic growth, and in India, with less outstanding growth rates, great difficulties are met in weaning enterprises from reliance on well-protected domestic markets.

All three economies – like many others NICs – have begun in the late 1970s to meet new problems enforced by the rise in oil prices and by the less encouraging conditions of world demand. The need for reorientation of policies is coming to be recognized. Thus all three countries appear to have reached a certain turning point in their paths of development.

The remarkable transformation of **South Korea** (ch. 7), still a fairly typical low-income mainly agricultural economy in the early 1960s, is attributed by **Kim** to the deliberate strategy of expansion of labour-intensive manufactured exports (following a rather short period of import substitution in some consumer goods). The external environment – the rapid growth of international trade with increasing liberalization – was favourable; government policies, including an investment policy channelling savings into the development of export-related industry, together with the encouragement of entrepreneurial abilities, stimulated the rapid exploitation of the nation's latent comparative advantages.

In the early 1970s, the economy began to encounter difficulties: the prospect of a withdrawal of American troops led to the development of national defence industries, as well as reducing a useful inflow of dollars; the slowing down of world trade, the rise in oil prices, the growth of protectionism and increasing international competition in South Korea's main export lines, induced a diversification of production and exports towards machinery, electronics, ships, steel, and, as noted above, the creation of an export-oriented motor industry.

It has become clear that the strategy of development which has so far proved successful will not ensure continued progress in the more difficult circumstances expected for the 1980s. Although a long-term strategy has not yet been officially formulated, **Kim** outlines some main features of the policy reorientation required to maintain fast and balanced growth. These include:

(1) less direct concentration than in the past on export promotion ('the first engine of growth') and more emphasis on what he describes as the 'second engine of growth', namely improvements in social conditions and infrastructure, and the expansion of productive capacities for future export expansion in more advanced products;
(2) a restructuring of the financial machinery to induce an investment pattern in line with market forces, and removing the incentives (such as low preferential interest rates) to over-investment which have led to excess capacity in some heavy industries;
(3) encouragement of foreign investment, especially for the transfer of technology;
(4) more manpower training to make fuller use of Korea's potential comparative advantage in the high quality of its labour force; and
(5) the promotion of intra-industry specialization through foreign investment and joint ventures, to meet the threats of protectionism in foreign markets. In a plea for international cooperation in development, the author holds that Korea and the other NICs 'with their high growth potential, can serve as "growth points" for the world economy'.

By contrast with Korea, **India's** postwar industrial development, as analysed by **Balasubramanyan** (ch. 8) was based mainly on a strategy of import-substitution enforced by quotas and industrial licensing (although the limits of this strategy were approached in the early 1960s). The strategy succeeded in creating a well diversified industrial structure, with a mature capital goods sector. The pattern of exports has also shifted away from the long-established textile industries towards engineering, chemicals, steel and clothing; and in some areas there have been significant competitive successes. But despite various incentives, the overall growth of both old and new exports has been very modest in comparison with that in the East Asian NICs.

Is there any prospect that India could move in the 1980s into a significantly faster growth rate than the 'respectable' 3½ per cent a year achieved on average for the last 30 years? **Balasubramanyan** discusses the necessary conditions for faster growth. In his view, such a shift of gear would require a drastic move away from the inward-looking attitudes, based on a philosophy of self-reliance, which have characterized past development. This implies not only more measures for direct export promotion: 'much more important are attitudes towards the role of competition and market forces in the development process'. Development has been impeded not so much by the import-substitution strategy in itself as by restrictions on the private sector and an excess of 'bureaucratic decision-making' often leading to monopolistic practices and lack of dynamism in the application of India's considerable technological and entrepreneurial abilities. But economic performance could also be assisted by a more positive attitude towards collaborative foreign investment especially for the improvement of technology and for raising the quality of India's industrial products to world market standards. Mrs Gandhi's new government has not, at the time of writing, declared its economic strategy. The author believes that India has the potential to achieve the expansion of industrial exports necessary for more rapid economic and social progress. But he takes the view that although the growth of new export lines may continue at recent rates, India is unlikely to be willing to depart in a major way from the paths so far followed and so to emerge as a major exporter in the foreseeable future.

Brazilian industrialization, too, has been fostered by a highly protective strategy – although originally based upon the incomes generated by Brazil's outward-oriented response to the expansion of world demand for coffee (and, later, cotton) from the end of the nineteenth century. In ch. 9 **Campos** and **Valentino** display the various phases of the import-substitution strategies pursued. They note particularly how the logic of indiscriminate import substitution, while leading to fast industrial growth in quantitative terms, impeded the quality of production by depriving industry of the inputs and capital equipment needed for competitive development. These difficulties led to efforts to widen the industrial base by increased domestic production of capital goods and to diversify the exports of manufactures. To these aims could be added increased production for the basic needs of the population rather than of non-essential consumer goods. The promotion of non-traditional exports has been marked by some notable successes and by a big shift in Brazil's export structure. In these developments, foreign investment in Brazilian industry played an important but not, in the authors' view, a dominant part.

The period of the 'Brazilian miracle', from the mid-1960s to the mid-1970s, showed fast growth and a slowing down of the earlier rates of damaging inflation. But the successive increases of oil prices, in a particularly oil-intensive economy, together with the increasingly unfavourable international environment, exposed the weak points of the earlier strategies. Oil imports and the service of the large foreign debt threaten to eat up an alarming proportion of export revenue. As in other NICs, a reorientation of long-term strategy clearly became necessary. A new strategy of 'structural transformation' is in progress, aiming at maintenance of growth (rather than deflationary restraints), together with progressive improvement of the current balance by 'a combined effort of import restraint, import-substitution and export-diversification'. Features of the new long-term strategy include a better coordinated and more selective system of export promotion, based on more cooperation with the private sector and less reliance on government subsidies; and a new stress on the neglected improvement of agriculture including the important effort to expand sugar planting for production of alcohol fuel which is expected to save a substantial part of the oil import bill. The authors recognize that such strategies involve extensive additional investment, including more foreign participation for improving technology, and may imply a continuing strain on the balance of payments until they pay off.

Part IV Policy responses in the old industrial countries

The varying mixtures of import-substituting and export-promoting strategy as displayed in the three NICs can be matched by the varying and changing mixtures of protectionist and free trade policies – defensive and offensive strategies – adopted in the old industrial countries.

The three chapters in Part 4 are concerned with these policy issues in each of the major 'old' – but still dominant – industrial areas: Western Europe, North America and Japan. While the central theme is the economic relations between old and new, it is clear that these relationships are only one element in the problems of policy which the Western industrial countries have experienced in recent decades and will continue to meet in the 1980s and beyond. Nor can it be said that explicit and clear strategies for the 1980s have yet been formulated in many of the industrial countries.

In his analysis of **Western European** experience, policies and prospects, **Plessz** (ch. 10) displays a significant comparison between the three industrial areas. On the one hand, the influence of the NICs on the foreign trade in manufactures of Western Europe as a whole (although differing widely amongst countries and sectors) has been much less, in proportions of total trade, than on North America or Japan. This contrast applies to trade in both directions (it applies even if the Southern Europeans whose links with industrial Western Europe are naturally stronger than with North America or Japan are included among the NICs). On the other hand, in his view, the fears of NIC penetration of domestic markets and the various protectionist measures adopted to reduce it, have been, on the whole, stronger in most of

Western Europe than in North America or Japan. A number of explanations (not necessarily in order of importance) are offered for this apparent paradox:

(1) the moderate degree of NIC penetration is itself the result of the defensive actions taken;
(2) the Western European response has been aroused as much by success-ful NIC competition in third markets (remembering the example of Japanese expansion) as by penetration of European markets (to some extent, it is European protectionism which has reinforced the NICs' export efforts in other areas);
(3) positive responses – the shift of West European industry 'up-market' and into the industrial growth points – have obviously not been missing; yet 'the adjustment mechanism was blocked' within European manufacturing, especially after 1973, by the slow growth of demand, by occupational rigidities, and, indeed, by a certain 'growth pessimism' about the future, which strengthened the defensive preferences for 'a bird in the hand' over 'two in the bush';
(4) this negative reaction was reinforced by the strength of the business, labour and community interests concerned with maintaining what it was feasible to keep of the existing industrial structure; those con-cerned with the opening of new markets – including transnational corporations involved in Third World operations – have not been able to exercise a countervailing power against the protectionists to the same extent as in North America (see also **Baldwin/Bale**, ch. 11) or Japan.

All this, of course, is qualified by the wide range in the reactions of the individual West European countries and governments. As the author says, 'it would be a dangerous oversimplification to try to identify a single European "response" to the NIC "challenge"'.

Plessz sees, however, encouragement in the changing attitudes of Western European governments, despite their actual defensive measures: this has been expressed, for example, in the OECD discussions directed towards the formulation of 'Positive Adjustment Policies'. He suggests that the balance of interests and attitudes is changing; in particular, current economic conditions are arousing general unwillingness to accept the heavy budgetary and inflationary costs of excessive support of existing but not fully rewarding activities. Whether these more constructive trends will allow the integration of the industrial newcomers 'into the kind of mutual rela-tionships existing among major industrial countries' can be taken, in Plessz's view, as a 'test of the dynamism of Western capitalism'. As an alternative scenario, which might come about if Western European governments prove unable to control the internal pressures for maintaining a defensive stance, he suggests that the NICs might join in a series of regional 'growth poles' in which Western European countries, in their 'rapidly spreading mood of self-fulfilling growth pessimism' might have no place.

Baldwin and **Bale** (ch. 11) describe the variety of forms taken by policy responses to the high level of manufactured imports from the NICs into the **United States**, and to the lower but increasing level into **Canada**. (In the US, particularly, the gross import figures may exaggerate the actual effect on the US economy: because of the large extent of sub-contracting, off-shore assembly, etc. organized by US firms, the proportion of value added by the NICs themselves in the recorded imports from them may be relatively small.) On the whole, it appears that US protective measures – apart from the longer-term Multi Fibre Arrangement – are more often explicitly temporary, designed to 'buy time' for adjustment to market conditions, than the well-stocked armoury of Canadian measures which are particularly well-equipped. The more positive policies attracting attention are the systems of 'adjustment assistance' adopted in both countries in the early 1960s; these make provision for financial aids to firms and workers displaced by imports (not only imports from NICs). In comparison with those of the US, the Canadian programmes are designed to direct aid and advisory services to those firms which exhibit a capacity for effectively competing with imports, rather than simply to compensate for displacement. The fairly elaborate rules governing such assistance are described in some detail. The conditions for assistance were originally somewhat restricted in application, but have now been significantly eased. Nevertheless, the results in the US are summarized by the authors as 'modest and of marginal assistance to trade adjustment'.

Baldwin and **Bale**, taking up a theme which can apply to most industrial societies, ask why the merits of trade liberalization, despite widespread support among economists, have failed to achieve public support. They are not satisfied with the usual economists' explanation – namely that market imperfections, and especially lack of information, allow the vested interests of those producing for the domestic market and suffering substantial damage from imports to override politically the diffused, individually small, and not easily identifiable damage to consumers and exporters who might gain additional markets in the countries supplying the imports: nor are they satisfied with the implied remedies – better information, more perfect markets and countervailing political action by consumers.

As a politically more realistic explanation, the authors suggest that workers and consumers not directly damaged by imports put less weight on the diffused, but recognized, costs to themselves of specific protectionist measures than on the longer term dangers of allowing vulnerable industries to decline (another aspect of the case for 'a bird in the hand' rather than 'two in the bush'). Further, the dangers of liberalized imports may include a risk to their own jobs and incomes. Thus, protection of endangered sectors may be regarded as a kind of 'collective good', or a form of social insurance, the cost of which is justified on welfare grounds. If this is a fair representation of public attitudes, the authors suggest, then the realistic political approach to a liberal, commercial policy must improve positive adjustment strategies to prevent serious injury to particular groups 'as the cornerstone of trade policy rather than as an "afterthought" introduced to gain more support'.

The story of rapid structural change in **Japan** is well-known. **Okumura** (ch. 12) concentrates his attention mainly on an analysis of the part played in recent Japanese development by economic relations with the four East Asian NICs. From one angle, these four NICs may be regarded as export competitors with Japan – a second generation of Asian competitors following the Japanese pattern of penetration into world markets. In fact, as the author indicates, Japan has succeeded in keeping pace with the East Asian NICs in OECD markets. This parallel advance has been achieved by rapid adjustment of Japan's export structure; Japan has shifted from textiles and other consumer goods (including radios and household durables), as the NICs moved into these markets, to machinery and vehicles. From another angle there is the evolving pattern of direct relations between Japan and the Asian NICs accounting (in 1978) for 15 per cent of Japan's total exports but for only 7 per cent of her imports and thus contributing half of Japan's total trade surplus. In this trade, too, a clear division of labour emerges: Japan imports simpler and low-priced light industry products and exports more complex engineering products and industrial inputs.

The author describes two important features of the mechanism of the Japanese adjustment process – in which, of course, the effect of trade with the Asian NICs is only one element. The first is the rather systematic withdrawal from industries particularly affected by imports, in particular textiles and clothing but also simple consumer durables. In textiles, after some hesitation, the need for a permanent reduction of capacity has been accepted and embodied in a scrapping scheme supported by legislation; it is complemented by moves in the industry towards up-market specialization. (The freezing of shipbuilding capacity is another example but that is more a consequence of the collapse of world demand than of NIC competition.)

The second feature of the adjustment process is the rise in Japanese industries' direct investment abroad. Investment began with sales subsidiaries for Japanese exports, and spread into overseas production, particularly of the products vulnerable to import competition; it is often organized as 'co-production', some components being supplied from Japan, or in the form of specialization in coordinating overall production between home and overseas plants. As in Europe and America, Japan's industrial investment abroad has been criticized as 'exporting jobs' to the detriment of domestic industry. **Okumura** (ch. 12, section 12.4) has provided interesting and valuable new information on the activities of Japanese subsidiaries abroad. This shows, in particular, that the bulk (over 60 per cent) of Asian subsidiaries' sales go to the home market in the host countries, the rest being about equally divided between sales to Japan (mainly agricultural and mining products which Japan lacks) and to third markets. Moreover, these subsidiaries buy from Japan nearly half of their purchases. A 'boomerang' effect may exist but is probably less important, even for the Japanese economy itself, than the contribution made to industrial development of the host countries.

The author expects that the NICs' import penetration of the Japanese market will increase and that the Japanese government – despite some pressure for protection from the Japanese textile industry – will continue to take an attitude of 'benign neglect' (unless imports should reach proportions undermining smooth restructuring). Thus Japan's response, and the prospect of continued economic expansion, must rely largely on pushing forward on the 'frontiers of technology', e.g. into the information-oriented industries. At the same time, the author holds that Japanese industries can at least maintain their competitiveness in automobiles, in much of engineering, and in higher qualities of steel and chemicals. To smooth the 'inevitable structural transformation' – in new and old industrial economies generally – they urge a 'rational synchronization' of structural change, especially of large investment projects; this would require at least a full exchange of information and expectations between industrial policy-makers in both groups of countries. Recognizing that such exchanges at a world level would take long to establish, he suggests beginning on a regional scale; thus Japan could cooperate in formulating future development patterns with other countries in the Pacific area – an area which 'may well hold the best hope of fast expansion in the world economy in the 1980s'.

Part V   Can the old system work? Is a new one possible?

In ch. 13 **Hager** reflects on earlier chapters and sees a certain contradiction in approach. There is broad agreement on the purely statistical fact that the effect of NIC competition on total output and employment in the old industrial countries is so far only marginal – quite a minor element among the many economic problems facing these countries. Further, several authors regard this competition less as a 'threat' than as an opportunity for raising economic efficiency through an improved international division of labour as the circle of industrializing economies widens. Yet the tenor of the discussion indicates a widespread pessimism, induced perhaps by the increasing pressures for meeting the uncertainties of the future by defence rather than defiance, about the prospect that the opportunities will in fact be taken. Thus those who venture policy recommendations face a dilemma. They may, like the authors of some chapters, press hard for acceptance of the rational solutions long offered by economic theory for the progress of the world economy: the demolition of both external and domestic barriers to the free movement of goods and services and factors of production for instance. Or, taking into account the strength of the many resistances to such optimizing solutions, they may seek 'second-best' ways of accommodating national and international policy to political and social realities which may be irrational but are unlikely to go away.

As a first step towards expressing his own approach to a solution, **Hager** suggests a number of reasons (some also appearing in other chapters) for scepticism about the 'easy optimism' of the approach through general liberalization. Among them are:

- The small overall effect of NIC competition masks heavy imports in some individual products. The real fear derives from extrapolation of recent trends to a much stronger future impact and uncertainties about which sector this future impact will affect inhibits a confident industrial response.

- Reasonable expectations that total trade between old and new industrial countries will finally reach equilibrium mask the big disequilibria, which may well persist, for individual countries, thus increasing the obstacles to attaining an international consensus on policies of liberalization.

- The implicit assumption that trade liberalization simply represents an acceptance of inevitable market forces ignores the extent to which the expansion of NIC (and other countries') exports has itself been 'managed' by their deliberate policies (including subsidies); the appropriate response need not, therefore, be blind acceptance but a matter for political choice.

- Liberal acceptance of manufactured imports is not automatically a particularly unambiguous contribution to the much larger problems of Third World development. At the centre of these problems is the expansion of employment, to which the growth of manufactured exports to the old industrial countries cannot, in the best of circumstances, give more than marginal help.

- Recommendations that all the old industrial countries have to do is to 'shift resources' into high value-added, high technology, high wage and fast growth activities ignore the limited range of such activities and the limited employment which they offer. Such recommendations are rarely specific enough to be convincing, relying perhaps on the assumption that God (or appropriate demand elasticities) will provide a match between increasing employment opportunities in the new growth sectors and declining demand for labour elsewhere.

- Trade theories resting on the achievement of equilibrium by progressive international equalization of productivity wages are not wholly convincing. The old industrial countries are the *unionized* part of the world where labour oligopolies determine labour costs but are losing to other areas the scarcity value of education and skill.

Recognition of the realities of life, however, leads **Hager** to conclude that 'there is little alternative to trying the optimist approach for all that it is worth, until trade reaches higher levels and the doubts expressed. . . are settled one way or another'. The 'cold shower hypothesis' may work in facilitating adjustment. But, even then, alternative strategies are available which are not in conflict with a general 'commitment to the market'. He stresses the urgent need – especially in view of present expectations of slow growth – for the international community to 'be seen to tackle potential trade problems in a constructive manner'. He sees possibilities, even if they are regarded as 'second-best', in a common response defined as 'conditional adherence to free trade based on a shared concern for order which is ultimately political!'. This implies that while most trade will continue to be conducted within the GATT framework, departures from it will be necessary when margins of tolerance are reached. Such departures should certainly be minimized and be subject to international consultation.

The heart of the argument, for any single developing country, is that an export-led and NIC-type strategy which seems reasonable for the country in isolation may be seen as unrealistic when aggregated with the strategies of competing countries and when confronted with the limits on the capacity for adjustment of the hoped-for industrial markets. (Much the same can apply, *mutatis mutandis*, to strategies for an industrialized country.) International consultation, based on exchanges of information and expectations – especially for costly long-term investment projects – may be useful to avoid foreseeable shocks and incompatibilities. In particular, NICs – and potential NICs – have a strong interest in respecting the thresholds of tolerance if open markets are to be maintained. The value of such a mutual accommodation of strategies is recognized – if not fully applied – among OECD countries but needs to be extended much more widely. **Hager**, like **Okumura** (ch. 12), envisages, for example, the possibility of such an accomodation between a dynamic Pacific community and a stagnating Atlantic area.

The editor may be allowed a few concluding remarks, which do not attempt to cover the whole of the constructive debate.

One intention (as outlined at the beginning of the Introduction) was to define actual and likely future 'strategies' in both the old and new industrial countries and the consequences for relations between them. If this aim is not fully achieved, it is simply because clear strategies have not been evolved in many countries. It clearly emerges that the actions of governments and industrial organizations in the old industrial countries have been determined – as is inevitable – by conflicting pressures, internal and external. At the level of high principle, the prevailing attitude continues to be, for the most part, adherence to the liberalization of trade and acceptance of the need for long-term adjustment as the international economic landscape changes. In practice, this has become what **Hager** describes as 'conditional adherence to free trade'. It has been modified by the various internal pressures for resisting disturbances and by the common, if not universal, attitude of national governments that the game should be played according to the rules – but only so long as the rules are observed by all important players.

Thus differences of opinion about the correct policies to be pursued by the 'West' centre in part on the choice between the complete freeing of markets and the continuation of defensive interventions to hold back market forces; but it may be more important that they concern differences about what *mix* of acceptance of market forces and intervention is to be desired or, indeed, is practicable. 'Strategies' become pragmatic. In fact, tactics may seem to override strategy. But a built-in bias towards the free trade approach remains – even if described as 'managed free trade'. Again, the need to promote the long-term adjustment of the old economies to the entry of present and potential NICs on the market is also accepted (as Dr Johnson advised his friend who enthusiastically professed her 'acceptance of life', she couldn't really do otherwise). The issue is how long is long-term? 'Adjustment' involves a temporary social cost, and perhaps a net economic cost, which may or may not be offset by the long-term gains. Blind submission to market forces (whose long-term vigour may not be predictable) can cause economic as well as social waste. Moreover, what may be perceived as a 'market force' by one partner experiencing a sudden incursion of competitive imports, may in fact be a positive state-supported strategy, unjustified by pure economic considerations, on the part of the other. Is it necessarily rational on economic grounds even for a rich society to yield to the state-supported strategies of another (even a poor one)?

The answer must be that it depends on the circumstances. And these must include the farsightedness and objectivity of the policy-makers and their ability to consider not only direct economic consequences but also indirect social and economic gains and losses – 'externalities'. Policy-makers, whether in the public or private sector, can make errors. But 'market forces' are not always irreversible. It is doubtful whether any *general* answers can be given to these questions. Again, pragmatism must serve. The same point is made in the OECD report, *The Case for Positive Adjustment Policies* (referred to by **Plessz**, in ch. 10). There is no valid general case for or against government intervention. Solutions are essentially pragmatic, 'adjustment is not an end in itself, it is a means of increasing economic and social welfare'[5].

Similarly, the analysis of NIC experience and policies suggests that the choice between import-substitution and export-led growth is rarely clear. NIC policies, also, represent a mix, although the shift of emphasis towards export promotion, with varying degrees of success, is common enough. The difficulties of running the two horses in harness – a too well-fed import substitution horse impeding the pace of his partner – are obvious. Attention may be called, however, to one case which may justify at least temporary use of protection for the development of an export capacity. While the growth of manufactured exports from India has not been outstanding, there has been a striking expansion of the export of Indian technology (in know-how, licensing, turnkey factories, civil engineering and consultancy, especially to other developing countries): India is a leader among developing countries in this field. This expansion is attributed to deliberate efforts to protect and promote the assimilation and adaptation of foreign technology by Indian enterprises and to establish an independent technological base. This might not have occurred if the easier path of passively depending on a continuous flow of imported technologies, by licensing or direct investment, had been followed[6]. Successes in this less familiar opening for use of the unexploited technological capacity of developing countries have also been achieved by other NICs (e.g. Argentina, Brazil, Mexico, South Korea and Taiwan).

A second illustration of the difficulty of drawing a firm line between import-substituting and export-promoting strategies arises from the trend towards the expansion of intra-industry trade. In many advanced products, the growing complexity of the manufacturing process, coupled with the need for a large market to justify production, are together responsible for the expansion of intra-industry trade: it takes the form of manufacturing the components of a complex product – whether or not organized by trans-national enterprises – in a variety of locations, in some of which the local market would not be large enough for economic production. This means that concepts of specialization, of economies of scale and of the economic size of markets, must not be thought of simply in terms of nations, industries or final products.

There is a general consensus that the world-wide spread of industry, and the accompanying internationalization of industrial production, urgently requires a new thrust towards improved policy-management on the international level; moreover, this new thrust must concern business, labour and consumer interests as well as national governments. In particular, it is highly desirable to build up a continuing system of consultation and exchange of information about long-term policy intentions and expectations on a wider basis than that provided by existing international institutions. This is one way of smoothing the path towards integration of the young and the old partners in the world economy. NICs and potential NICs have a particular interest in the establishment of more effective, and multilaterally agreed, rules governing direct and indirect trade restrictions. Consultations based on a realistic appreciation of the pressures in both exporting and importing countries could diminish the ignorance and uncertainties which bedevil the possibilities of integration; they could also slow down the trend towards unilateral displays of protectionism.

Not too much can be expected in the short term. Plans and strategies cannot be harmonized if they do not exist, and if projections about the uncertain future of the world economy are no more than hopes – or fears. (It has been remarked that while policy-makers complain of their inability to formulate explicit strategies if economists refuse to commit themselves to forecasts, so economists declare themselves unable to forecast so long as policies remain indeterminate.) Individual nation-states can determine their own futures only within narrow limits. These constraints on effective policy-making can be loosened, but only if policies are much more firmly based than at present on the obvious truth of interdependence within the world economy.

References

1 Organization for Economic Cooperation and Development (OECD), *The Impact of the Newly Industrializing Countries on Production and Trade in Manufactures.* Paris, 1979.

2 Organization for Economic Cooperation and Development (OECD), *The Impact of the Newly Industrializing Countries on Production and Trade in Manufactures.* Paris, 1979.

3 Organization for Economic Cooperation and Development (OECD), *The Impact of the Newly Industrializing Countries on Production and Trade in Manufactures.* Paris, 1979.

4 See *Tables 5.1* and *5.2.*

5 Organization for Economic Cooperation and Development (OECD), 'Positive Adjustment Policies, some general issues'. CES/79.10, 2nd revision, para 12.

6 See S. Lall, *Developing Countries as Exporters of Technology.* Macmillan, London, forthcoming.

PART I

The nature of the new industrial countries: dependency or diffusion?

The role of economic policies

Bernd Stecher*

1.1 Introduction

Economists, at one time or another, have singled out a great variety of causes for underdevelopment and economic backwardness and have made various recommendations to policy-makers on how to improve the conditions for social and economic progress. Among these recommendations, appropriate policies for industrialization and international trade have been central. After several decades of experience of industrialization in many developing countries, there has emerged – as Keesing[1] well puts it – a considerable convergence of 'mainstream' expert views on what the policies ideally should be and on how – under given conditions specific to each country – improvements could be achieved. This statement does not preclude, however, occasional disagreements, even among these so-called 'mainstream' views – mainly when matters of application are discussed.

It is the purpose of this paper to review and assess the development process of the so-called newly industrializing countries (NICs) in relation to the policies that they chose. We do not propose to consider each NIC individually, but rather to examine the main thrust of their policies, and the differences and similarities between them, before assessing their effectiveness. We shall concentrate upon seven countries in the Third World: Brazil, Hong Kong, India[2], South Korea, Mexico, Singapore and Taiwan – which have been able to achieve higher growth rates of GDP and industrial output, to create employment opportunities more rapidly, and to increase import capacity more substantially, than the 'average developing country'; and even within the group of the NICs there have been considerable differences in performance (see *Table 1.1*).

This review is based upon the empirical findings of country studies carried out by various institutions, such as the OECD, the National Bureau of Economic Research and the World Bank; it draws especially on the results of a similar project carried out by the Kiel Institute[3]. The paper tries to summarize the postwar experience in economic policy-making without providing detailed case-by-case evidence. Nor have we attempted to com-

* Institute of World Economics, Kiel. I gratefully acknowledge helpful comments on an earlier draft by Juergen B. Donges, Ulrich Hiemenz and Dean Spinanger

Table 1.1 Growth performance and trade expansion in seven NICs, 1950–1977 (average annual growth rates, per cent)

	Period	Brazil	Hong Kong	India	South Korea	Mexico	Singapore	Taiwan
Real GDP	1960–1970	5.3	10.0	3.6	8.5	7.3	8.8	9.2
	1970–1976	9.8	8.2	3.0	10.4	5.0	8.6	7.7
Real GNP per capita	1950–1960	3.1	3.6	2.3	2.6	2.4	0.6	4.8
	1960–1970	4.8	6.4	1.2	7.3	3.0	7.5	6.2
	1970–1976	7.4	5.2	0.5	8.7	1.7	6.8	5.5
Labour productivity	1950–1960	3.4	5.1	2.9	3.1	3.0	..	5.2
	1960–1975	4.6	5.6	1.4	6.2	3.4	6.6	5.7
Manufactured exports[c]	1950–1960	3.0	6.5	-1.2	10.2[b]	2.9	1.8[a]	28.9
	1960–1975	34.4	16.7	8.5	57.6	19.8[d]	16.6	36.3
Total exports[c]	1950–1960	-0.6	5.2[a]	1.5	3.6	3.7	1.2	4.7
	1960–1970	5.0	12.7	3.1	35.2	3.3	4.2	23.7
	1970–1977	6.5	6.5	6.4	30.7	1.9	9.8	16.7

[a] 1956–1960
[b] 1952–1960
[c] SITC 5–8, excluding 67 + 68
[d] 1960–1974

Source: United Nations, Commodity Trade Statistics, various issues
International Bank for Reconstruction and Development, World Tables, 1976, Washington, World Development Report, World Bank Atlas, Washington, 1978
International Monetary Fund, International Financial Statistics, various issues
J. B. Donges and L. Müller-Ohlsen, Außenwirtschaftsstrategien und Industrialisierung in Entwicklungsländern, Kieler Studien 157, Tübingen, 1978

pare systematically the development of the NICs with the emergence of industrial countries during the last century (although this might afford a rather interesting test of parallelism in history); only occasionally has industrialization been considered in a historical perspective.

The pragmatic and non-historical approach has been preferred for several reasons. The economic and political environment of the eighteenth and nineteenth century differed fundamentally from post World War II conditions. Most of the developing countries of today were politically unimportant and economically far behind the industrialized countries: industrialization in the eighteenth and nineteenth centuries concerned only the political and economic giants of that time. Except for Great Britain, the degree of development within the group did not differ considerably, thus reducing the potential for imitation even more. Furthermore, those countries about to embark upon industrialization were political competitors, challenging Britain for political dominance. Consequently the industrialization policies adopted were not really comparable with the deliberate import substitution policies of the NICs; autarky was pursued, but the motivation was to reduce a dependency which had political effects.

Although this review – for the sake of analysis – categorizes the respective policies pursued as being either predominantly inward- or predominantly outward-looking, we do not intend to embark again on the old dispute of import substitution versus export promotion policies; both strategies can be regarded as being alternative ways of saving or earning foreign exchange. The purpose is, rather, to see whether inherent characteristics of the one or the other policy are responsible for significant differences in performance.

1.2 Basic strategy decisions

Until the early 1930s there was little disagreement among economists or policy-makers that the system of international division of labour then prevailing – industrial countries producing manufactures and developing countries supplying primary commodities – was more or less equally beneficial for both groups; this is at least suggested by the evidence of similar growth rates for exports of manufactures and of primary commodities between 1876 and 1929[4]. After the Great Depression, the structure of world trade changed to the disadvantage of the developing countries. Not only did the volume growth of primary commodity exports, except for oil, show a less favourable trend than that for manufactures, but also the developing countries' terms of trade deteriorated – a deterioration only temporarily interrupted by World War II and the Korean war.

The fall in import capacity, the increase in the real burden of servicing foreign debt and the war-caused shortage in the supply of manufactured goods stimulated the urge for economic independence in most developing countries. Industrialization seemed the appropriate course because it not only promised self-sufficiency for nations that had just regained political sovereignty, but it also offered external economies accruing from technical progress – as the history of the old industrial countries showed. Except for some Latin American countries that had already started to industrialize in the 1930s, most developing countries concentrated their efforts at industrialization in the late 1950s and early 1960s.

Broadly speaking, developing countries can choose between two approaches to industrialization: an import-substitution policy under which the respective country turns away from the international division of labour or an outward-looking policy of diversifying the structure of exports. The term 'import-substitution' has been bandied about freely by economists and policy-makers alike. It has not always been clear that expanding domestic production of particular goods (competing with imports) beyond the rate of increase of internal demand (thus reducing the share of imports in total supply) can be the result either of a 'normal' structural change (accompanying economic growth) or of deliberate policy. In the first case one could speak of a 'natural' import-substitution, or of what Hirschman has called 'import-swallowing': the increase in per capita income tends to widen the domestic market and at the same time changes the demand pattern. This implies that conditions for profitable private domestic production improve, thus stimulating domestic investment. The expansion of import-competing domestic production need not be stimulated by incentives but can follow the market, provided that there are domestic (or foreign) entrepreneurs willing to bear the risk of succumbing to competition from foreign suppliers. Import-substitution can also take the form of a deliberate policy to encourage industrialization; this involves considerable government intervention.

Until the early 1960s there was a rather wide consensus among economists, policy-makers in developing countries and experts in international organizations that a deliberate import-substitution policy was the appropriate route for industrialization in developing countries. This recommendation was followed by a majority of the developing countries. The first United Nations Conference on Trade and Development in 1964 (UNCTAD I) marks a turning point in international discussions on the 'appropriate' industrialization strategy. People became more and more convinced that markets closed by protective walls have not very often favoured long-term prospects of economic development, and that outward-looking policies should be pursued instead. Although the idea of an export-oriented industrialization was given considerable attention in the continuing discussions, as well as being implemented in actual policies, it has never remained undisputed; even free traders have argued that an export-oriented approach would not be feasible for countries at an initial phase of their development: that is, countries without infrastructure and without sufficient spirit of enterprise among potential industrialists, such a spirit being especially necessary for the extremely risky export business[5].

Except for Hong Kong and Singapore, the industrialization of the countries reviewed reveals a great deal of similarity. This holds true not only of the spontaneous nature of industrialization during its early phase (resembling what happened in the old industrial countries during the late eighteenth and early nineteenth centuries); it applies to the underlying policies during the deliberate phase of industrialization and also to the emphasis initially placed on import-substituting activities and later on transferred to the export of manufactured products[6]. Import-substitution, however, is not enough to provide an adequate growth stimulus to the economy in the medium and long run, because its dynamism depends on the growth rate of domestic demand which in most developing countries is relatively slow.

In recognizing the limited growth potential of this kind of import-substitution, political authorities started to strengthen industrial growth by deliberately pursuing supply-oriented decisions. The development plans of the 1950s reveal considerable sensitivity to the need for incentives to investment in those industrial activities where the respective country's comparative advantage seemed most likely to lie; but the policies actually pursued in those years were scarcely based on the criteria for efficient specialization in manufactures. In most of the countries reviewed, there was in the 1950s a lack of coordinated industrialization policies. The measures taken were the result of sequential decision-making, sometimes by politically competing authorities, in response to shifting circumstances[7]; the measures were applied sporadically rather than steadily, very often in the form of emergency actions. In some countries, this has led in effect to a rather selective encouragement of industrial activities; in others, incentives were granted across the board, following the motto 'what can technically be produced has to be produced'. Only Taiwan and South Korea seem to have followed a more rational strategy, because they tried to concentrate on policies corresponding to their comparative advantages, i.e. on light and relatively labour-intensive industrial activities: these are industries where production – in spite of low output volumes – could be run reasonably efficiently because of the low capital requirements.

This is the general pattern of early industrialization by import-substitution (although from sometimes different motives) by which the old industrial countries, including Japan, developed. The only exception is Britain, which led the world economy of the nineteenth century. Among the NICs reviewed here, Hong Kong and Singapore (in 1965 after her separation from Malaysia) do not fit the pattern; in these countries, policy-makers – in view of the narrow domestic market – decided not to follow an import substitution policy but rather tried to orient manufacturing industry towards the world market[8].

1.3 Salient features of import-substitution policies

In accordance with this general strategy choice, governments in most of the NICs under review relied greatly on the restriction of manufactured imports as a device to encourage industrialization. The principal instruments of import restriction have been tariffs, import-licensing and a system of multiple exchange rates. The level of protection was on average higher than that prevailing in most developed countries when they were in their initial phase of industrialization. A glance at the history of protection – briefly recorded in the well known study by Little, Scitovsky and Scott – shows that apart from a very few countries (Russia, United States, Spain and Portugal) nominal tariff protection during the nineteenth and early twentieth centuries was far less than might have been justified economically by welfare-theoretical arguments[9]. Japan's economic history in particular is an example of industrialization with negligible tariff protection.

The structure of nominal protection in the NICs shows a high degree of similarity: highest tariff on consumer goods, lower for intermediate products and lowest for capital goods. This refers only to nominal rates of tariff. To assess the encouragement of a specific industrial activity it is insufficient, however, to consider only the amount by which a tariff raises the price of the industry's product. What matters for resource allocation is the extent to which the value added, in domestic prices, exceeds the value added at world prices. This so-called effective protection is an increasing function of the nominal tariff on the output and a decreasing function of input tariffs, given the amount of value added; for any nominal tariff the effective protection is greater the smaller the proportion of value added in a particular industry[10]. Other things being equal, the allocation of resources among industries will depend on the structure of effective rates of protection: between any two industries factors of production will tend to move into the one that benefits from higher protection.

Empirical studies show that effective protection on average exceeded nominal tariff rates in the seven newly industrializing countries[11]. Further, the complex systems of protection applied in each country were handled in a way that neglected the structure of actual and/or potential comparative advantage. This holds true not only for tariffs but also for quantitative restrictions; in all but two countries (Hong Kong and Singapore) such restrictions were applied. These measures pose additional allocational problems to an economy, because quota-type protection (as compared with tariff-type protection) eliminates the price-mechanism. The protective effect of a given quantitative restriction is greater, the faster domestic demand is expanding, because when the relevant quota is filled, the import supply tends to become price-inelastic.

As Donges's survey of industrialization policies in developing countries (based on the results of the Kiel Project) shows, in virtually all NICs governments put much emphasis on investment licensing[12]. They were obviously convinced that licensing could help attain other domestic goals – such as the promotion of a regionally balanced industrial development – and would more effectively allocate resources in accordance with public welfare than the market would do. The empirical results, however, were not in line with these expectations: the systems applied did little to avoid regional imbalances (most striking in Brazil) and resulted in discrimination among export activities (India being the country where policies were most biased against export trade).

The credit and fiscal incentive systems applied in most of the countries played a similar and crucial role, the most common instruments being income tax exemptions, preferential credits and accelerated depreciation allowances. As in the case of import licensing, government authorities proceeded in a rather arbitrary way when deciding the grant of the respective incentives. Investigations of the effectiveness of these fiscal and credit incentives tend to support the presumption that they did not lead to economically rational investments which would otherwise not have taken place[13].

In spite of some of the above-mentioned weaknesses, these policies have promoted industrialization and have considerably influenced the pattern of import-substitution: in all the selected NICs which pursued this type of policy, the share of manufacturing in total real value added increased during the 1950s, most strikingly in Brazil and South Korea. In all the countries, import-substitution was most marked for consumer goods, and occurred occasionally even at higher stages of manufacture – in capital goods and the intermediate sector. At the end of the 1950s the opportunities for further import-substituting industrialization for consumer goods seemed very limited, except in South Korea; here the import proportion of domestic supply was still about 20 per cent. *Table 1.2* shows that the share of manufacturing as a whole in GDP increased – rather moderately in Brazil, India and Mexico, more significantly in South Korea and Taiwan.

In spite of faster growth rates of real GDP per capita, and of real manufacturing output, than the average for developing countries during the import-substitution phase of the 1950s (*Table 1.1*), rates of labour absorption in industry have generally been disappointing: employment in manufacturing grew less rapidly than did the urban labour supply and the ratio of manufacturing employment to total employment remained also unchanged[14].

Except for Korea and Taiwan, which succeeded in avoiding the most severe mistakes when designing their policy framework, by the end of their inward-looking strategy phase the countries under study faced manifold problems which seem typical results of an excessive application of import-substitution[15]. They can be summarized as follows:

Table 1.2 Selected economic indicators, 1955, 1960 and 1977

		Brazil	Hong Kong	India	South Korea	Mexico	Singapore	Taiwan
Population (million)	1977	107.1	4.4	608.1	35.3	59.9	2.3	16.0
GNP per capita (US$)[a]	1977	1390	2590	150	810	1110	2890	1180
Share of manufacturing in GDP (%)	1955	22	29	··	10	24	··	17
	1960	26	32	14	12	23	12	22
	1977	28	36	16	25	28	25	37
Share of manufacturing employment in total labour force (%)	1955	14	50	10	7	19	18	10
	1960	15	52	11	9	20	23	11
	1977	20	57	11	33	25	32	27
Share of manufactured exports[b] in total exports (%)	1955	1.7	75.4	49.3	5.9	9.4	11.3	18.7
	1960	2.0	91.4	43.5	13.8	11.7	19.7	27.7
	1977	28.1	93.1	45.0	82.7	37.8[c]	43.0	82.9
Share of manufactured exports[b] in manufacturing output (%)	1970	5.2	70.0	8.9	39.8	5.3	43.3	49.1
	1975	13.7	77.7	9.5	35.7	15.5	65.0	47.4

[a] At current market prices
[b] SITC 5–8, excluding 67 + 68
[c] 1974

Source: As for Table 1.1

- The insulation of the domestic economies from foreign competition provided domestic manufacturers with opportunities to price their products at higher levels than might have been possible under free trade conditions and to do less to improve efficiency and to meet international quality standards than under competition.
- The protective systems led to a wide range of levels of effective protection, thus allowing some import-substitution industries to use more resources than others to save a unit of foreign exchange; this implies a waste of resources and a loss in overall productivity.
- Tariff and other import restrictions generated overvalued domestic currencies which allowed relative prices to move in favour of inward-looking producers, hence discouraging exporters.
- The combination of relatively low tariffs on capital goods and the undervaluation of foreign exchange kept the price of imported investment goods below their scarcity value, hence increasing capital intensity in production at the expense of employment creation.

In conclusion, this review of the import-substitution phase in the NICs suggests that the policies applied created undesired side-effects, in general causing considerable costs to the economies by the misallocation and waste of resources, by bias against the use of labour, by discouragement of exports, by loss of output and, therefore, of savings. These effects have brought the industrialization process – in some countries sooner, in others later – up against both a balance-of-payments constraint and a market-size constraint[16].

1.4 The move to export promotion policies

By the early 1960s governments in most of the selected countries began to redesign their industrialization efforts and to set up policy frameworks more appropriate for integrating the young industrial sectors into the world economy.

In the new policies introduced in the early and mid-1960s, exchange rate measures played a central role. While some of the countries began with a substantial formal exchange rate devaluation, others tried not only to tackle the current (protection-caused) overvaluation of their domestic currency but also to take precautions against a new overvaluation resulting from domestic prices rising faster than those of their trading partners[17]. Brazil's (discretionary) crawling peg-system is familiar. South Korea applied a similar system. Compared with the abrupt devaluations practised in most developing countries, the advantages of the peg-systems soon became obvious: actual and potential exporters could be sure that their price-competitiveness would not be artifically changed to their disadvantage. Moreover, because devaluations took place in small steps, stabilization policy could be pursued gradually and the political resistance of pressure groups could be contained.

In general, exchange rate policies were accompanied by a restructuring of the protective system. Quantitative import restrictions were reduced, and import tariffs gradually cut. As a result of these liberalization efforts, the conditions for exploiting the manufacturing export potential, which had been built up during the import-substitution period in many of the NICs, definitely improved; a lower level of protection and a better inter-sectoral distribution of effective protection, however, does not automatically lead to equal business opportunities for (still) import-substituting and (already) export-oriented activities. The remaining protection leaves prices of inputs higher than in a free trade situation; an exporter who has to be competitive at given world market prices, but has to use import-substituted (more expensive) inputs, is discriminated against. Many countries have tried to overcome this spill-over problem by granting export-subsidies to neurtralize the disadvantages to exporters accruing from protection. In some cases, export incentives, even exceeding the amount necessary to compensate for the discrimination effect, were granted. This points to a specific promotional attitude by policy-makers in the NICs which can be justified economically by reasons similar to those advanced in the 'infant-industry' argument. The range of policies most commonly adopted, both for compensating and promoting export industries, was rather broad: for example, draw-back schemes, exemptions from duties, remissions of customs duties for specific imports, income tax exemptions for earnings from exports[18]. The success of such measures was striking. All the NICs have been able to realize an enormous increase of their manufactured exports (*Table 1.1*) and at least to maintain the growth rate of real GDP achieved during the import-substitution period. Especially impressive were the export performances in Brazil, South Korea and Taiwan[19].

Success in export expansion has not only diversified the NICs' structure of exports considerably but has also led in some cases to slight increases in shares of world exports. This faster growth of manufactured exports, as compared with the growth of world trade, suggests other factors at work than effective export policies. *Table 1.3* shows the results of a 'constant market share analysis' for the period 1962–1976[20]. This method allows identification of the contribution of various determinants to export expansion:

(1) the relative growth of world demand for all manufactures;
(2) the relative growth of world demand for specific products;
(3) the relative growth of demand in a specific region for a specific product; and
(4) a residual which expresses domestic changes in costs, prices, quality, i.e. competitiveness.

Assuming a çonstant share in world trade for each country, the actual export development can be traced back to these four elements. *Table 1.3* shows that the expansion of manufactured exports from Brazil, Hong Kong, India and Mexico can mainly be attributed to the trend of world exports. In all countries except India, the regional and commodity structure of the exports proved unfavourable as compared with prevailing demand trends; for Mexico this was especially the case in the early 1970s. In South Korea, Singapore and Taiwan the growth of manufactured exports would have been

Table 1.3 *Percentage contributions to total export growth*

Country	Period	Trend of world exports	Commodity structure	Regional structure[b]	'Competitiveness'
Brazil	1965–1972	79.1	–31.0	–1.1	53.0
	1973–1976	113.1	–36.7	6.4	17.3
Hong Kong	1962–1975	76.8	–11.7	–0.8	35.7
India	1962–1975	226.0	–37.5	6.5	–95.0
South Korea	1962–1975	1.5	–0.1	–0.1	98.5
Mexico	1965–1972	146.9	–49.4	–35.8	38.3
	1973–1974	292.9	–109.4	–47.7	–35.8
Singapore	1962–1975	22.7	–1.5	–4.7	83.5
Taiwan	1962–1975	13.6	–1.6	–2.6	90.6

[a] Excluding SITC 22, 67, 68 and 9
[b] According to the following pattern of destinations: USA, Canada, European Community, EFTA, other Europe, Eastern Europe, Japan, Australia and New Zealand and South Africa, other Africa, Middle East, other Asia, Asian centrally planned economies, Latin America

Sources: United Nations Conference on Trade and Development, *Handbook of International Trade and Development Statistics,* various issues
United Nations, *Yearbook of International Trade Statistics,* various issues
J. B. Donges and L. Müller-Ohlsen, *Außenwirtschaftsstrategien und Industrialisierung in Entwicklungsländern, Kieler Studien* **157**, Tübingen, 1978

much slower if these countries had not significantly improved their competitive position. In other words, even if the international environment had been less favourable, South Korea, Singapore and Taiwan would most probably have experienced a considerable expansion of their manufactured exports, simply because these countries proved able not only to concentrate industrialization efforts on activities with potential comparative advantage but also to realize substantial productivity growth, a prerequisite for competitive pricing in international markets.

In addition to the right basic choice of industry, and product-mix, policy makers seem to have been quite successful in adopting appropriate policies to support effectively the growing 'export-mentality' of local entrepreneurs. Such policies in these countries were favoured by the existence of a rather developed institutional infrastructure, of administrative abilities and of a good supply of risk-taking entrepreneurs. The pursuit of appropriate policies and the adequate entrepreneurial response may perhaps be regarded as a very characteristic reference to the 'diffusionist' theory. The very high level of aggregation in the analysis, and the arbitrary choice of the period (determined by the availability of statistics), does not allow more detailed conclusions; it is remarkable, however, that the broad picture of the relative importance of the factors mentioned (ranking: trend of world exports, competitiveness, commodity composition, regional structure of exports) is confirmed by the more disaggregated export-analyses in the individual country studies carried out in the Kiel Institute.

The results of this 'constant market share analysis' – crude as they are – at least tend to confirm the view that the policies pursued by the NICs have been effective in that the manufacturing sector as a whole has improved its competitive position. The method is not able, however, to show how the manufacturing sectors in the selected countries have specialized, or how competitive individual industrial branches have become during the export promotion phase of industrialization. Answers to these questions can be found by an approach based on the assumption that comparative cost advantages eventually materialize in trade flows: a country will export predominantly those goods of which the production is in line with prevailing comparative advantages, while it will import mainly those which can be produced domestically only at higher costs because of comparative disadvantages.

Empirically, the sectoral pattern of national specializations can be determined by Balassa's concept of 'revealed comparative advantage' (RCA). The concept has been adapted to measure the difference, in a given country, between a given sector's foreign trade position:

$$\left. \frac{x_{ij} - m_{ij}}{x_{ij} + m_{ij}} \right\}$$ net exports of sector j of country i as a proportion of the trade turnover of sector j

and the foreign trade position of the country's whole manufacturing sector:

$$\left. \frac{\sum_j (x_{ij} - m_{ij})}{\sum_j (x_{ij} + m_{ij})} \right\}$$ sum of net exports of all manufacturing sectors of country i as a proportion of trade turnover.

This difference is a measure of each sector's relative net export performance (although it does not of course show whether the actual trade pattern is 'optimal'). The performance of each sector has been scaled from + 100 (meaning exports but no imports of the sector's products) to − 100 (imports but no exports)[21]. Calculations have been made for three of our selected countries: Brazil, India and Mexico. The results for a number of products are shown in *Table 1.4*. Because the competitiveness of a sector varies with

Table 1.4 Structure of comparative advantages in the manufacturing sector, 1965 and 1976 in trade with developed (DC) and developing (LDC) countries

SITC	Brazil 1965		Brazil 1976		India 1965		India 1973		Mexico 1965		Mexico 1974	
	DC	LDC	DC	LDC	DC	LDC	DC	LDC	DC	LDC	DC	LDC
51 Chemical elements and compounds	-19.4	-71.9	-74.0	-84.2	-85.8	-47.7	-91.1	-48.4	8.0	-24.8	-5.6	-4.7
52 Mineral tar and crude chemicals and coal, petroleum and natural gas	-100.0	-100.0	-100.0	-100.0	49.1	100.0	-100.0	-100.0	14.8	—	-17.6	100.0
53 Dyeing, tanning and colouring materials	-11.8	-38.5	-84.6	-21.8	-86.4	-78.0	1.0	-47.7	-100.0	-34.0	-49.6	-32.6
54 Medicinal and pharmaceutical products	0.1	-28.7	-65.6	-36.2	-47.9	12.1	-61.0	83.3	17.2	2.0	25.4	23.2
55 Essential oils and perfume materials; toilet, polishing and cleansing preparations	34.8	100.0	30.7	-14.8	59.1	-6.9	42.8	-13.1	19.6	-2.8	18.1	-66.4
56 Fertilizers, manufactured	-100.0	-100.0	-100.0	-84.8	-100.0	-100.0	-100.0	-91.5	-100.0	-50.4	10.5	65.0
57 Explosives and pyrotechnic products	-100.0	100.0	54.5	100.0	-100.0	—	-100.0	100.0	-100.0	—	4.1	8.7
58 Plastic materials, regenerated cellulose and artificial resins	-100.0	100.0	-71.4	-46.6	-93.3	100.0	-93.3	-12.2	-100.0	100.0	-90.4	-33.7
61 Leather, leather manufactures, not elsewhere specified and dressed fur skins	93.7	—	97.8	-64.0	99.6	100.0	99.9	100.0	51.0	—	42.7	100.0

Table 1.4 (contd.)

SITC	Brazil 1965		Brazil 1976		India 1965		India 1973		Mexico 1965		Mexico 1974	
	DC	LDC	DC	LDC	DC	LDC	DC	LDC	DC	LDC	DC	LDC
62 Rubber manufactures, not elsewhere specified	-100.0	100.0	0.6	48.9	36.0	100.0	-14.5	100.0	-10.4	100.0	-15.7	100.0
63 Wood and cork manufactures (excluding furniture)	95.1	100.0	93.6	27.1	-100.0	100.0	73.4	100.0	53.4	-100.0	67.1	-61.4
64 Paper, paperboard and manufactures thereof	-100.0	-100.0	-30.5	-22.3	-100.0	100.0	-96.4	-26.9	-70.2	-60.8	-92.4	50.6
65 Textile yarn, fabrics, made-up articles and related products	89.6	100.0	70.4	48.4	92.8	58.8	97.5	97.9	57.1	-20.4	68.2	53.9
66 Non-metallic mineral manufactures, not elsewhere specified	8.3	-48.3	23.1	-19.3	63.0	-16.2	19.7	-9.5	33.9	76.6	40.8	29.2
67 Iron and steel	8.2	98.7	8.2	19.3	-79.4	100.0	-77.4	87.8	15.0	93.3	-28.5	-7.3
69 Manufactures of metal, not elsewhere specified	-83.7	44.6	-45.8	55.0	-78.7	-3.1	4.8	84.6	-2.8	86.9	17.4	77.6
71 Machinery, other than electric	-81.4	-1.4	-59.6	31.7	-98.8	-2.5	-92.4	74.7	-88.3	-5.9	-67.7	-19.8
72 Electrical machinery, apparatus and appliances	-93.2	-7.6	-34.9	-7.9	-98.4	-1.9	-89.7	80.4	-93.0	38.5	-66.0	-4.8
73 Transport equipment	-77.3	62.7	-32.1	89.7	-98.9	-3.0	-85.1	63.5	-95.9	-72.9	-25.6	74.3

81 Sanitary, plumbing, heating and lighting fixtures and fittings	100.0	—	58.6	100.0	-100.0	100.0	55.4	100.0	-100.0	100.0	51.1	-55.3
82 Furniture	—	—	84.3	89.5	-100.0	100.0	-35.6	100.0	61.6	—	63.0	-100.0
83 Travel goods, handbags and similar articles	—	—	91.1	-20.7	100.0	—	100.0	100.0	45.7	-100.0	64.0	-67.3
84 Clothing	—	—	87.0	79.3	100.0	100.0	99.7	100.0	10.0	-62.9	61.0	-68.5
85 Footwear	100.0	—	99.9	74.5	100.0	100.0	100.0	100.0	34.6	-100.0	29.2	-94.9
86 Professional, scientific and controlling instruments, photographic and optical goods, watches and clocks	-100.0	38.5	-87.3	-58.8	-88.3	100.0	-80.2	82.0	-83.0	11.5	-89.7	-7.4
89 Miscellaneous manufactured articles, not elsewhere specified	-13.2	-26.1	8.5	-21.2	30.9	45.0	62.2	33.2	15.3	31.6	11.7	19.5

Source: Calculated from United Nations, Commodity Trade Statistics and Yearbook of International Trade Statistics, various issues
J. P. Agarwal, H. Rodemer, Die Veränderungen internationaler Standortbedingungen und ihre Konsequenzen für Entscheidungen privater Investoren, Kiel, 1977 (unpublished)

the trading partner's degree of industrialization, the RCA figures have been computed to separate trade with developed countries from trade with other developing countries. The following summary results emerge:

(1) Most improvements of the competitive position in trade with developed countries took place in the relatively labour- and raw material-intensive branches of the SITC groups 8 (miscellaneous manufactures) and 6 (manufactured goods classified chiefly by material).

(2) Comparative disadvantages in trade with developed countries continued to exist in the capital-intensive branches of SITC group 7 (machinery and transport equipment), although in some cases (India and Mexico) it was considerably reduced.

(3) The more advanced the respective country in industrialization (see *Table 1.2*), the more the labour-intensive branches lost competitiveness in trade with developing countries.

(4) Leather manufactures, wood, textiles, clothing and footwear are the branches in which the development of the RCA-position was most stable over time.

The altogether rather satisfactory development of exports following the shift in industrialization policies in the NICs (especially in South Korea and Taiwan) does not mean, however, that the measures taken were optimal. Analysis of the Indian experience shows, for example, that decision-makers have carried the expansion of exports in some branches (e.g. machinery, transport equipment) beyond economic rationality – with the consequence that domestic resource costs of producing and exporting manufactures exceeded the respective foreign exchange earnings considerably[22].

It may be useful to conclude by bringing the NICs' emergence as dynamic exporters of manufactures into a more general perspective. A cursory examination of international trade and output statistics shows that the NICs contributed considerably to structural change in the world economy. The share of all NICs' industrial output in world industrial output nearly doubled between 1963 and 1977, amounting to 6 per cent in 1977; the seven countries under review accounted for about 40 per cent of developing countries' total industrial output. The NICs' share in world exports of manufactures trebled between 1963 and 1976 (from 2½ to over 7 per cent)[23]; these seven NICs concentrated about 70 per cent of all manufactured exports from the developing world.

1.5 Concluding comments

The experience of the newly industrializing countries strongly supports the view that – given the decision to exploit the gains of a deeper integration in the world economy – a wide range of policies can be adopted in developing countries to accelerate their industrialization. This view, however, has been increasingly challenged by political economists, as well as by representatives of developing countries, during the last 10 years. Although their arguments for rejecting an outward-looking approach, and favouring 'de-linked', 'dissociated' (selectively or universally), or similarly labelled forms of industrialization, are essentially the same, the political and economic origins of their thinking vary considerably[24]. In summing up the various shades of basically similar arguments, three main lines can be singled out[25].

(1) The international division of labour systematically discriminates against developing countries.
(2) Increasing protectionist attitudes in industrialized countries, following slackening economic growth, must limit the absorption of manufactures from developing countries.
(3) Outward-looking industrialization does not meet the need in developing countries for a vigorous attack on underdevelopment and poverty.

The first argument may be true of the early phases of development when there are large differences between developed and developing countries in their respective factor endowments, implying a complementary trade pattern. But it becomes less true as developing countries move away from primary products and labour-intensive manufactures towards more sophisticated products, providing opportunities for intra-industry trade. This stage is now coming closer in the NICs whose experience has been reviewed above. The often emphasized risk of a consequent over-supply of labour-intensive products on the world market would be averted as the developed countries move up the scale of sophistication in their own production, leaving room for the 'late-comers' to specialize in less sophisticated products.

As regards the second argument, there is no doubt that protection in the developed countries, together with the current recession, has limited the scope for export expansion by the NICs. But it seems inappropriate that developing countries should for this reason resort to inward-looking policies. The longer-term experience of the NICs as shown in this paper offers considerable encouragement to outward-looking policies of export expansion.

As regards the third argument, the evidence does not suggest that inward-looking policies, directed towards an industrialization 'de-linked' from the world economy, have resulted in a more equitable distribution of the fruits of growth than outward-directed development paths. All depends on the basic political background and on the capacity of the policy-makers to design and execute their policies in accordance with explicit goals. There is no reason why such development policies should not combine the economic advantages of competition and of an efficient allocation of resources – such as are available to a competitive open economy – with an improved income distribution.

44 *The role of economic policies*

References

1 D. Keesing, *Trade Policy for Developing Countries*. World Bank Staff Working Paper No. 353. Washington, August 1979, pp. 55f.

2 The inclusion of India in this group of NICs might be surprising, given the relatively moderate average growth of real GNP (especially on a per capita basis) and of export expansion in manufactures after World War II. This choice seemed justifiable for two reasons: India, although mainly emphasizing agricultural development, has implemented extensive industrialization programmes which have created a rather diversified industrial sector; and the industrialization policies pursued, however, have at the same time been rather biased towards import-substituting activities thus providing a kind of negative element causing inefficiencies and considerable economic costs.

3 I. Little, T. Scitovsky, M. Scott, *Industry and Trade in Some Developing Countries, A Comparative Study*. Oxford University Press for the OECD, London, 1970.
J. N. Bhagwati, *Foreign Trade Regimes and Economic Development: Anatomy and Consequences of Exchange Control Regimes*. National Bureau of Economic Research, Special Conference Series **11**, New York, 1978.
J. N. Bhagwati, *Foreign Trade Regimes and Economic Development: Liberalization Attempts and Consequences*. National Bureau of Economic Research, Special Conference Series **10**, New York, 1978.
B. A. Balassa *et al.*, *The Structure of Protection in Developing Countries*. Johns Hopkins University Press, Baltimore and London, 1971.
B. A. Balassa, *A 'Stages' Approach to Comparative Advantage*. World Bank Staff Working Paper No. 256, Washington, May 1977.
H. Hughes, *Trade and Industrialization Policies: The Political Economy of the Second-Best*. World Bank Staff Working Paper No. 143, Washington, February 1973.
J. B. Donges and L. Müller-Ohlsen, *Aussenwirtschaftsstrategien und Industrialisierung in Entwicklungsländern*. Kieler Studien **157**, Tübingen 1978 (reviewing the empirical results of 15 country-studies).

4 R. Prebisch, 'Towards a New Trade Policy for Development'. In *Proceedings of the United Nations Conference on Trade and Development*, Geneva, 23 March–16 June 1964. *Vol. II: Policy Statements*. New York, 1964, p. 12.

5 For completeness, it should be added that recent discussions about a New International Economic Order have finally provided an additional variant of the issue without really being, however, a comparable strategic option because it is based on a change of the existing political and economic environment. According to these ideas, developing countries should aim at realizing a structure of specialization deviating considerably from what would arise under free trade conditions; global investment plans and patterns of international trade flows negotiated between governments should replace private investment-decisions as the basic element of the allocation mechanism.

6 See J. B. Donges, 'A Comparative Survey of Industrialization Policies in Fifteen Semi-Industrialized Countries'. In *Weltwirtschaftliches Archiv*, **112** (4), Tübingen, 1976, p. 629.

7 See Keesing, op. cit., p. 137.

8 See J. Riedel, *The Industrialization of Hong Kong*. Kieler Studien No. 124. J.C.B. Mohr Tübingen, 1974; and D. Lotz, 'Singapor: Ein Beispiel für exportorientiertes Industriewachstum', *Die Weltwirtschaft*, Tübingen, 1978, Heft 1, pp. 162f.

9 See I. Little, T. Scitovsky, M. Scott, *Industry and Trade in Some Developing Countries, A Comparative Study*. Oxford University Press for the OECD, London, 1970, Table 5.1 and pp. 164f – D. Keesing, *Trade Policy for Developing Countries*. World Bank Staff Working Paper No. 353. Washington, August 1979, pp.56f.

10 See W. M. Corden, *The Theory of Protection*. Oxford University Press, London, 1971.

11 See J. B. Donges and L. Müller-Ohlsen, *Aussenwirtschaftsstrategien und Industrialisierung in Entwicklungsländern*. Kieler Studien **157**, Tübingen, 1978 (reviewing the empirical results of 15 country – studies) p. 60.

12 J. B. Donges, 'A Comparative Survey of Industrialization Policies in Fifteen Semi-Industrialized Countries'. In *Weltwirtschaftliches Archiv*, 112 (4), Tübingen, 1976.

13 See A. O. Krueger, *Foreign Trade Regimes and Economic Development: Liberalization Attempts and Consequences*. National Bureau of Economic Research, Special Conference Series, 10, New York, 1978.

14 See J. B. Donges, 'A Comparative Survey of Industrialization Policies in Fifteen Semi-Industrialized Countries'. In *Weltwirtschaftliches Archiv*, 112 (4), Tübingen, 1976, p. 642.

15 See B. Stecher, *Erfolgsbedingungen der Import-substitution und der Exportdiversifizierung im Industrialisierungsprozess. Die Erfahrungen in Chile, Mexiko und Südkorea*. Kieler Studien No. 136, Tübingen, 1976, pp. 12f.

16 B. Stecher, *Erfolgsbedingungen der Importsubstitution under der Exportdiversifizierung im Industrialisiereungsprozess. Die Erfahrungen in Chile, Mexiko und Südkorea*. Kieler Studien No. 136, pp. 20f.

17 See A. O. Krueger, *Foreign Trade Regimes and Economic Development: Liberalization Attempts and Consequences*. National Bureau of Economic Research, Special Conference Series, 10, New York, 1978, chs. 5 and 6.

18 See Organization for Economic Cooperation and Development (OECD), *The Impact of the Newly Industrializing Countries on Production and Trade in Manufactures*. Paris, 1979, section IV.

19 See J. B. Donges, 'A Comparative Survey of Industrialization Policies in Fifteen Semi-Industrialized Countries'. In *Weltwirtschaftliches Archiv* 112 (4), Tübingen, 1976, p. 653.

20 The absolute change of manufactured exports during a period 0 to 1

$\left(\sum_i \sum_j x^1_{ij} - \sum_i \sum_j x^0_{ij} \right)$ can be decomposed as follows: $\sum_i \sum_j r x^0_{ij} +$

$$(1)$$

$$\sum_i \sum_j (r_i - r)x^0_{ij} + \sum_i \sum_j (r_{ij} - r_i)x^0_{ij} + \sum_i \sum_j (x^1_{ij} - x^0_{ij} - r_{ij} x^0_{ij})$$

$$(2) \qquad\qquad (3) \qquad\qquad (4)$$

See E. E. Leamer and R. M. Stern, *Quantitative International Economics*. Allyn & Bacon, Boston, 1970, pp. 171f.

21 The RCA-concept was originally developed by B. A. Balassa, 'Trade Liberalization and "Revealed" Comparative Advantage'. *The Manchester School of Economic and Social Studies* 33, 1965, pp. 99f. The concept assumes that there are equal export prices for all countries of destination and that a country's imports from all sources are equally influenced by protection, transport costs, etc. Calculations provided in *Table 1.4* were made according to a modified formula:

$$RCA_{ij} = \left[\frac{x_{ij} - m_{ij}}{x_{ij} + m_{ij}} - \frac{\sum_i (x_{ij} - m_{ij})}{\sum_i (x_{ij} + m_{ij})} \right] \times \left[\frac{100}{1 \text{ or } \begin{smallmatrix} + \\ - \end{smallmatrix} \ast \frac{\sum_j (x_{ij} - m_{ij})}{\sum_j (x_{ij} + m_{ij})}} \right]$$

* + if the first term within the first [ ] is greater than the second (i.e. if net export performance of sector *j* is better than average); − if the first term is less than the second (net export performance worse than average).
x_{ij} exports of commodity *j* by country *i*
m_{ij} imports of commodity *j* by country *i*

22 See R. Banerji, *Exports of Manufactures from India: an Appraisal of the Emerging Pattern.* Mohr, Tübingen, 1975, pp. 223f.
23 See Organization for Economic Cooperation and Development (OECD) *The Impact of the Newly Industralizing Countries on Production and Trade in Manufactures.* Paris, 1979, Tables 1 and 2; and World Bank, *World Development Report, 1979,* Washington, 1979, Annex tables.
24 For a critique of *laissez-faire* in international economic relations and the foundations for a de-linked approach see C. Diaz-Alejandro, 'Delinking North and South'. In *Rich and Poor Nations in the World Economy* (A. Fischlow *et al.*, eds.), Council on Foreign Relations. McGraw-Hill, New York, 1978, pp. 8f.
25 This categorization of arguments draws on J. B. Donges, L. Müller-Ohlsen, *Aussenwirtschaftsstrategien und Industrialisierung in Entwicklungsländern.* Kieler Studien **157**, Tübingen, 1978 (reviewing the empirical results of 15 country-studies), p. 167.

Cultures and Growth

Henri Aujac*

2.1 Purpose and organization of the study

Ignorance of the links between, on the one side, a country's culture and the social order structuring its society and, on the other, the suitability of the country for one or other type of industrialization, is no doubt the chief cause of the checks experienced by some developing countries in their attempts to industrialize. Iran is a good example; but analogous cases, if less spectacular, can be found throughout the world, notably among the Islamic countries, in black Africa and in Latin America.

We propose to display some of these links, in particular:

- A country's culture and its prevailing social order largely determine its suitability for industrialization and, moreover, condition quite strictly the possible modes of industrialization: some cultures and some social orders favour industrialization, others do not.
- Reciprocally, some forms of industrialization destroy the prevailing culture and social order without replacing them with new ones; the society is then threatened by chaos or regression. Industrialization in this case destroys the society.

To deal with these various points, we shall briefly describe the concepts used and expound the methodology which seems appropriate; we shall then illustrate our approach by a number of examples.

We will take first two countries, France and Japan, which industrialized a long time ago; to analyse how industrialization is linked with the culture and social order, countries must be chosen in which industrialization already has a fairly long history. Of course, it is true that these examples are specific and that conclusions drawn from them cannot be applied incautiously to the industrialization of today's developing countries: in these two old countries the state, the nation, the people, the race and the culture have become intermingled, which is not true of a number of today's developing countries.

We will then consider Brazil, a country of recent industrialization, to bring out how difficult it is to build up simultaneously an industry and a

---

* Scientific adviser to the Chairman, Bureau d'Information et de Prévision Economique (BIPE) Neuilly-sur-Seine, and Director of Studies at the Ecole des Hautes Etudes en Sciences Sociales, Paris

social order – even in a country already endowed with a culture. Industrialization seems the easier task; by contrast, to build up a nation demands much time and great efforts. The mode of industrialization adopted may promote, or it may retard, the construction of a nation. Finally, by taking as an example the Ivory Coast, a country only now at the very beginning of industrialization, we shall express a certain apprehension: the mode of industrialization adopted – of a Western type – has so far led to remarkable achievements on the economic level; but is it not tending to destroy, without being able to replace, the social order and culture?

It seems quite plausible that, in a given country, the prevailing cultural and social order cannot fail to influence the sub-sector formed by the industrial society: a culture and social order take centuries to establish and even the oldest industrial societies have existed for less than two centuries; even in these societies, it is not so long ago that the industrial population became superior to the agricultural.

Culture – that is the totality of the intellectual character of a population, and the body of social, religious, ethical, scientific and technical features which constitute the culture – was established in the course of a country's history at a time when its people were struggling to escape from ancestral terrors and to overcome the horrors of famine, war, disease and death. This culture is based on behaviour, hopes and beliefs taught by very long experience to individuals and groups; the culture so formed allows the organization of a generally acceptable community life and promotes relationships between individuals and groups and relations with the outside world.

Such a culture both sustains and is sustained by the general social order structuring the society. This order is made manifest in customs and an informal system of law as well as in organizations and institutions and in the differentiation of social groups; almost always it incorporates a constitution explicitly defining each group's rights and duties. This general social order, more or less accepted by all, is the result of the society's history and the outward expression of its culture.

A general social organization always involves a hierarchical ordering of society, on occasion quite strict, into groups or classes. Less than two centuries ago in every country, and in many countries today, there is a 'Prince', (i.e., a power centre) at the peak of the 'social pyramid', a Prince who is sometimes considered as having divine characteristics.

It is of interest for our purpose to ascertain the values attached to this general social order. Briefly, they are altruism and devotion to the group. Whether in the family, the army or the nation, each individual is obligated to sacrifice his personal interest and, if necessary, his life for the advantage of the group whether small or large, which claims his loyalty; in return, the group, whether it be the nation or the family, owes its members a duty of protection and succour. Religion is often capable of smoothing the interpersonal relationships which every state establishes by the very fact of its existence.

Within the general social order a series of special orders may be distinguished; these are either *de facto* orders, which are not explicitly structured and involve persons with common intellectual or material interests, or special orders engendered by the various institutions.

An 'industrial organization', when it exists, is one of these special orders. In general, its beginnings are timid. Once established, it grows and, within the society at large, generates a new society structured by industrial enterprises, banks, trading firms, transport enterprises, etc., each run by specific actors in the industrial world. Depending on the political regime, these firms may be private enterprises run by capitalists, or state-owned firms run by the bureaucracy; in any case, the corresponding industrial organization determines the hierarchical position of the various participants, in particular that of firms' executives and their workers and employees: the managerial class commands the workers and sets working objectives and discipline, and fixes wages, more or less strictly, depending on the times and the system.

We may examine the industrial order of a liberal capitalistic state as an illustration. The motivations and values used as norms in this order are indeed special. The goal of the industrial capitalist is financial profit; the value recognized by society is money; the relationships between firms and men who run them are governed by competition; moreover, competition exists within the firm between executives seeking to rise to the top of the structure. The principle of the relationships between management and labour is simple: capitalists can exist only if they can preserve the greatest difference between the prices at which they sell the production of the firm and the wages they pay to their workers; in the short term at least, the interests of labour and management are contradictory.

The ethic of this industrial world is thus different from that of the general social organization because it stresses such qualities as individualism, the importance of the leader, the pursuit of personal interest, the need to struggle against others, and the reduction of values to an equivalent in monetary terms.

It can readily be seen how diferent the general social organization, as analysed above, is from the pitcture of the liberal, capitalistic, industrial organization we have presented. To a certain extent, they are incompatible[1].

So history has seen the formation of a number of different cultures and social orders, and, often, industrialization has equally taken different forms. It would be interesting, but it is not our purpose here, to establish a correspondence between each culture and social order on the one side, and, on the other, the associated mode of industrialization. For the present, we shall try to analyse the relationship between these two concepts but restricting the discussion, for convenience, to the liberal capitalist mode of industrialization, which is only a special case – one of the possible modes. These relationships can be various.

One kind of culture and general social organization may favour the creation and development of industrial organization: we will therefore call it an 'industrializing culture and social order'. Another type of social order may be unfavourable. The conditions to be satisfied if a culture and social order is to be considered as industrializing, will be examined below.

By contrast, it should first be stressed, to avoid mentioning it again, that an industrial organization, which has succeeded in emerging through favourable circumstances, may turn out to be completely incompatible with the culture and the general social order into which it was born. It may then either generate a new general social order which is more favourable, or replace it to become itself the new culture and the new general social order. In the Communist Manifesto, Marx and Engels give the example of the substitution of an industrial, bourgeois organization in place of the feudal general social order which it destroys. This illustrates one kind of possible relationship between the industrial and the general social orders. It sets out a view which has not yet been justified by the facts: almost 150 years after Marx and Engels wrote these lines, the industrializing bourgeoisie, as they perceived it, has nowhere yet succeeded in altogether destroying the previous culture and general social organization[2].

In what conditions will a general social order foster the birth and growth of industrialization of the liberal capitalist type? To answer this question, we must discover the conditions to be fulfilled by a developing country in order to interest rich countries in investing there[3]. This type of industrialization is obviously very special because foreign investment and capital are involved but it shows what the promoters of the industrial order demand from the general social order – demands which are expressed quite bluntly, and sometimes with a degree of cynicism. Some of them relate to problems arising from the foreign nationality of the investor, which are of little concern to us here: for instance, a favourable climate in which foreign investors are accepted, if need be as participants in joint ventures; or the provision of guarantees for the repatriation of profits. Other demands, however, reveal requirements felt by any industrial organization which the general social order is expected to meet. These include, among other things:

(1) The public authorities must be strong and effective enough to maintain order and, if possible, the stability of the currency.
(2) The society must be stable enough, politically and socially, human rights sufficiently respected, and political circles sufficiently honest, respected and respectable, to eliminate the possibility that revolutionary parties can establish themselves and foment rebellion.
(3) The general attitude towards a Western-type civilization – that is to say, the profit motive and the consumer society – must be favourable.

(4) Transport and communication networks must be cheap and effective.
(5) Manpower must be abundant, active, capable, submissive and inexpensive.

There is one last necessary condition for the development of the country to be autonomous:

(6) The values of the traditional social organization should permit or, even better, stimulate dynamic people to enter business, as a means to financial gains and power.

Conditions (1) and (2) imply that the general social organization of the country considered must be vigorous and comprise a relatively strict and accepted hierarchy in which the Prince, the power groups or the ruling classes uncontestedly dominate 'the people' who supply manpower.

Conditions (3) and (6) stress that there must be at least minimal compatibility between the values of the society at large and those of the industrial society. For example, industrialization will be difficult if the society as a whole believes that trading, manufacturing and banking are disreputable, or if it condemns the lending of money at interest.

Condition (5) is obviously essential and is often satisfied. At the start of the industrialization process, the first workers are peasants; indeed, infant industries often first appear in rural areas – sometimes to escape the rules of corporations which protect workers – and create a labour force working in both field and factory. This rural labour force, trained by centuries of agricultural toil, has almost all the necessary qualities from the outset. The permanent threat of starvation has taught it that permanent activity and infinite patience are the source of its daily bread. Farmers know that the fruit of their immense toil is at the mercy of random destruction by an act of God – blight, storm, hail, banditry, etc. – that it is absolutely necessary to be content with little, and that when a catastrophe occurs, the only recourse is to heaven and its representatives on earth – or to rich landlords, men of a superior breed whose way of life and reactions are so strange that they seem to live on another planet. Whether toward heaven, the clergy or the landlord, obedience is the only effective behaviour, and the only possible one.

Energetic, obedient and undemanding, the labour force originating in the rural environment has thus many of the basic qualities required. It nevertheless suffers difficulties in adapting to the yoke of working hours and working discipline and especially to the pace of activity necessitated by industrial production. Above all, technological progress today increasingly requires workers to have professional qualifications beyond those of someone migrating from a rural environment. Nowadays, it is the professional qualifications of the labour force which determine what technologies can be introduced in a given country. Adaptation and qualification take time: several years in some cases, a whole generation in others.

The case discussed here occurs frequently in countries which have been industrialized for quite a while; the farmer has moved from field to factory with practically no transition. But peasants sometimes leave the countryside to seek employment in towns and find none, pile up in the suburbs, rapidly lose their earlier qualities of skill and conscientiousness and become unsuitable for industrial tasks. This phenomenon is frequent today in the developing countries.

So we can understand that the characteristics of the culture and of the general social order directly influence the birth and development of industrial organization; and there is reason to believe that only some of these orders are 'industrializing'. This working hypothesis will now be illustrated using concrete cases.

2.2 France and Japan: Two comparable cultures with different modes of industrialization

France

Until the French Revolution, society was subject to the authority of a monarchy which had ruled by divine right for 10 centuries. French society was composed of three sharply demarcated hierarchical orders: the clergy, followed by a nobility established by birth and land ownership, and, at the bottom of the pyramid, the 'Third Estate', that is to say the 'people', comprising the mass of the peasantry and the bourgeois classes – handicraft workers, traders, businessmen, lawyers, notaries, doctors, bankers, ship-owners, etc. God's will, birth and land ownership were the legitimating basis of this order which determined social prestige and power. The values cherished by this society were military and feudal: submission to the will of God and the King, respect of and for religion, honour, one's word, the hierarchy, fidelity to one's superior, the protection of the weak, and a degree of distrust for newly acquired social position or wealth. Relationships between men in this type of society were the opposite of those prevailing in a developed commercial and industrial society.

The financing of the whole system was based on the exploitation of the peasantry who could be 'taxed and put to forced labour at will' paying farm rents and sharecropping dues to the nobility and a series of direct and indirect taxes to the royal tax inspectors. The peasants were extremely poor, living on the border of famine, and incapable of constituting a market of any kind.

This social organization was unfavourable to industrialization for both economic and cultural reasons, namely:

- Markets were local and not very dynamic; transport was dangerous and expensive, and business hampered by excise taxes.
- In the towns, the strict rules of the guilds limited the volume of production and the number of apprentices. This effectively stopped any growth or development of the economy.
- The nobles, although enjoying the highest incomes, were debarred from business or industrial activities. At best, without derogation to their rank, they could indulge in foreign trade or in branches of business such as mining and metallurgy which were considered direct extensions of agricultural activity.
- The most prized investment, yielding prestige and wealth, was land purchase, and the purchase or construction of castles, following the royal example. Savings were thus channelled chiefly to property and only limited resources were devoted to handicraft and manufacturing trades.

In spite of these handicaps, manufacturing and handicrafts developed. Some rich members of the bourgeoisie became interested in new industries, in particular textiles, and they evaded the corporative rules by employing the rural peasants in their homes. The bourgeoisie would supply the raw materials and market the finished products.

The royal power also generated a limited degree of industrialization in response to two areas of concern. The desire for power led the King, often at war to extend or defend his kingdom and in need of arms and warships, to establish arsenals and foster the development of privately-owned arms factories, while the desire for wealth implied the circulation of a substantial quantity of gold, to be seized in case of need; thus the foreign balance had to be positive. However the King, the court, the nobility and the rich bourgeoisie were accustomed to importing luxury goods from abroad. These goods had to be produced in France, and as private firms were incapable of doing so, the royal manufactories had to be created for the purpose.

In short, industrialization was begun under the monarchy. However to accelerate this process, it would have been necessary, among other things, to abolish corporative regulations, to permit handicraft workers and industrialists to produce and to use the labour force as they saw fit, to channel available capital to their activities, to do away with the internal customs and to improve transport. We shall see how far the Revolution of 1789 contributed to meeting these conditions.

The bourgeois revolution of 1789, at least in appearance, destroyed the general social organization of the monarchy and replaced it by a new one: the orders were abolished, the King was executed, and many of the nobility fled the country. All citizens were proclaimed equal before the law. The change, nevertheless, was not as deep as it seemed. The new order was, indeed, not based on birth, but the concept of power and privilege through land ownership remained intact. The bourgeoisie became landed proprietors, bought castles and tried to reinstate the old system, but this time to their own benefit. In addition, the aristocracy which had returned to France after 1815 were reasonably successful in reconstituting their former landed property rights. Instead of a substitution of the nobility by the bourgeoisie, the two classes merged, the bourgeoisie taking the nobility as its model and adopting land ownership as the outward sign and justification of its membership of the highest class.

Thus, the change in the general social order was restricted to the higher classes. By contrast, things hardly changed for the labouring classes. Indeed, for some, conditions worsened, as they were no longer protected by corporate regulations. However, living conditions did improve for the peasants, who were freed of all tax to the local seigneur; many purchased small holdings – becoming 'lords of their own domains' – to which they held a fierce attachment.

From an economic viewpoint, the bourgeoisie had achieved the abolition of the guild rules, which had hamstrung freedom to establish enterprises and to exploit the labour force. Does this mean that the conditions for true industrialization had now been satisfied?

In reality some characteristics and values of monarchical times remained deeply engraved in the collective memory, subsisting for 150 years, or from four to five generations, up to World War II; even today, there are still traces of them:

- As regards the exercise of royal authority, the collective subconscious remembers that the subject owes obedience to the state, and in particular to the head of state, and that in return the state has a duty of protection and assistance.
- The ownership of land rather than other property remained pre-eminent in conferring social prestige long after the revolution, and still survives today. For more than half a century after the revolution, only those who were able to prove high enough landed incomes were entitled to vote and thus able to exercise political power. Because of this, for a good part of the nineteenth century, industrial activity was seen basically as a means of becoming rich faster, in order to purchase domains and castles and thus gain access to privileged status[4].

A few teachings still remain as vestiges of the guild regulations and their spirit: the golden rule of a society '*á la française*' is to live, however modestly, and to let live. Too overt a search for financial profit, in particular through competition – branded in short order as 'unbridled' – is viewed as almost tantamount to usury and as almost contemptible. Such attitudes, which are quite common, are obviously not likely to generate much industrial dynamism.

It is not surprising that in these circumstances French industrialization, except for some rare periods of its history, has recorded only a moderate rate of growth.

There have, however, been periods of strength, of which we may distinguish five:

(1) In the period of the First Empire, as under any authoritarian system, the regime wished to mask the absence of freedoms by an increase in general welfare; this, coupled with the absence of British competition during the continental blockade, led it to promote industry.

(2) The restoration of absolute monarchy in 1815 and – even more – the regime of Louise-Philippe (July 1830) helped the business world to seize political power, while the development of the railways stimulated that of industry.

(3) Under the Second Empire, France reached the stage of an urbanized society, with further substantial industrial development.

(4) In the 1890s the second 'Industrial Revolution', under the Third Republic, was based on the development of electricity, chemicals, the automobile and aviation – developments intensified during World War I and immediately after.

(5) We must wait until 1947 for the next surge in industrial progress – a surge of unprecedented magnitude and duration. It can be attributed to a variety of causes and conditions:

   (a) people who had suffered severely from wartime privations and still held modest expectations, while scarcities brought high prices – conditions favouring capital accumulation;

   (b) a well-qualified labour force but a stock of capital equipment badly in need of modernization;

   (c) American aid under the Marshall Plan, which very soon after the war put abundant capital at the disposal of the government for promoting industrial reconstruction;

   (d) the planning system of Jean Monnet which provided capital to industry, but only for projects introducing modern techniques and international competitiveness – conditions favourable to the creation of a modern and efficient production capacity; and

   (e) finally, a country which had lost the battle of 1940, which had known privation and which had seen its factories, its railways, its industry and agriculture in ruins, was able – despite profound political divergences – to find itself united in attacking the priority task of reconstructing the national economy.

During the process of industrial development, the proletariat expanded, as did the trade unions and political parties favourable to labour. First came the Republican party during the July Monarchy, then the socialist party, followed by the Communist party under the Third Republic. From the Revolution down to our time, the general social organization of French society was – or more accurately, appeared to be – threatened by working-class claims only on very rare occasions: during the 1848 revolution, the Paris Commune in 1870, the take-over of power by the Popular Front in 1936, when France was liberated in 1945, and in May 1968. Whenever conflicts of interest between the commanding capitalistic minority and the submissive majority have appeared insoluble within the industrial order, the reaction of the ruling classes has been sharp and often bloody, and – what concerns us here – has quickly produced a reinforcement of the general social order by a return to the former monarchic-style order. In other words, when capitalists and business leaders are incapable of maintaining their domination over the working class and thus no longer control the industrial order, the mobilization of the old organization, which is still the structuring element of society as a whole even if masked, secures their victory.

Several conclusions seem to flow from this rapid overview of the history of French industrialization:

- The often lengthy religious, political and social history which preceded industrialization progressively forged a national culture, to wit, a set of morals, behaviour patterns, relationships between men, and values. Experience proves that this culture changes its basic features only slowly, over several generations. It thus closely conditions the pace and mode of industrialization, as well as the type of industrial society which can develop in the country. From this standpoint, French culture still transmits values which do not correspond to those of a dynamic industrial society.
- To endure, that is to maintain capitalistic domination over labour, to be able to accumulate capital fast enough, and to counterbalance the discipline forced upon workers by an adequate distribution of wealth, the industrial order needs the support of a solidly grounded general social order. The older the order, the more solid it appears. It is the ultimate but up to now unshakable support for the defence of the industrial order.

Japan

The situation in Japan toward the middle of the nineteenth century was similar in many ways to that prevailing in France a hundred years earlier. The general social order was still strong, but it was beginning to deteriorate through the influence of the monetary economy. It consisted of

(1) an emperor, of divine descent, respected by all, but enjoying no real power;
(2) a shogun, always a member of the same family, holding authority and with an efficient government organization at his disposal which allowed him to dominate the nobility of 'Daimyo';

(3) the lords and vassals constituting the samurai, a military class which learnt the techniques of management in the shogunate administration and formed a set of competent, patriotic and reforming men who were to play a decisive role in Japan's industrialization; and

(4) the people, the majority being peasants working on the lands of the samurai, together with handicraft workers, traders, etc.; their level of education was higher than in Europe at the same period; almost half the population was literate.

Religion and education taught that society is necessarily a patriarchal and hierarchical organization, in which an individual has value only inasmuch as he contributes to the welfare of the community as a whole. The social system was financed by farmers who paid extremely heavy taxes, sometimes amounting to over 50 per cent of their harvest, to the emperor, the shogun and the samurai. Such a social structure is not particularly conducive to industrialization. Corporative regulations limited the development of handicrafts and small industry. The samurai, an active and dynamic class, could not conduct business: their code of honour forbade profit-seeking and taught them to hold money in contempt. Nevertheless, the development of the monetary system eroded this general social order somewhat, for instance by enriching traders and by fostering a certain development of handicraft and even of industrial activities, ruining a number of the samurai in the process.

The main participants in the beginnings of industrialization towards the middle of the nineteenth century were rich peasants and certain samurai. They might be taken as the advance signs of the rise of a bourgeois society, but they were weak, and the shogunate order still remained intact as an extremely centralized feudal organization. So one might have forecast that, as in France, Japan's industrial development would remain restricted; but one would have been wrong, and we now turn to the reasons.

The arrival of American (1854) and British (1866) fleets at the Japanese ports to open up the country to foreign trade had two consequences: it was to generate an upheaval in the general social order, and it led to Japan's rapid industrialization.

It was the samurai military class which wrought both changes. The shogun, who had accepted the foreigners' demands, lost status. The emperor retrieved power, assisted by young samurai, who were versed in business matters, competent and ardently patriotic. This involved a return to the old feudal system which had been adulterated by the shoguns' ambitions: the restoration of the Meiji. Several revolutionary measures were taken: farmers became owners of the lands they tilled, all men were declared to be equal, and education became available to all. In practice, the change does not really seem to have affected the traditional order. The samurai remained in control of the levers of power. The peasant's lot did not improve materially for an income tax replaced the old taxes – an exchange of one burden for another.

The samurai drew two lessons from the entry by force of foreign warships into their ports: freedom of trade meant that industrial countries with a fleet of warships could force less-developed countries to open their borders to them; and to remain independent, the country must acquire military strength. This implied a powerful arms industry. At this point, the conditions for rapid industrialization had been satisfied:

- The ruling class had set itself an aim: the country's independence. This could not be achieved without a powerful industry.
- This class held large financial resources, much greater than the rich traders or wealthy handicraft workers could mobilize to equip heavy industries.
- The workers accepted the aims set by the ruling class, and were ready to pay the price in terms of effort.

Industrialization gathered pace thereafter with great efficiency: arms industries, shipyards, steel plants, and the many activitires generated by the navy and the army were rapidly established. In parallel, a major effort was undertaken to improve the country's infrastructures with the building of rail and road networks, ports, etc.

Thus, within a few decades Japan became a great industrial power, with features that may still be observed today in the Japanese economy. These include a traditional industry, especially in textiles and food, with small and average-size firms; and a modern industrial sector comprising heavy industries, transport industries, mechanical industries, etc., using modern techniques and structures which were set up by the state in the form of powerful public corporations and then resold cheaply to a capitalistic family.

As industrialization proceeded, both the male and female labour force increased greatly but its composition has unusual characteristics. The Meiji Restoration did not bring about a rural exodus and the dawn of industrialization took place in traditional industries in rural areas using the especially submissive female labour force. Only towards the end of World War I did the number of male workers equal that of women, mainly through the development of heavy and arms industries.

Only a small percentage of the labour force was unionized, and the unions were ineffective. From the outset, the development of unions was opposed by the government in the name of military imperatives: in 1900, unions were even abolished, together with the then nascent Democratic Socialist party. The union movement recovered strength after World War I, but was torn by internal disputes and ideological discussions. It was repressed in 1931, when the military order took over, and finally abolished in 1937 when it was replaced by an official union which supported austerity and work in the name of solidarity with the fighting forces.

Thus, during the whole Meiji period, and until 1945, the general social order remained unchallenged. The industrial order developed within it, with no urgent social problems raised by the struggle between capitalists and workers. The still neo-feudal state generated first state then private, capitalism – dynamic and with modern structures – by providing funds, markets and a cheap and docile labour force. The authorities used the centralized administration, inherited from the shogunate period, with considerable efficiency and drew full benefit from the lessons taught by the foreigners: navies and armies open external markets; power derives from the use of the most modern techniques and is based on the country's industrialization.

A half-century earlier, France had experienced the bourgeois revolution; because the social fabric was impregnated by the monarchical order, it could build up only a not very dynamic industry based on private ownership of the means of production, consisting mainly of small- and medium-size firms. By contrast, Japan, attacked by Western imperialists, recovered its strength by returning to its previous mode of social organization, the imperial feudal order. The state devoted its efforts and abundant financial means to the creation of a powerful, dynamic industry with the most modern structures and techniques, in order to procure the arms needed to make other nations respect its boundaries and the to secure *lebensraum*. Thus two societies, quite similar at the outset, yielded two very different patterns of industrialization: in France, where the bourgeois seized power, industry grew at a moderate pace; in Japan, the warrior class took over authority and modern-style industrialization was introduced directly.

It may be interesting to analyse the links between culture, the general social order and the industrialization policy since the end of World War II. In 1945, several Japanese towns were destroyed, some by atomic, others by phosphorus bombs. The war was over. American forces occupied the country, with General MacArthur acting as proconsul. For the second time, foreigners were to produce a radical change in Japan's general social order. MacArthur took the following measures in particular: the Empire was abolished and replaced by American-type democratic institutions. Freedom was granted to found unions and political parties; the large family businesses of the heavy and modern industrial sector were broken up; and Japan was obliged to do away with its armed forces and arms industry. The general social order seemed to be deeply shaken. It has lost its traditional legitimacy: the Emperor was no longer divine but the US occupation authorities carefully preserved the monarchy while abolishing its powers.

In fact, here again, we have a great upheaval which had no very visible effects on social organization. The habits and beliefs forged by centuries of an earlier social order cannot be changed instantly. The Emperor had indeed lost his antique prestige and there had been some renewal of the ruling classes, but a capable administration, a direct inheritance from the Meiji epoch, still controlled the country's destiny, collaborating closely with the business world – the heads of the large banking, commercial and industrial firms. The population, trained by long practice in a quasi-military discipline and supervised by political parties of which the largest were financed by business interests, integrated willingly into the industrial order.

Today, the position is what one would expect if there had been no significant changes since the Meiji Restoration and the military period, but nevertheless, with one basic difference: the military-style leadership of the state and the Zaibatsu has been put to the service of other aims, not military but civilian; the twin objectives being to raise Japanese living standards and to conquer foreign markets in order to pay for essential imports. The second of these objectives is pursued according to the rules of military strategy: technical superiority will bring victory; production as a whole must be maintained at a reasonable level as regards both the techniques used and the labour force applying them; the resistance of foreign competitors must be studied in all fields, in order rapidly to concentrate resources in quantity where a breakthrough appears possible. Western observers agree that the large Japanese firms do not apply the criteria used in Western countries in deciding on their investments. Japanese investments are, to quote François Perroux, 'wagers on new structures', whereas French investments are calculated on the basis of discounted present values and marginal criteria. Indeed, in a society in which large business concerns and the planning authorities collaborate closely, two or three large firms may decide simultaneously to make identical investments, and then compete fiercely with each other. A firm which has beaten its Japanese competitors need have no complexes about its ability to sell on world markets.

Thus the situation is what one would expect if the executives of the large Japanese firms, like the top civil servants, thought of the struggle for world markets as if it were a military struggle: a war must be won and to do so the necessary means must be provided without regard to expense. Victory will recompense the initial sacrifices – and with great profit; by contrast, defeat means ruin.

Such a strategy can be executed only for so long as capital accumulation remains substantial, and while the labour force accepts lower living standards compared with immediate opportunities, knowing that to sacrifice the present to the future is the only way to obtain a greater rise in living standards in the long run; or more simply, the sacrifice is an unavoidable necessity in a country that is deprived of basic raw materials.

Does this mean that there are no imminent dangers? The old general social order is still preserved in the collective memory and still protects the industrial order efficiently. Its legitimacy has nevertheless been seriously eroded. A generation has gone by since the end of World War II, and another will pass before the capitalistic industrial order can take control of the labour force without the help of the traditional social order. It is then that the difficulties will no doubt occur.

Be this as it may, Japanese history from the Meiji Restoration up to the end of World War II shows clearly that the general social order, the expression of a very ancient culture, having forgotten none of the lessons of history, closely conditions the form of industrial development.

2.3   Brazil: A culture coexisting with the difficult search for a social order and for industrialization[5]

Originally a Portuguese colony, Brazil became independent in 1822 after the transfer of the Portuguese court to Rio de Janeiro in 1807. So Brazil appears quite early on as a fully-fledged, independent state. The population, whether it be white, black or yellow, consists of immigrants or the children of immigrants, but all speak the same language. Racism is unknown. All possess or have assimilated a similar culture and generously share mutual beliefs: no one doubts that he is part of the nation.

However, for obvious reasons, a general social order covering the whole of this immense country was not formed by inheritance from the past, as occurred in France and Japan. It had to be created *ex nihilo*, and the effort to do so is relatively recent, dating back mainly to the years after World War I.

There have been not one but several general social orders which were established at various periods and in different regions, as mining and agricultural activities brought settlers and workers to different parts of the country. It is possible, very schematically, to distinguish two or possibly three general social organizations, each relating to a region. Some of their characteristics still subsist today.

The general social order of the North-East region, based on sugar growing, prospered between approximately 1600 and 1700. The type of development was the great estate using a large slave labour force, consisting of some Indians but mainly of black labourers brought from Africa. The corresponding social organization is simple: at the top the white land-owner and below the many slaves working for him. The type of human relationship is patriarchal, quasi-feudal and precludes racism. This society has the features of a stationary community, ruled indolently by rich and undynamic landowners[6]. This neo-feudal type of social order is unpropitious terrain for industrialization.

The general social organization of the Southern regions is a composite of two different activitires: mining and agricultural production. Gold mining (1780–1795) developed in the Minas region and attracted a large number of adventurers – energetic and often unscrupulous, but dynamic speculators. The general social order which was established comprised a few landlords who managed to take over the land, a relatively large number of adventurers of all kinds, and a few black slaves working in the mines. The gold and diamond deposits were soon worked out, but new, large and diversified mineral resources soon replaced them. This mining period, which is still with us today, generated an active and dynamic population favourable to risk and change. The numerous small mining centres have been converted into small industrial centres.

Coffee was produced in the São Paulo region; its great era of prosperity lasted from approximately 1830 until the 1930 crisis. Coffee brought great wealth to the region; but the market for this product is speculative, and subject to successive crises and booms. A traditional-type social order was established by this crop: namely, the estate owner with a particularly abundant labour force[7]. This type of social order, as we have seen, is not particularly favourable to industrialization; nevertheless, coffee growers have considerable speculative propensities which, allied to knowledge of world markets, can be an excellent asset for potential industrial production. The 1930 crisis imperilled this social order and, quite paradoxically, it generated the birth of small landed estates and industrial take-off. Some landlords were forced to divide up their land. This led to the creation of a class of small owners, conservative politically but dynamic as regards their farming practices, who rapidly diversified their crops to include cotton, tobacco and vines. Above all, and this is mainly what concerns us here, the landlords, whose incomes had declined but who were still very rich, decided to invest in building, commerce and industry.

In this way, industrialization began in the São Paulo region from 1930 onward, with considerable support from the state, as will be seen below. The São Paulo region, by contrast to the North-East region, was populated by small as well as large land-owners, as well as by heads of firms and dynamic, speculative businessmen versed in the mechanisms of international markets and attached to Western cultural values.

Accordingly, of the different social orders which had been created in the various regions, only those generated by mining and coffee cultivation were capable of triggering a process of industrialization, but for different reasons and following different paths[8]. Moreover, the regions developed independently of one another. Regional governments dominated either by landlords or business circles were relatively powerful, the central power weak. Great diversity was thus to be observed among the various regions; nevertheless, any inhabitant of a given region still felt strongly that he belonged to the same nation and culture.

On the basis of, or together with, these different regional social orders, could a general social order be established covering the whole population? Two political forces took the matter in hand in the period after the end of World War I: the President of the Republic and the Army.

First, Brazilian nationalism began to emerge in the political, social and economic fields under the presidency of Gaetulio Vargas. The strengthening of the central government involved the subordination of the regional parties dominated by the great landlords. Vargas succeeded in endowing Brazil with a constitution in July 1934, with the help of the middle class, the 'lieutenants' in the army, and also, the trade unions. The authority of the central government was reinforced and the regional parties rendered almost powerless. At least in theory, the state's authority was secured over the whole of Brazil's territory.

On the social side, Vargas instigated a new policy, 'populism', which aimed to satisfy the demands of the working class and to unify them at national level. Social measures were taken that were ahead of the times: education was reorganized to enable the largest possible number to benefit from it, and social legislation was passed in favour of unions and workers. On the economic side, various measures were taken first to surmount the 1929 crisis and later to foster the country's development.

In 1930, Vargas had to deal with the problems of an economy which had been deeply shaken by the world crisis. Coffee prices had collapsed, and the São Paulo region was threatened with bankruptcy. The President succeeded in stabilizing the price of coffee by organizing the destruction of stocks and by limiting the number of plantations. This preserved internal demand and fostered the development of small industrial firms, mostly located around São Paulo, which began to produce goods that had formerly been imported from abroad. These firms reinvested their profits, to their own benefit and to that of the region.

Vargas's development policy for Brazil was to promote the country's economic integration by abolishing the customs barriers among the states, and to follow a course which, from then onward, was to be one of the characteristics of Brazil's mode of industrialization: on the one hand, he invited foreign investors, mainly American, into Brazil; on the other hand, he attempted to preserve Brazil's resources and the sectors deemed to be strategic, by creating the first national planning organizations, and by launching national corporations covering areas such as steel and energy. Vargas's successors followed the same general line. Sometimes they stressed the value of foreign capital for Brazil's development (even if provided by multinational, mostly American companies); at other times Brazil's interest in retaining control of the key sectors and in pursuing a more autonomous development was emphasized.

Secondly, the Brazilian army has always been characterized by the intellectual quality of its officers and by the extent of the duties they believe they owe their country. Officers have always considered that their role goes beyond their purely military function, and includes the achievement of national unity as well as responsibility for the proper social and political organization of the nation. The general staff together with the officer corps (the 'military Sorbonne') has thus played a prominent role in Brazil's social and economic development, at least since the end of World War I.

Both these centralizing forces, in attempting to create a general social organization applicable to the whole country, have pursued the same objectives, but at different levels: the population and the elite. Most of the time, they have helped one another, but at times have acted at cross-purposes. Nevertheless, the main principles they follow remain the same:

- At the political level, to strengthen national feeling by extending the availability of education, raising the standard of living of the population and emphasizing the international role which could be played by Brazil as the dominant South American country and as supporter of the United States in the ideological struggles between 'Western' ideas and communism (or, at least, ideas judged to be communist);
- From an economic viewpoint, to raise living standards of the population and strengthen the country's potential by industrializing; this is easier to achieve than agricultural reform which has still not really begun. Industrial development is financed and carried out mainly by drawing on foreign investment and techniques, but the sources are being diversified as much as possible, e.g. Japanese investment, but German technology for the nuclear programme. Nevertheless, future opportunities must be preserved by maintaining strategic production and wealth under the control of the Brazilian government.

As a consequence of the errors made by the Government, which in spite of its good intentions had pursued a policty leading to a very fast inflation and the cessation of growth, the army seized power in 1964, intending to return it to civilian authority as soon as possible. It has not yet, 15 years later, managed to do so, and the difficulties have, if anything, intensified.

One of the sources of present problems may be the difficulty of pursuing several objectives at the same time: regional social orders are being replaced by a national order; yet before this general order has been established, discipline must be maintained in the industrial social order while business circles are divided into two groups, one associated with international capitalism and the other linked with national activities. At the same time, working class movements and unions have put forward ideas which are no doubt in advance of the real state of development of the country.

2.4 Ivory Coast: a remarkable economic success but a society at risk

The Ivory Coast was progressively populated over the course of its history by tribal migrations going back several centuries. The population was divided into a multitude of ethnic groups and tribes, each having its own dialect, culture and deities, and also its own forms of social organization: some patriarchal and dominated by elders, others based on a prototype of state organization.

France, the colonial power, had begun to structure the Ivorian territory by establishing a centralized administrative organization. Nevertheless, it

left the country with almost no industry. In the general trend to de-
colonization which followed World War II, the Ivory Coast obtained its
independence from France in 1960 without an armed struggle by a Liberation Front. Elsewhere, it was this struggle that united the various sections of
the population and generated the birth of national feeling.

When the first President of the Republic, Felix Houphouët-Boigny, took
power (and he was still President in 1980) the Ivory Coast for practical
purposes had neither a general social order nor an industrial order. With a
remarkable political instinct, the President set himself the task of unifying
the country by creating a national sentiment and sense of solidarity between
the different members of the community. This was accomplished by a rapid
betterment of the population's living conditions, by development of certain
agricultural products for export such as coffee, cocoa and oilseeds, by
prospecting for and exploiting mineral resources, in particular, iron ore and
oil, and by rapid industrialization. An exceptional rate of growth over a long
period allowed a general social order and industrial order to be created in a
country where they had not hitherto existed, but they had to be constructed
in order to meet the aim of the country's social and political unification.

A few remarks may be made on the method used to graft a general social
order and an industrial order onto the basis provided by the general social
organization of the various ethnic groups. The experience of the Ivory Coast
appears to be particularly relevant.

The general social orders, each corresponding to an ethnic group, were
very diverse, but all had this in common: they were based on the institutions
of the extended family and of the tribe. Relationships between men are very
special in this institutional environment: the spirit of solidarity which unites
a family and a tribe is a basic moral value. Each member of the group, if he
works at all, works for the community and not for himself. Healthy youths
and adults take responsibility for the aged and the infirm. It is the duty of a
wage-earner to provide for the upkeep of a large number of relations who do
not work – and sometimes do not want to. The family's activities moreover
do not go beyond providing for the basic needs of its members, with no
surplus. Furthermore, strict rules govern relationships between the various
members of the family: the elders have the authority and the young are
allowed very little initiative. It can be observed that such a general social
order is not really suitable for promoting a Western-type industrial society.
The solidarity which unites the members of a family limits economic
competition, the fruit of the individual's work is handed over to the
collectivity, and the most dynamic element – youth – is prevented from
acting.

It was President Houphouët-Boigny's view that in these circumstances he
could attack the problem of introducing an industrializing social order by a
strategy aimed at destroying the existing social orders based on ethnic
groups by adopting legislation which by-passes the traditional family and
deals only with the rights and obigations of the Western-type small family

cell. To implement the President's plans, the young should be educated in a Western fashion; and administrative authority would operate on the basis of Western motivations once the young had been freed from traditional and family constraints and had become Westernized (the young Ivorian administration is a carbon copy of the French administration and needs a large number of executives, trained in the French approach to government). This implied introducing the incentive system based on personal profit, and promoting the training of Western-type managers to become business experts and profit-seekers, thus giving the finishing touches to the industrialization process under way.

Together with the conditions needed for the development of an industrial order, an Ivorian nation is to be created by introducing a unified legislation which the Ivorians must accept to replace the diversity of the old local customs. With the passage of time, all the features which constitute the specificity of an Ivorian member of an ethnic group will disappear, and the state will then have Ivorians of a similar nature – which can only increase the efficiency of the nation's economic performance.

The price to be paid by the population for this policy to succeed is rather high. For example there is conflict between the older and the younger generations over such features as new marriage customs where the old practices like the dowry, polygamy and preferential marriage are disappearing. The security granted by the family and the tribe to the old and infirm will cease. The direct contact of much of youth with Western civilization will have significant and possibly dramatic consequences on culture and beliefs.

Nevertheless, it is still too soon to draw conclusions from this fascinating experiment. The President's ability and the exceptional growth in the last few years have enabled the Ivory Coast to progress in line with the President's plans, but will the roots of the new general social order be established deeply enough? The industrial social order is not yet in place, as Ivorian executives to supervise industry are in too short supply and young people are not yet really attracted to the engineering sciences. Some young people, freed from tribal restrictions and tribal solidarity, seem to seek money by speculative rather than productive activities and adopt the behaviour typical of *nouveaux riches*. Some young women react to their liberation from family constraints by refusing to have children.

The experiment under way is indeed fascinating, but there is an obvious danger: that of unstructuring society by destroying the old order before any type of order, whether a new general social order or an industrial order, has been established to replace it. The situation would become especially precarious if economic growth were to stop or, even worse, if a crisis arose. There would doubtless then be reason to fear that rivalries among ethnic groups attempting to appropriate the state's resources might destroy the still fragile, new social order which is now being created.

2.5   Conclusion

Clearly, there is no way of drawing firm conclusions from the four examples discussed earlier, two of them mere outlines. But our goal, less ambitious, was only to seek a link between the general social order and a society's aptitude for industrialization. The examples seem reasonably convincing.

In France, the social order under the Bourbons proved relatively unpropitious to the development of industrialization, notwithstanding attempts by the monarchy to promote it. This social order made way for a bourgeois social organization, but rather than destroying its predecessor the new order grafted itself onto it. Under the new system, industry and the industrial order took root, but the process of industrialization was not particularly dynamic. The bourgeois order in France has a low propensity to industrialize.

In Japan, the feudal social order lasted until quite recently. Initially, it was not a favourable terrain for industrialization, but it became so once the ruling class of nobles came to believe that rapid industrialization was the condition of national independence. The social order as a whole was mobilized to achieve this end, and industrialization followed rapidly. The Japanese social order is strongly conducive to industrialization.

Several specific social orders appear to exist in Brazil. There is a lively sense of national identity, but the concept of the nation as the overall social order, imposing itself on the population at large and transforming it into a fairly structured and organized whole, hardly applies, or has begun to do so only very recently. The state and the army have done their utmost to promote a social order which would secure the stable domination of capitalism, and of industrial leaders over the working classes. Two questions are: who will draw advantage from the new order, and which class will exploit the now docile labour force for its own ends? The answers will obviously depend on the form finally taken by the general social order now being established, and by the institutions or groups to emerge as playing commanding roles: the state, the army, the national industrial groups or the multinational corporations. Clearly the type of industrialization will depend on which comes to the top.

In the Ivory Coast, the traditional general social order has not been destroyed by the bourgeoisie, but by the state, which has accepted the close link between the nature of the social order and the scope for industrialization. In its view, the traditional social order is incompatible with industrialization, and, consequently, must be destroyed – implying an onslaught against such institutions as kinship and the tribe. If, as the government hopes, the overall social order takes the shape of a liberal society, the population will become true Western-style consumers and producers, and industrialization can begin; but perhaps there will no longer be a 'living society'.

Several conclusions may be drawn from this comparison of social experiences.

The history of countries that have been industrialized for a long time seems to show that there is a certain link between the culture, the general social order and the scope and methods of industrialization. Some cultures and social orders are 'industrializing', others less so, or not at all.

It is worth remarking that the bourgeois social order, as an approximation to the ideal of a liberal society, is not the only way of promoting industrialization. Japan provides the example of a nation where the survival of feudal social relationships has been consistent with, and indeed has actively fostered, intense industrialization.

The leaders of some developing countries accept the close link among the culture, the general social structure and their nation's scope for industrialization, but they appear convinced that only a liberal social order will produce this result. This may be an error. The establishment of the new general social order must be based on the ruins of the old order and of the old cuture, and it cannot be attained in the short-term.

Experience shows, *pace* Marx and Engels, that the bourgeois social order has not succeeded, even today, in destroying and supplanting the archaic social order in the long-industrialized countries[9]. It is the earlier order which has enabled industrialization to go forward by securing the domination of the working classes by capitalists (or by the state bureaucracy). The industrial order on its own has never succeeded in becoming the general social order. In some countries, at certain times, when it seemed close to achieving this goal, the working classes have effectively resisted their subjugation by the ruling classes, engendering a decline in the rate of increase of the stock of capital and, with it, economic stagnation.

A working hypothesis flowing from these observations seems worth testing, namely, the extent to which the history of a long-industrialized country discloses the following pattern. It may begin with a stable monarchical or feudal society not particularly conducive to industrialization. At some point, usually for non-economic reasons, the ruling class opts to promote it. The process gets under way, engenders the industrial order, and proceeds without particular difficulties so long as the general social order guarantees satisfaction of the necessary conditions for the accumulation of capital, that is to say the domination of the workers by the economic ruling class (which is not necessarily the political leadership).

However, with the passage of time, this general social order loses its vigour, in part as an effect of the growth of industrialization itself. The political and economic leaderships tend to amalgamate at this stage, notably when a democratic system takes over from a royalist or feudal regime. The industrial order is then left alone to maintain discipline in the factories and the wage system, but performs this function inefficiently; this is because the working class can impose its own laws through the electoral system – which it could not have done under a monarchy or in a feudal society. At this point, productivity falls, stagnation sets in, and decadence begins[10].

This is not to say that a politico-economic system is utopian if its general social order and its industrial organization are based solely on democratic principles, for example a society of the 'self-management' type. But the fact remains that no such society has yet seen the light of day. Once the earlier social order – admittedly taken by many to be based on an 'illusion', to use Marx's expression – has lost its strength, the proper functioning of the industrial order and the accumulation of capital can be maintained only by governmental control backed by police truncheons.

In practical terms, any assessment of the scope for the development of a given country, less-developed or other, should take into account its general social order, and ascertain how far its structure and the aspirations of the dominant groups lend themselves to the growth of industrialization. It should be noted that the end-purpose of industrialization and its form may differ from the models so far offered by our experience of Western-style development and industrialization. In many developing countries there are, today, examples of a denial that development necessarily means industrialization along the lines followed by the Western world.

This raises a difficult, but fundamental problem that the West will have to face: the emergence of societies, doubtless industrial, but also involving other forms of activity to satisfy other individual and collective demands, and, above all, seeking to achieve ends other than the sole pursuit of economic wealth. This has always been so; what is new is that these will be powerful societies, capable of bringing into question the dominating position now held by the societies of our Western world, and, in the more or less distant future, forcing our Western societies to adjust to *their* values.

References

1 The difference would, at least in theory, be smaller if the industrial order had sprung from the desire of the Prince to have, say, a powerful arms industry. Industrial organization would then be directly at the service of the general social order. This would also be true if firms were nationalized bodies – provided that individuals and groups are, rightly or wrongly, certain that the nationalized industrial order thus created is in harmony with the standards they recognize: to wit, the values of the general society to which they belong, and that it operates to their advantage, and not only to that of their governing bureaucracy.
2 We believe that, on the contrary, the industrial order is expanding not in opposition to, but sheltered by, the general social order, by using certain of its structures, in particular the hierarchical institutions, which are favourable to it. When these institutions prove too weak, the industrial order is often unable to force its own hierarchy onto society other than by terror, and it is then threatened with chaos.
3 'A peaceful Asia beckons investors'. *Fortune*, October 1977.
4 Admittedly some entrepreneurs actively sought the status of industrialist – many were Protestants – but they magnified it by giving it a social meaning. The industrialist's function is to provide working-class families with their daily bread and, only incidentally, to make a profit. By acting thus, these industrialists have,

doubtless unconsciously, tried to reconstitute, but this time at the factory level, the relationships that bound men during the monarchy.

5 For Brazilian economic development, see also Chapter 9 of this work.

6 In the eighteenth century, competition from Antilles sugar dangerously threatened this society's economic foundations. The crisis was to last a long time. The landlords, who controlled the local government, saved themselves from bankruptcy by even greater exploitation of the labour force. The crisis worsened after World War I and yet again after 1940. This last blow put the social order to the test: peasant leagues were formed which were moreover advised by the sons of rich families unable any longer to bear the contrast between the wealth of some and the wretchedness of most. These leagues demanded the redistribution of land.

7 Until the early 1900s, the field-workers were mainly black slaves, either from the North-East region or imported illegally from Africa. But then whites began to enter (Europeans, Mediterraneans and Lebanese) and then, finally, Asians (the Japanese). Whatever the colour of their skin, these workers were treated with equal harshness.

8 It should be recalled that the golden age of rubber production was between 1850 and 1914. It contributed to the discovery of the Amazon but generated no industrialization.

9 Similar conclusions would no doubt be drawn from scrutiny of the history of Great Britain and Germany. The case of the United States is of particular interest and should be studied from this standpoint.

10 This problem is closely related to those raised by Theodore Geiger, assisted by Frances M. Geiger, in their interesting study *Welfare and Efficiency*, National Planning Association, Washington D.C., 1978.

Select Bibliography

France

L. Bergeron, *Les capitalistes en France: 1780–1914*. Gallimard-Julliard, Paris, 1978.

L. Girard, M. Bonnefous and J. Rudel, *1848–1914*. Editions Bordas, Paris, 1966.

G. Lefranc, *Les organisations patronales en France*. Payot, Paris, 1976.

J. M. Mayeur, F. Bederidan, A. Prost and J. L. Monneron (Preface by C. Morazé), *Histoire du peuple francais*. Nouvelle librairie de France, Paris, 1964.

A. J. Tudesq and J. Rudel *1789–1848*. Editions Bordas, Paris, 1964.

Japan

H. Brochier, *Le miracle économique japonais*. Calmann-Levy, Paris, 1965.

R. Guillain, *Japon troisième grand*. Seuil, Paris, 1969.

N. Jequier, *Le défi industriel japonais*. Centre de recherches économiques, Lausanne, 1970.

C. Sautter, *Le prix de la puissance*. Seuil, Paris, 1973.

P. Van Thuan, *La construction du Japon moderne*. Centre de recherches européennes, Lausanne, 1966.

Brazil

C. Furtado, 'Au Brésil: économie, politique et sociéte'. *Annales Economies, Sociétés. Civilisation*, Juillet-août 1966.

M. Lannou and N. Lecocq-Muller, *Le nouveau Brésil*. Armand Colin, Paris, 1976.

M. Niedergang, *Les 20 Amériques latines*. Editions du Seuil, Paris, 1977.

M. Schooyans, *Destin du Brésil*. Editions J. Duculot – Gembloux, Belgium, 1973.

A. Touraine, *Les sociétés dépendantes*. Editions J. Duculot-Gembloux, Belgium, 1973.

Ivory Coast

H. Bourgoin and P. Guilhaume, *Côte-d'Ivoire: économie et sociéte*. Stock, Paris, 1979.

Theories of diffusion and dependency

Ambassador Roberto de Oliveira Campos
and Dr Raphael Valentino*

3.1 An introductory appraisal

To a certain extent, the debate between 'diffusion' and 'dependence' recalls the medieval controversy of nominalism, which opposed the two truths – the philosophical and the theological. William of Ockham, an important spokesman for nominalism, held that reason had to capitulate when faced with revealed truth. For nominalists, general concepts were mere figments of the imagination; they did not exist in reality but only in terminology. It is not intended to dwell upon the subtleties into which such a conception developed, especially the doctrine of transubstantiation. But it should be stressed that dependency theories have tried to weaken the concept of industrialization as a general category by distinguishing between dependent and independent industrialization and refusing to ascribe to the former the nature of a development process.

Philip J. O'Brien has rightly pointed out that in unsophisticated hands the danger is that dependency can easily become a pseudo-concept which explains everything in general and hence nothing in particular. 'In the hands of some Latin-American writers, the theory of dependency is used as a *deus ex machina* explanation for everything which seems to be wrong with Latin American society.'[1] O'Brien is right in adding to his criticism of the dependency theory that instead of offering a synthesis of the historical process, it is merely a descriptive catalogue of different types of dependency. In this connection, he singles out Canada as an eloquent counter-example to the dependency theory, because it is an obvious instance of a structurally diversified country with high per capita income levels – and yet it is described as a 'dependent' country.

By transmuting the familiar distinction between developed and underdeveloped countries into a new verbiage, which contrasts 'dependent' with 'independent' development, the real issues of underdevelopment, one of the major challenges of our epoch, are conceptually blurred, leaving us with the additional quandary of explaining why some dependent countries are rich and others poor. For it is not very illuminating simply to argue, like

* The same authors also contribute Chapter 9, which deals specifically with Brazilian development.

Theotonio dos Santos, that dependency is the 'conditioning structure of poverty'[2].

We do not mean to ignore some analytic contributions brought to light by the modern controversy on industrialization which divides 'diffusionists' from 'dependentists'. But we cannot escape the impression that to a certain extent those new labels evoke the old antagonism between structuralists and monetarists on the sources and cure of inflation. As Joseph Schumpeter used to repeat, it is essential not to throw away the analytical baby with the philosophical bath-water – or rather with the ideological bath-water in this case.

The theoreticians of dependency appear to suffer from a taxonomic as well as ideological bias. The ideological bias is implicit in the notion that dependent development involves residual imperialist exploitation, while the 'pure' economic analyst would regard it merely as a transitional phase in the process of development, thus adhering to a phased rather than to an ideological view of things.

The taxonomic approach lies in interpreting dependent development as a fatalistic qualitative category, while for the analytical economist, it is merely an instance of 'how-much-moreness' – countries evolving from dependency to interdependence (independence remaining a utopian goal) along a continuous path of industrialization and technological absorptions.

In his lucid essay *Imperialism and Capitalist Industrialization*, Bill Warren has adequately refuted the Marxist *prophétisme sinistre*, which predicted the non-development of the Third World[3].

> 'Despite statements and predictions to the contrary, the underdeveloped world, considered as a whole, has made considerable progress in industrialization in the postwar period. In fact, already by the 1950s, the Third World accounted for a higher proportion of the world's manufacturing output than it did pre-war. Whereas in 1937 the developed capitalist countries accounted for about nine times the manufacturing output of Latin America, Africa and Asia, by 1959 the ratio had been reduced to seven to one.'

Moreover, he goes on to say, 'this tendency for manufacturing output to grow faster in the underdeveloped world than in the developed capitalist world continued into the 1960s, with Third World manufacturing output growing at about 7 per cent per annum between 1960 and 1968, when in the advanced capitalist world it grew at about 6 per cent'. This was despite the fact that during the 1960s industrial growth in the developed capitalist world was exceptionally high by historical standards.

Moreover, periods of higher growth in manufacturing production of the underdeveloped world do not necessarily coincide with periods of high growth in manufacturing production in the industrialized countries. This could be presented in a simplistic way as independence rather than as dependence.

Warren does not neglect, in his analysis, such objections as the argument that this apparent success is attributable to the high statistical growth rates associated with very small industrial bases and can therefore be regarded as misleading; or, alternatively, that in terms of output per head the record of the underdeveloped countries compared with the developed capitalist countries is rather poor. Figures for individual countries make clear the ability of many underdeveloped countries substantially to diversify their industrial basis and to maintain, over a sustained period, much faster rates of growth of manufacturing output than the already industrialized economies (see *Table 3.1*).

Table 3.1 *Annual rates of growth of manufacturing for selected countries 1960–1977 (%)*

	1960–70	1970–77		1960–77	1970–77
Brazil	4.8	10.7	Pakistan	9.4	2.2
Chile	5.5	3.6	Panama	10.5	. .
Iran	12.0	16.7	Peru	7.2	. .
Iraq	5.9	11.5[b]	Philippines	6.7	6.8
Ivory Coast	11.6[a]	7.9[a]	Singapore	13.0	9.0
Jamaica	5.6	0.6	Taiwan	17.3	12.5
Jordan	9.9[a]	. .	Thailand	11.0	11.2
South Korea	17.2	19.3	Turkey	10.7	. .
Malaysia	. .	12.3	Venezuela	6.2	6.8
Mexico	9.4	6.0	Zambia	. .	3.7
Nicaragua	11.1	6.3			

[a] Industry
[b] 1970–1976

Source: World Bank, *World Development Report 1979*, Annex Table 2 and (for Brazil 1960–1970) APEC, *A Economia Brazileira e suas Perspectivas*, various issues

Furthermore, Warren stresses that this industrialization has been taking place in a period where neither war nor world depression acted to 'cut off' the Third World from the advanced capitalist countries. And yet it is this cutting-off that some consider crucial in explaining such industrial progress as has been made (in partial exception to this 'developing underdevelopment' and 'increasing polarization' thesis.) One of Warren's conclusions deserves special mention:

'Certainly, the growth of manufacturing output per head in the underdeveloped countries does lag behind that of the imperialist world, *in part because of the unprecedented postwar rates of population growth in the former.* But to take the growth of manufacturing output per head as a basis of comparison is to apply an extremely demanding criterion of performance. . . . From the point of view of living standards, per capita growth rates are the most relevant criterion. However, *from the perspectives of the distribution of world industrial power and the growth of the market* (which are more relevant to the problem at hand) *total, rather than per capita growth rates are the central issues*.[4]

(emphasis added)

If we look at countries of the socialist periphery – presumably immune from capitalist dependency – we can easily see that liberation from the 'imperialist centres of industrial power' has not meant liberation from the strains and limits of development and industrialization. The Cuban case is very seldom discussed in the light of the dependency theory, because many advocates of such theory argue that this country is deemed to have achieved the pre-conditions for development, although the implementation of its development has not yet come, 20 years after the revolution. Quite often, ideological sympathy for the Cuban experiment prevails over economic objectivity in assessing its developmental impact.

3.2   Reverse dependency

'Reverse dependency' is the other side of the coin. President Kennedy remarked once that the most dependent powers in the world are the super powers. Raymond Aron had already stressed that while from 1920 to 1929, imports and exports of raw materials in the United States were practically in equilibrium, from 1949 onwards the country has become an importer of the first rank. In 1973, Raymond Aron pointed out that for strategic materials, the percentages of American imports as a ratio of total consumption were as follows: 24 per cent for tungsten, 100 per cent for columbium, 75 per cent for nickel, 100 per cent for chrome and 100 per cent for cobalt[5].

If we were to list 'dependency handicaps' of the Soviet Union, a very basic one – foodstuffs – could certainly come first. Both China and other socialist countries have come to acknowledge 'dependency' on the market economies for accelerating industrial modernization. The oil crisis, the consequent relapses of the world into mini-recessions and maxi-inflations and the 'currencies warfare' (*'la guerre des monnaies'*, as Raymond Aron labelled the present monetary disorder) are further evidence of a begrudgingly recognized interdependence of economic fortunes in both a positive and a negative direction.

Perroux's concept of industrialization, which is one of the leading forces behind the diffusionist approach, is today more real than ever (if we are to avert a replay of previous economic crises in the world). According to Perroux, within the framework of his theory of the 'growth poles', industrialization means reshaping economic and social structures under the influence of technological processes. The main consequences of this restructuring are:

(1) its irreversibility;

(2) geographical and sectoral movements of workers;

(3) invigoration of the external sector for the implantation of economies of scale to overcome the smallness of domestic markets; and

(4) technological and financial interdependence among world centres to ensure the continuity of the process[6].

One paradoxical note, in our present time of dilemmas and reversions, is the reversal of fears between industrialized and developing countries. The dependency theory was a reaction of the premature against the mature. By an odd transmigration of irrational economic anxieties, some of the advanced industrial societies are now afraid of their own de-industrialization and of the industrial onrush of the emerging countries.

Since 1945, the dichotomy – industrial/pre-industrial – has become the keynote of any classification of societies. As Ernest Gellner pointed out, this new dichotomy has not only outranked previous ones – such as democracy, capitalism and socialism – but has also been imbued with a sense of exclusivism. And Gellner goes on to emphasize that 'the consequence was a view which like that of the Enlightenment and unlike the intervening Evolutionism, was a two-term one' (i.e. industrial versus pre-industrial societies), and one which locates the crucial transition somewhere near the present time rather than at the beginning or the end of an evolution in time. The Enlightenment's romantic regret has been associated with progressive hope within the framework of a new vision which takes over from the nineteenth century a far richer sense of the diversity and complexity of social forms. Furthermore, contemporary history has made it quite clear that development is not a single path. As Gellner notes, 'unilinealism has now died many, many deaths'. Development is indeed a complex network of routes. Even Marx's 'pre-capitalist social formations', Gellner adds, if plotted on paper, would not look like a single road but more like the Southern Railway's commuter network[7].

Our sketch of the Brazilian stages of industrialization in Chapter 9 provides a counter-illustration to unilinealism and evidence of the wide range of possibilities for coexistence among several formats of industrialization within the same country. Perhaps from such an experience useful lessons can be derived for creative coexistence between industrialized and industrializing countries.

3.3   Foreign trade constraints: protectionism in the aftermath of the oil shock

After a moderate (and perhaps temporary) triumph of the spirit of negotiation in the political field, the shock of adjustment to the new distribution of economic power has reintroduced into the international scene the threat of another modality of Cold War – the Cold War of Protectionism – now between the North and the South. 'Non-proliferation' has been one of the main catchwords for international political development, whereas 'proliferation of underdevelopment' has emerged as an unsavoury potential outcome of this confrontation. As a consequence, even the art of economics has, in some cases, reversed its basic aims and, instead of pursuing welfare in spite of scarcity, has become a weapon of scarcity against welfare.

It has been repeatedly stressed that the mercantilist writers wrote for the short-run situation that confronted them but there is considerable evidence that they did not seem to be aware of any distinction between desirable practice to meet a temporary situation and permanent policy. In speaking of a revival of mercantilism, we mean a resurrection of selfish, unenlightened short-term policies which survive much longer than their doubtful economic wisdom would warrant. Inflation, misdirection of labour and failed attempts to maintain a high employment level, have been some of the consequences. But let us take the assumptions of the present neo-protectionism and test their effectiveness against the background of economic performance.

The NICs have become a sort of 'phantom of economic freedom'. The way the industrial countries view the NICs would deserve a film by Buñuel, perhaps in the wake of *That Obscure Object of Desire*, in which an aged gentleman and a young lady chase and reject each other for the wrong reasons.

The OECD study – *The Impact of the Newly Industrialized Countries on Production and Trade in Manufactures* – dealt with a restricted list of countries which, the study itself recognizes, are far from being homogeneous[8]. The OECD study includes within the category of NICs: Brazil and Mexico from Latin America; Greece, Portugal, Spain and Yugoslavia from Southern Europe and the Mediterranean; and Hong Kong, South Korea, Singapore and Taiwan from East and South-East Asia.

Table 3.2 *NICs' share in world exports of manufactures to selected areas (%)*

	1963	1973	1976
NIC exports to:			
Industrial countries[a]	2.6	7.0	7.9
Developing countries, of which	4.7	7.2	8.1
OPEC	3.9	5.9	6.4
Others	4.9	7.6	8.6
Eastern bloc	1.3	2.5	3.1

[a] OECD minus Australia and New Zealand

Source: Organization for Economic Cooperation and Development (OECD), *The Impact of the Newly Industrializing Countries on Production and Trade in Manufactures*. Paris, 1979, Table 30

The supposedly alarming fact about the NICs (in some minds) is that their share of OECD imports of manufactures grew from 2.6 to 7.9 per cent between 1963 and 1976 (see *Table 3.2*).

In fact, this is a false alarm. Firstly, the low-base argument is not to be neglected (as opposed to the non-growth prophecy, as discussed above), because the NICs started from a very low base indeed. Secondly, the OECD study itself stresses that the NICs have an overall deficit in trade in manufactures; this deficit more than doubled in current dollars between 1963 and 1973, although declining somewhat in 1976 (*Table 3.3*). Furthermore, we should not be deluded by global figures for the NICs as if they were a metaphysical entity. Brazil, like the European NICs, experienced a very large increase in her deficit over the period. Finally, the present new wave of protectionism is based on a static profile of world demand and neglects the role of innovation.

Table 3.3 *NICs' trade balances in manufactures[a] ($ billion)*

	1963	1973	1976
Greece	−0.46	−1.53	−2.27
Portugal	−0.08	−0.48	−0.90
Spain	−0.69	−1.55	−1.11
Yugoslavia	−0.24	−0.95	−0.99
Brazil	−0.73	−3.02	−4.56
Mexico	−1.03	−1.38	−1.85
Hong Kong	−0.07	0.05	0.99
South Korea	−0.22	0.53	2.45
Singapore	−0.19	−1.24	−1.40
Taiwan	−0.08	1.27	2.50
Total	−3.79	−8.30	−7.14

[a] Exports fob less imports fob

Source: Organization for Economic Cooperation and Development (OECD), *The Impact of the Newly Industrializing Countries on Production and Trade in Manufactures.* Paris, 1979, Table 34

The best conceptual framework for understanding the present dynamics of international trade is that of an international product cycle, which covers a vast network of migration of technologies, parts and sub-parts of products in order to maximize comparative advantages. The US–Mexican twin plants in the border area provide a textbook illustration of one country using labour-intensive components to be assembled on the US high-wage side. This instance, among many others, emphasizes the role of foreign investment, and its potentialities for joint-ventures, maximizing the power of the growth-engine of international trade.

The greatest protectionist superstition is job destruction as a consequence of low-cost imports from the NICs. Once again, the argument is based on a double fallacy: it is not true and if it were, it would be economically unwise. Let us take the factual point first. As Vincent Cable pointed out, much of the steam behind the recent campaigning for import controls has been built up by citing the very large loss of employment in sectors such as textiles and footwear; in the former, 400 000 jobs were lost in the EEC between 1973 and 1975 alone, almost 15 per cent of the (1975) labour force. 'It was invariably inferred', Cable writes, 'that "low cost" imports were responsible. However, this is to disregard other factors at work, notably the influence of falling demand in a recession, the influence of trade between developed countries, and the influence of rising labour productivity.' The last of these is particularly important, Cable adds, since in a growing economy, even in the absence of trade, the low productivity, labour-intensive sectors can expect to lose manpower to higher wage and higher productivity sectors. And Cable concludes emphatically and realistically: 'Indeed, LDC–DC trade is in a very real sense catalysing changes that would have taken place anyway and are regarded as generally desirable.'[9]

A number of studies[10] of the employment effect of imports from developing countries have demonstrated two things:

(1) Unemployment caused by imports from developing countries is quite small in comparison with that resulting from labour productivity. For example, a study for the Federal Republic of Germany – which had one of the highest rates of growth of imports from developing countries – estimates the gross number of jobs displaced in 1962–1975 as 133 000, while 6½ million were displaced by increases in labour productivity and about 1.6 million were displaced by imports from other sources[11]. Similar results are shown by studies for the United Kingdom.

(2) Losses of jobs resulting from imports from developing countries are largely offset, in some cases more than offset, by gains in *exports to* developing countries. This implies, of course, displacement of labour between industries but on balance a shift from low-skill to high-skill occupations[12].

Similarly, a recent study by the Consumers' Association in Great Britain points out that at present the NICs are major importers of manufactures and most of them run large trade deficits with the industrialized countries. 'The money they earn from exporting textiles, clothing and so on', the study stresses, 'is used to finance imports.' If they are not to be allowed to increase their exports then they will cut back their imports from the industrialized countries. Every extra £6500 worth of goods that Britain exports is worth a new job in a British factory. An increase of one-tenth of 1 per cent of total exports creates 40 000 new jobs[13].

The second fallacy of the unemployment superstition reflects a distrust of economic and technological progress. The fear of the NICs' competition stems from the negative desire to freeze low competitiveness as it is, ignoring the possibility of positive adaptation through the development of new products and improvement of skills, as some industrial countries – notably Japan – have tried to do. Migrations and cross-fertilization of technologies, circulation of skills and *specialisation en finesse* are entirely disregarded on the social grounds of a 'charitocracy' (dictatorship of economic charity), which protects the non-competitive from the winds and virtues of competition.

In sum, fearing the industrial onrush of the NICs seems a curious revival of the pristine Luddite movement, this time running from the old industrial centres to the new industrial periphery. But a puzzling question remains, noted by Cable: if the threat of the NICs is exaggerated and mutual trade in manufactures is generally beneficial, why do most Western governments seem to act as if the opposite were the case? The answer he provides to such a question is that if the real costs of NIC competition to Western economies are small, the benefits are also small, at least in the short term, compared with the difficulties of assuaging the interest groups affected[14]. As a consequence, many Western countries have adopted the 'salami tactics', i.e. increasing their protectionism by one thin slice at a time, in the hope that no individual slice will provoke great retaliation or de-stabilize the system. In the long run, however, 'salami tactics' are an anti-growth strategy and still more than that, a self-denial of the liberal mind in the Western world.

3.4 By way of conclusion: Who's afraid of the NICs?

In an illuminating article, Professor Ralf Dahrendorf points out that if one listens to the signs of the times in the Western industrialized world and even outside it, it seems clear that we are not about to enter another age of national economic miracles[15]. Accordingly, cooperation seems to re-emerge as a dominant value in economic strategies in this post-miracle age, where interdependence definitely takes over from old dreams of self-sufficiency.

The economically unified world in which we live now requires a fundamental choice by the industrial countries – adaptation or retreat. If they are to relapse into protectionism, they should bear in mind that national economies are based upon interconnected industries; to protect one part entails the need for protection of the next link in the chain, and so on. Protectionism feeds protectionism and ends up in self-insulation and growing inefficiency. It would be deeply regretted if the external environment were to force the NICs into defensive forms of economic primitivism. In the light of previous experience of world crises and recessions, let us not forget Hegel's warning as qualified by Marx: all facts of great importance in world history occur, as it were, twice – the first time as tragedy, the second as farce. And what about the next round? This is our final question.

References

1 P. J. O'Brien, 'A Critique of Latin American Theories of Dependency'. In Ivar Oxaal *et al.*, *Beyond the Sociology of Development*. Routledge & Kegan Paul, London, 1975, p. 12.

2 T. dos Santos, 'The crisis of development theory and the problem of dependency in Latin America'. In H. Bernstein, *Underdevelopment and Development*, Penguin, Harmondsworth, 1973.

3 B. Warren, 'Imperialism and Capitalist Industrialization', *New Left Review* 81, September-October 1973, pp. 3/43.

4 B. Warren, 'Imperialism and Capitalist Industrialization'. *New Left Review* 81, September-October 1973, p. 7.

5 R. Aron, The Imperial Republic; the United States in the World, *1945–1972*. Winthrop, Englewood Cliffs, N. J., 1975, p. 165.

6 F. Perroux, *Pouvoir et Economie*, Paris, 1973.

7 E. Gellner, *Contemporary Thought and Politics*, Routledge & Kegan Paul, London, 1974, p. 128.

8 See Organization for Economic Cooperation and Development (OECD), *The Impact of the Newly Industrializing Countries on Production and Trade in Manufactures*. Paris, 1979, p. 47.

9 For a thorough criticism of anxieties about the NICs, see V. Cable, 'Britain, the New Protectionism and Trade with the Newly Industrializing Countries'. In *International Affairs* 55(1) January 1979, p. 1.

10 See Organization for Economic Cooperation and Development (OECD). *The Impact of the Newly Industrializing Countries on Production and Trade in Manufactures*. Paris, 1979, Annex II for a survey and summary of a number of such studies.

11 F. Wolter, 'Adjustment to imports from developing countries'. A paper presented to a symposium at Kiel, December 1976.

12 B. Balassa, *'The Changing International Division of Labour in manufactured goods'. Banca Nazionale del Lavoro, Quarterly Review* 130, September 1979, p. 243.

13 Consumers' Association, *The Price of Protection – A Which? Campaign Report*, London, 1979, p. 27.

14 V. Cable, 'Britain, the New Protectionism and Trade with the Newly Industrializing Countries'. In *International Affairs* 55(1), January 1979, p. 9.

15 *Sunday Times*, 30 December 1979.

4

Dependency in the 1980s

Otto Kreye*

The 1960s and 1970s saw a rapid industrial development in the developing countries; this was especially reflected in the rates of growth of manufacturing industry. Between 1960 and 1970, output of manufacturing industry in the developing countries grew by 6.4 per cent a year; between 1970 and 1976 this rate accelerated to 7.5 per cent. By contrast, the rates of growth in the western industrial nations fell from 5.8 to 3.4 per cent between the same periods[1]. Employment in manufacturing industry in the developing countries increased by 3.8 per cent a year between 1960 and 1970, and by 6.2 per cent in the period 1970–1976, whereas employment in manufacturing in the industrial nations stagnated in the 1960s and actually fell in the first half of the 1970s[2].

Whereas growth in the developing countries in the 1950s and early 1960s was characterized primarily by import-substitution, the development of the latter half of the 1960s and the 1970s saw a growing role for industrial production for foreign markets – so-called 'export production'. In the meantime, production for import-substitution and production for export have, in practice, become considerably interwoven[3].

The rapid industrial development in the developing countries was by no means confined to a few countries; it could be observed in most of the countries of Asia and Latin America, and in a growing number of African countries. In addition, development was not restricted to light industry but could also be found in the sphere of heavy industry; in fact, heavy industry grew at an above-average pace in the developing countries, with a rate of 9 per cent per annum between 1960 and 1976[4]. A significant share of the world output of the traditional light industries, in particular textiles and garments, and parts of the electrical engineering industry, and a by no means negligible share of heavy industry, in particular steel and shipbuilding, are now accounted for by sites in the Third World. In addition, examples of very modern industrial production can now be found in the Third World: drilling rigs for offshore work are constructed in Singapore, ground-stations for satellite communications are put together in Indonesia, and modern aircraft, such as helicopters, are manufactured in Brazil.

Modern industrial sites have been established in almost all developing countries in the 1960s and 1970s and equipped with the facilities and modern

* Max-Planck-Institut zur Erforschung der Lebensbedingungen der Wissenschaftlich-technischen Welt, Starnberg FRG. The paper was translated by Pete Burgess, London.

infrastructure to allow industrial production to take place. Finally, rapid industrial growth was by no means confined to manufacturing. Other new and old sectors, such as agro-industry and the extractive industries, also exhibited fast rates of growth. Moreover, the tendency for rapid industrial development was scarcely interrupted by the massive economic crises of this period, such as the recession of 1974/75.

Of course this overall portrayal of the growth of industry in the Third World hides a number of regional differences. Nevertheless, it does not detract from the general validity of the claim that there is a strong tendency towards the industrialization of the Third World *in toto*, and by implication a tendency towards a new international division of labour, in the course of which countries that formerly supplied only agricultural products and raw materials now supply agricultural products, raw materials *and* industrial goods[5].

4.1   Industrialization and social development

One of the axiomatic beliefs of conventional development policy is that through industrialization the developing countries will attain one of the basic preconditions for overcoming underdevelopment. However, the reports on the social situation in the developing world, published by several international organizations at the end of the 1970s, reveal that rapid industrial development in the developing countries is not necessarily linked with a general improvement in the social condition of the majority of the population of these countries. In fact, statistics on the development of employment and incomes, nutrition, housing, etc. show that in many regions the social condition of a large part of the population has worsened, not merely relatively, but in absolute terms. This applies even to the most advanced NICs – for example Brazil, Mexico, India, South Africa, South Korea and Tunisia.

In a report for the World Conference on Employment, Income Distribution and Social Progress and the International Division of Labour held in 1976, the International Labour Office (ILO) stated:

'More than 700 million people live in acute poverty and are destitute. At least 460 million persons were estimated to suffer from a severe degree of protein–energy malnutrition even before the recent food crisis. Scores of millions live constantly under a threat of starvation. Countless millions suffer from debilitating diseases of various sorts and lack access to the most basic medical services. The squalor of urban slums is too well known to need further emphasis. The number of illiterate adults has been estimated to have grown from 700 million in 1962 to 760 million towards 1970. The tragic waste of human resources in the Third World is symbolized by nearly 300 million persons unemployed or underemployed in the mid-1970s.'[6]

Less than two years after this report, the ILO revised the figures and arrived at the new result that, 'according to latest estimates there are one to one and one-half billion people unable to fulfil even the minimum of their basic needs'[7].

In the World Bank's first *World Development Report* in 1978, the President, Robert McNamara, concluded in his Foreword:

'The past quarter century has been a period of unprecedented change and progress in the developing world, and yet despite this impressive record, some 800 million individuals continue to be trapped in what I have termed absolute poverty; a condition of life so characterized by malnutrition, illiteracy, disease, squalid surroundings, high infant mortality and low life-expectancy as to be beneath any reasonable definition of human decency'[8].

The same picture can be found in the numerous analyses and reports of social development in the developing countries recently published by a number of other organizations, such as the Food and Agriculture Organization (FAO), the United Nations Conference on Trade and Development (UNCTAD), the regional organizations of the United Nations and the regional development banks.

4.2 The transnational organization of production

We are faced with two questions. Why have industrial development and social development diverged so greatly in the countries of the Third World? Will these opposing tendencies continue in the 1980s? An analysis of the conditions, structure and results of industrialization in the developing countries allows a provisional answer to these questions.

The industrialization of the developing countries is taking place in the conditions of a transnationally integrated economic system which remains dominantly a *capitalist* one[9]. In particular, it is taking place within an existing world market for labour and production sites, as well as within world markets for capital, raw materials, technology and semi- and fully-manufactured products which have existed for decades, or even centuries.

Industrialization in the conditions of a transnationally integrated economic system is, as a consequence, basically the outcome of the opportunities and necessity to undertake the transnational organization of production. A leading international business consultancy organization some years ago coined the concept of 'world-wide sourcing' to illustrate the necessity for the transnational organization of production.

'The entire world [has become] a single uninterrupted continuum not only from a sales standpoint but also from a sourcing one . . . companies look world-wide not only for men, materials and the money to run their businesses, but also for manufacturing resources. In the short run this means sourcing decisions from existing manufacturing capabilities; in the long run it means locating the company's assets in the best possible location for profit world-wide – one of the most important types of major decisions that a company must make. . . . "Sourcing" can mean:

(1) the movement of components or semi-finished goods from one part of the company's operations to another, e.g. for final assembly;
(2) the movement of finished goods from a plant to a sales point;
(3) the purchasing of products or services from non-company sources;
(4) the selection of the appropriate plant of a major supplier;
(5) the purchasing (or borrowing) of manpower and services; and
(6) the locating of production facilities in the best places to serve regional or global marketing needs.'[10]

The industrialization of the developing countries in the 1960s and 1970s is to a great extent the result of investment decisions made with these considerations in mind. This applies not only to export-production, but also to a large part of that portion of production characterized as 'import-substitution', in the overall context of which tariff and non-tariff barriers to trade, often singled out as the main reason for 'import-substitution', feature as merely one factor among the hundreds assessed in the decision-making process[11].

Frederick Clairemonte said of the production of bananas that it was not *countries* which produced bananas but rather *enterprises* within those countries: the same applies to industrial production. It is not the *countries* of the Third World which produce cars, electronic components and steel but rather *enterprises* within their borders. It is not the developing countries which produce cars, but firms such as General Motors, Volkswagen and Mitsubishi who are increasing their output in Brazil, Nigeria and South Korea; it is not developing countries who assemble electronic components but firms such as General Electric, Siemens and Sony who assemble these components in Mexico, South Korea and Taiwan. It is not developing countries which make steel, but firms such as United Steel, Mannesmann and Kawasaki who make steel in Brazil, the Philippines and South Korea. Even where domestic firms produce for the domestic market, or even for foreign markets, this production – often carried out under licence or commission – is always the production of a *firm in* a (developing) country, and not that *of* a (developing) *country*.

The objectives of the production carried out in private enterprises are as much a datum as the conditions in which it takes place. Goods are produced for markets – and must be produced for markets which are likely to offer adequate effective demand – regardless of whether these markets are at home or abroad. Furthermore, production takes place at sites that allow it to yield a profit. Many such sites are now to be found in the developing countries.

However, markets are still predominantly located in the industrial countries, with only a small fraction in the developing countries. Despite their massive needs, the masses of the population in the developing countries – for the most part without any money-income worthy of note – do not constitute such an effective demand and, as a result, do not represent a market for which goods can be produced – now, or, probably, in the future[12].

As with any other private economic activity, the industrial production carried out by firms in the developing countries cannot and will not be directed towards solving the problems of these societies, on pain of commercial extinction. By the same token, such firms cannot and may not base their calculations of financing, production, technology, purchasing and sales, and in particular, decisions where to declare, distribute and reinvest profits, on the conditions and needs of individual societies. Correspondingly, a form of industry has arisen and is in the process of growing up, which only incidentally accords with the needs and possibilities of the host country, and then often only to a limited extent and for a limited time span. As a consequence this is a type of industry which is integrated with the rest of the local regional economy only to an incidental and limited extent. More often industry has developed, or is developing, which represents merely a non-complex, unintegrated partial process of production, or a mono-industry. Such industry has developed, and is being established, because firms have found, and are finding, that favourable conditions for their processes exist at the respective sites in developing countries. At present the most important of these conditions are cheap labour, accessible raw materials, energy and industrial estates. In addition tax, credit and customs benefits are also significant.

The building-up of industrial sub-manufacture in the developing countries within the context of the transnational organization of production is one of the most evident manifestations of the process of the industrialization of the Third World. Such processes can be found in both light and heavy industry. Peter Drucker characterized this form of the transnational organization of production as 'production sharing'[13], an expression which, however, serves to emphasize that this form of the division of labour does not embrace 'decision sharing' or 'consumption sharing'.

It does not require a lengthy argument to show that non-complex and unintegrated sub-manufacturing processes or mono-industrialization do not represent an adequate basis for overcoming underdevelopment, and hence for solving the social problems of the Third World. This is all the more so if, as is the case in the majority of developing countries, these processes remain outside national control. It is not the countries, but the firms in these countries which control production, technology, management and marketing – and, as a result, the application and distribution of the company's output and earnings. Whilst the phase of import-substitution made it clear that production under licence cannot lead to the development of independent national industrial production, 'export production' has removed the element of national control even more. Whereas firms producing for local markets are forced to submit to national control to at least some extent – inasmuch as local restrictions apply to all firms they do not affect competition – in production for foreign markets firms are often able to avoid national controls, since production for the world market often allows them to locate export manufacturing at sites where national control is weak or non-existent.

To the extent that industrial production in the developing countries is controlled by foreign enterprises, whether directly through equity holding, or indirectly through management agreements, production under licence or production on contract, the technology, management, marketing – and hence the use and distribution of earnings – are almost exclusively under the control of foreign enterprises. And, in fact foreign firms do account for a high share of economic activity in many developing countries. With a few exceptions, industrial production by foreign firms has not opened the door to either modern technology or markets. Even in situations where the transfer of technology to developing *countries* is unavoidable for certain specific operations, firms make sure that their technical lead remains secure. C. Lester Hogan, Vice Chairman of the Fairchild Camera and Instrument Corporation, has discussed with commendable candour just how firms maintain their technical superiority, and perpetuate the technological dependency of the developing countries:

'We must keep in mind that in high technology areas the technology changes so rapidly there is always a strategic time to sell. When newer processing techniques are beginning to blossom in the laboratory, the sale of present technology can do little to hurt us in this country.'[14]

A typical instance of continuing technical dependency, even with advanced industrial production in a branch, can be seen in the example of the South Korean electronic industry as outlined by the Korean Exchange Bank:

'At the end of last year [1976] 118 firms used foreign, mainly American and Japanese technology, principally in the production of parts and components. . . . In spite of relatively low requirements of fixed capital, why does the Korean electronics industry rely so heavily on foreign capital? The answer lies in the fact that foreign corporations always tie capital participation to transfers of technology. Furthermore, the small size of domestic firms leaves little room for independent technological development. This further encourages the inflow of technology and leads to the neglect of domestic research. This vicious circle has left the Korean electronics industry with a low level of technology . . . . The technical dependence on both Japan and the USA poses a threat to the continued growth of the industry. These countries' technical control over the Korean electronics industry could deal a crippling blow unless the industry devotes sufficient resources to the research and development of its own technology. Especially to lessen the reliance on Japanese technology which soon becomes outmoded, the industry is encouraged to go directly to the sources of new technology, if necessary through joint-ventures.'[15]

Access to foreign-controlled markets, and sources of raw materials and energy, remains effectively barred to the developing countries, even with advanced forms of import substitution and export production. What is decisive, however, is that the earnings of foreign-controlled production in the developing countries, regardless of whether this is directed at local or foreign markets, can be protected from local control, and hence local taxation or redistribution. Legal instruments, such as the use of tax-havens, transfer-pricing and the imposition of licence fees are the mechanisms usually favoured. In the last 25 years this has created a situation in which the growth of industrial production in the developing countries has been accompanied by a continuously rising outflow of economic surplus in the form of open, or hidden, transfers of profit from these countries. Such outflows are increasingly placing these countries' capacity for extended economic reproduction in doubt. Inadequate domestic rates of saving, mounting indebtedness and corresponding balance-of-payments deficits are the visible expression of this development.

The case of Mexico – one of the most advanced industrialized countries of the Third World – clearly shows that despite a high share of industrial production in the generation of GDP, and despite a development of industrial production in at least nearly all of the traditional industrial branches, industry has failed to develop complex local structures, remains horizontally unintegrated and is instead vertically integrated into the world market, and hence highly dependent. Such a form of industrial development is hardly able to contribute to the improvement of the social situation of the bulk of the population of this, and other, countries. One comment on the level of Mexican industrial development may be cited.

'For two decades manufacturing industry was built up through the importation of entire factories and assembly facilities, but these plants remain dependent on component parts from abroad. In the case of finished goods the Republic has not fulfilled export expectations, as its products do not measure up to the quality of products from the recognized industrial countries. Industry, in the real sense of the word, does not yet exist. As in the case of other developing countries, this development has placed Mexico in a dilemma: to grasp that the mere setting up of assembly lines does not mean that a true industry can be created where there was none before.'[16]

The 1979 OECD report *Interfutures* had the following to say on Mexico's industrial development.

'Industrialization is relatively advanced, Mexico being the third largest industrial producer in the Third World (11.2 per cent of Third World production in 1973 – excluding China – and 0.8 per cent of world production). However, the characteristics of the mode of industrialization are comparable with those of Brazil: a domestic market confined to the highest income brackets, excessive protection leading to inefficiency, control over growth exerted by the multinationals and, above all, investment which generates few jobs.'[17]

Another report on the social situation in Mexico drew the following picture:

'Unemployment and underemployment have expanded to include more than half the workforce and prices have rushed ahead of wages. For millions it has meant less to eat . . . . More than 100 000 children die here each year because of the relationship between malnutrition and transmittable diseases . . . . And, of the two millions or so who are born each year, at least one and a half million will not adequately develop their mental, physical and social functions.'[18]

The concerns of capital valorization and the satisfaction of social needs are not one and the same thing; however, despite its simplicity and correctness, this long-standing truth is intended to remain unknown in the interest of the expansion of capital. The following experience related by the President of Tanzania, Mwalimu Julius K. Nyerere, confirms the view that follows of the Chairman of a US transnational corporation.

'The motive of private investment is the making of profit. Anyone proposing to build a factory demands four things: assured, adequate, and cheap power and water supplies; a labour supply which is disciplined and with an adequate skill component; the existence of an effective market, and easy access to it; and fourthly, economic and political stability, with especial reference to low taxation, profit repatriation, and the availability of adequate consumer goods and services to provide incentives for senior management. . . .

By its very nature, therefore, foreign capital will only find poor countries attractive in those areas where returns are immediate and very high. These are not usually the most useful investments. Any other kind of foreign investment has to be induced by promises of tax exemptions, and of priority over even the most essential provision of services to our people.

Some poor countries have nevertheless decided to pin their faith in private enterprise as the basis of their development strategy. They have given the tax-holidays demanded, guaranteed the export of profit, endeavoured to prevent the growth of trade unions which would demand dignity and decent conditions for the employees in such firms. But they remain poor nations. Even if a small group of their citizens become wealthy, the people as a whole remain undeveloped. To their other problems is added that of gross internal inequality, with – sooner or later – its consequent political instability. . . .

But private enterprise will not make the quantity of investment required to overcome our poverty; it will not do the priority jobs in our nations; and, to the extent that we attract it by promising to leave it uncontrolled and untrammelled, it will add to our social and cultural problems.'[19]

'In looking at society and its needs for goods and services, it is clear that the private sector does not and cannot fill the entire bill. To be really efficient, the private sector has to operate with a return on investment and in its own self-interest. By doing so, the private sector certainly provides benefits to the rest of society. But it cannot equitably distribute the proceeds to that society nor can it guarantee the security and welfare of the total community. That has to be done by some other body.'[20]

4.3   A critique of export-led growth

After it had become clear for all to see that the strategy of *industrialization* through import-substitution did not allow a complex, integrated industrial system to develop in the developing countries, and after it also became clear that the strategy of *development* through import-substitution had finally come to grief[21], a new strategy was proclaimed for the developing countries: industrialization through the growth of exports and development through export industries.

It is no accident that the World Bank has now placed itself in the forefront of the criticism of the policy of import-substitution and made itself one of the chief advocates of production for export. The World Bank argues that an improvement in the situation of the balance of payments and employment in the developing countries will come about if the handicaps placed in the way of production for export are reduced relative to production for the domestic market. Donald Keesing of the staff of the World Bank gives the following advice:

'Production sharing is very important for developing countries, but the big impact comes on their overall industrial development, by increasing their ability to pay for imports, by overcoming bottlenecks, by giving them greater flexibility in terms of output mix and scale in face of the constraints imposed by their domestic demand, by allowing them to make better uses of their labour and other resources, and by improving what they learn and how fast they learn it. This helps to accelerate their overall growth and development, which in turn helps to provide jobs as well as opportunities for productivity growth.'[22]

Instead of explaining the changed conditions on the world market which made industrial production for export both possible and necessary at sites in the developing countries, the political and academic advocates of the strategy of development via export-led growth dedicated themselves to legitimizing the actual process of export-industrialization as it took place, declaring that the Age of Development had now at last come about for the Third World, and that the welfare-effects of industrial development would now be inevitable. The countries of the Third World are promised that export production and export-led growth will extend the narrow limits of their internal markets, that they can attain high domestic rates of savings and investment, that access will be available to modern technology which will in turn facilitate rapid strides forward in productivity, and that, finally, the associated economic and social infrastructure will develop in such a way as to lay down the foundations for a comprehensive development[23].

The actual process of 'export-led growth' is now confirming what was already theoretically apparent: the promises of development through export-industrialization cannot be and have not been fulfilled. To reiterate, export-industrialization, even more than import-substitution, means that it is not the countries, but the companies, who determine rates and sites of saving and accumulation, access to markets and technology and productivity. The countries do not experience the promised effects. Instead of higher rates of saving and capital accumulation, they experience a bigger drain of capital, and, consequently, falling rates of domestic savings and capital accumulation; instead of access to new markets, they discover that they have no control over 'their' markets. Instead of access to modern technology, they experience the destruction of domestic initiatives for the development of an autonomous technological development. Instead of developing a broad social and economic infrastructure, the developing countries are obliged to finance an industrial infrastructure which does not serve the requirements of a developing economy, and may often actively impede the development process.

4.4 Prospects for development in the 1980s

In attempting to give an indication of the prospects for industrial, and beyond that, social development in the developing countries in the 1980s two further considerations are of key importance: firstly, the far-reaching structural changes which are taking place throughout the world in agriculture, set in motion in particular by capital-intensive production techniques; and secondly, the wave of rationalization affecting nearly all branches of industrial production which have received their special impetus from the new possibilities offered by electronics, together with the global increase in capacity which will come about in connection with it.

One consequence of an increase in the capital-intensity of production, including agricultural production, in the developing countries is an accelerated release of labour which has reinforced, and will continue to reinforce, the battalions of the industrial reserve army of labour on the world market for labour; this will intensify the competition between the developing countries for labour-intensive export industries. The efforts of such countries as Bangladesh, Sri Lanka and Egypt to become new sites for export-industries are one expression of this development. Moreover, this form of competition for labour-intensive export-industries among the developing countries is increasingly spreading to the socialist countries, including China, who also offer their labour forces on the capitalist world market for export production.

Despite a further extension of industrial production, especially export production, at sites in the Third World, its growing dispersion and unequal distribution will mean that industrial production will remain relatively slight in the majority of developing countries, and may even decline. At the same time a few countries can be expected to experience a considerable extension of their industrial production. The supply of cheap labour will, however, induce a settlement of new industries only if it can be linked with attractive provision of raw materials and energy.

Whilst there are indications that certain traditional industries will increasingly produce for the world market from sites in the developing countries – principally, steel production, vehicle manufacture, shipbuilding and some sections of the chemical and mechanical engineering industries – there are other indications to show that in other branches – which moved to sites in the Third World in the 1960s and 1970s – such as textiles and garments, precision engineering and optics, and electrical engineering – production might decline. The possibility and necessity to automate, through the introduction of robots, will in many cases lead to a shifting of what were labour-intensive processes back to the traditional industrial sites. Many companies have long had plans, at least on the drawing board, for manufacturing equipment which is intended to make even unskilled, cheap labour superfluous in the 1980s. For example, specialists in the garment industry claim, contrary to common belief, that rationalization has scarcely begun, and that the next step will be at least the introduction of semi-automatic production processes. The electrical engineering industry is also a source of announcements to the effect that the previously manually accomplished operations of soldering and assembly in the manufacture of integrated circuits can be profitably eliminated through the introduction of automation. It is therefore reasonable to expect that in countries such as Malaysia, Mexico and South Korea hundreds of thousands of unskilled workers, at present carrying out these tasks manually, will become superfluous – that is to say, unemployed.

Because the wave of rationalization is associated with a considerable extension of capacity in many branches, industry is expecting to be faced with the emergence of substantial over-capacity. However, there are no indications that it will not be the production facilities in the Third World which corporate strategies will declare as the first to be made obsolete. The outcome will be that the process of industrialization in the Third World will continue to develop unevenly, both regionally and sectorally, despite the probable globally higher rates of growth of industrial production in the Third World. The possibility of a small number of developing countries acquiring at least a partially integrated and semi-complex industry capable of some degree of autonomous development cannot be excluded: this stage might conceivably be reached in South Korea and Taiwan. However, such an outcome is not a systematic product of the tendencies towards industrialization in the Third World: it is much more certain that, in view of the given conditions on the world market, a complex, integrated industry, capable of autonomous reproduction will not come about in the majority of developing countries.

The dependency of the process of industrialization in the developing countries on corporate calculations and corporate decisions will persist, regardless of the good intentions of development policy and strategies. Corporate calculations and decisions are, in turn, dependent on the changing conditions of the capitalist world market. Firms are compelled to respond flexibly to changing conditions, new opportunities and exigencies. Social considerations, or, in other words, the hopes of development policies, cannot feature as an element in these calculations, and do not do so. It is therefore not surprising that the scenarios of international organizations, such as OECD, suggest that despite the advancement of industrial development in the Third World, the problems of povery and misery will endure for large sections of the population, not only up to the end of the 1980s, but beyond to the year 2000. What is more astonishing is that the mode of production that makes such developments inevitable is not once questioned by the authors of such prognoses – not even at the intellectual level, let alone in a practical–political sense in the democratic process. Despite their recognition of the possibility that underdevelopment will mean civil wars, wars between countries, revolutions and counter-revolutions, their silence on the given mode of production remains unbroken.

'What then is the overall picture of the Third World at the end of the century revealed by an analytical approach? How far does it add to, and confirm, the picture given by the worldwide scenarios?

An analysis by country and by region reminds us, firstly – if this were necessary – of the possibility of more or less fundamental *socio-political upheavals* affecting one Third World country or another, and occasionally upsetting the economic and political equilibrium of a whole region. Such upheavals can take many forms: civil wars between different ethnic groups; border conflicts between countries; revolutions and counter-revolutions. . . .

Revolutionary upheavals will bring about changes in development strategies and in relations with the developed countries. But there is no certainty that they will result in more efficient management, nor that, despite the opposition to past development strategies which they express, they will result in greater attention to the needs of poorer segments of the population.'[24]

References

1 United Nations Conference on Trade and Development (UNCTAD), *Handbook of International Trade and Development Statistics, 1979*. New York, 1979, p. 534.
2 United Nations Conference on Trade and Development (UNCTAD), *Handbook of International Trade and Development Statistics 1979*. New York, 1979, p. 536.
3 As a consequence it is often virtually impossible to differentiate between industrial development for local and foreign markets. Besides, both production for the local market (import-substitution), and for foreign markets (export-oriented production) are production for the world market, which, regardless of the location of production, constitutes a unity of foreign and local markets.
4 United Nations Conference on Trade and Development (UNCTAD), *Handbook of International Trade and Development Statistics 1979*. New York, 1979, p. 534.
5 F. Fröbel, J. Heinrichs and O. Kreye. *The new international division of labour*. Cambridge University Press, Cambridge, 1980.
6 International Labour Office. *Employment, Growth and Basic Needs: A One World Problem*. Geneva, 1976, p. 3.
7 *Süddeutsche Zeitung*, 9/10 December 1979.
8 World Bank, *World Development Report 1978*. Washington, 1978.
9 The capitalist economic system has been a global one from its inception. The international integration of economic activities, latent at the outset, had long become a reality by the middle of this century. The fact that the internationally integrated economic system does not have a correspondingly internationally integrated political system often obscures the real situation.
10 Business International Corporation, *Solving Worldwide Sourcing Problems*. Management Monographs No. 53, New York, 1971, pp. 3–5.
11 Business International Corporation, *Decision Making in International Operations: 151 Checklists*.
12 This applies also to domestic private or public enterprises. As far as governments of some countries tried to protect or to direct domestic industrial activities, an industry capable to compete on the world market did not develop, or international organizations, as for instance the International Monetary Fund, became active in order to secure that national protectionist policies did not 'damage' too much international integration and did not last for too long.
13 P. F. Drucker, 'Production Sharing'. *Wall Street Journal*, 15 March 1977.
14 C. L. Hogan, 'Production Sharing and the Multinational Corporation', *Journal of The Flagstaff Institute* 1, 1979, p. 15.
15 Korea Exchange Bank, 'Electronics Industry in Korea'. *Monthly Review* 9, 1977, pp. 11–12.
16 'Blick durch die Wirtschaft', *Frankfurter Allgemeine Zeitung*, 4 October 1976.
17 Organization for Economic Cooperation and Development (OECD), 'Interfutures: Final Report'. *Facing the Future: Mastering the Probable and Managing the Unpredictable*. Paris, 1979, p. 215.
18 *International Herald Tribune*, 9 March 1978.
19 M. J. K. Nyerere, 'The Third World and the International Economic Structure'. *Internationales Afrika-Forum* 2, 1976, pp. 159–160.
20 W. F. May (chairman, American Can Co.), 'Executive Viewpoint'. *Business International*. 12 January 1979, p. 12.
21 See, for example, the special issue of *World Development* (1&2) 1977, 'Latin America in the Post-Import-Substitution Era'.
22 D. B. Keesing, 'Production Sharing: Implications for Trade between Developing Nations and Developed Nations', *Journal of the Flagstaff Institute* I, 1979, p. 25.
23 See for example, G. M. Meier, *Employment, Trade and Development, a Problem in International Policy Analysis*, Sijthoff, Leiden, 1977.
24 Organization for Economic Cooperation and Development (OECD), *Interfutures: Final Report, Facing the Future: Mastering the Probable and Managing the Unpredictable*. Paris, 1979, p. 229.

PART II

The new industrial countries in the world economy

5

Pessimism and a way out

Helen Hughes[*]

Although it is clear that the industrial market economies will not dominate world production and trade for ever, or even, as history measures time, for much longer, they will still be the major actors on the world stage in the 1980s. In the 1950s and 1960s, when they were growing rapidly, they were able to adjust fairly smoothly to the growth of the developing countries. But in the 1970s the industrial countries began to be faced by internal structural weaknesses. These were exacerbated by the petroleum price increases, so their growth decelerated sharply. Moreover, because the industrial market economies still contribute so heavily to trade and other international economic flows, their economic problems have slowed market expansion for the developing countries.

Whether the industrial countries can improve their economic policies sufficiently to accelerate their growth is thus an important issue for the 1980s. However, the growth of the developing and centrally planned economy countries does not simply, or even mainly, reflect trends in the world economy. These countries are engaged in a strong growth process of their own, and they can do much to affect their own economic growth and welfare regardless of the industrial market economies' performance.

The industrial economies' problems, and the developing countries' growth prospects, can be understood only in a long-run context. Section 5.1 therefore examines the changes in long-term global production and competitiveness for both the industrial and the developing countries, although it must be stressed from the outset that differences among countries within these groups are often as great as the differences among the groups. The responses of the international economy to those changing production patterns are indicated in section 5.2. Section 5.3 explores some scenarios and their policy implications for the 1980s.

[*] Economic Analysis and Projections Department, The World Bank. I am indebted to my colleagues in the Department for many insights and for the statistical base for this paper. The views, however, are my own, and should not be attributed to the World Bank.

5.1   A retrospective view

The roots of the industrial revolution now sweeping the developing countries lie in eighteenth century Britain, but the world-wide pattern of industrialization has been uneven. The first wave of growth in British manufacturing (with accompanying changes in other sectors) was followed in the nineteenth and early twentieth centuries in continental Europe and in the countries of European settlement. The first socialist country, the USSR, began to rebuild its economy in the 1920s. But some countries – principally in southern Europe and in Latin America – did not undertake industrialization until the 1950s. Development has also been very uneven within individual countries, frequently leaving backwaters even in highly industrialized states.

Technological innovation (in the broad sense which includes industrial organization) has played a key role in each phase, establishing the leaders to which the other countries aspired to 'catch up' by increased productivity in the pursuit of higher living standards. It was, of course, Schumpeter's linking of the importance of technological innovations with Kondratieff's statistical observations that brought the 'Kondratieff cycle' into economic analysis. A more up-to-date version might link successive technological waves with the economic policies required to catch up to the technological leader in that wave[1]. For technological change is not the only driving force of the industrial process. It has become increasingly evident that national and international economic policy (again broadly defined to include such areas as education and industrial relations) is at least as important.

The unexpected and unprecedented growth of the world economy from the 1950s to the mid-1970s has been well documented[2]. Compared with an estimated 1–2 per cent growth in the nineteenth and early twentieth centuries, the post-World War II growth of the industrial countries looks spectacular indeed. The use of official rather than purchasing power exchange rates, of Laspeyres indexes not corrected for quality and preference changes to measure prices, and of indirectly derived Paasche indexes to measure output, not only distorts comparisons between levels of income among countries at a given time but also understates true growth rates, particularly of such countries as the Federal Republic of Germany and Japan, which caught up rapidly in the 1950s and 1960s, and the rapidly growing developing countries[3].

Many factors – including vastly improved technology, improvements in mass education and hence in 'human' capital, accelerated capital accumulation and investment, structural shifts that moved a significant proportion of the workforce from low productivity agriculture to high productivity manufacturing and service activities, the movement of women from household to remunerated work, and flows of temporary and permanent immigrants – have been identified at one time or another as a principal cause of growth after World War II. The remarkable freeing of capital and trade flows following the

Table 5.1 *GNP and GNP per capita growth trends (average annual percentage growth rates in 1977 US$ at official exchange rates)*

	GNP			GNP per capita		
	1950–60	1960–70	1970–78	1950–60	1960–70	1970–78
Industrial market economies	4.2	5.0	3.4	3.0	3.9	2.6
European centrally planned economies	6.1	6.1	5.5	4.3	4.9	4.6
Capital surplus petroleum exporting economies[a]	..	11.7	9.0	..	7.8	5.3
Developing market economies[b]	5.0	5.7	5.5	2.7	3.1	3.1
People's Republic of China	9.0	5.0	6.0	6.7	3.0	4.6

[a] Iran, Iraq, Kuwait, Libya, Oman, Qatar, Saudi Arabia and United Arab Emirates. Note that population growth includes immigrant inflow.
[b] Spain, Portugal, Greece, Yugoslavia and all countries of the Mediterranean; Asia and Oceania, except Japan, Australia, New Zealand, and the People's Republic of China; the Middle East and Africa except those countries noted in [a] and Central and Latin America and the Caribbean

Source: World Bank data, March 1980

dismantling of exchange and other controls on capital movements in the market economy industrialized countries, the Dillon and Kennedy rounds of trade negotiations, and the additional fillip given to intra-European trade and capital flows by the formation of the European Free Trade Area and the European Economic Community have clearly played a role. But all of these explanations are not unlike the blind man's description of an elephant.

The underlying force which brought these trends to fruition was the world-wide focus on social progress (albeit in varying degrees in different countries) underlined by a greatly improved policy formulation and administrative capacity on the part of governments. The economic crisis of the 1930s had given rise to changing social perceptions, and these were strengthened by World War II. The unemployment and social waste that had prevailed for centuries became unacceptable, and the wartime economies demonstrated that national economic management was possible without destroying an essentially market-oriented system. The fear of renewed depression was still strong in the 1950s, and it stimulated political pressures for domestic policies aimed at full employment, rapid growth and, in many countries, social welfare[4]. The protectionism of the 1930s was seen as one of the important causes of a miserable, stagnating world economy. The liberalization of the international movement of goods and factors of production was thought essential to growth; and growth became so rapid that the costs of liberalization were so exceeded by its benefits that further liberalization was encouraged. For most of the industrialized countries, moreover, catching up to the United States's productivity and living standards meant following an easily defined growth path. In the developing countries the internal pressures for catching up were even stronger, and they were endorsed internationally with the spread of social welfare ideals. Once poverty became unacceptable in a national context, inequality among nations also became of concern, leading to a substantial lobby for economic assistance to the developing countries.

Why did these sources of growth dry up in the industrial countries in the 1970s? Why did the increase in the price of petroleum, instead of leading to policies that would foster a new technological wave, become so serious an adjustment problem? How were the developing countries affected?

Industrial market economies

A number of social, political and economic factors came together in the industrial countries in the late 1960s and early 1970s to induce economic doldrums. The impetus for growth was eroded. High general standards of living made growth less attractive to the higher income groups. Indeed, for the upper and even the middle classes, growth was eroding the privileges of wealth which they alone had previously enjoyed[5]. The Club of Rome translated the concerns of the very rich into a finite view of the earth's resources, and although this was quickly shown to be erroneous, new variants continue to appear[6]. Growth became identified with the destruction of the 'natural' environment. Yet because of the growing awareness of environmental problems, more has been done in recent years than at any other time in history to reduce water, air and other types of pollution, to limit population growth, and to alert policy-makers to the need to improve the environment.

The gains in economic equality have been reflected in the much greater strength of lower income groups acting through trade unions or farm groups. They are not satisfied with their admittedly larger 'slice of the cake', wanting to increase it by appropriating a larger share of the national product, by increasing that product, or both. Where trade union, farmer, business and other groups have a short-term horizon, the emphasis tends to be more on the 'share of the cake' rather than on higher productivity to increase the cake's size. The slower the growth the sharper is the conflict over sharing its benefits. The conflict has become even more acute with the increased cost of petroleum. Such social conflict is the principal cause of inflationary pressure and it frequently leads to a monetary irresponsibility which fuels inflation further. Monetary restraints and other deflationary policies (which have often been 'too little and too late') result in even less willingness to part with some of the slowly growing 'slice of the cake'. Social services have been greatly improved in most countries. There is a welfare cushion of some sort for the very poor and the unemployed, but unemployment has grown – partly, indeed, because of this cushion. But the unemployed are not powerful politically, and so, together with groups such as old people on fixed incomes, they have paid most of the costs of the social tug-of-war. It is only when conflicts arise over the prices of particular goods and jobs, as in the clothing, footwear, textile, steel or shipbuilding industries, that the concern with employment tends to become dominant, because attention is clearly focused and both workers and owners of capital are involved[7]. The national characteristics of such pressure groups as trade unions, employers' associations and farmers' cooperatives have a major influence on the outcome of these socio-economic struggles. Growth policies have thus been easier to implement in countries with strong, centrally managed, productivity-oriented industrial trade unions, such as the Federal Republic of Germany, than somewhere like the United Kingdom with its highly fragmented craft and mixed unions[8].

In many countries the pendulum has swung too far from the 1930s. Governments which set out to achieve efficiency in production and equity in distribution have started to confuse the two objectives by using production policies for welfare ends. This has led to the nationalization of bankrupt firms and to public guarantees, subsidies and similar measures which have undermined the competitiveness of the productive sectors[9]. In some countries taxation appears to have reached the long-threatened levels at which it inhibits productivity and entrepreneurship, often undermining national probity as well.

But to acknowledge something of an 'over-kill' in government activities does not mean that governments have no important role to play in economic growth. With growing investment lead-times in major industries, notably energy, and with growing economies of scale in such industries as computer and aeroplane manufacturing, encouraging more monopolistic structures of production, governments can no more abdicate their role in long-run economic planning and arbitration among conflicting economic interests than they can afford to abandon market mechanisms. The art is to balance market forces with government intervention so as to arrive at the best – not the worst – of these two worlds.

Governments can act only if they quickly reach a working consensus, and if they are staffed by capable and honest civil servants. These conditions are most readily achieved in small and relatively homogeneous countries. In a liberal international trading environment these same small countries can simultaneously benefit from the economies of scale that come with participating in the international economy. It is thus not surprising that small countries rank high among those that have grown most rapidly and become the wealthiest[10].

In contrast, the two large blocs in the world economy, the United States and the European Economic Community, have found policy determination and implementation increasingly difficult. Until the 1950s, the United States was the only industrialized market economy with its own large market, accordingly reaping unique benefits of scale and competitiveness. This no doubt had contributed to its rapid growth in the nineteenth century, and to its technological and organizational leadership in the first half of the twentieth century. But the countries that participated in the international liberalization of trade in the 1950s and 1960s acquired these same advantages of access to large markets. Their governments do not, however, have the policy-making disadvantages of needing to create an economic consensus among constituencies as diverse as the northeastern, southern, mid-western, and western states of the United States. In the United States, moreover, the division between the executive and the legislature exacerbates the geographic heterogeneity, and the politicization of the higher echelons of the public service has reduced its professionalism, increasing the difficulties of policy formulation and implementation. The United States thus had difficulties in absorbing the costs of the war in Vietnam, it has problems handling defence and welfare and other public expenditures, and it has been unable to evolve an energy policy to encourage a new wave of technological innovation. The members of the European Economic Community, ignoring the costs of economic integration in the mistaken belief that political cooperation requires economic unification, have locked themselves into a highly uneconomic agricultural policy. With every additional step they take toward the harmonization of monetary and other policies, and with the expanding role assumed by their parliament and bureaucracy, they are following the United States's path toward a breakdown of effective policy determination and implementation.

European centrally planned economies

The European centrally planned economies performed well in the period of reconstruction, repairing the very great damages of war and rapidly raising living standards in the undeveloped Balkans. After these basic tasks were accomplished, the difficulties of central planning in increasingly complex societies began to emerge in the 1960s, although their rates of growth have remained significantly higher than those of the industrial market economies.

In the early postwar years, the centrally planned economies relied heavily on their ample labour supplies, moving labour from agriculture to manufacturing to increase productivity. Now these excess labour resources have been drawn down, and the workforce is growing very slowly. Compared with the situation in the market economy countries labour productivity is low, so that labour shortages rather than unemployment tend to be the problem in a number of industries.

These countries' strength lies in their mineral raw materials and basic manufacturing industries, but the emphasis on physical planning, and the lack, until recently, of the social pricing of capital, labour and raw materials, have led to very high capital output ratios and high energy intensity. Limited

participation in international trade severely curtailed technological development. Agricultural production is still unsatisfactory, with a heavy and
growing dependence on imports from the industrial market economies.
Meanwhile, a vocal demand for high quality consumer goods and services is
putting pressure on production. Service activities in particular lag behind
those in the industrial market economies, with slow growth leading to the
frustration of the expectation of catching up with higher living standards, and
hence to political difficulties.

The centrally planned economies recognized these problems, and the
technological lags at their core, and began to borrow heavily in the 1970s to
upgrade their technology through capital goods imports. But in the short
run, debt service problems have exacerbated the almost chronic balance-of-
payments difficulties between East European countries and the industrial
market economies. Net petroleum exports, boosted by increasing prices,
and recent high gold prices have helped the bloc as a whole, but at the cost of
an increase in the USSR's economic power in relation to the other countries.
Balance of payments problems could become even more difficult for the East
European countries, other than the USSR, as their energy needs grow and
supplies (in the case of Romania) decline. And yet to continue to accelerate
technological change, particularly in a more economic use of materials,
labour and energy, they will need to continue borrowing to import more
capital goods as well as agricultural products. Servicing their borrowing
while paying for imports requires a growing export volume. Much will
depend on the USSR's investment in petroleum, gas, coal and hydro-
electricity, and on its exports of energy to the other East European countries
and to market economies. Its resources are well established, and modern
technology could increase output relatively quickly, but it is not clear that
appropriate policies will be followed to increase output and exports.
Continued high gold prices would also be helpful, for the USSR supplies
about 30 per cent of the new gold coming onto world markets. For the other
East European economies, any substantial increase in exports must be
expected to come in manufactured products. A number of the recent capital
import agreements with the Western countries include export arrangements
to repay the investments (which are officially regarded as trade credits).
However, such contractual arrangements cover only a small share of the
Eastern European centrally planned economies' total exports, so they will
have to supplement them with more traditional, relatively labour-intensive
exports. Such trade will increase adjustment pressures in the industrial
market economies and will compete with imports from the developing
countries.

Developing countries

Although the detailed objectives and policy approaches may appear to vary
greatly from country to country, the growth of the developing countries is

part of the process of catching up with the countries enjoying the highest standards of living. Definitions of countries as 'developing', particularly those with relatively high productivity and living standards midway in the development spectrum, reflect at best the analytical purpose being pursued but more often political convenience. So do the definitions of 'new' and 'old' industrial countries[11]. Industrialization, like the development of which it is part, is a continuum along which the differences between the countries barely emerging from primitive agricultural production and such 'new' industrial countries as Spain or Singapore are much greater than those between the latter and the 'old' industrial countries. Moreover, countries such as India and the People's Republic of China, though still poor and predominantly agricultural, are also 'new' industrial countries in the sense that they have large, sophisticated and, potentially, internationally competitive industrial sectors[12].

The developing countries have compressed into 30 years the development that took the 'old' industrial countries 200 years to accomplish. It is impossible to illustrate this process quantitatively because data that understate the growth of such countries as Germany and Japan distort it even more for countries that had very low economic levels at the end of World War II. The outlines, however, are clear, and growth rates as conventionally calculated give some rough indications of relative magnitudes (*Table 5.2*).

Table 5.2 *GNP growth of developing countries by principal regions[a] (average annual percentage growth rates using 1977 US dollars at official exchange rates)*

	GNP		GNP per capita	
	1960–70	1970–78	1960–70	1970–78
Africa south of the Sahara	4.4	4.4	1.9	1.6
Middle East and North Africa	4.2	7.1	1.5	4.4
South Asia	4.3	3.5	1.8	1.3
East and Southeast Asia, and Oceania	6.8	8.0	4.2	5.7
Latin America and Caribbean	5.9	5.6	3.2	2.9
Southern Europe	7.1	5.1	5.6	3.5

[a] Excludes capital surplus petroleum exporting economies
Source: World Bank data, 1 March 1980

The poor countries south of the Sahara, which lacked physical and social infrastructure, entrepreneurs and administrators and were politically very underdeveloped, have had the hardest struggle. These economies are still predominantly agricultural, and harvests tend to dominate performance. The drought in the Sahel, for example, was substantially responsible for keeping the 1970s growth rates no higher than in the 1960s. Mineral development has helped some of these countries, particularly the petroleum rich ones. Although this group includes the poorest developing countries, other countries such as Nigeria, the Ivory Coast and Kenya have had considerable industrial growth.

The large poor countries of South Asia grew relatively slowly also, but for different reasons. Pakistan and Bangladesh have suffered from severe political problems, with estimated growth rates falling from 7.3 per cent in the 1960s to 4.1 per cent in the 1970s for Pakistan and from 4.1 per cent in the 1960s to 2.1 per cent in the 1970s for Bangladesh. India came to independence with a relatively good infrastructure and well developed human resources, but its size and heterogeneity made it difficult to create a meaningful political consensus for rapid growth. The development of agriculture to the point of self-sufficiency has been long and painful. Poor monsoons in the early 1970s (also in part responsible for the low Pakistan and Bangladesh growth rates) led to a fall in growth rates from 4.0 per cent in the 1960s to 1.4 per cent in 1970–1974. It is widely thought that for may years food aid was a major factor in hampering agricultural development. By the mid-1970s self-sufficiency in food was achieved, and from 1974 to 1978 growth rates rose at an average of 5.6 per cent despite fluctuating climatic conditions. Infrastructure development, particularly in transport and energy, however, has been slow in India. Manufacturing production has grown at only 4.5 per cent a year, and the manufacturing sector is still very inefficient despite the advantages of a large domestic market.

With agricultural development well advanced, an industrial structure in place, and a healthy balance of payments situation (based to a large extent on workers' remittances and non-factor service exports), the possibilities for accelerating growth in India must again be examined. Can the infrastructure bottlenecks be overcome or is decision-making too centralized for this to be done in so large a country? Can the success in agriculture be translated into industrial growth by appropriate policies? Can the more rapidly developing states develop even faster and the poorer ones start to catch up with them by pursuing better policies? Is the need for a greater push at the centre or for a move toward a more federal structure? Specifically, why can India not attain growth rates of from 8 to 10 per cent a year[13]?

Petroleum production and price increases and other mineral finds have been important in North Africa and the Middle East, where performance has otherwise been disappointing in relation to the level of economic development at independence. Industrial growth has been rather slow, and industrial output is by and large not competitive with the old industrial countries. However, the direct and indirect effects of the petroleum price increases led to a substantial increase in growth for this region in the 1970s. The capital surplus petroleum-exporting countries, which are also located in this region, grew more slowly in the 1970s than in the 1960s when the rate of increase of their volume of petroleum exports peaked.

Latin America has had a longer history of political independence than more developing countries; nevertheless as late as the 1950s it was still relatively backward economically. Argentina and Chile were (together with Australia and New Zealand) among the highest income countries in the world in 1900 and were taking the first steps towards industrialization, but by the 1950s they had become 'developing' countries. Latin America is richly endowed with natural resources (including petroluem) and, tother with the islands of the Caribbean, it is well located to exploit North American markets. But despite a heavy emphasis on industrialization after World War II, and considerable industrial growth, overall economic growth has been slow, and it has been marked by high capital and import intensity. Latin American development has been hampered by political instability, and the region has been the victim of an inward-looking politico-economic ideology which long precluded effective participation in international trade. Political instability made adjustment to changing circumstances difficult and resulted in low growth in the 1970s. There were some exceptions. Brazil, a country heavily dependent on petroleum imports, nevertheless averaged 9.2 per cent growth in the 1970s compared with 6.1 per cent in the 1960s[14].

The East Asian countries have been the outstanding performers, with Korea, Taiwan, Hong Kong and Singapore – the remarkable 'gang of four' – being the fastest growing group of developing countries. Two are city states with little alternative to export-oriented manufacturing development, but Taiwan and Korea have demonstrated the value of paying attention to all sectors and to a balance betwen domestic and externally oriented policies, although Korea may have overbalanced its economy in the direction of exports[15].

The growth of the East Asian countries has also been relatively rapid. They all have rich resource bases. They have pursued relatively balanced economic policies so that they now have well developed infrastructure, agricultural and manufacturing sectors. Indonesia, because of relatively poor policies, has been one of the slower growers of this group, despite its petroleum exports. The Southeast and East Asian countries as a group grew faster in the 1970s than in the 1960s, with the petroleum importing countries in the lead.

For several of the Southern European countries, the 'developing' label is more political than analytical. It is not surprising that they have been in the forefront of those catching up, with per capita incomes coming close to, and in the case of Spain even passing, those of lagging industrial countries. Their economies have always been closely linked with Western Europe and several are expected to join the European Economic Community as they graduate from developing status. However, this close connection, and their approach to the upper end of the catching up curve, meant that their growth was substantially slower in the 1970s than in the 1960s. These countries' weight in total developing country income (about 20 per cent) depressed the developing countries' overall growth rate in the 1970s. If the Southern European countries are excluded, the developing countries' GNP growth in the 1970s was about the same as in the 1960s. However, relatively high population growth rates have meant that per capita income grew only in East and Southeast Asia and in the Middle East and North Africa.

China, the largest of the developing countries, has long been an enigma, although it is now coming into the international economic orbit. Chinese data are so dubious that they must be taken with a larger than usual pinch of salt. However, China, like the European centrally planned economies, apparently found the first stage of putting a war-torn country on its feet relatively easy, but then began to face a more difficult situation. Its technology is very outdated, and it is therefore competitive internationally only in relatively simple labour-intensive manufactures where its low labour costs are a major advantage. Central physical planning is running modernization plans into serious problems. If China continues to move into the world economy – and powerful political forces, including the army, are backing this – it will have to become a major exporter to purchase modern technology. Because it will need raw materials, including petroleum and coal, for rapid domestic industrial growth, it is doubtful that significant volumes will be available for export. The emphasis is likely to be on the export of labour-intensive manufactures which could be expanded quickly around the Hong Kong and Macao bases without major changes in the domestic economy.

The developing countries' catching-up process typically seems to have a slow start while human and physical resources are being accumulated and political cohesion is being achieved. This is frequently followed by a rapid 'Rostowian' take-off period[16], when a country makes a rapid transition (which it is impossible to measure realistically) to being 'industrial'. It then follows whatever short (cyclical) and long-term (Kondratieff) waves dominate the high income, industrial countries' growth paths at that time. The growth process is not linear but 'S'-shaped, but the curve is not smooth. There is much variation among countries, with some graduating from being 'low' to 'middle' and 'high' income countries quickly, while others take a long time and some become stationary or even decline for a period. Low income countries with appropriate policies thus grow faster than middle income countries with inappropriate policies.

In the development process, political stability matters a great deal. The lack of natural resources it not a serious barrier to growth if human resources are available. In fact, having natural resources can be a problem if human resources are inadequte: some of the countries with the greatest development difficulties and the slowest growth, including Zaire, Zambia and Peru, are resource-rich countries. Very large size, again, can be a handicap in spite of the gains from economies of scale from a large domestic market. Not only India but also Indonesia, Nigeria, Pakistan and Bangladesh seem to have been handicapped by their large and heterogeneous political bases. By contrast, in the liberal trading environment of the last 30 years, a small domestic market does not necessarily result in serious problems. A good location can help, but whereas some small Mediterranean countries have taken advantage of their proximity to Europe, most countries in Central America and the Caribbean have failed to take advantage of the United States's market. Some island economies such as Mauritius are growing strongly; others are not. Being landlocked is a handicap if surrounding countries are poor; but it should be remembered that the world's highest per capita income country, Switzerland, is landlocked.

Large injections of aid in per capita terms (for example in Taiwan and South Korea) and access to international capital markets have helped many countries, but others have failed to achieve sustained growth despite large aid and commercial capital inflows. Breaking through balance-of-payments constraints is important, but the claims made for 'outward-oriented' industrialization strategies and export growth have greatly exaggerated the importance of exports in development. Rapidly growing countries were the ones which have introduced social infrastructure policies to overcome human constraints, agricultural policies to break rural production bottlenecks, industrialization policies that lead to internationally competitive costs of production and appropriate physical infrastructure investment and policies. Their policies (and implementation) were not perfect but they were sufficiently competent to release the pent-up energy inherent in the catching-up process. A few countries, including Singapore and Malaysia, have been successful in attaining growth with equity by accentuating 'trickle down' effects by careful attention to access to public goods; but most have paid little attention to welfare. Some, such as Sri Lanka and Tanzania, have traded off growth for equity. Some countries achieved neither growth nor equity. All the rapidly growing countries used market mechanisms as well as government intervention. Hong Kong and Singapore, for example, often regarded as *laissez-faire* economies, had very considerable public works and housing programmes which interacted with private sector growth. Indicative planning played a particularly important role in Singapore's development. The rapidly growing countries avoided the shibboleths of the right as well as of the left, while narrow-minded ideologies have had a poor growth record. There are, evidently, many paths to rapid economic growth; countries must be selective and choose the one that suits their particular economic, social and political conditions and levels of development.

The changing structure of production

Whatever the data used, the developing countries' share of the world's production is very small. At official exchange rates, the developing countries (including China and the petroleum exporting capital surplus developing countries) account for some three-quarters of the world's population but have less than one-quarter of its income. Their increase in the share of income since the 1960s has not, in conventional measures, been very large (*Table 5.3*).

Table 5.3 *The distribution of world population and GNP by regions*

	Population 1978 (%)	GNP 1960 (%)	GNP 1970 (%)	GNP 1978 (%)
Industrial market economies	17	72	70	66
European centrally planned economies	9	9	10	11
Capital surplus petroleum exporting economies	a	a	a	2
Developing market economies, of which	51	14	15	17
Africa south of the Sahara	8	2	2	2
Middle East and North Africa	2	1	1	1
South Asia	22	2	2	2
East and Southeast Asia	8	2	2	3
Latin America and Caribbean	8	5	5	6
Southern Europe	3	3	3	4
People's Republic of China	22	4	4	5
World	100	100	100	100
(number in millions)	4081			
(value US$ billion)		3277	5505	7628

a Less than 1%

Source: World Bank data, March 1980

Conversion to purchasing power parity figures would increase both the rate of growth of the developing countries' GNP shares and the size of their shares in 1978, although it would leave their production share still far below that of their population share. Data for such a conversion are not yet available, but preliminary indications are that the more rapidly growing countries are catching up with the industrial countries and that this process is accelerating. It is being reflected in, and stimulated by, international economic flows.

5.2   The international economy

The liberalization of the flows of trade and capital after World War II, and a return to the high volumes of migration reminiscent of the nineteenth century, contributed to a rapid spread of technology, gave countries an opportunity to exploit economies of scale and specialization beyond their own borders, and enabled the developing economies in particular to avoid balance-of-payments constraints and to augment their savings through trade and borrowing.

Trends in trade

The industrial market economies have accounted for almost two-thirds of world trade throughout the 1960s and 1970s, with the developing economies (including China and the capital surplus petroleum exporting economies) taking up nearly a third, leaving a very small share for the European centrally planned economies (see *Table 5.4*).

Table 5.4 *Composition of world exports[a], 1960, 1970 and 1977 (%)*

	1960	1970	1977
Industrial market economies	62	64	63
European centrally planned economies	8	7	8
Capital surplus petroleum-exporting economies	4	6	6
Developing market economies	26	23	23
People's Republic of China	b	b	b
Total	100	100	100
US$ billion	150	375	1344

[a] Merchandise trade and non-factor services. Non-factor service data for the centrally planned economies had to be estimated from very partial information
[b] Less than 1%

Source: World Bank data, March 1980

The commodity composition of trade has changed sharply. *Table 5.5* indicates an increase in the share of fuel exports, resulting from the increase in both volume and price. The increase in the share of manufactures occurred mainly in the 1960s; it is considerably understated by the use of conventional Standard International Trade Classifications 5 to 8 (minus 67 and 68) to represent manufactures, and 0, 1, 2 and 4 to represent raw materials, because the latter include an increasing proportion of processed, that is manufactured, products.

Table 5.5 *Composition and growth of world merchandise exports by commodity groups, 1960, 1970 and 1977 (%)*

	1960	1970	1977	Average annual growth rates 1960–77
Agricultural products	30	21	17	4.7
Metals and minerals	8	7	4	4.1
Fuels	10	9	20	6.4
Manufactures	52	63	60	8.9
Total	100	100	100	7.2
US$ billion	128	313	1120	

Source: Based on UN trade data, March 1980

The growth rate of global exports peaked at about 7½ per cent a year in the 1960s and then fell to about 6½ per cent in the 1970s. The capital surplus petroleum exporting developing economies' exports increased rapidly in the 1960s when the volume of petroleum consumed and traded internationally increased sharply, then maintained their share in the 1970s with the petroleum price increases. The other developing countries' share of total trade, however, declined, largely reflecting the decline in the developing economies' share of primary product exports. Latin America in particular in the 1950s and 1960s lost a substantial share of its agricultural temperate climate exports to the industrial market economies. Not all of the decline was the result of the exporting countries' neglect. The introduction of the European Economic Community's Common Agricultural Policy, and agricultural protectionism in the other industrial market economies, severely restricted the markets for a number of products, notably sugar and beef. Latin America also lost some of its share of mineral exports to other developing countries. Thus Latin America's share of world merchandise exports fell from 12 per cent in 1950 to 8 per cent in 1960 and to about 5.5 per cent in the 1970s. Its exports of petroleum and manufactures did not grow rapidly enough to make up for the export losses in agricultural products and minerals. The neglect of trade during the 1950s and most of the 1960s was part of the policy-mix which had caused most Latin American countries' growth to lag substantially behind that of other countries at similar and lower levels of development. Apart from petroleum and minerals, most of the African countries had a poor export performance during the 1950s and 1960s, so that their share fell from about 5 to 4 per cent between 1950 and the late 1970s. Only Asian countries increased their share, from about 13 per cent in 1950 to about 15 per cent in the late 1970s. This change represents two trends: a loss in South Asia's share of trade and a gain by the East and Southeast Asian countries in agricultural, mineral and particularly manufactured exports.

The developing market economies' share of world exports of processed raw materials and manufactured products rose from about 10 to 20 per cent between 1960 and 1977, with rapid rates of growth in East and Southeast Asia, in several of the Southern European and Mediterranean countries and in some Latin American countries. The developing economies' exports of manufactures alone (as conventionally defined) grew at about 15 per cent a year between 1960 and 1973, and at more than 12 per cent a year in the second half of the 1970s. The entry of developing countries into world trade in manufactures began on a small scale in the 1950s when Israel and Hong Kong were the only significant exporters. Taiwan followed in the early 1960s and then South Korea, Singapore and the Southern European countries in the mid-1960s. Colombia was the first of the Latin American countries to attempt to facilitate non-traditional exports by a change in exchange rate policies combined with high export incentives. Brazil followed. By the early 1970s, enthusiasm for exports of manufactures had become the new conventional wisdom. Although the 'gang of four' – Hong Kong, Taiwan, South Korea and Singapore – continued to dominate the developing countries' exports of manufactures, more than 30 developing countries were exporting more than $100 million of manufactures annually by the early 1970s. The number of countries exporting manufactures has continued to grow, and so has the diversity of the products exported. While some relatively advanced industrial countries such as India continue to lag in exports of manufactures – exporting less than Hong Kong, for example – others, such as Malta and Mauritius, are rapidly becoming significant exporters. The notion that the more industrialized developing countries are the only ones causing the adjustment problems in industrial countries is misleading. In 1978, manufactures (as conventionally defined) accounted for about a third of total developing country exports and the proportion is growing.

The market conflict between the industrial and developing countries is, moreover, not new. Despite the trade liberalization movement of the 1950s and 1960s, developing countries faced protectionist measures against their exports almost from the start. In fact there is a continuous history of protectionism against developing countries from the time the first 'developing' country, Japan, came on the market with a large volume of low cost products in the 1920s. It is salutary to recall that the trade diversion policies pursued by the United Kingdom, France and the United States in their home and colonial markets in the 1920s were precursors to the protectionism of the 1930s, and contributed to Japan's involvement in World War II. Protectionist measures against Japan were continued as soon as it came back into world markets in the 1950s, and they were extended to include the rapidly expanding East Asian exporters by the 1960s[17].

Several characteristics of developing country exports of manufactures contribute to the industrial countries' difficulties in adjusting to them. Developing countries tend to come in at the bottom of the market with very low cost products, reflecting their low wage scales. Once production and marketing problems are overcome by developing country (or transnational corporation) entrepreneurs, exports can be increased very rapidly because labour supplies are ample. For this reason it also takes time for costs of production to rise, although growth eventually increases per capita incomes and forces countries to move into other, less labour intensive products. But this process may take a long time, particularly in relatively large countries where pockets of poverty may remain for long periods. In any case, other, still low income, developing countries can come into the export market, again with low costs and prices. Also, in contrast to the trade among the industrial countries, the initial effect tends to fall on entire industries such as clothing, textiles and footwear which employ the least skilled workers. These are often women who are denied entry into skilled trades and, as secondary income earners, have low geographic mobility. Whereas adjustment to less labour intensive production is relatively easy within industry groups such as metal working, glassware, or pottery which produce a range of products with broadly similar skills, it is difficult when a whole large industry employing marginal workers is affected. Adjustment is also easier within a transnational corporation's organization. Japan has been particularly successful in utilizing its large corporations which cover a range of activities to bear the costs of adjustment[18]. But when a relatively large industry is being phased out, the least efficient and financially weak firms, employing the least skilled and enterprising workers, are usually the last ones left. If such firms are geographically concentrated, adjustment becomes particularly difficult because whole regions begin to decline. Some of the adjustments resulting from changes in technology, tastes and trade among industrial countries, of course, also have certain of these characteristics, but rarely do they have all of them, and they usually do not have them to the same degree. In the 1950s and 1960s, when the industrial economies' growth was rapid, the adjustment process nevertheless worked quite well, even in clothing, textiles and footwear where the labour force characteristics that make adjustment difficult were concentrated. The developing countries' expansion went almost unnoticed in some industries with the industrial economies' production in those industries being almost phased out. Some articles of sports equipment in the USA are an example.

Although adjustment has had its difficulties, protectionism against developing countries should not be exaggerated. In the mid and late 1970s, the developing economies' exports of manufactures to industrial market economies continued to grow more rapidly than did industrial countries' exports to each other. More protectionist action was taken against other industrialized countries than against the developing or centrally planned economies. Some of the developing countries' influence on the production of the industrial market economies took place through competition in new markets, particularly in the Middle East. Thus trade among developing economies, which had been declining in the 1950s and 1960s, turned around sharply in the 1970s with about a quarter of their total exports and about a third of their manufactured exports and services going to other developing countries[19].

The movement of labour

The industrial countries of 'new settlement' were traditionally countries of immigration, and they still have relatively low ratios of population to land. The United States continues to attract migrants from the developing countries, particularly from Latin America. The ending of the colonial era, and the associated political settlements, also led to some migration to other industrial countries, principally France and the United Kingdom. With full employment in industrial countries in the 1960s, a new type of short-term immigration began to flow to the rapidly growing countries of northwestern continental Europe. Germany and Switzerland were the principal host countries for these 'guest workers'. There were also some flows of workers among developing economies, particularly in Africa where imperialist interests had rarely coincided with traditional patterns of culture. But there has also been a considerable movement of migrants within Latin America. The rapid economic growth of the low population petroleum exporting countries of the Middle East led to a new wave of migration from neighbouring states and from South Asia in the late 1960s and 1970s. To the individuals concerned, the benefits of such migration evidently exceeded the costs. There have always been more applicants than places for short- and long-term migration, and the pressure of illegal migration has been very strong, and in the United States successful to a considerable degree. The United States admits some 400 000 people a year legally, but estimates of illegal immigrants, mainly from Latin America, residing in the United States range from 2 to 4 million people or more. There were about 6 million temporary migrants in Europe in the mid-1960s, with as many dependants. Estimates suggest that about 2 million people have migrated in Africa (including to South Africa) and 3 million in Latin America. Immigration into the Middle East involves some 2 to 4 millions[20].

Although migrants have for the most part come into the workforce at the lowest prevailing wages and for the least attractive jobs, both wages and jobs were more attractive than those in their home country. The European host countries also pay substantial social security benefits to the migrants, either together with their wages or as a lump sum on their return home. While living conditions for temporary workers are usually inferior to those enjoyed by the local population, they are rarely as bad as – and are often much better than – those in the home country. The workers accumulate considerable savings and they usually return to their home country with new skills and sufficient capital to improve their living standards markedly. For permanent migrants, the industrial economies offer an unequalled opportunity to attain the industrialized countries' living standards, generally within a generation.

Given the advantages to the migrants, it is curious to find opposition to migration in both the home and host countries. In the home countries it has been argued that emigration drew away the relatively skilled workers. The 'brain drain' argument, which is the extreme form of this argument, is much more persuasive in pressing for wiser education policies in developing countries than for taxation of emigrants[21]. Agricultural production was said to suffer. But many of the returning workers contributed new entrepreneurial and skilled inputs in the home country. Workers' remittances have had a favourable effect on the balance of payments of the developing countries bordering the Mediterranean, some Caribbean and Latin American countries, and Middle Eastern and South Asian countries. In 1977 workers' remittances and (net) private transfers contributed some $16 billion to developing country foreign earnings; this compared with only some $7 billion in official transfers[22]. Workers' remittances were particularly valuable for the low income South Asian countries which have not been able to formulate and implement appropriate policies to stimulate exports.

In the host countries, employers were keen to secure additional labour in tight market conditions. It has been argued that the encouragement of such immigration delayed technological change, investment and increases in productivity in the industrialized countries; if true, migration thus contributed to the competitiveness of developing country exports by avoiding the substitution of capital for labour through new technology.

There seems little doubt that migration is a very efficient – perhaps the most efficient – means of raising living standards for poor people. But although labour is a substitute for capital and trade in economic terms, it is quite different from other factors and outputs of production in human terms. Migration leads to social conflicts. Short-term migration which generally separates men from their families has undesirable social effects on both the home and the host countries. Social problems became evident in Europe in the early 1970s and came to a head in the mid-1970s recession when the number of short-term migrants was sharply reduced. It is thus usually argued, even by ardent economic liberals, that trade, together with the export of capital and associated technology from industrial economies, is socially more desirable than the migration of people from developing to industrial countries[23].

Debt as an engine of growth

The dominance of the Harrod–Domar growth model, with its central emphasis on (physical) capital investment, led to a concern about the lack of domestic savings in developing countries after World War II. Domestic savings could be supplemented by foreign capital flows, and these became even more desirable because development was seen to put pressure on the balance of payments. But this was easier said than done. Although the former 'metropolitan' and other relatively high income countries acknowledged (whether for reasons of conscience, humanity or political interest) some responsibility for helping the developing countries to catch up to their living standards, the aid flows that taxpayers would support were not likely to be enough to close the 'two gaps' as was thought necessary for development. In the early 1950s, it was thought difficult, if not impossible, for the developing countries to attract private capital to supplement aid flows. They were not thought to be creditworthy, except for short-term borrowing for trade[24]. Aid flows, in part grants and technical assistance but predominantly 'soft' loans made directly or through multilateral lending institutions, were thus the dominant capital flow to developing countries.

By the mid-1950s it seemed possible that private direct foreign investment flows could become available to developing countries. Transnational corporations were beginning to have a major influence on the transfer of 'packages' of technology, management and capital, first from the United

States to the fast-growing industrial market economies, and then more widely. Many transnationals had links with the former colonial and semi-colonial countries, mainly in the exploitation of natural resources and in public utilities. But some of these corporations had been closely associated politically with the foreign rulers, and almost all had appropriated high resource rents from their exploitation of mineral and other natural resources and monopoly rents from public utilities. The developing economies wished to appropriate these rents for themselves, and the transnationals' investment moved to manufacturing and allied industries, such as banking, insurance and advertising, which were beginning to flourish with high protection and other incentives.

Because it was feared that developing countries could not attract direct foreign investment, they were advised to introduce not only guarantees that capital and profits could be repatriated but also a wide range of taxation, credit and other inventives to attract foreign investment. The developing countries, taking this advice, began to compete against each other in giving incentives to foreign firms, eroding their own revenues and creating monopolistic rents, particularly where protection was high. Some industrial countries, because they regarded foreign investment as aid, assisted such investment by subsidies, further distorting market signals. A wave of 'defensive' investment by the major international corporations mainly interested in consumer goods followed[25], but most of the transnationals did not permit their subsidiaries and associated companies to export from developing (and other host) countries.

The conditions under which such foreign investment took place added to the conflicts and difficulties already engendered by investment in minerals and other natural resources. The corporations were seen to be earning high monopoly rents and hindering export efforts. Many corporations refused to permit host country participation in the form of ownership or management. Where they combined with local elites they used their political power to seek even higher protection and other subsidies. Where the corporations of one country dominated foreign investment in another, fears of political dependence were added to fears of economic domination. An acrimonious debate about the effects of private direct foreign investment thus pervaded the 1950s and 1960s. Although many countries such as South Korea followed Japan in industrializing almost entirely without foreign investment, and although in countries such as Brazil or Argentina, where foreign investment was relatively heavy, it accounted only for a small proportion (usually less than 25 per cent) of total investment in manufacturing, it has taken years to sort out the balance of costs and benefits associated with direct private foreign investment.

Under pressure from domestic groups protesting against distortions in the movement of jobs to developing countries, the 'home' countries, led by the United States, moved toward neutral treatment of foreign investment. The danger of under-investment at home because of the attractions of high monopoly profits abroad was a factor. The developing countries ended the transnationals' role in public utilities and reduced their direct role substantially in natural resource exploitation. Conditions in manufacturing have become more competitive in many developing countries, thereby reducing monopoly rents. In the late 1950s, some transnationals actively began to seek low-income country location for the manufacture of the labour intensive components of their products both for their home and export markets. They then began to permit subsidiaries to export from developing (and other) countries. Local participation in ownership and management began to increase, with a movement toward the 'unbundling' of the foreign investment package. European, Japanese, and transnationals from developing countries diversified the sources of direct foreign investment. Contrary to the fears expressed in the past, nations can control transnational corporations and ensure that the social and economic benefits of their activities exceed the social and economic costs in home and host countries[26].

In the 1960s, export credits, fostered by mercantilist industrial governments, sometimes in the guise of aid, added to the flow of funds to developing countries (see *Table 5.6*). Official credits were part of concessional flows, but the impetus for private credits, soon to become dominant, was commercial. Though they were theoretically intended merely to offset the long-term nature of returns on capital goods imports, export credits, by subsidizing long-term interest rates, in fact became hidden export incentives in industrial

Table 5.6 *Composition of net capital flows to developing countries, 1960–1962 and 1976–1978 (%)*

	1960–62	1976–78
Aid	59	33
Other concessional, mainly official	7	12
Private non-concessional, of which	34	55
Direct investment	20	14
Export credits	7	12
Financial flows	7	30
Total	100	100
US$ billion annual average	9	67[a]

The figures for 1976–1978 cover flows from OPEC and the centrally planned economies as well as from the DAC and India, Ireland, Israel, Luxembourg, Spain and Yugoslavia. For OPEC, the three-year totals were an estimated $13.6 billion in net bilateral and multilateral aid and an estimated $4.4 billion in net non-concessional flows, together representing about 9% of the entire net flow. For the centrally planned economies, the figures were $2.5 billion and $3.2 billion, respectively, or about 3% of the total. Comparable information on OPEC and CPE flows is not available for 1960–1962.

[a] 75 in 1978

Source: OECD, *Development Cooperation*, (Paris) *passim*

countries. The developing countries benefited from the subsidy, but it was 'tied'. By the mid-1960s, export credits were being pushed out to the developing countires in such volume that they led to severe repayment problems in a number of countries. It was only toward the end of the 1960s, when both the sponsoring and receiving governments became more mature in their use of export credits, that the problems associated with them were overcome.

In the late 1960s the more rapidly developing countries began to have access to the expanding international capital market. The loosening of capital flows among industrial countries, the excess of savings over investments in some countries, and the particular circumstances that led to the creation of the Eurodollar and Eurocurrency markets, came just as the more rapidly growing developing countries were ready to borrow directly from financial institutions. The increase in petroleum prices, and the transfer of some of the petroleum rents from the consumers in the industrial economies to the producers in developing economies, led to a rapid growth of the international capital market. The developing countries (and the European centrally planned economies) took advantage of the greatly increased international liquidity, generally to avoid retarding their development. When countries borrowed to avoid adjusting to the increase in petroleum prices they ran into trouble, but in the main the flow of capital contributed to the maintenance of growth in developing countries in the 1970s, incidentally maintaining the export markets of the industrial countries. The share of industrial economies' merchandise exports going to developing countries rose from about 20 per cent to about 25–27 per cent.

It is ironical that the complaints of the developing economies' lack of access to capital markets in the 1950s and 1960s should, in the 1970s, turn into a fear that they have accumulatd too much debt. It has now been argued for several years that the developing countries have borrowed so much that a large number will go bankrupt, one precipitating others in a domino fashion. It is feared that this will shake the world economy and bring on another financial collapse such as that of 1929 (a view particularly favoured at the end of 1979). The banks that have lent to the developing countries are said to be 'overexposed' in developing countries so that they too will go bankrupt, also in a domino fashion, contributing to the collapse of the entire international financial structure. Even if an international crisis of this dimension does not occur, disaster is nevertheless around the corner because the developing economies and 'the banks' are now so vulnerable that the international capital markets will stop functioning – or, put more crudely, 'will stop recycling the petrodollars' and the savings of industrial countries.

It is by definition true that, having acquired access to capital markets, the developing countries have acquired debt liabilities. The question that should be asked is whether their debts are excessive in relation to the productivity of the financial projects and to the national income growth of the borrowing countries. This is the 'solvency' equivalent of a private enterprise's borrowing. Just as there is no optimal gearing ratio for a firm, there is no optimal debt level for a country.

A second question relates to the management and servicing of the debt and related balance-of-payments issues. This is a 'liquidity' problem. The developing countries have been fortunate to have been borrowing in a period when interest rates (and other costs of borrowing) have lagged behind inflation, thereby transferring income from lenders to borrowers. They have also been fortunate because it has been a period of high world savings and liquidity, so that in addition maturities have been relatively long, often of more than 10 years' duration. Even more important (and in contrast to borrowing from industrial countries' official sources), the liquidity of the private market has made for ready refinancing facilities and relatively easy debt management. The healthy world trade situation, even in the 1970s, together with the borrowing developing economies' rapid export and GNP growth, has made their debt highly productive and manageable.

It has been clear for some time that although the developing countries' debt has been increasing – they owed nearly $400 billion gross at the end of 1979 – there is no debt problem for developing countries *as a whole*. The ratios of debt to exports and to GNP increased in the 1970s but they are still relatively low, for both the low income and the middle income countries. The

Table 5.7 *Developing country debt exposure indicators, 1974 and 1978 (%)*

	1974	1978
Debt/GNP		
Low income economies	20	23
Middle income economies	16	23
Debt exports		
Low income economies	153	169
Middle income economies	60	90
Debt service exports		
Low income economies	10	14
Middle income economies	11	17
Interest payments/exports		
Low income economies	3	5
Middle income economies	3	5
International reserves/debt		
Low income economies	24	33
Middle income economies	74	47
Total debt outstanding (US$ billion)		
Low income economies	30	55
Middle income economies	120	270

Source: World Bank. Debt figures relate to public and publicly guaranteed private debt and debt not guaranteed by the developing countries.

petroleum exporting countries – mostly classed as middle income – account for more than a third of the developing countries' total debt. For the low income countries official reserves have risen to 33 per cent of debt, while for the middle income countries they have fallen from their high, export boom, level of 1974 to just under half of their debt in 1978. Some developing countries – mainly the capital surplus petroleum exporters and, paradoxically, the low income economies – hold foreign assets (including exchange reserves) in excess of their debts. The middle income countries' debt (including that of capital deficit petroleum exporters), on the other hand, exceeded their total banking and gold reserves (valued at current prices) by some $60 billion.

Debt exposure is high for some countries, but for the most part these are the countries that invest their borrowings productively and manage them well. Some badly managed or politically troubled countries, ranging from the very poorest to some relatively high income economies, have had both solvency and liquidity problems. They have not invested well, and they have not paid attention to export growth and balance-of-payments management. Debt service ratios (the ratio of interest and amortization to total exports) are not very useful indicators of the debt situation. Some countries with very high debt service ratios (and very high petroleum import bills) have managed their balance of payments by rolling over their debt. For these countries, interest payment to export ratios are better indicators of liquidity than are debt service ratios. The well managed countries have maintained high reserves and good relations with their banking suppliers. Certain other countries, with relatively small debt service payments and low petroleum imports, have nevertheless found themselves in trouble.

Similarly, the lending programmes of the banks operating in the international sphere have been sound on the whole. Most refinancing arrangements have been made on mutually beneficial terms, and losses have been negligible. The developing countries accounted for about half of all international borrowing in the late 1970s, but their borrowing represented only a small proportion, certainly less than 20 per cent, of total global capital flows (including capital flows between industrial market economies).

5.3   Scenarios for the 1980s

Economists are congenitally myopic. Following the industrial economies' difficulties in handling the economic problems that became increasingly pressing in the 1970s, when rising petroleum prices exacerbated inflationary pressures, economists agreed that a deep recession during 1980/81 was inevitable, (particularly in view of the 1979 petroleum price increases). Such a recession is already doubtful. It was also agreed that recovery would be sluggish at least during the first half of the 1980s, and probably beyond that into the 1990s. The principal institutions that engage in global economic forecasting have been reducing the growth rates in their projections for the 1980s. The LINK system projections have become very bleak, with growth of less than 1 per cent predicted for 1980 and 1981. The World Bank official growth projections have been progressively reduced during the last three years, from about 4.5 per cent a year for industrialized and 5.8 per cent for industrializing economies to about 4.0 per cent and 5.3 per cent, respectively, for the 1980s[27]. The OECD 'Interfutures' report presented several scenarios, including one of relatively high growth of about 4.3 per cent a year for the period 1975–2000 although this was not thought to be the most likely outcome. The Interfutures growth scenarios postulated that with a less 'material goods oriented world', and with the breaking up of the international economic system either into major geographic regions or into the 'north' and the 'south', long-range growth rates for the industrialized economies were more likely to be between 3 and 3.5 per cent[28]. Recent discussions have become even more pessimistic, with much talk about a '2 per cent' future for the market economy industrial economies in contrast to the '4 per cent' past of the 1950s and 1960s. Low growth in industrial countries is expected to reduce the developing economies' growth because they are thought to be highly dependent on the market economy industrial countries through access to markets for their exports, aid and other capital transfers and, to a lesser degree, through the effect of workers' remittances on their balance of payments.

A '2 per cent' future

The more pessimistic of the current prognosticators are suggesting a long-term, if not permanent, return to pre-World War II growth rates. The disillusionment of the rich with growth and material possessions plays an important role in these views. In the terms of the Interfutures report, this outlook postulates a rapid adoption of new 'post-materialist' values, with a new emphasis on the quality of life and leisure. These are equated with less economic activity, opposition to new forms of energy that may be damaging to the environment, and a disenchantment with industrialization which, in a breathtaking leap of logic, is equated with economic activity. Instead of being a bugbear, 'de-industrialization' becomes a desirable objective. A large number of complementary, though often implicit, assumptions postulate that productivity will fall with lower working hours, that a leisure oriented and non-materialistic society will be a non-consuming society, and that better environmental conditions can be achieved without investment[29].

Another variant of the low growth scenario is built around the likelihood of political conflict between Western and socialist countries, between 'the North' and 'the South', or as a result of further political crises in the Middle East which would sharply curtail petroleum supplies.

A third version suggests a polarization of trade and other economic relations around three regional groups of countries: North and South America; Western Europe, Africa and some parts of the Middle East; and Japan, Australasia and Asia. The European Economic Community's policies are widely perceived to be heading in this direction with the inclusion of several South European countries, the Community's complex of relationships with the Maghreb countries, and the colonial-type negotiations recently concluded with the (predominantly African) group of Lomé countries – leading to increasingly inward-looking and protectionist policies. North America would follow its historical orientation toward Latin America. Australia and New Zealand would join Japan in an updated version of an Asian co-prosperity sphere. These scenarios reflect some current trends, but they are not altogether persuasive. India and China do not fit easily into them. In contrast to the European Economic Community, the United States has been very supportive of liberal international economic relations. It can be argued that, as its share of world output shrinks further as other countries' shares grow, the United States will become more susceptible to regional protectionist views. Proposals, albeit still vague, for a northern American common market embracing Canada, the United States and Mexico hint in this direction.

Most versions of the '2 per cent' world scenarios blame the increasing price of petroleum for the market economy industrialized countries' low growth. They argue that the industrialized countries will not be able to handle the current and prospective price increases, staggering along a 'stagflationary' path as petroleum producers deliver price blow after price blow. It is maintained that the major industrialized countries will not be able to implement policies that will contain inflation, damp down the use of energy in the short run, and mobilize a major investment in petroleum substitutes in the long run. It is again being argued, as in 1974/75, that the petroleum producers, and the funds that petroleum rents create even if recycled to other countries, will not create sufficient demand to offset the industrial economies' low growth. Most industrial economies are expected not to imitate what the developing countries did in the 1970s – to borrow from the petroleum exporters' accumulation of funds to overcome short-run balance-of-payments problems – but rather to continue to follow mercantilist and deflationary policies which will reinforce each other across the Atlantic and reach to Japan. The 'instability of the international monetary system' will then take the blame for the irresponsible actions of its member countries.

There can be little doubt that slow growth would make more difficult the adjustment of industry (and of agriculture and services) to technological innovation and to changes in taste and mutual trade, as well as to the competition of the developing and centrally planned economies. Adjustment to trade with the developing countries is only a small component of the total adjustment continuously taking place in the industrial economies; but it is politically the easiest to avoid. In an efficient country, increases in imports lower costs and prices and lead to further exports; but adjustment costs do exist, and governments that cannot handle inflation and other internal economic problems are likely to turn to subsidizing their less competitive industries with tariffs, non-tariff barriers and domestic subsidies. In the absence of imaginative national employment and investment policies, weak, confused and partial adjustment policies which often resist change may be expected to continue if growth is slow, despite their high economic costs. Such policies would lead to some reversal of factor proportions in competition with low labour cost countries but, more commonly, to the propping up of inefficient firms and workers in 'senile' industries. Just as 'infant' industries have taken a long time to grow up in the slowly growing developing economies, so 'senile' industries would take a long time to die in slowly growing industrial ones, although handsome rents would be earned in the meantime. The vested interests so created would begin to present a formidable barrier to further liberalization. Indeed, if low growth becomes sufficiently widespread, a return to protectionism would be likely. This would again take decades of negotiations to remove.

A return to a '4 per cent plus' future

It has been widely argued, on a variety of assumptions, that continuing productivity increases and national income growth rates of some 4.2–4.5 per cent a year would be required in the industrial market economies, during the 1980s, to mop up existing unemployment and to provide jobs to new entrants (including women) into the workforce[30]. Given zero population growth, such national income growth rates imply substantial improvements in living standards whether in the form of increased material goods, increased leisure, an improved environment, or, as is most likely, some combination of all three. Some changes in national accounting methods will be needed to capture this improved 'quality of life' in the measurements of national income and its growth. It seems that current growth rates already understate growth in comparison even with the 1960s, because the benefits of such 'outputs' as cleaner rivers are not fully measured. If they could be fully measured, 3–4 per cent growth in the 1980s, as conventionally recorded, might not be so much less than the 5 per cent of the 1960s as it appears to be.

Discussion about the policies required for '4 per cent plus' growth continues, despite current pessimism[31]. The mix of policies needed would, of course, vary from country to country with the particular problems of each. However, the broad outlines are well known. It is clear that no one policy – monetarist, Keynesian, trade policies or any other – would suffice. To carry through appropriate policies it would be necessary to cajole strong vested interests into moving to new positions. Among the most important policies are those concerned with persuading various interest groups that they have more to gain from containing inflation than from letting it continue at high and fluctuating rates. To be effective, 'income' policies would require some form of political compact, so that the different groups concerned would be convinced that their shares of the costs of containing inflation are fair. The political leaders of those developing countries that experienced high inflation rates in the 1960s are no doubt amused to see countries which then lectured them about their iniquitous and spendthrift ways now themselves unable to handle inflation. Until it is resolved which sections of society will pay, and in what measure, for rising petroleum prices and the poor policies of the 1970s, the likelihood of a return to a '4 per cent plus' future will remain dim.

Containing inflation also requires monetary and fiscal responsibility. Appropriate monetary policies are particularly difficult to devise in countries that have high rents from petroleum, such as the United Kingdom. Fiscal responsibility (in the sense that national expenditures, whether social or political, have to be paid for) appears to have become very difficult to enforce in such countries as the United States. Taxation policies should now be reviewed in many countries. Trade policies, too, have an important role to play in stimulating efficiency and productivity through competitiveness, and thus in interacting with other policies in damping down inflation. Protection should be reduced in agriculture and services as well as in manufacturing. For some of the market industrial economies, as for many of the developing and socialist economies, international borrowing would be desirable (and given international liquidity, available) for financing the deficits; this would bridge an adjustment to higher petroleum prices and more efficient production.

The current economic situation favours a positive approach to growth. Investment has been relatively low for more than a decade, retained earnings are high in many countries in spite of somewhat eroded business profits, and there is ample international liquidity. It is clear than in an economic, as distinct from an engineering, sense many industries are running close to capacity. But, at the same time, there are signs of shortages of capacity in some metal industries, in many engineering industries, and in such new industries as microelectronics. All the industrial economies need a major investment programme in energy conservation. Some countries, notably the United States, need a major investment drive in alternative energy production. Social investment is required in low productivity countries in re-educating and restructuring the labour force and in changing the character of education and training for new entrants. The range of improved sectoral policies needed to support and complement macroeconomic policies is wide and varies from country to country.

Growth policies have an international component. Beggar-your-neighbour protectionism, the export of unemployment through inflation by the larger economies, and disruptive exchange rate fluctuations have no place in a rapidly growing international economy. With growth, such problems become easier to handle. Instead of moving toward more protectionism the international community should become seriously concerned with the evolution of the post-Tokyo round codes of conduct on non-tariff barriers in international trade which hide protectionism.

A return to a '4 per cent plus' growth would thus mean the continued improvement of all the productive sectors, including agriculture, manufacturing, infrastructure and services. There would be a reduction in the output of industries, and more particularly of those firms that cannot compete internationally and a shift of workers and other resources to those that can. It is unlikely that a large volume of low-quality textile, clothing or footwear production would survive in the industrial market economies, given the competition from the developing and centrally planned countries; although some firms would no doubt continue to operate successfully because of specialization, proximity to the market and factor reversal. Movements within such basic industries as steel, such capital goods industries as shipbuilding, and such durable consumer goods as motor vehicles, would be likely, with increasing trade in industrial parts and components, particularly between the more industrialized planned economies and the developing countries and among the latter. The European Economic Community's Common Agricultural Policy, and the agricultural protectionism of Japan and the United States, would have to be dismantled. The trends toward the confusion of efficiency in production and welfare in consumption would have to be resolved and the subsidies to production phased out.

Energy policy remains critical. The problem is not a long-run shortage of energy, but rather the political insecurity of supplies in the short run. This can be overcome only by investment in the production of petroleum and its substitutes. Until recently this has been clearly perceived by the dominant OPEC producers, which therefore tried to keep the price of petroleum below the level at which investment in substitutes would become profitable. Some industrial economies, notably the United States and until recently Canada and Australia, foolishly gave the OPEC cartel *carte blanche* to increase prices by their lack of domestic energy policies. But substitutes are generally regarded as becoming economic (taking into account full environmental costs) when petroleum is priced somewhere between $45 and $50 a barrel (in 1980 prices). It would have been beneficial to the consuming countries to have steadily brought up prices to these levels by taxation ahead of OPEC action. Some moved along this path, and so continued to appropriate substantial portions of petroleum rents to the public purse and to stimulate investment both in alternative energy sources and in the more economic use of commercial and domestic energy. Because of the long lead-times in energy investment, energy conservation is particularly important in the short run. But the 1970s were a period of missed opportunities in the industrial economies, with immediate political objectives clouding long-term perspectives. The attempts to hold down energy prices during 1977 and 1978 thus inevitably led to price increases in 1979. Although the 1979 petroleum price increases were not as steep as those of 1974[32], petroleum prices are now finally coming close to the point at which the signals for investment in substitutes are becoming clear even in the United States. Coal and coal derivatives, heavy oils, oil tars and oil sands are becoming competitive alternatives to petroleum. The recent increases in petroleum prices are thus likely to achieve what years of exhortation failed to do. The appropriate policy would still be to bring the price of petroleum for consumers to that of substitutes over a period of, say, from 3 to 5 years, and to appropriate the difference in taxes; but in view of the political difficulties in industrial countries there is probably a case for arguing that the sooner the international price goes up to about $40 to $45 a barrel, the better. Any effects on the price system could be handled in the context of the policies outlined, with investment in energy conservation and production contributing substantially to overall growth.

Policies for growth see the emphasis on the quality of life and the improvement of the environment not as a brake but as a stimulus. A high quality of life requires a meaningful involvement in productive social goals as well as the consumption of leisure. In fact, more leisure means more consumption, though not necessarily of material goods. And access by the mass of the people to a highly improved environment requires very high productivity growth. In some industrial countries enormous investment is needed to reverse urban blight and to improve access to, and the quality of, such public goods as mass transportation and street safety.

The return to higher growth seems such an attractive alternative that it is likely to be followed by a number of countries; it is difficult to grasp why others think it so far out of reach. The new growth pessimism appears to be in part, perhaps not altogether consciously, a counter-revolution against the erosion of wealth wrought by the social and economic revolutions of the past 30 years. In a stagnating world there would be less access to the 'top'; in contrast, the continuation of growth would mean more equality of opportunity. The principal problems of growth are ideological and political rather than economic. Politicians, unwilling to do the hard political work of persuading vested interests to accept short-term sacrifices for long-term gains, call for international summits. Thus in the 1980s, as in previous decades, there is likely to be a wide range of economic performance.

Prospects for developing countries

The growth of the developing economies, like that of the industrial economies, will continue to be determined largely by their own policies. In that sense, they have been 'de-linked' from the industrial economies ever since they won independence; developing countries are not as dependent on the industrial countries for growth now as they were in the colonial period because their decisions are made by their own governments. Some are, it is true, still heavily influenced by certain industrial countries (both market economy and centrally planned), some by transnational corporations, and some by other developing countries, but this is their choice, or at least that of their ruling interest groups. The relatively strong growth of the developing economies in the 1970s bears out their independence and the strength of the impetus towards catching up with the industrial economies.

Aid is important for welfare (for which it is only rarely given), and it can be important for growth. Access to trade and capital markets is even more important to growth. Therefore, a return to rapid growth in the international economy would help the developing countries. With unchanged domestic policies, a return to '4 per cent plus' growth in the industrial countries could mean as much as a percentage point increase in overall developing country growth, and perhaps as much as two percentage point increases for small and medium-sized countries with export-oriented economies. But developing countries could achieve these, and even larger, increases without much growth in the international economy merely by changing their domestic policies. Indeed, the pressure of relatively slow growth in the industrial countries could be helpful in pushing them in these directions. The ratios of imports to national income growth and of investment to output growth can be reduced substantially in many countries without reducing growth itself because the capital–output, capital–labour and import–growth ratios are very high in many developing countries. Slow growth in the industrial economies could thus, paradoxically, lead to a more rapid growth in developing countries. Rapid expansion of trade among developing countries could compensate for other lags in world trade. The growth of large countries – India and China particularly – is for the most part independent of global trends, yet these countries have the heaviest weight in overall developing country growth and a great potential for increasing trade between developing countries.

As a group (even apart from the capital surplus petroleum exporters) the developing countries are relatively well endowed with energy resources. While only some 15 developing countries are petroleum exporters, another 10 or 20 have substantial proven domestic petroleum and gas reserves, and others are now discovering them. Several are known to have coal reserves, and others will find them in the future. Their potential for hydro-electricity has yet to be exploited. The smallest and poorest countries that do not have energy resources are also small energy users; large petroleum imports are concentrated in a few, for the most part rapidly growing countries, such as Brazil and South Korea. In countries with serious petroleum import cost problems, such as Turkey, the cause of difficulties is not so much petroleum imports as internal inefficiency and bad export and balance-of-payments management.

The rapidly growing developing countries were able to export goods and services to the Middle East petroleum-rich countries, and some of the poorest receive substantial workers' remittances from them. The developing economies' trade with the 'high absorbing' petroleum-rich countries such as

Mexico and Indonesia is expected to grow rapidly in the 1980s. Trade with the industrial countries could also expand, even if the more pessimistic scenarios for their growth as a whole materialize. This would help even the small poor countries highly dependent on one or two primary export crops.

The current upswing in terms of trade for primary producers has already alleviated some of the impact of higher petroleum prices for many petroleum-importing developing countries. There are prospects, particularly if the higher growth scenarios (in real terms) are realistic, that this upswing will hold in the early 1980s at least, for it reflects the low investment levels of the 1970s. In the longer run trade is of course much more important for a healthy balance of payments than are capital flows, and developing country exports to each other contribute to the capacity to import just as much as do exports to the industrial countries. If the developing countries pursue the trade opportunities that are likely to open up in the 1980s, their trade outlook will be promising.

Even if the developing countries' current account deficit reaches levels of $60–$70 billion in 1980 (about 5 per cent of their GNP, as was the case in 1974) it seems likely that it can be financed without an undue strain on the international financial system. For small and very poor countries, aid from the industrial and petroleum exporting countries will have to play the main role. For the middle income countries the international capital markets can be expected to handle the situation. Although interest rates are now positive when adjusted for inflation, they are still not high. Loan maturities, which were averaging 10 years in 1978 and 1979 for good borrowers, have shortened somewhat, but this is not of great concern to those developing countries managing their debt by year-to-year refinancing arrangements. So long as these countries continue to grow soundly, they cannot be regarded as having reached the limits of borrowing. Some of the international banks (or their governments) may consider their exposure excessive in some countries, but new banks, including some from the Middle East, are becoming increasingly active[33]. It will be interesting to see whether, on balance, the developing countries that have borrowed heavily in commercial markets will do better or worse than they did when their borrowing was accompanied by the homilies of bilateral and multilateral aid institutions. For countries that have used borrowing in the past to avoid rather than stimulate adjustment to changing world conditions, the situation will of course be very different. They will find themselves in serious difficulties, stemming primarily not from petroleum import costs or high debt service, but from years of inappropriate economic policies. Hopefully such policies will now be changed. Thus high liquidity in international markets holds dangers for borrowers as well as for lenders. While developing countries will have to continue to deal with various shocks in the international economy, and those with inappropriate domestic policies will continue to find it difficult to do so, as a group they can be expected vigorously to continue their catching up process.

It was estimated in the mid-1970s that an increase in developing economy growth could lead to a 'not negligible' increase in the growth of the industrial market economies[34]. By the mid-1980s the weight of the more rapidly growing developing countries in the world economy will be somewhat greater if trade and capital flows continue to be liberalized. If India and China grow rapidly and participate strongly in international trade, the 1980s will see an even quicker evolution of the international economy than did the 1960s and 1970s. The potential for an impetus to further growth in the industrial countries resulting from a catching up by the developing economies would then become substantial. The industrial and developing economies are linked through trade and capital flows from which all participants benefit.

However, countries are not dependent on each other for the quality of their economic performance. Each country has to make its own policy decisions and take the responsibility for them. Greater competitiveness and stability in the international economy will follow from better national performance. The larger economies carry not only greater weight but also greater responsibility. The 1970s saw an excess of international summits, conferences and exhortations which dealt in generalities designed to avoid the hard political decisions which must be taken at the national level to set economies on faster growth paths. Hopefully the 1980s will see a focus of attention on national problems and technical issues, such as the implementation of the GATT codes of conduct and the IMF's substitution account, which can have a practical effect on improving international economic relations.

References

1 See W. Hager, ch. 13 of this work.
2 See D. Morawetz, *Twenty-five Years of Economic Development, 1950–75*. The World Bank, Washington, D. C., 1977 for a brisk summary.
3 See I. B. Kravis *et al.*, *A System of International Comparisons of Gross Product and Purchasing Power*. The World Bank, Johns Hopkins University Press, Baltimore and London, 1975 and I. B. Kravis *et al.*, *International Comparisons of Real Product and Purchasing Power*, The World Bank, Johns Hopkins University Press, Baltimore and London, 1978, for an indication of the distortions introduced by the use of official exchange rates in international comparisons. Such distortions are not removed by the use of domestic currency growth rates to estimate past growth (see I. B. Kravis *et al.*, 'Real GDP per Capita for More than One Hundred Countries'. *The Economic Journal* 88, June 1978, pp. 215–242), for these also underestimate the growth of countries moving from simple, non-monetized to industrial economies. Current work by Kravis, Heston and Summers, and by Robin Marris, is seeking to identify the character and magnitude of such underestimation of growth. The catching-up process, which is underestimated by growth rate measurements, whether in local or international currencies, is fully captured only when countries revalue their currencies against those with which they are catching up.
4 See H. W. Arndt, *The Rise and Fall of Economic Growth: A Study in Contemporary Thought*. Longman Cheshire, Melbourne, 1978, particularly chs. 3, 4 and 5 for the post-World War II ideology of growth as expressed in the writings of English-speaking economists.

5 See H. W. Arndt, *The Rise and Fall of Economic Growth: A Study in Contemporary Thought*. Longman Cheshire, Melbourne, 1978 for a discussion of the decline of the importance of growth as an economic and social objective. E. J. Mishan, *The Costs of Economic Growth*. Staples Press, London, 1967, states the case against the erosion of privilege by growth. F. Hirsch, *Social Limits to Growth*. Harvard University Press, Cambridge, Massachusetts, 1976, emphasizes the positional limitations which affect middle class attitudes to growth. W. Beckerman, *In Defence of Economic Growth*. Jonathan Cape, London, 1974, on the other hand, puts the case for continuing growth.

6 D. H. Meadows *et al.*, *The Limits to Growth: A Report for the Club of Rome on the Predicament of Mankind*. Universe Books, New York, 1972, started a debate which quickly negated, on the basis of careful research, the Report's findings. Organization for Economic Cooperation and Development (OECD). *Interfutures: Final Report, Facing the Future: Mastering the Probable and Managing the Unpredictable*. Paris, 1979, sums up the case against the 'finite world' concept.

7 See the rapidly growing literature on the political economy of protectionism following R. E. Caves, 'Economic Models of Political Choice: Canada's Tariff Structure'. *The Canadian Journal of Economics* **IX**, May 1976, 278–300.

8 See M. Olson, 'The Political Economy of Comparative Growth Rates'. University of Maryland, November/December 1978 (mimeo). It is interesting, however, that the shop stewards' hold on trade unions seems to be weakening as rank and file workers perceive that their interests sometimes coincide with national ones.

9 The public ownership of enterprises has, of course, always combined social, economic and even political objectives to some extent. Perhaps that is one of the reasons why (apart from 'natural' monopolies) it has only been successful in special circumstances in market economies. In the United Kingdom 'de-industrialization' has somewhat confusingly been blamed for much of the falling efficiency that has resulted from the mixing of productive and welfare policies. See for example F. Blackaby (ed.), *De-Industrialization*. National Institute of Economic and Social Research, Economic Policy Papers **2**, Heinemann Educational Books, London, 1979.

10 The liberalization of trade and capital flows has noticeably reduced the interest in the economic size of countries in recent years. A questioning of the impact of size on policy formulation would, however, seem in order in view of the increased attention now given the latter.

11 For differing definitions of newly industrializing countries, see introduction to this volume, p. 2f.

12 See H. Hughes, 'Industrialization and Development: A Stocktaking'. *Industry and Development* **2**, United Nations, New York, 1978, pp. 3–29.

13 See ch. 8.

14 See ch. 9.

15 See ch. 7.

16 W. W. Rostow, *The Stages of Economic Growth A Non-Communist Manifesto*. Cambridge University Press, London, 1960, while not applicable in detail, contains the germs of important observations about the nature of economic growth.

17 D. B. Keesing and M. Wolf, 'Textile Quotas Against Developing Countries: A Study of Managed Trade'. World Bank, Washington D. C., March 1980 (mimeo).

18 See ch. 12.

19 B. Balassa, 'The New Protectionism and the International Economy'. *Journal of World Trade Law* **12**(5), 1978, and R. Blackhurst, N. Marian and J. Tumlir, *Trade Liberalization, Protectionism and Interdependence*. GATT Studies in International Trade, Geneva, November 1977, for example, give great emphasis to the extent and impact of 'new protectionism' and appear to have exaggerated its extent. The International Monetary Fund's *Annual Reports of Exchange Restrictions, 1975–1978 passim*, have noted that most protectionist action was turned against industrial market economies. J. Riedel and L. M. Gard, 'Recent Changes in Industrial Protectionism: An Assessment of the Implications for Developing Countries'. World Bank, Washington D. C., October 1979 (mimeo), give a balanced account which warns of the dangers of protectionism but does not encourage export pessimism in the developing countries. (For the importance to developing countries of manufactured exports see ch. 1, especially *Table 1.3*.) For the importance of inter-developing country trade see H. Hughes, 'Inter-developing Country Trade and Employment'. International Economic Association Sixth World Congress, Mexico City, August 1980.

20 Based on World Bank data.

21 See J. N. Bhagwati and M. Partington, *Taxing the Brain Drain: A Proposal*. North-Holland, Amsterdam, 1976, and J. N. Bhagwati (ed.), *The Brain Drain and Taxation: Theory and Empirical Analysis*. North-Holland, Amsterdam, 1976; see also United Nations Conference on Trade and Development (UNCTAD), *The Reverse Transfer of Technology: Economic Effects of the Outflow of Trained Personnel from Developing Countries*. United Nations, Geneva, TD/B/AC, 11/25, 1972.

22 It is impossible to distinguish clearly between 'workers' remittances' which are mainly manual workers' remittances, and 'private transfers' which are transfers by higher income groups, in balance-of-payments data. They should be taken together as they are here. The figures are based on International Monetary Fund balance-of-payments data.

23 See H. Hughes and G. Ohlin, 'The International Environment'. In J. Cody, H. Hughes and D. Wall (eds.), *Policies for Industrial Progress in Developing Countries*. Oxford University Press, London, 1980, for an elaboration of the competitiveness and complementarity among migration, trade and capital movements.

24 Short-term credit of less than one year's duration, which is generally used for trade purposes, is not included here. Where it is used for long-term purposes and builds up to substantial sums, it usually becomes 'long-term' debt and appears as such in debt data. For a more detailed account of the growth of capital flows to developing countries see H. Hughes, 'Debt and Development: The Role of Foreign Capital in Economic Growth'. *World Development* 7, pp. 95–112.

25 S. Hymer, *The International Operations of National Firms: A Study of Direct Foreign Investment*. MIT Press, Cambridge, Massachusetts, 1976.

26 The debate and ensuing literature about direct foreign investment and transnational corporations is too vast to note here. K. Billerbeck and Y. Yasugi, 'Private Direct Foreign Investment in Developing Countries'. *World Bank Staff Working Paper No. 348*, July 1979, provide an up-to-date summary view. For an expression of a highly critical view see ch. 4 in this book.

27 See World Bank, 'Prospects for Developing Countries, 1978–1985', and *World Development Reports, 1978* and *1979*, Washington 1977, 1978 and 1979.

28 Scenario BI with growth rates averaging 3.4 per cent from 1975–2000. For other B and the CI (North–South conflict) scenarios, see Organization for Economic Cooperation and Development (OECD), *Interfutures: Final Report, Facing the Future: Mastering the Probable and Managing the Unpredictable*. Paris, 1979.

29 This is equivalent to *Facing the Future*, Scenario A, and the World Bank 'base case' scenarios. It is usually assumed that working hours will continue to decline slowly and that women's participation rates will continue to rise slowly, but neither of these assumptions is essential to the proposition.

30 See Organization for Economic Cooperation and Development (OECD), *Interfutures: Final Report, Facing the Future: Mastering the Probable and Managing the Unpredictable*: Paris, 1979.

31 See for example, H. Giersch, 'On the Future of the World Economy – An Optimist's View'. *The World Economy* 2(3), September 1979.

32 Prices doubled from an average of about $14 a barrel in 1978 to about $28–$30 a barrel in 1980, compared with the rise from $6 to $18 a barrel from 1973 to 1974, all in 1980 prices.

33 In 1974/75 it was thought that the international capital market would not be able to handle the developing countries' borrowing requirements. When it became clear in 1976 that the private markets were responding better than official donors to the developing countries' needs, the imminent collapse of the international capital market began to be predicted. Basically such views reflect a lack of understanding of the evolution of international capital markets and their interaction with developing countries. However, these views have also been fuelled by such interest groups as banks seeking a 'safety net' which would absolve them from all responsibility for lending, yet insure their loans in all circumstances. The argument has even been used as a case for more aid. However, such prophecies add to the developing countries' cost of borrowing and, at worst, could become self-fulfilling.

34 J. Holsen and J. Waelbroeck, 'LDC Balance of Payments Policies and the International Monetary System'. *World Bank Staff Working Paper* No. 226, February 1976.

6

Industrial strategies in textiles and clothing and motor cars

Geoffrey Shepherd*

6.1 Introduction[1]

The emergence of the Newly Industrializing Countries (NICs) as important exporters of manufactures has been encouraged not only by the increasing postwar liberalization of the trade regimes of the industrial market economies (hereafter referred to as 'industrial countries'), but also by a perceptible improvement in the speed at which technologies and 'know-how' have been internationally transferred, partly via multinational corporations (MNCs). In the 1970s NIC export prospects have dimmed as adjustment problems and defensive intervention in the industrial countries have grown, a result of the recession since the mid-1970s, of the unabated pressure on employment levels from continued productivity gains and of the growing divergence in the competitive capacities of different countries. The weaker industrial countries find themselves under pressure both from the technology leaders above and from the NICs below.

This paper examines the emergence of the NICs on world markets, and the adjustment problems of industrial countries, through the study of two sectors: textiles and clothing and passenger motor cars. Textiles and clothing are characterized by the relative export success that developing countries as a group have achieved, the size and high political profile of these industries in the industrial countries, and the high degree of regulation of world trade that exists through the Multi Fibre Arrangement (MFA). Motor cars are characterized by the high and enduring degree of world oligopoly in the industry; only Japan has succeeded in breaking into this oligopoly since World War II, though some NICs are now making an attempt. These characteristics to an extent make both industries unique. Nevertheless they illustrate a range of problems that are likely to confront a world trading system facing increasing international competition *and* recession.

6.2 Textiles and clothing

Most branches of textiles, and particularly clothing, remain low wage and labour-intensive industries in comparison with other manufacturing activities. Plant economies of scale are limited, especially in clothing and knitting,

*Deputy Director, Sussex European Research Centre, University of Sussex

132

but economies associated with long production runs are more substantial. The textile and clothing industries produce goods which range from being highly standardized to fashion-differentiated, the degree of differentiation increasing with successive stages of production. While the textile industry – far more than clothing – has a number of relatively large firms which may appear to enjoy dominant positions on narrowly defined sub-markets, both textiles and clothing have essentially competitive structures as a result of their process and product characteristics: there is significant ease of entry for new firms on national markets (though this does not in practice happen too much in declining industries), while any tendency to national oligopoly is dissipated by significant amounts of international trade. Different national textile and clothing industries display markedly different degrees of vertical and horizontal organization. This survey will tend to concentrate, within textiles, on the cotton industry (which is a major processor of manmade, as well as cotton, fibres) and on the clothing industry (including knitted clothing); these are the industries which have faced the most significant NIC-related adjustment problems.

Pressures for adjustment

The principal adjustment pressures on industrial countries have been transmitted through international trade. Substantial trade liberalization since World War II has resulted in large increases in trade among industrial countries (see the evolution of OECD textile and clothing imports by source, from 1963 to 1977, in *Table 6.1*). Trade liberalization has also been one of the factors in the industrial countries' large increases in imports from low-wage countries (i.e. the developing world – including the 'transitional' countries of Southern Europe – and the centrally-planned economies). In terms of types of products, nothing approaching the complete specialization of textbook trade theory appears to have occurred. Even now, the average share of developing countries in industrial countries' textile and clothing markets does not exceed 10 per cent (it was 3 per cent in textiles and 9 per cent in clothing in 1975 according to *Table 6.2*). Trade among industrial countries remains absolutely more important than imports from developing countries even if the very large amounts of intra-EEC trade are excluded. Of course, the developing countries' share would be larger in the absence of restrictions, but several industrial countries nevertheless remain strong exporters. Developing countries are stronger in exports of clothing than of textiles (see *Tables 6.1 and 6.2*), of cotton than of manmade fibre textiles, and of standardized than of fashion-differentiated products.

Substantial technical changes have occurred in traditional processes, in substitute processes and in raw materials, so far with a greater effect on textiles than on clothing. In the cotton system a postwar backlog in modernization investments (in Europe rather than the US), continuous

Table 6.1 OECD imports of textiles, clothing and transport equipment by area of origin, 1963, 1973 and 1977 ($ billion)

	Textiles (SITC 65)			Clothing (SITC 84)			Transport equipment (SITC 73)		
	1963	1973	1977	1963	1973	1977	1963	1973	1977
Industrial countries, of which	3.2	11.6	15.3	1.2	5.7	9.2	5.4	39.0	68.6
North America	0.2	1.0	1.3	—	0.2	0.4	1.2	13.4	20.5
Japan	0.3	0.7	0.7	0.1	0.3	0.3	0.1	4.3	10.6
Other OECD^a	2.7	9.9	13.3	1.1	5.2	8.5	4.1	21.1	37.5
Eastern bloc countries	0.1	0.7	0.8	—	0.5	1.0	—	0.4	0.7
Developing countries, of which	0.7	3.2	4.1	0.3	4.2	9.3	0.1	0.9	2.3
Southern Europe	0.1	0.6	0.8	0.1	0.7	1.4	0.1	0.5	1.4
Brazil and Mexico	—	0.2	0.3	—	0.2	0.3	—	0.1	0.3
Far Eastern NICs	0.1	0.9	1.1	0.2	2.8	5.8	—	0.1	0.3
Other	0.5	1.5	1.9	—	0.5	1.8	—	0.2	0.3
Total imports	4.0	15.5	20.3	1.5	10.4	19.5	5.5	40.3	71.6

^a Excluding Southern Europe

Source: Calculated from Organization for Economic Cooperation and Development (OECD), *The Impact of the Newly Industrializing Countries on Production and Trade in Manufactures*, Paris, 1979, Annex Table 1

improvements in conventional techniques and the commercial availability, from the 1960s, of newer techniques have provided the opportunity for continuing high productivity gains and labour-shedding. Synthetic fibres were first commercially introduced after World War II. Until the 1970s at least, the industrial countries had a clear comparative advantage in producing these fibres whose versatility in processing and end-use permitted a rapid

Table 6.2 *Trade in textiles and clothing as a percentage of apparent consumption in major industrial countries, 1959/60 and 1975 (based on value)*

	Textiles		Clothing	
	1959/60	1975	1959/60	1975
Imports, by origin				
EEC–6[a], of which	6.1	11.6	2.4	14.7
Developing countries	0.9	4.1	0.6	6.4
Other countries	5.2	7.5	1.8	8.3
UK, of which	14.0	31.8	9.5	31.6
Developing countries	5.2	5.4	3.9	13.3
Other countries	8.8	26.4	5.6	18.3
US, of which	5.5	6.2	3.5	15.3
Developing countries	1.6	2.5	0.8	10.0
Other countries	3.9	3.7	2.7	5.3
Japan, of which	1.1	5.3	1.4	15.3
Developing countries	0.1	2.2	0.7	9.1
Other countries	1.0	3.1	0.7	6.2
Total[b], of which	3.0	6.0	1.7	13.3
Developing countries	1.6	3.3	1.0	8.6
Other countries	1.4	2.7	0.7	4.7
Exports				
EEC–6[a]	19.5	20.5	8.3	11.8
UK	30.7	32.8	8.6	18.9
US	5.4	8.8	1.2	2.5
Japan	44.0	20.3	103.4	11.1
Total[b]	13.1	13.7	3.2	5.4

[a] Original founder-members; excluding trade between them
[b] Excluding trade between EEC, UK, US and Japan

Source: UNCTAD, *Handbook on International Trade and Development Statistics: Supplement 1977*, Geneva, 1978, Table 7.1

substitution for natural fibres in high-income markets. The textile industries of the industrial countries were initially able to capture much of this revolution, not only in their traditional branches such as cotton, but also in the rapid development of newer branches, such as knitting. With few significant new fibre developments, these advantages are now gradually coming to an end and synthetic fibres are becoming increasingly important in

NIC production. So far, the clothing industry has been minimally affected by technical change: the central sewing processes have defied automation, although intense efforts are now under way to bring electronics to bear, while the synthetics revolution has had little direct effect on the industry.

The final important source of adjustment pressure has come from the sluggish growth of textile demand in industrial countries. Textiles and clothing do not have high income-elasticities of demand. Moreover, the prolonged recession since the mid-1970s has reduced sluggish growth to stagnation.

Textile and clothing industries in the NICs

The growth of developing country textile exports is long-standing. India, Japan and China were becoming strong exporters of cotton cloth in the interwar period, but this was interrupted by the spread of protectionism in the 1930s. In the 1950s Japan and India re-emerged as strong exporters, to be joined by Hong Kong, which had inherited textile entrepreneurs fleeing with some of their equipment from the Chinese mainland. Their export strength prompted their major markets, the US (for Japan and Hong Kong) and the UK (for India and Hong Kong) to negotiate 'voluntary' export restraints with them in the late 1950s. During the 1960s and 1970s these exporters were joined by a large number of new suppliers from most parts of the developing world. This rash of new suppliers prompted the importing countries to formalize their import restraints within the framework of an international agreement: the Long-Term Arrangement for International Trade in Cotton Textiles (LTA), negotiated in 1962 for five years but eventually extended until 1973, was designed to provide a legal sanction for import controls, but also to encourage the more restrictive importers, principally the EEC countries, to carry more of the import burden. As manmade fibre textiles from Japan and the NICs in turn became a problem for importing countries from the later 1960s, the LTA was replaced by the MFA in 1974. The 1978 MFA extension to 1981 was accompanied by the EEC's negotiation, or imposition, of a substantially more comprehensive (by country and product) and restrictive (in terms of permissible import growth) set of limitation agreements with developing and centrally-planned exporters. Spreading trade restrictions have severely constrained the level of imports from developing countries, substantially frozen the shares in this of individual exporters and restricted the access of new entrants.

A relatively large number of countries is involved in exporting, most of them higher-income developing countries, though some of them – such as Egypt, Morocco and Ivory Coast – might have difficulty in coming under even the most liberal definition of newly industrializing countries. In spite of this variety, a small number of NICs dominates trade; this is particularly true of clothing, where three East Asian countries – Korea, Hong Kong and

Taiwan – account for some 60 per cent of developing country exports to the OECD and the Southern European NICs (Spain, Portugal, Greece and Yugoslavia) another 15 per cent. The East Asian NICs are less dominant in textiles, where South Asia (India and Pakistan) and Latin America (Mexico and Brazil) are correspondingly a little more important.

The general reasons for the extent and limitations of the export success of developing countries in textiles and clothing, in terms of the process, scale and product characteristics of textiles and clothing, have already been mentioned. Greater developing country export success in clothing than in textiles, in spite of the latter's greater product standardization, partly reflects the greater labour-intensity of clothing and the ability of high-wage textile industries to contain their cost disadvantage with a stream of machinery improvements substituting capital for labour.

In assessing differences between developing countries, it is useful to distinguish between 'overspill' exporters, exporting on the basis of processed domestic raw materials or of a large domestic market, and 'export-oriented' countries exporting more strictly on the basis of their factor endowments and a conscious exploitation of world demand. On the whole, the East Asian, and to a lesser extent Southern European, NICs would tend to be classified as export-oriented, the South Asian, and to a lesser extent Latin American, NICs as overspill exporters. The major overspill exporters are more or less self-sufficient in cotton fibres, notably India, Pakistan, Egypt, Brazil and Mexico. For some of them, most notably India, protection of domestic cotton-growing interests has led to fiscal discrimination against manmade fibres which exporters have been unable to circumvent. An equally important characteristic of overspill exporters is the marginality of the export market: these countries tend to export what they produce for the local market. Thus, they are far stronger in cotton and weaving than in manmade fibres and knitting, in textiles than in clothing (domestic incomes are too low to sustain a large ready-to-wear clothing industry), and in low-quality rather than in sophisticated goods. The strengths of the export-oriented countries are the other way around, and they also export significantly higher proportions of their output. In addition, there are systematic differences in techniques and factor use. While export-oriented countries tend to pay higher wages than *some* overspill exporters, they make up for this with more modern machinery, higher labour efficiency, higher capacity utilization and generally better management; as a result they produce the same product significantly more cheaply[2].

The export-oriented strategy is partly the result of specific policies which allow exporters access at world prices to imported inputs and machinery, encourage local production of inputs at or near world prices, and offset the attractions of heavily protected domestic markets through export subsidy and promotion schemes. In addition to these price-related policies, some export-oriented economies tend to place a political emphasis on exporting;

this emphasis can be seen institutionally, in Korea for instance, in a strong government foreign marketing effort, the activities of large private trading houses, and the consensus achievable through strong industry associations. The relative smallness of the Asian NICs clearly also provides a strong motive for exporting.

The debate on the role of industrial countries' initiatives in the export success of developing countries reflects some disagreement and incomplete evidence. At the governmental level, national policies in importing countries have been important in encouraging certain national sources of supply. US political commitment to non-communist East Asia in the 1950s and 1960s appears to have been important in granting Japan, Hong Kong, Korea and Taiwan the market access for textiles and clothing mostly denied them in the more protectionist EEC. Commonwealth preferences encouraged the initial foothold of Commonwealth countries in the UK market in the 1950s. The EEC's more recent tariff preferences to Mediterranean countries and Japan's creation of an economic hinterland in the East Asian NICS (though less supported by *formal* measures) have had a similar effect.

Foreign investment and sub-contracting

Private-sector initiatives from industrial countries in the creation of low-wage export capacity have taken the form of direct foreign investment and international sub-contracting[3]. Some foreign investment has had the traditional motive of seeking to get behind protective barriers; French textile investment in francophone Africa, the world's least developed textile producing region, is an example of this (and is now resulting in a trickle of exports back to the EEC). The major reason for Japanese foreign investment in textiles, mostly in Southeast Asia, was at first to assure an offtake for Japanese synthetic fibres, but these kinds of investments by large Japanese groups have increasingly had an export motive. For many years Japan and Hong Kong have invested to set up 'quota-hopping' export facilities in countries with more liberal access to North American and Western European markets[4]. The United States and the Federal Republic of Germany, the two largest clothing importers from developing countries, have invested in foreign clothing production mainly for re-export to the home market, the US mainly in the Carribean and Southeast Asia and the Federal Republic of Germany in Southern Europe. The firms involved have not *led* the process of creating export capacities in NICs; rather, they have reacted defensively to the success of the export-oriented NICs.

International sub-contracting in clothing has probably been the single most important external stimulant to developing-country exports. Its two major variants are: the world-wide 'sourcing' activities of major retailing groups in importing countries' (department stores, mail-order houses and clothing chains); and the outward-processing activities largely carried out by clothing producers. The major retail groups have set up world-wide buying networks which probably now account for a major part of NIC clothing exports.

Outward processing exists chiefly because some countries, notably the US, the Netherlands and the Federal Republic of Germany, have tariff provisions requiring duty payment, under certain conditions, on only the foreign value-added content of an import. Typically, pre-cut fabrics are exported for processing in low-wage locations and subsequently re-imported; the low-wage country contributes little more than unskilled labour, while the industrial country exercises almost complete managerial control, as it would in a direct foreign investment. Indeed, this kind of sub-contracting is an alternative to export-oriented foreign investment and has been motivated by similar defensive considerations[5].

Outward processing alone is not a dominant vehicle of NIC clothing exports; in the Federal Republic of Germany, the country where it is by far the most important, it accounted in 1976 for 15 per cent of imports from developing countries. It has been calculated that some 40 per cent of all West German clothing imports are attributable to the foreign activities of West German clothing manufacturers: outward processing, foreign investment and arms-length sub-contracting[6]. It appears that the majority of German clothing imports from developing countries are, in part at least, the result of the international activity of German firms. Nevertheless, an important distinction should be made between international arrangements such as outward processing and foreign investment in clothing, where exporting countries are largely dependent on specific importing-country firms, and looser forms of sub-contracting such as international sourcing where, even if the buying house dictates patterns, many exporting countries are still largely independent in determining their long-term marketing and product quality strategy.

To our two categories of 'overspill' and 'export-oriented' exporters we might add a small third category of small 'dependent' countries that have developed clothing export industries largely as a result of initiatives from industrial countries' clothing manufacturers and importers: Malta, Morocco and various Caribbean countries would come into this category.

Adjustment in industrial countries

Some of the problems faced by industrial countries in the changing world textile and clothing economy can be seen in the evolution of their output, employment, productivity and trade balances (see *Table 6.3* for 1973–1978 trends in major countries). After moderate expansion up to the early 1970s, at best stagnant levels of output have been the general case since 1973 in the major industrial countries[7]. In spite of recession, productivity has continued to grow, typically by from 2 to 5 per cent per annum. Combined job losses in

Table 6.3 *Structural change in the textile and clothing industries in major industrial countries, 1973–1978*

	Federal Republic of Germany	France	Italy	UK	US	Japan
Index of output, 1978 (1973 = 100)						
Textiles	96	90	97	87	96	92
Clothing	87	98	98	103	108	93
Index of employment, 1978 (1973 = 100)						
Textiles	74	81	84	82	87	71
Clothing	76	84	92ᵃ	90	90	108
Index of labour productivity, 1978 (1973 = 100)						
Textiles	131	110	116ᵃ	105	111	128
Clothing	115	116	124ᵃ	118	119	87
Employment losses (−) or gains (+) in 1973–78 as % of 1978 employment in manufactures						
Textiles	−1.6	−2.5	−1.2ᵇ	−1.4	−0.8	−3.0
Clothing	−1.2	−1.0	−0.5ᵇ	−0.5	−0.6	+0.3
Trade balance ($ billion)						
Textiles 1973	0.30	0.29	0.62	0.19	−0.36	1.32
Textiles 1978	−0.21	−0.26	1.86	−0.45	0.01	2.33
Clothing 1973	−1.63	0.45	1.11	−0.38	−1.88	−0.20
Clothing 1978	3.81	0.25	3.00	−0.48	−4.67	−0.75

ᵃ 1976
ᵇ 1973–1976

Sources: W. Kurth, *Textiles and Clothing; a National and International Issue.* Paper prepared by OECD Directorate for Science, Technology and Industry for International Symposium on Industrial Policies for the 1980s, Madrid, 5–9 May 1980, Tables I, II and III
GATT, *International Trade 1978/79*, Geneva, 1979, Appendix Table A.6

textiles and clothing in the period 1973–1978 were equivalent to around 3 per cent of the total manufacturing labour force for the Federal Republic of Germany, France and Japan and from 1 to 2 per cent for Italy, the UK and the US; but these aggregate figures hide sub-sectoral and regional variations, and the rate of job loss has become a sharpened economic and political issue in most industrial countries. Changes in the trade balance differed among countries and sectors: bright spots were improved Japanese balances in textiles and Italian balances in textiles and clothing; dark spots were deteriorating US, West German and Japanese balances in clothing, and French and UK balances in textiles. (The German trade balance in textiles, which was improving up to 1976, fell into deficit in 1977 and 1978, but recovered into substantial surplus in 1979.)

There is little solid evidence on the economic and social cost of this general picture of decline. Until the 1970s, in spite of the intense pressures for protection in many countries, textile employment losses seem to have been absorbed by the dynamism of the rest of the economy (even in the semi-depressed regions of a slow-growing country like the UK), while in most countries the clothing labour force was not declining. In the 1970s the rate of job losses has accelerated and the absorptive capacity of the manufacturing sector has weakened, but the extent of the unemployment problem remains unclear, though it has grown as a political issue. A number of studies have concluded that the employment effect of trade with developing countries has so far led to minimal job losses compared with productivity-related losses[8].

The various adjustment pressures faced by industrial countries in recent decades have resulted in the emergence of a number of different strategic responses. These responses have been reflected both in private-sector strategies and in government intervention objectives in a way that is difficult to disentangle. A useful generalization about comparative strategies has been made in a recent study by CEPII (Centre d'Etudes Prospectives et d'Informations Internationales). Japan, the Federal Republic of Germany, the Netherlands, the US and Austria–Switzerland were observed over 1964–1974 increasingly to have specialized in upstream products – manmade fibre production and textiles – at the expense of downsteam products – clothing and made-up goods. Great Britain, Belgium, Southern Europe, Italy and France, on the other hand, showed no clear specialization trend between the vertical stages of production[9].

We may also characterize specific strategies as defensive or offensive. By further classifying them into five sub-strategies we shall see that no country has opted solely for the one or the other. Defensive sub-strategies are

(1) a *protective* strategy: defence of the domestic market through protection (and subsidy), an option pursued by virtually every country and most tenaciously by the UK and US, followed by Italy and France;

(2) a *low-wage* strategy: all EEC countries employ many immigrants in textile and clothing industries, while Italy's recent export success has been partly built on 'black' labour avoiding payment of some taxes and social security contributions and union agreements; and

(3) a *mass-market* strategy: frontal competition with low-cost, standardized imports by means of capital-intensive, highly rationalized mass production in textiles (the UK, Japan and US). While offensive in its apparent intent of regaining competitiveness with imports, this strategy has often invoked a defensive infant-industry argument for protection.

Offensive sub-strategies are

(4) a *specialization* strategy: national adjustment to areas of greatest comparative advantage within textiles and clothing, a strategy involving increased exports and, often, imports (Federal Republic of Germany, Italy and Japan);

(5) an *internationalization* strategy: international adjustment through foreign investment or sub-contracting (Japan, the Federal Republic of Germany, and, in part, the US); and

(6) a *diversification* strategy into non-textile or non-clothing areas: an option which appears to have been pursued to any extent only in Japan.

While the two country groups are in practice more difficult to distinguish than are export-oriented and overspill exporters among the NICs, the same basic dichotomy of outward- and inward-oriented economies can be perceived. We shall briefly characterize the evolution of West German and UK strategies, as polar examples of this dichotomy, and add comments on some other major countries.

By the late 1950s the United Kingdom suffered a substantial penetration of NIC imports as a result of its then generally liberal trading stance and its Commonwealth obligations. This 'cold shower', however, failed to solve the cotton industry's chronic problems of overcapacity, fragmentation and poor management. One of the country's two leading manmade fibre producers, Courtaulds, fearing the loss of its domestic markets, formulated a mass-market strategy, bought its way massively into the textile, and, partly, the clothing, industry and obtained a government commitment to infant-industry protection from major sources of low-cost imports. This strategy, which came to dominate government and industry thinking, never really succeeded in its original aim of achieving competitiveness without quota protection. As a result, protection has become progressively heavier to the point where – though the UK for historical reasons is a relatively high-level importer from developing countries – the industry and the government see protection as a fairly permanent feature. Even with this protection, the industry still appears uncompetitive in trade with other industrial countries.

(In ch. 10, section 10.4, Plessz points out how, as a result of increasing restrictions under the MFA, the UK, among other importing countries, has tended to shift its imports from non-European to European low-cost suppliers, rather than improve its own share of the market.) There are arguably bright spots, however: the industry has largely succeeded in solving its long-standing structural problems. It remains to be seen whether it can capitalize on its relatively low (by EEC standards) wages to increase its exports, at least within a protected European environment – a strategy which has already been a partial success for the clothing industry.

The Federal Republic of Germany's markets, unlike Britain's, were initially protected, opening up to competition with other industrial countries in the 1950s and 1960s and to NIC competition in the later 1960s and 1970s. In the 1960s, the dominant strategy in textiles was, as in the UK, that of the mass-market. But in the face of the continued liberalizing of the market, this strategy had resulted in the collapse or near collapse of many leading firms by the mid-1970s. (By and large, the regional governments and banks resuscitated or restructured these firms.) Meanwhile, parts of the textile industry had gradually been converting to a specialization strategy, a conversion more or less complete by the later 1970s; this strategy is heavily based on medium-sized, technologically advanced and flexible production units highly concentrated on quality fashion fabrics and both special household and industrial markets. The result has been a very large increase in textile imports *and* exports.

In clothing, the West German strategy has relied more on internationalization than specialization. Foreign investment and outward processing have been supported by the government in the form of special outward-processing arrangements, additional to normal clothing quotas, a concession available only to clothing manufacturers; thus manufacturers have been able to cross-subsidize domestic production, including exports, from imports. In spite of these 'offensive' elements, clothing quotas, though they grew in the 1970s, restricted imports more than in textiles, presumably with the intention of permitting a politically tolerable rate of decline in the clothing industry. The Federal Republic of Germany has also administered the growth of its quotas to favour its Eastern and Southern European economic hinterland (importers of German fibres and textiles), at the expense of the East Asian NICs (importers of Japanese and American fibres and textiles). The relatively liberal growth of imports from developing countries appears, however, to be coming to an end: recession and employment decline have prompted strong pressure for protectionism and the government has acquiesced, in spite of its publicly announced distaste for them, in the EEC's new restrictive MFA quotas.

It is tempting to ascribe German and UK performance, in terms of efficiency in resource allocation, to the pursuit, respectively, of liberal and protectionist policies. While this reasoning cannot lightly be dismissed, it could equally plausibly be argued that intervention *followed* strategic failure in the UK, while the Federal Republic's earlier protection may have set the stage for its later competitive stance.

In textiles and clothing Japan stands between the NICs and other industrial countries with its historical export strength on the one hand, and its rising real wage (like the Federal Republic) on the other. Its textile industry has declined rapidly, but within the industry a remarkably fast decline in traditional sectors has been offset by continued strength in synthetics. The pattern, including some liberalization of the import regime, parallels that of Germany. This industry's decline has been smoothed by effective voluntary and government-inspired scrapping schemes. On the basis of a large domestic market, advanced textile technology, and a wage not yet among the highest, Japan aims to pursue an eclectic strategy of mass production *and* up-market specialization. (For a fuller account of the Japanese textile strategy, see ch. 12, section 12.3.)

As a result of a large internal market and consistently heavy protection, international trade has played a relatively unimportant role in the US textile industry, although this has recently become more significant in clothing imports (see *Table 6.2*). The large market has also helped the US achieve a high level of rationalization in textile production which in turn has led to high levels of labour productivity. The substantial devaluation of the dollar in the 1970s has seen the US emerge as potentially one of the most competitive high-wage textile producers. The US and Japan have probably been the most successful countries in pursuing a mass-market strategy; in this light, the UK failure reflects its low productivity performance, in part based on the small size of its domestic market, plus a comparative lack of attention to product up-grading.

Italy, like France, has historically relied on heavy protection, although much liberalization occurred in both countries in the 1970s. But Italy's export success has relied on other factors: it followed an aggressive 'labour-intensive' strategy based partly on a sophisticated system of technically advanced, cooperating – yet competing – small-scale production, partly on the low wage of 'black' labour (particularly in clothing), partly on a good design capability, and partly on protection in its major export markets as a result of import controls operating against other low-wage countries.

6.3   Passenger motor cars[10]

Until the early 1970s, car output grew considerably faster than the economy in Western Europe and came to account, in the four larger car-producing countries, for from 5 to 8 per cent of manufacturing output, employment and investment, over 10 per cent of manufactured exports, and a substantial amount of derived demand for other industrial goods. Japan, and more recently a number of NICs, have sought to establish car industries which would play the same dynamic role in the economy.

Production of cars is characterized by important plant economies of scale and engineering skill requirements, but an equally important characteristic of the industry is its 'strategy-intensity': one model of a car will typically take five years to get from conception to production and subsequently have a life equally as long (the life-cycle of an engine could be nearer 20 years). In this process the importance of correct decisions – about model and major component specifications and about the right range of models – as well as the capacity to make a high, long-term investment in design and tooling-up, are key factors in success. The car is in some senses a standard, mature product, the internal combustion engine having undergone few major modifications in

Table 6.4 *Trade specialization ratios in passenger cars for major industrial countries (% based on number of units)*

		1963	1973	1978
Federal Republic	P/C	182	163	127
of Germany	I/C	10	34	35
	E/C	92	97	62
France	P/C	134	152	148
	I/C	13	25	27
	E/C	47	77	75
Italy	P/C	110	115	108
	I/C	19	26	38
	E/C	29	41	46
United Kingdom	P/C	155	106	78
	I/C	5	31	51
	E/C	59	36	30
Spain	P/C	84	125	154
	I/C	16	3	3
	E/C	—	28	57
United States	P/C	97	83	80
	I/C	5	21	26
	E/C	2	4	6
Japan	P/C	106	146	200
	I/C	2	1	2
	E/C	8	47	102
All industrial countries[a]	P/C	108	107	107
	I/C	13	27	33
	E/C	21	34	40

P/C: Ration of production to consumption × 100
I/C: Ratio of imports to consumption × 100
E/C: Ratio of exports to consumption × 100

[a] Includes Spain and all intra-country trade

Source: Calculated from Table A9 of GATT, *International Trade 1978/79*, Geneva, 1979

Table 6.5 *Car production by major firms in major countries, 1978[a] (thousands)*

	General Motors	Ford	PSA[j]	Renault	Volkswagen	Fiat	Others	Total production
United States	5284	2557	—	(164)[k]	40	—	1 131[m]	9 176
Canada	572	377	—	(34)[k]	—	—	179[m]	1 162
Brazil[b]	165	125	—	—	480	95	3	868
Mexico	20	35	—	14	94	—	80	243
Argentina	*	*	29	28	18	22	2	134
Andean Pact Countries[c]	*	—	*	*	*	*	—	—
West Germany	953	544	—	—	1641	—	752	3 890
France	*	*	1869	1242	—	—	—	3 111
Italy	—	—	—	—	—	1247	262	1 509
United Kingdom	84	324	196	—	—	—	619[n]	1 223
Spain/Portugal	*	261	206	235	—	284	—	986
Benelux	*	266	*	(64)[l]	*	—	—	330
Sweden/Finland	—	—	—	(182)[l]	—	(72)	254	254
Japan	(103)[g]	(493)[b]	—	—	—	—	5 380[h]	5 976
Australia	116	108	—	—	—	—	12	236
South Africa[d]	18	28	12	—	25	7	77	167
Poland	—	—	—	—	—	[292]	35	327
Yugoslavia	—	—	11	34	10	197	—	252
East Germany	—	—	[*]	[*]	—	—	170	170
Romania	—	—	[*]	[72]	—	—	—	72
Others	—	—	—	—	—	—	1 693[e]	1 693
Total[f]	7212	4660	2323	1553	2308	1852	11 871	31 779

* Assembly or engine plant existing or planned
( ) Total production of a separate firm in which the firm in the vertical column has a minority interest
[ ] Total production of a separate firm with which the firm in the vertical column has a buyback or cooperation agreement (n.b. cooperation agreements among Western European and North American firms have not been recorded)
a Car production figures for 1978; however ownership–cooperation links for early 1980
b May include some assembly, rather than full production; General Motors and Ford figures are estimates
c Venezuela, Colombia, Chile, Peru and Ecuador
d May include some assembly, rather than full production; figures are for 1977
e Of which USSR 1300, Czechoslovakia 175, China 100, South Korea 80, India 38
f Totals for individual named firms cover only majority holdings. Figures in ( ) or [ ], totalling 1476, are included in the 'Others' column.
g 34 per cent of Isuzu
h 25 per cent of Toyo Kogyo
i PSA is the holding company for Peugeot, Citroen and Talbot
k Renault owns 22.5 per cent of American Motors
l Renault is acquiring 20 per cent of Volvo
m All or mostly Chrysler
n Of which British Leyland 612; British Leyland will produce Honda cars under licence from 1981
p Of which Toyota 2162, Nissan 1883, Honda 653

Source: Based on data in D. T. Jones, (Reference 1); some figures are preliminary estimates.

this century. Nevertheless, the product is differentiated by size, by degree of luxury, by degree of innovation incorporated in the product, as well as by brand image. The scale- and strategy-intensity of car production has led to a highly oligopolistic organization of the world car industry: nine firms based in only five countries (but producing in many more) account for four-fifths of world production of cars. (*Table 6.5* provides a breakdown of major firms producing in major countries.)

Production consists of a discrete number of vertical stages from tool-making through components and sub-assemblies (e.g. engines) to final assembly. These stages may be reflected in a predominantly horizontal form of organization – giving rise to substantial sub-contracting relationships in some firms in the United Kingdom, the United States or Japan – or in a vertical form of organization as in France and Italy. Whatever the structure, the national links between the various stages are strong: expansion or contraction in national car assembly will have an immediate effect on activity at other stages.

From the end of World War II until the mid-1960s there was a certain stability in the structure and prosperity of the non-Communist world's car industry. Since then, pressures have arisen for substantial modifications. Probably the most important change is the fall in the growth of demand for cars which has occurred in the industrial countries in the 1970s as a result of the saturation of markets, the post-1973 recession and the rising cost of oil. Demand for cars in the OECD area is unlikely to grow at more than 2 per cent per annum in the coming years. Growth in NICs such as Brazil and Spain is likely to be considerably faster.

After several decades of slow technical progress in the industry, the signs are that as a result of increasing international competition, greater need for fuel economy, legislation affecting pollution and safety, and the scope offered by electronics, innovation is accelerating both in products (for example, more fuel-efficient engines, replacement of mechanical by electronic functions, etc.) and in processes (for example, automation of assembly, both substituting capital for labour and increasing flexibility).

The key factors in the changing international pattern of production and trade are the unification of the world market, the spread and changing character of foreign investment, and the emergence of new independent producers. The dramatic fall in levels of protection since the 1930s, the growing ease of international communications and the 'internationalization' of taste are increasingly making for one world market in cars. The commitment of the major US car firms to a vast programme of downsizing will increase this unity and probably improve the international competitiveness of the US. This unification is evident, not only from the dramatic increase since the 1960s in the ratio of international trade to production (see *Table 6.4*), but also from the level and growing integration of the foreign investments of major US and EEC producers (see *Table 6.5*).

The world-wide spread of the industry

Three successive stages of foreign investment in cars can be distinguished: dependent, independent and inter-dependent. The first stage is investment abroad in foreign assembly facilities dependent on components supplied by the headquarters firm. This move has very often been motivated by foreign erection of trade barriers against imports and has remained a typical form of foreign investment in developing countries. At the second stage foreign subsidiaries are a good deal more self-contained, though the foreign investment motivation is similar. This independent stage, only possible in larger, more sophisticated host economies, was typical of US car investment in Western Europe from the 1920s to the late 1960s. The third stage is investment in a number of countries in an integrated plan of production in which components or models are exchanged internationally. This stage is motivated more purely by cost-minimization, either through the choice of low-cost production locations or through economies of scale based on more complete international specialization. It was introduced for North America with the US–Canadian automotive agreement of 1965. It was adopted by Ford as a Western European strategy in the late 1960s, and by General Motors in the early 1970s, and is now being copied by several European firms on a Western European level (for instance, Renault and Peugeot–Citroen) or on a wider international level (for instance, Volkswagen and Fiat). This increasing international integration has resulted in the emergence of Brazil, Spain and Mexico as potentially important NIC exporters of cars and components within an MNC strategy. These cases are further discussed below.

Various forms of international integration short of majority-owned foreign investment have developed. First, minority shareholding is becoming increasingly important: for instance, the two major US car companies (General Motors and Ford), barred from majority ownership, have minority holdings in smaller Japanese firms. Second, limited cooperation agreements between firms have been made in Western Europe where economic nationalism has hindered the development of cross-border mergers: a joint venture in engine production by Renault, Peugeot and Volvo is an example of such cooperation. Third, French (Renault and Peugeot) and Italian (Fiat) car firms have made 'buy-back' agreements in Eastern Europe in which payment is received for a turnkey plant contract in the form of cars. These cars are then marketed by the French or Italian firms in the EEC or in their own export markets.

Only one major new exporter independent of the MNCs, Japan, has emerged since World War II. In the early 1960s Japan possessed only a fledgling car industry but its share in world production and exports of cars grew incredibly fast to around one-fifth by the end of the 1970s, and it will probably have overtaken the US as the world's largest producer in 1980 or 1981. Having penetrated those markets without car producers, or with weak car producers (entering the US, for instance, at a time when it was unable to compete in small cars), Japan is now beginning to penetrate the markets of more competitive producers such as Germany. So far, Japan's large car firms, Toyota, Nissan and Honda, have not invested significantly abroad, but they are likely to do so if the threat of import restraints in their major markets materializes. Honda has recently announced plans to build cars in the United States.

The only NIC currently planning to follow this independent strategy is South Korea. Until recently only an assembler of imported components, Korea began in 1976 to build up an independent car industry with an eclectic programme of buying design and management from Europe, and components from several sources, to produce its own model and subsequently raising the level of its domestic content. By the end of the 1980s it plans to approach an annual export volume of 150 000 cars and commercial vehicles, a modest target in comparison with Japan's past performance and Latin America's aggregate target of 700 000 for the end of the 1980s. Korea's attempt to emulate Japan is undoubtedy a high-risk strategy, given its reliance on one basic model so far. At the same time, Korea is being courted by the MNCs and may also hedge its bets with a partial MNC strategy.

That most NICs with export ambitions have chosen the strategy of MNC participation undoubtedly reflects the very high costs and risks of entry as an independent exporter. The strategy of MNC participation has shown a common pattern of development and of pitfalls complementary to the three stages of foreign investment. In the first stage, a number of firms, wholly foreign, local licensees or joint ventures, have set up highly protected, small assembly plants each producing a variety of models. Almost one hundred developing countries have reached at least this stage, but this development alone has not had major significance for the world car firms who have simply exported CKD (completely knocked down) kits for assembly, instead of the assembled car, with only marginal losses in unit export value.

Perceiving, in a second stage, that indeed assembly has had little positive effect on their own balance of payments, many of the more advanced or larger developing countries have put pressure on local assemblers gradually to increase the amount of local component manufacture (usually through government-set domestic-content targets). Because of the economies of scale in much component manufacture, governments have encouraged reductions in the number of firms and models. At this point, if they were not already dominant in the industry, the MNCs have become of key importance in providing the necessary technology. Host country ability to succeed at this stage is limited by the small size of the market, and by the way the 'deletion allowance' works. When a previously assembling country newly produces a component, it has been the practice of the firm supplying the CKD kit, in deleting this item, to reduce the price of the kit by an amount less than the average cost price of the component; under these conditions the achievement of domestic content becomes progressively more costly[11].

Perceiving, at a third stage, the high cost of domestic market-based domestic-content programmes, some NICs have sought to achieve economies of scale and, presumably, to offset the effects of the deletion allowance by negotiating with the MNCs an export role for themselves – a development in which MNCs themselves appear to have taken most of the initiative.

Brazil has sought to establish a car industry through policies of high levels of domestic protection and high domestic-content targets (90 per cent). It has now made agreements with all the major producers linking their export performance to tax exemptions on their imports. As examples of these agreements, Ford (Brazil) exports engines for assembly in North America in return for a quota of component imports at reduced tariffs and Volkswagen (Brazil) exports Beetles in assembled and CKD form to Third World markets and engines to Germany in return for a similar import deal. With broadly similar, protective, domestic-content and export-for-import policies, Mexico is embarking on exports to the US and Europe. Spain originally had a two-firm national car industry which has, however, been progressively multinationalized. It has established itself as the largest NIC exporter of cars by allowing entry to new multinational firms undertaking to export. Exports are almost entirely to the EEC where Spain has preferential access. Ford has led the way in integrating Spanish production (of its Fiesta) with European production. The prospect of Ford's strong position in an enlarged EEC is encouraging other producers, such as General Motors and Renault, to make similar deals with Spain (and more recently with Portugal) and has encouraged rationalization moves in the existing Spanish car industry.

The success so far achieved by Brazil, Mexico and Spain reflects the large size of their domestic markets (which has enabled them to trade MNC access to their domestic markets for their own access to world markets) and their favourable labour costs. This is likely to prove a strategy open to a limited number of countries (only Argentina, in the Third World, offers an equally large car market). Moreover, the MNCs will continue to exercise a strong control over the national industry, and it remains to be seen when the strategy will lead to a fourth stage of development of the car industry in these countries, that of an indigenous 'strategic' capacity in model and component design and marketing, a stage unlikely to happen in the 1980s.

The strategic option followed, in part at least, by several Eastern European countries (Yugoslavia, Romania, Poland and the USSR) of partially independent production of Western European models is something of a halfway house between the independent strategy of Japan and Korea and the MNC-dependent strategy of Brazil, Spain and Mexico. The most independent producers, in Poland and the USSR, are likely to develop substantial exports to Western Europe, free of the control of the MNCs.

Responses of the industrial countries' industries

Adjustment pressures in the car industries of North America and Western Europe began to be felt only in the mid-1970s and will intensify in the 1980s.

In rough order of immediacy the general pressures come from the sluggish growth of demand, the development of Japanese exports, the spread of MNC-dependent production, and accelerating technical change. National responses to these pressures are similar to those in textiles (see above), though in cars there is generally more of the 'offensive' and less of the 'defensive'. They can be characterized as follows:

(1) a *protective* strategy. Import protection, mostly through 'persuasion' rather than formal public arrangements, is practised by the United States, United Kingdom, France and Italy (the latter two very restrictively) against Japan. There is a tendency in Western European countries to discourage inward and outward foreign investment, the former to protect the national champions, the latter to protect national employment.

(2) a *frontally-competitive* strategy. This involves the exploitation of technical progress to automate domestic production and produce a continuing stream of minor product improvements, in order to maintain a domestic industry competitive across the range of the mass market. This strategy characterizes France and Italy, though these countries do not conceive it in isolation from internationalization (see (4) below).

(3) a *specialization* strategy. Germany is the only country where a shift in emphasis of domestic production to higher-value, more highly innovative and luxury cars is emphasized as an alternative to frontal competition.

(4) an *internationalization* strategy. Increasing international integration of car production, through majority- or minority-owned foreign investment, cooperative agreements or buy-back, is a strategy which is being hotly pursued by the car firms of all these countries, except the UK.

(5) a *diversification* strategy. This movement into other industries is of some importance to the major firms in Germany and Italy.

Until recently the American car industry has benefited from natural protection because the United States is the only country in the world which has a mass-market for large cars, so the industry has been able to achieve economies of scale from a very large domestic market. It has been able to translate its technical strength into a dominant world-wide foreign investment presence. Still potentially strong, the industry faces the problem of adjusting to the development of a domestic market for smaller cars. This market trend has encouraged substantial car imports and growing investment from Europe, led by Volkswagen, in the United States. It has also resulted in some weak 'voluntary' restraints on Japanese exports to the US which have not so far proved very effective. The industry's response, massive programmes to produce smaller cars, has been promoted by federal energy legislation. Most recently, the Government has moved, in an interventionist precedent, to rescue Chrysler, the firm most laggard in its downsizing programme and least successful in its foreign investment strategy. General Motors and Ford will move to integrate their US and foreign operations more completely and are likely, with their 'world cars', to strengthen their world position.

Until now German production has retained a considerable share of the domestic car market, in spite of the rapid rise in labour costs; but threats to export markets and the prospect of substantially increased import pressure, particularly from Japan, are obliging German producers to go up-market domestically and transfer production abroad. Volkswagen has ceded production of its 'Beetles' to its Brazilian subsidiary and is concentrating its German production, aided by component imports from Mexico and Brazil, on higher-value cars. The German up-market strategy has been consideraby helped by public R and D subsidies. The regional governments have, with the private banks, mounted several rescue operations – successful in the case of Volkswagen and BMW, unsuccessful in the case of Borgward.

The French car industry continues to develop with heavy government support for 'national champions' in the form of protection from imports and foreign investment, close government–industry cooperation – Renault is nationalized – and financial encouragement of mergers. The industry is a competitive producer of cars across a balanced model range, but it does have a government commitment to protect the market if Japanese imports grow. The main adjustment problem is to digest the extensive recent mergers which have resulted in the formation of Peugeot–Citroen and its take-over of Chrysler's European operations. While the two national champions have minority investments in North America and buy-back deals in Eastern Europe, the bulk of their internationalization effort – belated in comparison with Fiat and Volkswagen – has been centred on integrated production for Western Europe in France, Spain and, possibly for Renault, Portugal. This may evolve as a strategy of semi-protectionism at the (enlarged) EEC level.

As in France, Italy's national car market has been protected and continues to benefit from almost complete protection against Japanese imports. Fiat, Italy's largest non-publicly owned firm, has lost its past competitive advantages in small car production and design and is facing increasing problems of labour relations. In consequence it leads the EEC in its automation drive. With the development of integration, in the form of exchange of models and components among its domestic, Spanish and Brazilian plants and cooperating firms in Poland and Yugoslavia, Fiat's internationalization is more far-reaching, and less reliant on the home base, then Renault's or Peugeot–Citroen's.

The UK car industry is exceedingly weak: parts of its assembly activity are near to collapse, while the more competitive components industry would be unable to diversify its markets sufficiently fast to adjust painlessly. The degree of import penetration is high and growing. Export markets have collapsed, and the industry has gradually withdrawn from its major overseas investments and is itself becoming increasingly dominated by foreign investment. This weakness appears to be the result of many factors: poor management, particularly in the nationalized British Leyland, technical weaknesses, skill shortages and problems of labour relations – in short, the typical industrial problems of the United Kingdom. The industry has agreed 'voluntary' export restraints with Japan and the government has further supported the industry's survival with extensive subsidies. British Leyland has now secured an agreement to assemble a Japanese car (from Honda).

In the past, European car firms have received much more support, in the form of protection and subsidies, than their US counterparts. Indeed, government support has resulted in the Western European market continuing to support seven major producers: Volkswagen, Renault, Peugeot–Citroen, Fiat, British Leyland, Ford and General Motors. This number would undoubtedly be fewer by at least two, without such support. This national support imposes obligations on national firms (implicitly at least) to resist investing abroad where possible and to contribute to other government objectives, most notably regional employment creation. The degree of government support, hence of reciprocal obligation, appears strong in France and weak in Germany and Italy: hence there is a tendency in the latter countries for a greater internationalization of their operations.

6.4 Conclusions

In the industries we have looked at, two major factors have determined the degree of developing countries' export success: first, barriers to entry – hence oligopoly and MNC involvement – absent in textiles and clothing, but present and growing in cars; second, the extent to which general industrialization strategies are based on domestic market ('overspill') or exporting ('export-oriented'). In textiles and clothing, the most dynamic performance came from the export-oriented NICs of East Asia. In the MNC-dominated car industry, only a small number of NICs have become involved in exporting. Spain, Brazil and Mexico are pursuing a strategy, entirely within an MNC framework, in which exports can also be broadly characterized as spilling over from a large domestic market. The alternative route for establishing automotive exports is the more costly and risky independent strategy followed by Korea, although this will not be on a scale that is likely to affect world markets in the coming decade in the way that Japan's similar strategy did in the 1970s. In general, independent export-oriented countries – Asian NICs in textiles and clothing, Japan in cars – appear to have a more disruptive potential in international trade than either overspill or MNC-dependent exporters. This helps to make them more vulnerable to protection.

Sluggish demand growth, technical change and changes in trade patterns have affected both the textiles–clothing and car industries in the industrial countries, though the effects were felt later in the car industry. The NICs will continue to play a more marginal role in the adjustment problems of the car industry than in textiles. While competition among industrial countries is severe in both industries, this competition is ultimately a greater problem in cars.

The basic division in industrial countries' adjustment strategies is between those countries or industries that are adjusting to these changes and those that are protecting rather than adjusting. No country exclusively follows the one strategy or the other; nearly all provide non-tariff protection for their domestic markets to some extent. Nevertheless, a scale of countries dimly emerges. Germany (in textiles and cars) and Japan (in textiles), in a virtuous circle of rapidly rising output and wages, have opted for up-market specialization and transfer of production abroad, accompanied by a relative liberalization of import regimes. At the other end of the scale, the United Kingdom has become more protectionist in both textiles and cars. In the middle, the United States, France and Italy have been protectionist in textiles and clothing – though, as in the UK, this does not preclude all structural change; in cars, on the other hand, they are firmly engaged in a strategy of structural adaptation based on frontal competition (i.e. producing the same products more cheaply), though this does not preclude protection against Japan. At both ends of the scale strategies are consistent within a country, while in the middle this is less evident: the most striking paradox is in Italy's dual-economy, where the dominant strategy in textiles and clothing is based on low wages and small-scale production while an important part of the adjustment strategy in cars is based on advanced automation and internationalization. These broadly characterized national strategies are to be found to an extent in other industries; indeed, the countries at the top of the scale appear to have the greatest facility not only in adjusting upwards within industries, but also in moving into more sophisticated industries[12]. Overall, the interventionism of the non-adjusting countries appears to be as much the result as the cause of their failure to adjust. Protectionism is likely to continue to spread as long as these countries remain industrially weak; it is the strengthening, rather than outright decline, of import-competing industries which is more likely to abate the forces of protectionism.

References

1 This paper is based largely on research underway at the Sussex European Research Centre on structural adjustment and government intervention in Western European industry; in particular on D. T. Jones, *Industrial Adjustment and Policy: I. Maturity and Crisis in the European Car Industry*, Sussex European Paper No. 8, Sussex European Research Centre, University of Sussex, forthcoming and G. Shepherd, *How have the Industrialized Countries Addressed the Problem of Adjustment?*. Paper prepared for a Conference on International Trade in Textiles and Clothing, Brussels, 27–29 May 1980.

2 This is reflected in generally better rates of quota fulfilment. Export-oriented NICs also tend to have manufacturing sectors with low rates of effective protection – a proxy measure of economic efficiency – in comparison with overspill exporters.

3 For a thorough study of the extensive internationalization activities of the German textile and clothing industries, see F. Fröbel, J. Heinrichs and O. Kreye, *The New International Division of Labour*. Cambridge University Press, Cambridge, 1980.

4 Hong Kong is now the most important 'quota-hopping' country and is responsible for much of the export-oriented clothing investment in two of the newest suppliers, Sri Lanka and Mauritius.

5 The FRG's outward processing trade in clothing is almost entirely with Yugoslavia and Eastern Europe, while much of its export-oriented foreign investment is with Mediterranean countries. Unlike most other Mediterranean countries, Yugoslavia and East Europe (except for the GDR) face tariffs in Western Germany; they also place greater limits on foreign investment.

6 U. Schwarting, 'Strategies for Survival: The Example of the Clothing Industry'. *Intereconomics* 14(1), January-February 1979, pp. 15–19.

7 Much of Italy's export boom appears to have originated in the small-scale informal sector. Hence official output and employment figures are probably misleadingly conservative.

8 For recent estimates of sources of job losses in the clothing industry see J. De La Torré with M. Bacchetta, *Decline and Adjustment: European Policies towards their Clothing Industries*. INSEAD (European Institute of Business Administration), Fontainebleau, 1979. While technical change is clearly not unrelated to external trade pressures in a direct sense, much of this change in any one industry relates to wage and productivity developments in the economy as a whole. On the other hand, in Germany or Japan, it is precisely these rapid productivity gains which have led to big wage rises which have in turn led to a restructuring of the economy and its external trade pattern.

9 See ch. I of CEPII (Centre d'Etudes Prospectives et d'Informations Internationales), *Les Economies Industrialisées face à la Concurrence du Tiers-Monde: le Cas de la Filière Textile*. Paris, 1979.

10 See also pp. 352–356 of Organization for Economic Cooperation and Development (OECD), *Interfutures: Final Report, Facing the Future: Mastering the Probable and Managing the Unpredictable*. Paris, 1979.

11 This appears to be a form of transfer-pricing, though the CKD kit producers defend it on the grounds that handling charges are increased by partial deletions. There is a similar gap between average cost price and the price at which the car firms sell spare parts in all their markets.

12 For instance, Dosi describes the success of Japan in catching up with US semiconductor technology, the relative success of the Federal Republic of Germany (in European terms at least) and the failure of France, the United Kingdom and Italy to narrow the technological gap. See G. Dosi, *Industrial Adjustment and Policy II: Technical Change and Survival: Europe's Semiconductor Industry*. Sussex European Paper No. 9, Sussex European Research Centre, University of Sussex, forthcoming.

PART III

Prospects for the NICs: three country studies

7

South Korea

Key W. Kim*

For 17 years between 1962 and 1978 South Korea's real GNP grew at 9.9 per cent per annum. This rapid growth resulted in a more than threefold (3.2, to be exact) increase in per capita GNP at 1975 constant prices. The growth in GNP also brought about increasing employment opportunities. The 3.2 per cent unemployment level in 1978 was almost one-third of the 1962 level. During this period of high growth the country did not experience any serious deterioration in income distribution. On the whole, income distribution improved. Furthermore, for the period as a whole, both the real GNP growth rate and the ratio of investment to GNP showed rising trends (see *Figure 7.1*).

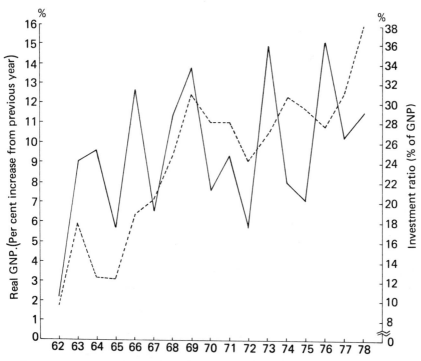

Figure 7.1 *Annual real growth of GNP and ratio of investment to GNP (at 1975 prices).*
———— *real GNP growth rate;* - - - - *ratio of investment to GNP*

* Director of Research, Korea International Economic Institute, Seoul

Table 7.1 *Ratios of investment and savings to GNP (% at 1975 prices)*

	Total investment	Domestic savings	Foreign savings	Marginal propensity to save
1962	9.6	−0.5	9.1	−153.8
1963	17.8	5.0	11.4	65.5
1964	12.4	7.7	6.0	35.5
1965	12.2	7.3	5.4	0.3
1966	18.8	12.2	8.0	50.7
1967	20.2	10.8	9.2	−10.0
1968	24.7	12.1	12.8	23.9
1969	30.8	15.5	13.6	40.1
1970	28.1	14.1	13.3	4.7
1971	28.1	13.2	15.4	4.0
1972	24.2	13.2	9.5	4.6
1973	26.9	18.0	8.2	50.6
1974	30.7	17.9	14.4	16.5
1975	29.4	18.6	10.4	28.6
1976	27.6	23.1	6.3	39.6
1977	31.0	25.3	6.2	46.6
1978	37.8	25.7	11.0	28.8

Total investment refers to gross investment including inventory changes. Foreign savings refer to the difference between total exports and total imports. The total investment ratio and the sums of savings ratios are not equal because of statistical discrepancies.

Source: Bank of Korea, *National Income in Korea* (various issues)

This remarkable economic progress was largely the result of an outward-looking development strategy in which a phenomenal expansion of exports played a key role.

In reviewing this progress, several questions naturally come to mind. What were the principal policies the government pursued? How successful were they? Will those policies work in the future? What are some of the changes in the current international environment that are highly unfavourable to Korea? What role should a country like South Korea play in the 1980s?

The present paper will touch upon all these questions. Its specific purpose is, however, threefold: to review the major government economic policies since the early 1960s; to make some guesses as to what policies South Korea is most likely to follow in the 1980s; and to suggest some ways of improving economic cooperation between a NIC like South Korea and the rest of the world in a new international environment.

7.1 Economic policies in the 1960s and 1970s

For the purpose of reviewing the major economic policies, the 17-year period can be broken into three sub-periods: 1962–1971, 1972–1978 and the period since January 1979.

During the period 1962–1971 the nation completed its first two five-year economic plans, the primary goals of which were to promote high growth through the expansion of labour-intensive manufactured exports. In the second period the government made strenuous efforts to accelerate the development of heavy and chemical industries, to a large degree as a response to drastic changes in the external environment. The last period since January 1979 may best be looked upon as one in which the government has been taking steps to rectify some serious structural distortions introduced into the economy in the course of the strenuous efforts to develop heavy and chemical industries during 1972–1978.

Entry into the world economy (1962–1971)

In 1961, one year before the First Five-year Plan was launched, economic conditions in South Korea were little different from those prevailing in any resource-poor, low-income developing country today. South Korea, already overpopulated, was experiencing an annual population growth of nearly 3 per cent. Per capita GNP at current prices was a meagre $82, permitting a negligible rate of domestic savings. The nation had no significant exports and had run chronic balance-of-payments deficits since liberation in 1945. In 1961 the country's exports amounted to less than one-quarter of its imports.

The challenge faced by South Korea at that time was how to promote high growth in such a way as to solve the problem of extensive unemployment and at the same time to improve the balance of payments.

The essence of the growth strategy followed during the first two Five-year Plans was to expand labour-intensive manufactured exports, in which South Korea enjoyed a comparative advantage. In order to carry through this strategy, the nation had to mobilize both internal and external resources to the maximum degree. To mobilize internal resources, the government revamped tax administration and raised the interest rates paid at commercial banks from 12 per cent to as high as 30 per cent. The results were an elimination of fiscal deficits and a dramatic rise in domestic savings (*Table 7.1*). For the three consecutive years from 1965, when the interest rates were raised, savings deposits in the nation's banking system nearly doubled every year. These became sources for funds which the government channelled into export-related industries.

To encourage the inflow of foreign capital, in 1966 the government passed a comprehensive Foreign Capital Promotion Act, under which the government was able to underwrite the risk borne by foreign investors.

The key measures that the government took to promote exports included the readjustment of the exchange rate. In 1964 the government adopted a uniform exchange rate system and devalued the currency by nearly 100 per cent, thus eliminating the bias against the trade sector stemming from the overvalued currency. In addition, the government adopted easy credit terms and tax rebates on materials imported for the production of exports. Furthermore, a number of free trade zones were established and customs procedures simplified. These measures enabled Korean exporters to conduct their business as if they were operating under a free trade regime[1].

The international environment during the 1960s was highly favourable to the growth of manufactured exports from South Korea. The original GATT rules were still binding on major industrial nations, and widespread resource nationalism was still unknown. As a result world trade was expanding at an unprecedented rate. During this period South Korea made excellent use of expanding markets abroad, particularly those in the United States and Japan which took about two-thirds of South Korea's total exports between 1962 and 1971.

The results of the government policies, together with the favourable international environment, surpassed all expectations. Exports at current prices rose from $55 million in 1962 to $1132 million in 1971, a more than twentyfold increase in 10 years. The share of agricultural and fishery products in total exports fell from 45 per cent in 1962 to 10.5 per cent in 1971, while the share of manufactured goods rose from 27 to 86 per cent.

There is little doubt that this rapid surge in manufactured exports served as the 'engine of growth' for the economy. Without it, the annual economic growth rate of 9.4 per cent in 1962–1971 could not have been achieved, and there would have been great difficulties in absorbing the fast growing labour force into gainful employment.

Simultaneous development of heavy industries and agriculture (1972–1978)

Compared with the previous period, 1972–1978 was a time when the external environment facing South Korea went through a series of drastic changes. Even before the nation launched its Third Five-year Economic Plan in 1972, there were a number of disturbing developments from the Korean viewpoint. In 1971 the Nixon Administration carried out its long-contemplated plan of reducing the level of US troops in South Korea by one-third. The move was interpreted by top policy-makers as the first of several moves toward the eventual withdrawal of all US troops in South Korea. Thus, fearing that the day might come when she alone would have to defend herself against possible invasion from the north, South Korea began to develop her own defence industries[2]. An announcement by Mr Carter during the 1976 presidential campaign that it would be his policy, if elected, to carry out total US troop withdrawal from South Korea only reinforced South Korea's resolve to develop her own defence industry.

The year 1971 was highly significant for South Korea for yet another reason. In that year the Bretton Woods system began to fall apart. The breakdown of the fixed exchange rate system had a twofold significance for

South Korea. Because the currency unit – the won–was rigidly pegged to the US dollar, any change in the dollar–yen rate or the value of the dollar against other major currencies meant an automatic change in South Korea's terms of trade with the rest of the world. The steady decline in the value of the dollar following the breakdown also meant an automatic devaluation of the won, a development which stimulated exports. In short, these currency changes acted as a powerful stimulus for South Korea to expand her exports and find new markets.

It was once believed that by discouraging the balance-of-payments adjustment process by means of the modification of exchange rates, the Bretton Woods system itself was the cause of rising trends in protectionism. According to this theory, the world would have witnessed a reduction in protectionist measures after the breakdown of the system. But what actually occurred was just the opposite.

The rising trends in protectionism after the breakdown forced South Korea to do two things: on the one hand to diversify her trading partners, and on the other to restructure the commodity composition of her exports in favour of more sophisticated, high value-added, industrial goods. The latter effort, combined with the desire to develop domestic defence industries, resulted in efforts to accelerate the growth of heavy and chemical industries including iron and steel, shipbuilding, machinery, electronics and petrochemicals – to a degree perhaps unjustified by South Korea's factor endowment.

The world-wide commodity boom of 1972/73 also had an effect on South Korea. By raising prices in world grain markets, it supported the argument that South Korea should develop her own agriculture, and in particular achieve self-sufficiency in major food grains. The goal of self-sufficiency was also argued in terms of its favourable effect on the balance of payments.

The quadrupling of oil prices in 1973/74 forced South Korea to respond to an alarming deterioration in her balance of payments in an unprecedented fashion, and not always with sufficient forethought.

The major policy adjustments to all these external and internal changes fell into three categories: determined efforts to accelerate the development of heavy and chemical industries; an all-out effort to diversify trade; and a policy of self-sufficiency in major food grains.

The development of heavy and chemical industries was already an important priority in the Third Five-year Plan. In the new political and economic environment just noted, however, the government deemed it necessary to give added emphasis to such development. The Heavy and Chemical Industry Development Plan, announced in 1973, called for an accelerated schedule to develop technologically sophisticated industries, not only to meet defence needs but also to upgrade the composition of exports in favour of high value-added products. Unfortunately, the Plan was drawn up on the assumption that world trade would continue to expand more or less at the same rate as in the 1960s.

In order to finance the accelerated development of heavy and chemical industries, the government established a National Investment Fund. This scheme mobilized not only all public employee pension funds, but also a substantial portion of private savings at regular banking institutions by requiring them to transfer automatically a certain percentage of their deposits to the Fund. The funds so mobilized were then channelled into heavy industry projects favoured by the government. When these funds proved to be insufficient to finance all such projects, the banking institutions were urged to make additional loans available on a preferential basis. On the grounds that the projects had long gestation periods, the loans were granted at very low interest rates. In fact, nominal interest rates charged on these loans were so low that their real rates often turned out to be negative.

Such low interest rates, of course, gave rise to a number of serious problems. In the first place they failed properly to reflect the opportunity cost of capital. This failure, together with the over-optimistic assumption regarding world trade prospects, led to unwise and excessive investment, particularly in power generators and construction equipment. Moreover, the very low interest rates caused a chronic excess demand for loans, which in turn served as a powerful force behind the expansion of domestic money supply. The availability of loans at low interest rates also led many project sponsors to underestimate other critical requirements for the successful development of heavy and sophisticated industries, such as the technical expertise and experience which other nations have only acquired over a long period.

Efforts to diversify trade took two forms. To circumvent quotas and other non-tariff barriers, South Korea developed new exports and upgraded the quality of existing products. In the area of new products, success was most noticeable in electronics, machinery, steel and shipbuilding. With their quality upgraded, traditional exports such as textiles, footwear and leather goods also performed very well.

To diversify markets geographically, efforts were directed initially to all regions. Latin American and African markets turned out to be the most difficult to penetrate. The easiest were in the Middle East and Europe. The share of commodity exports going to the Middle East rose from 1.8 per cent in 1973 to 11.7 per cent in 1976, and the share to Europe from 11.8 to 17.5 per cent.

In the Middle East, South Korea sold not only goods but also construction services. Gross earnings from construction in the Middle East rose from zero in 1973 to about $2.1 billion in 1978, and the total value of construction contracts won in the region by the end of 1978 was almost $15 billion. Construction activities in the Middle East had far-reaching effects. In addition to improving South Korea's balance of payments with the region, they provided opportunities for South Korean workers to learn skills and expertise in large project management in a foreign environment. Through this experience South Koreans have acquired a new comparative advantage in development projects in the Third World.

The immediate consequences of the participation in the Middle East were, however, a mixed blessing for the economy. For one thing, the departure of a large number of skilled workers to that region pushed up domestic wages. This, together with the growing demand for skilled workers in heavy industries, widened the wage differential between skilled and unskilled workers, which in turn had an adverse effect on income distribution. In addition, the sudden improvement in the balance of payments attributable to earnings from the Middle East led to the expansion of the domestic money supply and subsequent inflation. With a proper policy response this outcome could have been avoided, but the lesson was not learned quickly enough by a country which had been suffering from a chronic balance-of-payments deficit since the end of World War II.

When the Third Five-year Plan was being formulated, the growing gap in income levels between rural and urban households became a major social concern. When this was coupled, rightly or wrongly, with the effects of the commodity boom in the minds of top policy-makers the adoption of a policy of self-sufficiency in major food grains became inevitable.

Much has been written about South Korea's highly successful efforts to deal with the problem of urban–rural income disparity. One cannot overlook, however, the fact that these efforts failed to serve the long-term interests of the nation. While it is true that the gap in the level of income between the average urban and rural household had virtually been closed by 1977, a significant disparity has reappeared in the last two years.

The basic problem here stems from the major policy instrument used. The high grain price support programme led to a substantial budgetary deficit which aggravated inflationary pressures. By encouraging the production of grains at a time when consumer demand had already shifted to non-grain products, the price support programme created an imbalance in supply and demand conditions within the agricultural sector. Further, the programme tended to worsen the income distribution in rural areas by benefiting large farmers more than small farmers. Finally, it should be noted that the entire policy emphasis on grain production was a mistake in the first place because it diverted resources to an area in which Korea lacks comparative advantage.

Restructuring for continued high growth with stability (January 1979 to the present)

The three major policy thrusts just examined were to a large degree responsible for an average annual economic growth of 10.4 per cent between 1972 and 1978. Further, they brought about a significant structural change in the composition of exports. The share of heavy and chemical industrial products in total exports rose from 16.3 per cent in 1972 to almost 25 per cent

Table 7.2 *Share of selected commodities in total exports (%)*

SITC		1970	1971	1972	1973	1974	1975	1976	1977	1978
7	Machinery, of which	7.4	8.2	10.6	11.9	15.1	13.8	16.6	17.3	20.4
72	Electrical machinery	5.3	6.4	7.7	9.4	10.6	8.7	10.4	9.2	9.8
73	Ships and transport equipment	1.1	0.6	0.9	0.7	2.7	3.6	4.4	6.7	8.8
7 – (72 + 73)	Other machinery	1.1	1.2	2.0	1.8	1.7	1.5	1.7	1.4	1.7
67	Iron and steel	1.6	2.3	5.7	5.7	10.1	4.6	4.8	3.9	4.5
	Total machinery and iron and steel	9.0	10.5	16.3	17.6	25.2	18.4	21.4	21.2	24.9
65 and 84	Textiles and clothing	35.7	41.4	38.1	35.6	32.5	35.3	36.3	31.3	32.3
85	Footwear	2.1	3.5	3.4	3.2	4.0	3.8	5.2	4.9	5.4
03	Fishery products	4.9	4.0	4.3	4.3	3.8	7.1	4.1	6.9	5.0
	Others	48.3	40.6	37.9	39.3	34.5	35.4	33.1	35.7	32.3
	Total	100.0	100.0	100.0	100.0	100.0	100.0	100.0	100.0	100.0
	Total in million US$	835.2	1067.6	1624.1	3325.0	4460.4	5081.0	7715.1	10 046.5	12 710.6

Source: Bank of Korea, *Economic Statistics Yearbook* (various issues)

in 1978, as can be seen from *Table 7.2*. Both the high growth rate and the structural change were only achieved, however, at the cost of high inflation.

An important characteristic of the recent inflation in South Korea was the faster rise in prices of necessities than other goods. This made life difficult, particularly for the poor. In response, the government all too often resorted to price controls. But price controls led to the movement of resources away from the controlled sectors, thus making supply problems even more acute. By creating a permanent expectation of rising prices, inflation has retarded the growth of domestic savings. The slow growth of savings has further been aggravated by the policy of holding virtually all interest rates at regular banking institutions below the inflation rate. Moreover, the high rate of inflation, together with the rigid exchange rate regime, has resulted in a steady decline of export competitiveness.

The comprehensive stabilization programme introduced by the government in April 1979 was designed in large measure to deal with the causes as well as the consequences of inflation. In addition, the programme aims at restructuring the economy in such a way as to sustain high growth for at least another decade. The principal approach is to rely more heavily on the market mechanism to allocate resources both efficiently and equitably.

The programme thus had four major components: the tight monetary and fiscal policy designed to reduce excess liquidity in the economy; measures to correct structural imbalances caused by the past investment policy and the inflationary process itself; measures specifically designed to promote competition; and finally, a set of measures to help those who suffered most from inflation, the poor.

First and foremost among the measures designed to reduce excess liquidity was a reduction in the rate of growth of the money supply. In 1979 the target rate of growth in money supply, defined to include savings deposits, was 25 per cent against the actual 35 per cent growth in the previous year. In addition, the government made an effort to produce a budgetary surplus of some 150 billon won, or a little over 3 per cent of the total government expenditure for the year.

The measures designed to redress the structural imbalances in the economy included credit priorities in favour of light industries producing necessities for domestic consumption; the encouragement of non-grain production and mechanization in agriculture; programmes to modernize the domestic distribution network; and improvements in public transport.

Most important among the measures designed to bring about greater competition in the economy were price de-controls, removal of artificial barriers to entry which had existed in certain industries, and a speed-up in import liberalization. As a result of four rounds of price de-controls implemented since February 1979, the number of commodities subject to controls was reduced from 144 to 35. The speed-up in import liberalization was in the form of a reduction in tariff rates and a removal of licence requirements on many commodities. As a result, the liberalization ratio, that is to say, the number of commodities that could be imported without import licences over the total number of imported commodities, identified by the 4-digit Brussels Tariff Nomenclature classification, rose in 1979 to 69 per cent. Furthermore, the government announced its intention to liberalize 90 per cent of imports by 1981.

Lastly, the measures designed to help the poor included expansion of public works programme, exemption from tuition payments for children of low-income families, and direct cash payments to compensate for the reduction in real income resulting from price de-controls. Although the effects of these payments on the economy were not anti-inflationary, the government considered them necessary for reasons of equity and also a fair price to pay for the benefits to be derived from normalizing the relative price structure in the economy.

Economic management plan for 1980

During 1979/80 many changes have occurred in South Korea, obviously the most important being the death of President Park Chung Hee. Many had feared that the nation might suffer from social and political chaos following his death. However, the orderly transition to a new interim government justifies a degree of optimism for the future. To be sure, the relationship between the civilian government and the military is still somewhat uncertain. But in view of the overall political maturity of the people and the professional outlook held by the present military leadership, one is probably justified in expecting an evolution of the relationship clearly favouring civil supremacy in the not too distant future.

Among the external changes which have affected the country most, two developments should be considered: the continuing prospect of oil price increases and the deepening recessions in both the United States and Japan.

A number of oil price increases effected by OPEC during 1979, amounting to a total increase of around 75 per cent, brought about at least an 11 per cent rise in South Korea's domestic price level. The failure of the recent OPEC meeting in Caracas to come up with an agreement on the extent of oil price increases for 1980 poses an even more serious prospect. The implication South Korea drew from the Caracas meeting is that she must be prepared to pay an average of $30 per barrel of oil in 1980, and that even at this price she will probably have difficulties in securing the amount of oil needed in order to sustain growth. Even at $30 a barrel, South Korea's oil bill in 1980 would be as much as $6 billion, or a net increase of nearly $3 billion over 1979.

The worsening recessions in the United States and Japan are of no less concern to South Korea. It has been forecast that in 1980 real economic growth in the United States and Japan, South Korea's two largest export markets, will be 0.6 and 2.6 per cent respectively or only about one-half of the

1979 rates. With the deepening recessions in the two countries, it will not be at all realistic for South Korea to expect exports to grow in real terms in 1980.

In a highly export-oriented economy such as South Korea's the demand for new investment is of course closely tied with the growth of exports. The investment demand in the country is already weak for yet another reason. Many of the large industrial projects started in recent years are now in the process of coming on stream, and in 1980 there may well be considerable excess capacity in some of the heavy industries (as already noted). This is not true, however, in light industries.

The level of domestic consumption has held up rather well in 1979. However, South Korea could not rely on an increase in consumption to maintain growth in 1980. In a year when she will have to transfer almost another 5 per cent of GNP to oil producers in the Middle East and elsewhere, South Korea cannot afford a rise in domestic consumption.

What does the government intend to do in the light of these gloomy prospects? The South Korean government clearly recognizes that it must deal with the economic difficulties this year in such a way that the nation's long-term growth prospects are not sacrificed. In other words, it is prepared to accept a certain trade-off between growth in the year 1980 and growth for the entire decade of the 1980s.

As far as the government is concerned, South Korea's long-term prospects have never been in doubt. During the 1980s South Korea will continue to benefit from all the sources of rapid growth which a country in the early stages of industrial development typically enjoys.

South Korea's labour force will continue to grow at around 3 per cent per annum, while her total population will grow at about 1.6 per cent per annum. These differential growth rates will present unusual opportunities as well as challenges. The challenges will be to provide enough jobs and housing. The opportunities will stem from a higher ratio of labour force to population, which will simply mean that the average individual worker will have fewer dependants to support; consequently the economy will experience a unique opportunity to increase aggregate savings and thus be in a position to finance growing investment requirements with minimum inflation.

During the 1980s South Korea will enjoy an unusual opportunity to raise productivity. There is in the world today a wide range of technologies which can be readily introduced into South Korea to improve productivity. South Korea can also raise productivity by shifting labour out of agriculture and other traditional sectors where productivity is low to modern sectors where productivity is high. The average annual productivity improvement in manufacturing for the past 10 years has been 11–12 per cent, while in agriculture it has been 3–4 per cent. The potential for productivity improvement through the reallocation of labour is particularly large because it was only in 1978 that the absolute number of workers in agriculture began to decline.

To make use of this potential for fast growth, the policy-makers believe it is essential that the nation should persevere with the stabilization programme initiated in 1979. To be more specific, the target for the growth of money supply in 1980 was set below 20 per cent. In addition, the government intended to make every effort to reduce its current expenditure. It also announced its intention to do everything in its power to decelerate the rise in nominal and real wages which has led to a decline in the competitiveness of the nation's exports. The maximum nominal wage increase the government recommended in 1980 is 15 per cent. The government announced its intention to pass the expected increases in the price of oil on to consumers without delay.

In order to deal with the prospect of increased unemployment resulting from the unfavourable developments in exports and heavy industries, the government will try to stimulate further investment in light industries, housing, public transport and manpower training.

According to the government, an increase in investment in light industry this year will not only redress the current overinvestment in heavy industries, but also prepare the country to resume export growth when the hoped-for world economic recovery takes place in 1981. An expansion of housing construction, particularly of small units, will incur a minimal increase in imports, but contribute significantly to the goal of maintaining high employment. Greater investment in energy-saving mass transport, which has been long overdue, is to be undertaken in 1980.

Policy-makers also feel that 1980 is a good year for the nation to undertake an extensive manpower training programme. In recent years there has been a shortage of skilled manpower in all categories in South Korea. In the opinion of many, undertaking an extensive manpower training programme at a time when workers are less intensively engaged in their existing employment is a good idea.

For exports, the government has tentatively set a $17 billion target for 1980. In view of the recession overseas, however, the government intends to keep this target very flexible. For imports, the government is realistic enough to accept a continued rise, probably to over $22 billion compared with $19.6 billion in 1979. The major cause of this rise will of course be the increased oil bill, and the need to import some equipment and materials not locally available which will be required for the investment programme in light industry, housing construction and public transport.

With poor export prospects and the increased import requirements, South Korea will probably incur a current account deficit of nearly $5 billion in 1980. With a deficit as large as this, there will be a great temptation to resort to direct import controls. However, to its credit, the government has already announced that it will not succumb to such a temptation. The reason is that such controls will result in the multiplication of red tape, an increase in arbitrary government decisions and new distortions in the relative price structure at a time when the country should be striving to remove precisely these forms of inefficiencies.

At present government economists estimate that with the economic policy programme just outlined, Korea will achieve 3–5 per cent real growth and the level of unemployment will be 5–6 per cent in 1980[3].

7.2   Probable policy reforms and growth strategy in the 1980s

Internal reforms

The present South Korean government is well aware that if the nation is to continue to experience high growth for another decade a series of basic internal reforms must be undertaken.

Among the items on the agenda for reform on the economic front, the restructuring of the financial sector ranks extremely high. The heart of the problem here has been the absence of interest rates that can equilibrate investment and savings. This was responsible not only for some ill-advised investment decisions but also for the chronic inflationary pressures.

Three groups have been against a financial reform focusing on interest rates: high officials at the Ministry of Finance, professional bank managers and the owners of large business groups.

Why high officials at the Ministry of Finance should object to such a reform is easy to understand. Once the interest rates at regular banking institutions are set at equilibrium levels, the power and prerogatives of these officials to influence the channelling of funds would be significantly diminished.

Professional bank managers have been against the reform for similar reasons. Once the interest rates they charge on their loans are determined primarily by demand and supply conditions, the opportunities for them to offer favourable terms for specific individuals or groups would be reduced. It should also be noted that, for professional bank managers working in a banking system that is for the most part nationalized, maximum profit criteria have little relevance.

That owners of big businesses have been against interest rate reforms hardly requires an explanation. They have been the principal beneficiaries of preferential loans granted by the banking institutions.

Who have been in favour of the reform, and what chance do they have? Within the government, officials at the Economic Planning Board (EPB) stand out as the most vocal group in favour of a reform, largely because the EPB is held responsible for any rise in general price levels. Furthermore, EPB officials in general know only too well that if the nation's economic growth falters for whatever reason, they will be held primarily responsible; hence, they have every reason to favour the efficient allocation of investment funds through the mechanism of equilibrating interest rates.

Outside the government, at least two groups are, or should be, in favour of interest reform: small businessmen and consumers. Small businessmen have long been discriminated against in access to bank loans. In fact, when the share of preferential loans to heavy industry rose, they were virtually squeezed out of the market for bank loans; and thus they have relied very heavily on non-bank loan markets, commonly referred to as the 'curb market' in South Korea.

South Korean consumers have never had much access to bank loans, and household consumer credit, as it is practised in industrially advanced countries, is still unheard of in Korea.

There is little question that until now the groups against interest rate reform have been dominant. But during the past few months the situation has changed significantly. Many policy-makers have had second thoughts about the wisdom of handing out preferential loans at low interest rates, and the large business groups have become the target of popular criticism for the manner in which they have amassed their fortunes in recent years. Business groups in particular are now under pressure to demonstrate that their competitive edge in business is not necessarily derived from preferential, low interest loans. In short, the chances for interest rate reform have never been better.

Crucial as it is, the interest rate reform will be only a part of the total effort to normalize the entire relative price structure in the economy. To this end, the government will soon have to face the need to evaluate its foreign exchange rate system. In the opinion of many, the nation's currency is far overvalued, and many also feel that the system of pegging the currency to the US dollar is at best obsolete. The government has been postponing a currency devaluation on the grounds that it would lead to further inflationary pressures, but this justifiation will weaken when the current stabilization measures take further hold on the economy. Devaluation of the currency thus appears to be only a question of time. In fact, a devaluation could be undertaken even at this moment, provided that it is coupled with an additional dose of stabilization measures. With regard to pegging, the logical choice seems to be the adoption of a 'crawling peg' to a currency basket weighted by the relative importance of major individual currencies in the nation's trade. Such a system will go far toward achieving greater trade diversification in an orderly fashion and easing balance-of-payments pressures[4].

Closely related to the changes in the banking system and foreign exchange rate regime is the question of opening up the domestic capital market to foreign participation. For South Korea to develop her financial sector to match the development in the real sector, it is important that she should begin to make preparations for full foreign participation. Although the government is acutely aware of the need to do so, the progress in this area will be slow at best. For one thing, South Koreans are not eager at present to allow foreign investors to reap high profits in the form of dividends on existing shares, which are basically the South Korean people's well-deserved rewards for their hard work. Furthermore, it is generally felt that liberalizing all capital movements should come only after the domestic money market has been made into a truly resilient mechanism capable of absorbing ordinary flows of funds.

South Korea's policy on foreign capital so far has tended to be rather conservative about direct investment and joint participation requirements. The government has preferred foreign loans to foreign investment, and joint ventures to full ownership.

It is very likely, however, that this policy will change soon for at least three reasons. As already noted, the government expected considerable difficulties with the balance of payments during 1980, and encouraging a greater inflow of direct foreign investment would be one way to deal with the problem. Secondly in recent years the government has keenly realized that direct foreign investment with or without joint equity participation is an excellent vehicle for the transfer of technology into the country[5]. Many government officials are now of the opinion that some of the costly mistakes in investment programmes in heavy industry in recent years could have been avoided if they had been undertaken in the form of joint ventures. Thirdly, in contrast to many other countries, there is very little fear in South Korea of being dominated by multinational foreign enterprises. So far, direct foreign investment has accounted for no more than 10 per cent of the total foreign capital commitment, which at present stands at about $14 billion.

An important reform is also needed in agriculture. The government feels very keenly the need to phase out gradually the high grain price support programme. As a matter of fact, the government started an effort in this direction in autumn 1979 when it eliminated the price support for the traditional brand of rice consumed mostly by high-income groups. It is not certain, however, that the progress will continue in 1980. South Korea expects to have a new constitutional referendum and a general election in 1981. At such a time, few political leaders would be willing to take such a courageous stand to eliminate the high price support for farmers who still account for nearly 40 per cent of the population.

In one critical respect, however, one need not be pessimistic about the chances for further agricultural reform in South Korea. More than 30 years ago, the country carried out extensive land reforms which resulted in substantial increases in output per unit of land. Now, many people, both inside and outside the government, keenly realize that what the country needs in the long run is a steady rise in per capita farm earnings through technical improvement and the movement of population out of agriculture.

To increase efficiency, government aid has been made available for such purposes as enlargement of farms, expansion of non-grain production and increased mechanization. Furthermore, the manpower training programme to be implemented in 1980 will concentrate heavily on the vocational training of youth in the farming community. Finally, it should also be noted that, powerful as it is, the agricultural lobby in South Korea is not as politically entrenched as it is in countries such as Japan.

Many people in South Korea have suggested that one area in which reform is needed is in labour–management relations. The reform needed in this area, however, is not what most outside observers might think, namely, greater freedom for union movements and minimum wages. If the primary goal of labour unions is to increase wages, it is not altogether certain that South Korea will need them. For three years between 1976 and 1978, the average nominal money wages in South Korea rose at 33 per cent a year, far outpacing the rise in labour productivity and the rate of inflation. These high increases in nominal wages occurred at a time when union activities were not prominent.

The explanation for this rapid wage increase, which led to the decline in the competitiveness of South Korean exports, is twofold. The government, through its Office of Labour Affairs, pressured employers for what amounted to minimum wages. Furthermore, when large business groups undertaking heavy industry projects offered high wages to young skilled workers, they also raised the wages for older workers in deference to the seniority system still prevalent in the country today.

What South Korea needs in the area of labour–management relations in the years ahead is not stronger unions but a greater role for competitive markets. A nation whose overall labour force is expected to grow at 3 per cent per annum can ill afford restrictions on labour force participation.

External constraints

Formidable at these internal reform tasks are, they pale in comparison with the serious external constraints Korea must face during the 1980s. The major constraints will be the supply of oil, protectionism and the balance of payments. In addition to these three constraints, which are largely economic in nature, South Korea will have to deal with the problem of defence in the 1980s as she has done during the past three decades.

For the supply of oil, South Korea is totally dependent on imports. Although South Korea and Japan have recently joined forces in offshore oil exploration south of Korea, it is not yet certain whether these efforts will be fruitful. South Korea has so far had to rely rather heavily on major international oil companies for her oil supply, but as the spot market prices of oil go up, the international oil companies are becoming more and more reluctant to conclude long-term contracts. Moreover, in view of their declining role as the distributors for oil producing countries, it is probably not in South Korea's long-run interests to rely too heavily on these so-called oil 'majors'. Thus there is an urgent need for South Korea to enter into direct agreements with oil producers abroad, and it is not at all certain that South Korea will necessarily be more successful than other non-oil producing countries in this task.

For a rapidly growing economy such as South Korea, the demand for oil is highly elastic with respect to GNP. Between 1971 and 1978, South Korea's total oil consumption rose 11.6 per cent per year, while the annual growth rate of GNP was 10.4 per cent. If this relationship holds in the future, growing unavailability of oil could mean, at least in the short run, a drastic reduction in growth. The slow projected growth for 1980, in large part a consequence of the rise in the price of oil and its effect on the balance of payments, is a sobering reminder.

As oil becomes increasingly scarce, it will of course make sense for the nation to develop substitutes such as nuclear energy, coal, tidal power and solar energy. South Korea has already made substantial progress with her nuclear energy programme. According to the current long-term energy plan, by 1991 Korea will have at least 16 nuclear power plants capable of producing around 13 per cent of her total energy requirements.

The experience of developing nuclear energy, however, makes one point abundantly clear: the nation will have to incur huge investment costs for developing alternative sources of energy. To undertake such investment, the nation must accept a slower increase, or even in some cases a reduction in consumption and must rely very heavily on foreign capital and technology. As regards coal, South Korea cannot be sure that the two countries which have the biggest coal reserves in the world, namely the US and the USSR, will be any more reliable as suppliers than OPEC countries are at present.

South Korea has been experiencing protectionist barriers to her exports most intensely in industrially advanced countries, which account for about three-quarters of her exports. The calculations by various economists in South Korea show that in order for South Korea to substain a 8–9 per cent economic growth rate, she will need an annual export growth of some 12–14 per cent[6].

During the 1960s and the first half of the 1970s South Korea's exports expanded at a rate from four to five times faster than the world average. Assuming that world trade grows at something like 4 per cent a year during the 1980s, South Korea will have to increase her exports by at least three times the world average rate in order to attain an 8–9 per cent economic growth rate. Although South Korea's share of world trade is presently about 1 per cent, it will indeed be very difficult in the present environment for South Korea to keep expanding her exports at the required rate. If protectionism continues to intensify in industrially advanced countries, South Korea will have to develop greater trade with countries in the Third World and possibly with socialist countries. However, the difficulties involved in such a course should not be underestimated.

The oil problems, and the pessimistic outlook for world trade, of course, give rise to the belief that the balance-of-payments pressures will become one of the most critical constraints on the management of the South Korean economy during the 1980s. In addition, it should not be forgotten that South Korea is still a capital-poor country in need of continuous inflows of foreign capital for investment in areas such as light industry, housing, public transport, education and environmental protection.

At its last meeting in Paris in June 1979, the International Economic Consultative Group for South Korea (IECOK) suggested that South Korea should seek approximately $4.5 billion in foreign capital a year, and expressed the opinion that South Korea would probably have no difficulties in obtaining this sum. Today, however, changed circumstances both inside and outside South Korea make this somewhat debatable.

Further, if the oil situation and the prospects regarding protectionism do not improve, the amount of foreign capital Korea will have to seek might become even greater. In attracting foreign capital, and for that matter in many other respects, South Korea has always been handicapped by the constant threat to its security from North Korea. Although recent US diplomatic initiatives for détente with China will be beneficial for South Korea in the long run, one cannot overlook the short-run dangers inherent in such moves. The regime in North Korea might very well become nervous about the possibility of losing Chinese support, and as a result take sides with the Soviet Union or even launch a pre-emptive strike against South Korea. These and other possibilities make it necessary for South Korea to enhance her defence capabilities, and in the foreseeable future the country will need to allocate 5–6 per cent of GNP for this purpose[7].

Probable strategy in the 1980s

Some time ago a foreign correspondent stationed in Seoul was surprised to learn that South Korea has no overall long-term economic plans as such. It was inconceivable to him that a country in which planning has played such an active part does not possess more than a Five-year Plan. South Korea is now (in 1980) in the fourth year of the current Fourth Five-year Plan, and the EPB will soon begin to prepare the Fifth Five-year Plan to be launched in 1982.

In spite of the great uncertainty regarding the world economy, it is possible to sketch broadly the major thrusts of the economic development strategy for South Korea during the 1980s.

First, there is little question that South Korea will continue to push for fast growth. Apart from the rich growth potential already noted, there are some compelling reasons why the country should follow a fast growth policy.

The 3 per cent annual growth in the labour force will leave no choice but a policy of growth to maintain employment. Fast growth is imperative, too, if the country intends to maintain a strong defence capability without serious adverse effects on domestic consumption. In addition, the South Korean people are well aware that their standard of living, measured in per capita GNP or any other indicator, is at best about one-seventh of that in advanced countries, and they know that they still have a long way to go before they can consider their standard of living adequate.

The manner in which Koreans will seek fast growth during the 1980s will be somewhat different from that of the 1970s. Although they will remain committed to the outward-looking development strategy, they will be more flexible with its implementation. Instead of pushing for fast growth through the expansion of exports regardless of the international economic climate, they will rely more frequently on what their economists now call 'the second engine of growth'. The basic idea of 'the second engine' is that in times of sluggish economic activity abroad, South Korea should concentrate on domestic improvements and the expansion of production facilities for future export growth[8]. Many Korean economists feel that the nation relied too exclusively on the 'first engine', i.e., the expansion of exports, during the past two decades; and that as a result, there was not enough time even to service that engine.

The policy of relying on 'the second engine' is already being implemented this year in the form of increased investments in housing, public transport, light industry and manpower training. But South Koreas have no illusion that the 'second engine' can be a complete substitute for the 'first engine' even for a single year.

It is also fully realized in South Korea that for a highly trade-oriented nation it makes little sense to emphasize exports over imports. Thus, in spite of the balance-of-payments difficulties South Koreans will experience in the next few years, they are not likely to resort to direct import controls. Furthermore, they will pay as much attention to the diversification of the sources of imports as to the diversification of markets for exports.

As long as the protectionist situation in the industrially advanced countries does not improve, South Koreans will persist in their efforts to increase trade with countries in the Third World and with socialist countries. Because of their geographic proximity, the high growth countries in Southeast Asia will become increasingly attractive potential markets for South Korea. Furthermore, South Korea is willing to open trade with China at any time. With the Southeast Asian countries, there is a high degree of complementarity, not only in terms of industrial needs but also in resource endowment; and perhaps a similar point can be made about the relationship between China and South Korea.

One way in which South Korea will try to deal with protectionism in the advanced countries will be to engage in more trade based on intra-industry specialization rather than on inter-industry specialization. The burden of adjustment on the part of the importing countries will on the whole be less when trade is based on intra-industry specialization. Korea's level of technology and the quality of the labour force are such that an increase in intra-industry trade between herself and other advanced countries is now quite feasible. One way in which this trade can be promoted will be for South Korea to participate in more joint ventures and also to encourage more direct foreign investment. Because of the current level of education and technology in South Korea, it will not be particularly difficult to pursue such a policy.

Because of her extremely poor resource endowment, South Korea will engage in what is known as 'resource diplomacy' to an even greater extent during the 1980s. In this effort, she will try to make the best use of her recent successful experience in overseas construction.

South Korea's greatest asset has always been her people. It is possible to show that in recent years investment in education, particularly in the post-secondary school levels, has been less than adequate[9] and South Koreans themselves are keenly aware of this problem. Thus, it is certain that during the 1980s they will devote greater resources to the improvement of human capital. Likewise, their industrial development in the 1980s will place more emphasis on skill intensities rather than capital intensities. They will try to remember the painful lessons learned from some of the capital intensive projects they launched in the late 1970s.

In income distribution, South Koreans are not likely to depart significantly from the main thrust of the policy followed in the 1960s and to some degree in the 1970s. The expansion of employment opportunities through maximum economic growth with price stability will be the key element in the policy for income distribution. In addition, government investment in education, technical manpower training, housing, public transport and health services will also be considered very important for equitable income distribution, and public investment in education and manpower training in particular will go a long way not only toward better income distribution but also in meeting the current shortage of technical manpower.

In their efforts to improve income distribution, South Koreans will try to avoid the unfortunate experience of some advanced countries with so-called welfare programmes. They realize that some of these programmes have had serious disincentive effects on work and savings. Further, these programmes have led to difficulties in industrial adjustments with adverse effects on the rapid expansion of world trade.

7.3   Suggestions for greater international cooperation

Remarkable though it was, South Korea's economic development over the past 17 years or so is not an isolated case. Many developing countries, now increasingly referred to as NICs, have experienced similar growth. In fact, the rapid economic progress attained by these countries in recent years should rightly be considered as one of the most noteworthy achievements of the world economy during the past two decades. Now, at the threshold of a new decade, the remarkable progress of the NICs is being jeopardized by the rise in the prices of oil, protectionism and a prolonged recession in the industrially advanced nations. Neither the NICs themselves nor the world as a whole can afford a halt to this progress.

For most of the NICs to continue with their high growth, they simply must find an alternative global framework for meeting their energy and other resource requirements. In this task they need cooperation and assistance from both developed and developing countries.

With regard to oil and other critical raw materials, it should be remembered that not long ago many resource-producing countries were dominated by the monopsonistic powers of the users in industrially advanced countries. Lately some resource-producing countries have succeeded in altering this situation by setting up their own monopolies. The result unfortunately has been bilateral confrontation, with consequent unsettling effect on prices and output.

What the world now seems to require is a partnership in the development of resources by both user and producer countries. A partnership of the kind suggested here will go far toward changing the confrontational setting. Furthermore, if this partnership is coupled with a greater willingness by the industrial countries to undertake more of their manufacturing activities in the resource-producing countries, the current conflict as to where the initial processing of resources should be done can also be reduced. With the reduction of that conflict, the industrial countries will no longer have strong incentives to engage in such age-old practices as tariff escalation. With a reduction in tariff escalation, industrialization will be accelerated in the developing world.

It has been widely accepted that, at the present level of technology, nuclear energy represents the most economical source for generating electricity. However, the availability of this source of energy to the developing countries has been limited, in part because of the non-proliferation policy being followed in some advanced countries. It would be a pity if the developing countries are denied the benefits of nuclear power as a result of this policy. What the world seems to need in this respect is an arrangement whereby the energy needs of the developing countries and the security concerns of the advanced countries are simultaneously fulfilled. One way this could be done would be for the advanced countries to specialize in the production of nuclear fuel and to make it available to the developing countries at an incremental cost. In return for this privilege, the developing countries would agree to inspection by the advanced countries to ensure proper use of the nuclear fuel. Such an inspection system, together with a concentration of facilities for the production of nuclear fuel in the advanced countries only, would go far towards meeting the non-proliferation objective[10].

A further suggestion relates to the ways in which protectionism might be dealt with in the future. Too many developing countries, including South Korea, tend to view their exports as being of marginal importance in terms of the effect on the importing countries. Clearly the fallacy of composition is involved here; and the exporting countries would do well to keep in mind that the adjustment burden tends to be greater when exports are increased too rapidly, and also, as already pointed out, when trade is based on inter-industry rather than intra-industry specialization.

The advanced countries on their part should take a more positive attitude toward their industrial adjustment policies. They should be more willing to hand over to the developing countries some labour-intensive industries in which they no longer enjoy comparative advantage.

Furthermore, they too should take note of the costs of adjustment they impose on the developing countries by sudden protectionist moves, which often lead to the shortening of the life of investment capital in the developing countries and force these countries to 'leapfrog' stages of industrial development beyond their capacity. All these lead to the high cost of industrialization in the developing world. What is required here seems to be a guarantee that, in future, individual advanced countries will not undertake sudden protectionist moves without compensating their trading partners for the damage done to them by such moves[11].

The rise in protectionism and resource nationalism in recent years has stemmed in no small measure from the highly unstable international monetary relations which have prevailed at least since the breakdown of the Bretton Woods system. The sudden shifts in the NICs' exchange rates which result from forces beyond their control have compelled them to change their trading partners in ways not easy for them. The world is clearly in need of a stable international monetary order to replace the current monetary disorder. In this regard, the recent developments regarding the EMS have been highly encouraging, and it is hoped that the EEC, the United States and other industrial countries will soon join forces to come up with an alternative to the present situation[12].

As for the future role of the NICs in the world economy, we may observe that in the 1950s and 1960s we lived in a bipolar world. Politically, there were only the American and Soviet blocs. Economically, there were only developed and underdeveloped countries. But the world today is no longer so simple. In addition to the advanced countries, there are the NICs, resource-rich OPEC countries, less developed countries and centrally planned economies.

Among these groups, the NICs have a unique role to play. With their high growth potential, they can serve as 'growth points' for the world economy. By actively expanding trade and other forms of economic transactions with the NICs, the industrially advanced countries can make fuller use of their productive capacities. The NICs can certainly make greater use of capital, technology and financial services supplied by the advanced countries.

The potential value of the NICs as 'growth point' countries is not limited to the advanced countries. Many developing countries should also look upon the NICs as potential markets for their exports. After all, the levels of income in the NICs are much closer to the levels of income in the developing countries than to those in advanced countries; thus, relatively speaking, the NICs have a higher demand for manufactured goods produced in the developing countries.

The developing countries should also look upon the NICs as a source of technology imports. Too many people still tend to regard technological cooperation as something that can take place only between a developed country and a developing country. This is clearly a misconception. Many NICs, including Korea, have had considerable experience in adapting the highly capital intensive technologies of the advanced countries to their own conditions, and they now have a variety of technologies which are better suited for conditions in developing countries. It is indeed a shame that greater use of these technologies is not being made at present.

An NIC such as South Korea can fulfil a useful role for the development of the world economy in yet another way. Thanks to her relatively abundant supply of skilled workers, South Korea has played an active part in various development projects, most notably in the Middle East. The valuable experience and expertise thus acquired should be used for the good of the world, not only in the Middle East but also elsewhere. Three-way cooperation among NICs, advanced industrial countries and the developing countries for projects in the Third World would represent an ideal form of cooperation; under such an arrangement all parties would be able to contribute their respective strengths.

The final suggestion goes beyond the realm of economics. The economic progress that the NICs have achieved in recent years has been in no small measure the result of the peace and security maintained by the superpowers of the world. For continued economic progress, especially in a country such as South Korea, a clear understanding of this point by the superpowers is essential. Without such an understanding, all the progress achieved so far can be lost overnight. With such an understanding, the NICs, including South Korea, will be able to devote more of their resources for the economic betterment not only of their own people but also of the people of other nations throughout the world.

References

1 C. R. Frank, Jr., K. S. Kim and L. E. Westphal, *Foreign Trade Regimes and Economic Development: South Korea.* National Bureau of Economic Research, Conference Series on Foreign Trade Regimes and Economic Development, South Korea, New York, 1975, pp. 197–200, and P. Hasan, *Korea, Problems and Issues in a Rapidly Growing Economy.* Johns Hopkins University Press, Baltimore, 1976, pp. 56–78, 93–94.

2 For the Korean government reaction to this move, see Park Chung Hee, *Toward Peaceful Unification: Selected Speeches and Interview.* Seoul, 1976, p. 7.

3 Since this paper was written, the Economic Planning Board has published the *Economic Management Plan for 1980* which gives a description of policy thrusts which is more or less the same as the one given by the writer: see Economic Planning Board, *Economic Management Plan for 1980*. Seoul, February 1980.

4 After this paper was written, on 12 January 1980, to be exact, the government devalued the won by nearly 20 per cent, and on 27 February 1978, the Bank of Korea announced a switch to a floating exchange rate system. For a description of the new floating system, see Economic Planning Board, *Economic Bulletin* (80–07), 7 March 1980, p. 3.

5 For an elaboration of this opinion, see the speech given by H. H. Shin, Deputy Prime Minister and Minister of Economic Planning, to the Asia-Pacific Council of American Chambers of Commerce on 19 October 1979, entitled 'Economic Prospects and Investment Opportunities in Korea', pp. 8–9.

6 E.g. Korea Development Institute, *Long-Term Prospects for Economic and Social Development, 1977–91*. Seoul, 1978, pp. 49–50.

7 Korea currently is devoting roughly 5 per cent of GNP to defence. The ratio is more or less in line with an understanding reached between the South Korean and the United States governments on the basis of the bilateral mutual security agreement currently in effect.

8 In the South Korean context the idea of the 'second engine' of growth was first fully explained at a seminar in Seoul given by Dr John H. Adler, formerly Director of the International Development Institute at the World Bank, under the auspices of the Korea International Economic Institute. For details, see J. H. Adler, *The Prospects of the Korean Economy in a World of Uncertainty*, Seminar Series No. 15, Korea International Economic Institute, Seoul, September 1978, particularly pp. 23–26. The reader might also like to note that the idea of the 'second engine' of growth is not altogether dissimilar to the countercyclical policy regime suggested for small open economies by A. Lindbeck in his 'Stabilization Policy in Open Economies with Endogenous Politicians'. *American Economic Review* 66(2), May 1976, pp. 1–19.

9 During the discussion of the present paper at the Sussex conference, Professor H. W. Singer went further and stated that South Korea has now completely lost her comparative advantage based on the abundance of human capital on account of her past neglect of investment in public education, especially on the secondary level.

10 For this idea I am indebted to Dr Jae-ik Kim, Director-General of Economic Planning, Economic Planning Board, Republic of Korea. For details, see his unpublished paper, 'Nuclear Energy and Small Developing Countries', read at the Williamsburg IX Conference, at Baguio, Philippines, 25–28 October 1979.

11 The source of inspiration for this suggestion is J. Bhagwati, 'Market Disruption, Export Market Disruption, Compensation, and GATT Reform'. In J. N. Bhagwati (ed.), *The New International Economic Order: The North-South Debate*. MIT Press, Cambridge Massachusetts, 1977, pp. 159–191.

12 For the current status and future possibilities of the EMS, see R. Triffin, *'The European Monetary System'*. Paper presented to the Second Conference on Integration and Unequal Development: The Implications of the Second Enlargement of the EEC, Madrid, 15–19 October 1979.

India

V. N. Balasubramanyan*

8.1 Introduction

The familiar image of India is that of a big, poor and primarily agricultural country. About one in six of the world's population lives there, and with a population of 650 million people India is second only to China in terms of total numbers. About 40 to 50 per cent of the population are physically deprived and absolutely poor, suffering from malnutrition, lack of adequate clothing and shelter. And with an income per head of less than $150 India is classified among the low income countries in the international league tables. Agriculture supplies 45 per cent of the national product, and 80 per cent of the population live in rural areas.

But this is only a partial image of India. Much less known is the fact that India at present ranks about fifteenth among the nations of the world in terms of industrial production[1]. And in most economic discussions it is India's programmes of industrialization over the past three decades, based on a policy of import-substituting industrialization, which have attracted most attention. Although the economic inefficiencies and social costs of import-substituting industrialization have been the subject of intense debate, the fact remains that the strategy has endowed India with a diversified industrial structure. The spectrum of industries she possesses range from steel and sophisticated engineering goods to traditional items such as textiles and leather goods. Moreover, India is also a country with a long tradition of industrialization and entrepreneurship dating back to the early nineteenth century when her cotton textile, jute textile and coal mining industries began.

India, however, is often classified among the developing countries that have come to be known as the newly industrializing countries (NICs). This may be a misnomer as there is nothing much new about India's industrialization. The characteristic that she shares with the NICs is her recent entry into the world markets as an exporter of non-traditional manufactures, notably engineering goods. Although India figures among the NICs as an exporter of manufactures, up to now she has had only the status of an 'also ran'. If dramatic export growth and a commitment to exporting are the hallmarks of an NIC, India barely qualifies. Nevertheless, because of her size, her

*Senior lecturer in economics, University of Lancaster

diversified industrial structure and her endowments of labour and industrial enterprise, she has all the makings of a new industrial exporting country. If India does emerge as such – matching the performance of her Asian neighbours, namely South Korea, Hong Kong and Taiwan – she could pose a major challenge to economic management in the developed countries. But the central issue is: will India in fact emerge as a major exporter of manufactures?

It is the purpose of this paper to analyse the prospects for India emerging as a major exporter of manufactures in the 1980s. This analysis has to be grounded in a review of India's economic performance to date, her recent export experience and the political and economic factors that have shaped her economic philosophy. Further, the recent return to power of the Congress party, headed by Mrs Indira Gandhi, has added a new dimension to the debate on the future course of the Indian economy.

8.2   The growth record since 1950

India's growth record since 1950, when the country formally embarked on a planned process of development, has been both remarkable and disappointing. Over the successive five-year plans India has achieved a rate of growth of around 3.5 per cent a year (*Table 8.1*). Admittedly this is disappointing when compared with the growth rates achieved by star performers such as South Korea, Taiwan and Mexico. Yet, it is remarkable because it was achieved in

Table 8.1 *India's net national product and per capita income (annual average growth rates, %)*

	Net national product	Per capita income
At 1960–61 prices		
1951–56	3.7	1.8
1956–61	4.0	2.0
1961–66	2.6	0.4
1966–67	1.0	−1.0
1967–68	9.0	6.9
1968–69	3.3	0.7
1969–70	5.5	3.8
1970–71	4.3	2.0
1971–72	1.7	−0.7
1972–73	−1.7	−3.8
1973–74	3.2	0.5
At 1970–71 prices		
1973–78	4.0	1.0

Data are for fiscal years beginning 1 April
Source: J. N. Bhagwati, N. Jagdish and T. N. Srinivasan: *Foreign Trade Regimes and Economic Development: India. National Bureau of Economic Research, Conference Series on Foreign Trade Regimes and Economic Development* 6, *India*, New York, 1975
Reserve Bank of India Bulletin (various issues)

the face of two wars, the severe droughts of 1965 and 1966, and the 1973–1975 emergency. Furthermore, it represents a significant acceleration over the annual growth rate of British India for the first half of the twentieth century estimated to be no more than 1 per cent.

A second feature of India's growth effort is her heavy reliance on domestic resources. She has been remarkably successful in steadily increasing both the proportion of domestic savings and investment to GDP (*Table 8.2*).

Table 8.2 *Domestic savings and capital formation in the Indian economy*

	Net national product at factor cost (current prices, Rs billion)	Net domestic savings as a percentage of NNP	Net domestic capital formation as a percentage of NNP
1960–61	132.63	9.2	12.0
1965–66	206.37	12.0	13.4
1970–71	344.12	12.0	13.0
1975–76	616.09	16.0	15.8
1976–77	665.61	18.7	17.2
1977–78	731.57	17.8	16.6

Data are for fiscal years beginning 1 April

Source: Reserve Bank of India Bulletin (various issues)

Although India's tax effort has contributed to this rise in savings, it should be noted that the appreciably high savings rate achieved during the late 1970s has been largely a consequence of the inflow of remittances from abroad and exceptionally good harvests.

Industrial performance over the successive plan periods has been notable for its continued acceleration and for a shift in the structure of production away from consumer goods to capital goods and intermediate goods. Industrial production increased at a compound annual rate of growth of 5.75 per cent over the first five-year plan (1951–1956), nearly 7.5 per cent over the second five-year plan (1956–1961) and close to 8 per cent over the third five-year plan (1961–1966)[2]. The post-1966 industrial performance has been less satisfactory and the growth rates do not exhibit a stable trend. During the period 1970–1977, the annual growth rate was around 2 per cent or less in two years, around 4 to 5 per cent in three years; 6 per cent in one year and 10 per cent in another year[3]. And the estimated growth rate for 1978/79 is around 8–10 per cent. For the period 1951–79 as a whole the overall industrial growth rate is around 5 per cent per annum. Available estimates also show that while the first five-year plan period, was characterized by relatively substantial import-substitution in the consumer goods sector, the second plan period, with its emphasis on investment in heavy industry, showed the lowest import-substitution in the consumer goods sector and the highest in the capital goods sector[4]. It is this pursuit of an import-substitution strategy over the past three decades which has endowed India with a mature capital goods sector; evidence can be found in the contracts that Indian companies have won in the Middle East to set up complete power projects and in their ability to manufacture complete textile mills and sugar plants. In machine tools, nearly 85 per cent of domestic demand is met by indigenous production.

India's agricultural performance has been less impressive. The long-term trend growth rate of agricultural output over the period from 1949/50 to 1977/78 has been in the region of 2.5 per cent a year: food grains production has increased at a rate of 2.5 per cent a year and that of non-food grains at 2.7 per cent (*Table 8.3*). In recent years agricultural production has registered impressive strides. Weather conditions have been an important factor, both in the lean years of the mid-1960s when there were two unprecedented droughts and in the recent dramatic increases in production. However, the 'Green Revolution', based on new varieties of food grains, spread from 1965/66, although mostly confined to wheat. The growth rate achieved is the result both of extensions of area under cultivation up to mid-1960s, and of increased yields per hectare. Since the mid-1960s there has been a slow-down in the growth of crop areas in all crops except wheat. Again it is in wheat that most gains have been achieved in yields. As India's growth prospects rely heavily on the performance of her agricultural sector, it is disconcerting to note that the 'Green Revolution' has been mostly a wheat revolution.

While India's external trade relations are discussed in greater detail later in this paper, a few salient points are noted here. Import-substituting industrialization with emphasis on heavy industry has been India's basic economic strategy. Quantitative restrictions on imports and an excessively detailed system of industrial licensing have been the major instruments of this strategy[5]. Thus India has a relatively low ratio of imports to gross domestic product – around 7 per cent. Much of the increase in the value of imports in recent years is accounted for by the increase in import prices, especially for petroleum and oil products. The structure of imports is heavily oriented towards capital goods, petroleum and oil products and raw materials. Until recently food was the only consumer good which was imported in any significant quantity (*Table 8.4*). More than half of India's imports originate from North America and Western Europe. In recent years, however, the share of Middle East and East European countries has shown an appreciable increase (*Table 8.5*).

The salient features of India's exports can be briefly noted. Exports account for a relatively low proportion of GDP (around 7 per cent) and India's share of world exports has steadily declined from 2.1 per cent in 1950/51 to around 0.5 per cent by 1975. Much of this decline was accounted for by the stagnation of her three major exports – jute manufactures, cotton textiles and tea. The share of these items in India's total exports had declined from 52 per cent in 1950/51 to 21 per cent by the mid-1970s. A recent feature of India's exports has been the addition of a number of quite fast growing new items. These

Table 8.3 India's agricultural production (annual growth rates, % per annum)

		Foodgrains		Non-foodgrains			All crops		
	Area	Production	Yield	Area	Production	Yield	Area	Production	Yield
1949/50–1964/65	1.2	3.0	1.8	3.1	3.9	0.8	1.5	3.2	1.7
1964/65–1976/77	0.4	2.6	2.2	0.3	1.5	1.2	0.4	2.1	1.7
1976/77–1977/78	2.3	14.8	12.2	5.1	12.2	6.8	2.9	13.9	10.7

Data are for fiscal years beginning 1 April

Source: Reserve Bank of India Bulletin, June 1978

Table 8.4 Structure of India's imports

	Total imports ($ million)	Food	Petroleum and petroleum products	Machinery and transport equipment	Ferrous and non-ferrous metals	Other	Total imports as % of GDP
				as % of total imports			
1950/51	1365.4	12.0	8.5	24.8	7.4	47.3	7.2
1955/56	1425.6	2.4	8.2	28.5	12.0	48.9	7.1
1960/61	2393.4	15.8	6.1	29.2	14.9	34.0	8.1
1965/66	2957.9	22.7	4.8	35.0	11.8	25.7	6.4
1970/71	2178.9	12.5	8.3	24.1	16.3	38.8	4.4
1975/76	6084.3	25.3	23.3	17.7	7.8	25.9	8.0
1976/77	5676.0	16.9	27.8	20.6	7.4	27.3	7.1
1977/78	7084.4	1.7	25.6	18.4	10.6	43.7	7.7

Data are for fiscal years beginning 1 April

Source: Monthly Statistics of the Foreign Trade of India, Ministry of Commerce, Government of India

Table 8.5 *India's imports by source*

	Total imports ($million)	North America	Western Europe	Middle East	Other Asia and Oceania	Africa (exc. UAR)	Eastern Europe and USSR
					as % of total imports		
1950/51	1365.4	22.7	32.1	..	..	13.0	1.1
1955/56	1425.6	14.7	47.9	10.3	18.5	7.0	1.6
1960/61	2355.4	31.4	39.9	6.5	13.6	4.6	4.0
1965/66	2957.9	40.4	27.8	5.0	13.1	2.6	11.1
1970/71	2178.9	35.9	21.4	10.2	10.6	8.0	13.9
1975/76	6084.3	29.4	23.6	22.6	11.5	1.8	11.0
1977/78	7084.4	18.4	29.2	22.4	15.3	4.4	10.3

Data are for fiscal years beginning 1 April

Source: Monthly Statistics of the Foreign Trade of India

Table 8.6 *Commodity composition of India's exports*

	1950/51	1955/56	1960/61	1965/66	1970/71	1975/76	1976/77	1977/78
				as % of total exports				
Traditional exports, of which	70.6	68.9	64.4	60.0	42.6	28.9	26.9	31.6
Tea	13.4	17.9	18.7	14.3	9.7	5.9	5.7	10.3
Jute manufactures	18.9	19.4	20.5	22.7	12.4	6.2	3.9	4.5
Cotton textiles	19.7	9.3	8.7	6.9	4.9	4.0	5.2	4.1
Non-traditional exports, of which	6.5	7.0	15.2	24.5	40.0	53.7	53.3	50.5
Iron ore	—	1.0	2.6	5.2	7.5	5.3	4.6	4.5
Silver	n.a.	n.a.	n.a.	n.a.	n.a.	4.3	3.3	1.5
Gems	n.a.	n.a.	—	1.8	2.7	3.7	5.6	10.1
Leather and leather manufactures	4.3	3.8	4.1	4.3	5.3	5.6	4.6	4.9
Iron and steel	0.3	n.a.	1.5	1.6	5.9	1.7	5.6	3.5
Engineering goods	0.1	n.a.	2.7	2.5	7.6	10.2	11.0	11.5
Chemicals	1.4	0.9	0.5	1.1	1.9	2.1	2.2	2.2
Clothing	—	—	0.1	0.8	2.0	5.0	6.5	6.1
Total exports ($ million)	1261.3	1278.9	1386.5	1691.8	2046.9	4672.1	5753.1	6287.1

Data are for fiscal years beginning 1 April

Source: Monthly Statistics of the Foreign Trade of India

include engineering goods, chemicals, handicrafts, garments, sugar, silver and iron ore and leather manufactures. A number of these new manufactures show a buoyant trend, and they have accounted for about 50 per cent of India's export earnings in recent years. Especially significant among these items is the growth in the exports of engineering goods, which account for around 12 per cent of the total export earnings (*Table 8.6*). The markets for India's exports are also much more diversified today than in earlier years (*Table 8.7*).

Table 8.7 *Direction of India's export trade (in value terms, $ million)*

	Total exports	To developed countries	To East Europe and USSR	To OPEC* countries	To other countries
			as % of total exports		
1950/51	1261.3	59.5	0.6	1.0	38.9
1955/56	1278.9	63.6	0.8	2.5	33.0
1960/61	1386.5	63.2	7.5	2.9	26.3
1965/66	1691.8	57.3	19.4	4.0	19.2
1970/71	2046.9	49.7	23.6	5.8	20.8
1975/76	4664.6	49.8	17.0	13.3	19.8
1977/78	6287.1	53.6	16.1	10.0	20.3

Data are for fiscal years beginning 1 April
* Includes only Middle Eastern OPEC and Iran

Source: Monthly Statistics of the Foreign Trade of India

Another important feature of the Indian economy in recent years is the growth in foreign exchange reserves. Over the past three years, the level of external reserves on average increased by $1.7 billion a year, and stood at $7.3 billion, equivalent to 11 months of imports, at the end of 1978/79. This increase in reserves has mainly resulted from remittances by Indians working abroad.

8.3   India among the NICs

The foregoing review points to the resilience of the Indian economy which has enabled her to register a respectable 3.5 per cent annual rate of growth in the 1960s and 1970s against heavy odds, to the sophisticated and diversified nature of her industrial sector and to the increasing importance of manufactured goods in her export trade. However, her growth and trade performance compare poorly with that of other NICs. The growth record of 3.5 per cent a year pales in comparison with the 7–9 per cent rates achieved by South Korea, Brazil, Singapore and Hong Kong over the same period. The story about the growth in labour productivity and exports is much the same[6].

Most disconcerting is the steady decline in India's share of world exports noted earlier. India lost ground to her competitors even in her traditional exports, such as cotton textiles (excluding garments), tea, and jute manufactures. The glaring loss of market share was in cotton textiles. While in 1953 India accounted for 58 per cent of all developing countries' exports of textiles, this share had fallen to 8 per cent by 1969. Both South Korea and Taiwan, starting from a 3 per cent share, overtook India over this period.

It is, however, India's exports of non-traditional manufactures which finds her a place among the NICs. Since the mid-1960s India has added a number of fast growing items such as clothing, chemicals, leather manufactures, handicrafts and engineering goods to her list of exports. But her export performance in most of these goods has lacked the dynamism and competitive strength displayed by the other NICs. The total value of India's clothing exports in the early 1960s was virtually the same as that of South Korea and Taiwan, but by 1970 her Asian competitors had left her far behind. Again, in the early 1960s India's exports of engineering goods surpassed those of South Korea and the Latin American NICs; but she lost ground to her competitors in the 1970s. In chemicals, India's exports rose slowly until 1967/68 but accelerated thereafter. But here again India's export performance has lacked the momentum displayed by her competitors (see *Table I.1* in the Introduction to this volume).

Indeed, the buoyancy displayed by India's exports of manufactures during the 1960s appears to have been the result of a number of fortuitous factors which gave her a temporary competitive edge in external markets. Engineering goods, which now account for over 10 per cent of India's total exports, are an example. India exports a diverse range of products, from simple consumer goods and metal manufactures to sophisticated capital goods, and these exports accelerated during the mid-1960s. But the acceleration was mainly because of the recession in domestic demand, to the closure of the Suez Canal in 1967 and to the heavy export subsidies afforded to the engineering industry. Faced with a stagnant domestic market during the recession of 1965–67, firms may have turned to external markets, often selling goods below their average costs of production in an attempt to recoup as much of the fixed costs of production as possible. The closure of the Suez Canal in 1967 improved India's competitive position in Asian and East African markets relative to her European and American competitors. Export subsidies may have been crucial to India's export effort since it is reported that domestic market prices of engineering goods tend to be around 50 per cent higher than world market prices.

It is also significant that much of India's engineering goods exports, about 70 per cent, are directed to the developing countries. Of these, the Middle East accounts for around 36 per cent (principally the OPEC countries), South East Asia countries for 22 per cent and Africa for 14 per cent. The next biggest customers are the East European countries, principally the USSR, with a share of around 16 per cent in recent years. One of the principal reasons for the growth of India's engineering goods exports to these countries is her bilateral trade agreements with the East European countries, and with the United Arab Republic, Sudan, Iran and Nigeria among the developing countries. Increased exports to OPEC have been a consequence of the demand boom in these countries. Again, though the absolute value of India's exports to these countries has increased in recent years, she has not improved her competitive position.

The record is much the same with regard to the exports of most other manufactured goods. Although the absolute value of India's exports has increased, she has lost ground to her competitors. Indeed, the story of India's export performance is one of lack of competitiveness in external markets. Competitiveness in this context includes both price and non-price factors. That domestic demand pressures, high costs of production, non-availability of imported inputs and the poor quality of goods exported have been the main factors constraining India's export performance is an oft-repeated theme[7]. It is also generally accepted that many of these constraints can be traced to India's pursuit of a strategy of import-substituting industrialization.

However, at the same time, it may be argued that India's past performance offers no guide to her future growth and trade prospects. Furthermore, though the strategy of import-substituting industrialization may have constrained her export effort, it has endowed India with a diversified industrial structure. And in recent years the foreign trade regime has been liberalized. This includes both liberalization of imports and the provision of various incentives for exports. Also, as stated earlier, mainly because of the inflows of remittances from migrant workers, India now has substantial reserves of foreign exchange. As Helen Hughes asks (in ch. 5), now that India has a basic industrial structure in place, agricultural development is on its way, and the balance-of-payments position is healthy, why should not India rise to a 8 to 10 per cent growth performance?[8].

No doubt India possesses many of the ingredients necessary for a sustained development effort. But the successful application of these ingredients may largely depend on her ability to move away from the inward-looking strategy of development. This does not necessarily mean that India should concentrate its whole development directly and exclusively on an export drive. It could, indeed, be argued that an export-led strategy is not wholly appropriate to a country of India's size and resource endowments. However, emphasis on exports must be one element in an outward-looking strategy of development. Much more important are attitudes towards the role of competition and market forces in the development process. Import-substitution has been only one of the features of her development strategy. Much more significant is the panoply of restrictions India has imposed on the private sector and the importance she has attached to bureaucratic decision-making in the development process. Is it likely that India will make a clean break from the inward-looking policies of the past? And do recent developments herald a new era in her development effort? Before we discuss these issues it is in order to analyse briefly the rationale for the inward-looking policies and to review some of their consequences.

8.4 The 'in-principle' principle

Self-reliance has been a major theme in India's economic policy. As Michael Lipton and John Firn put it 'Self reliance in the Indian context does not mean "let us do what we are good at doing", but rather "leave us all we are in principle able to do – the "in-principle" principle.'[9] It is this principle which underlies the inward-looking development philosophy of India, with its emphasis on import-substituting industrialization. The main features of this strategy, which have been described by Bhagwati and Desai in detail, are quantitative restrictions on imports coupled with a complicated and excessively detailed system of industrial licensing and foreign exchange allocation. In the initial years, when the new nation-state was charting its development strategy, there may have been a rationale for the 'in-principle' principle. The size of the country, her diverse endowment of resources, the trained cadre of administrators she had inherited from the British and the enthusiasm of a new nation-state for development may have been this rationale.

The consequences of the pursuit of indiscriminate import-substituting industrialization in terms of the establishment of privately profitable but socially unprofitable industries, high degrees of under-utilized capacity, adverse effects on agriculture and widespread resource misallocation have often been noted. That such policies have also hindered exporting is also well established in the literature[10]. We note only the main points here. Such policies have resulted in highly profitable domestic markets, the attractions of which militated against exporting. A World Bank study reports that in all cases other than textile machinery, the fob export price was well below the domestic price – the discount ranging from 20 to 50 per cent[11]. It was only when various export incentives were provided that export profitability was close to that of domestic sales. Bhagwati and Srinivasan also estimate that the purchasing power parity exchange rate for imports was consistently higher than that for exports throughout the period 1950–1970, indicating the incentive for producing import substitutes. Further, the 'in-principle' principle also required export items to be manufactured with domestically produced inputs irrespective of their quality and price. The effects on exports to highly competitive international markets are all too obvious. It is these factors which have contributed to India's lack of competitiveness in external markets.

These consequences of the inward looking philosophy of development were all too clear by the 1960s – none more so than the fact that the strategy has had little success in alleviating unemployment or inequalities. Why then did India persist with the strategy, whereas countries such as South Korea opted for 'outward-looking' strategies after the first phase of easy import-substitution in consumer goods? It is often argued that it is India's size, her relatively high land–man ratio and the heterogeneity of her population which led her to adopt 'inward-looking' policies of development while the adoption of outward-looking policies by South Korea and Taiwan is explained by their small size and the high density and homogeneity of their populations.

Admittedly these factors may have played a role in shaping the differing economic philosophies of India and the other NICs. Their relatively small size may have forced countries such as Taiwan, Hong Kong and Singapore towards exporting. And India may have turned inward because of her size and the geographical diversity of her regions. India is often referred to as a continental economy, a characteristic feature of which is a relatively low dependence on international trade. But large size and geographical diversity of regions are not the only characteristics of a continental economy. The regions must be interdependent, they must be at a similar stage of development in terms of income levels and the magnitude of resources they possess, and they must be knit together by an efficient system of transportation and communications. The United States may be one such classic case of a continental economy. But India, as yet, is far from being a continental economy in this sense. While some regions of India are highly developed, others are economically backward by most criteria of development. India could be described as a continent because of her size, but she is not yet a continental economy. Again, inter-country comparisons of land–man ratios, if they are to be meaningful, have to be expressed in terms of cultivable land per head of population. India's land endowment in this respect may not be much different from that of Korea and Taiwan.

In any case, even if India's geophysical characteristics did differ markedly from the other NICs, it could at best explain her low dependence on international trade. But her inward-looking development philosophy is not confined to restrictions on imports. It also includes a detailed system of industrial licensing and a panoply of restrictions on the activities of private enterprise. These restrictions, coupled with the quantitative controls on imports, have served to limit both domestic and international competition, providing entrenched firms with monopolistic profits. The pertinent issue is: why has India persisted with this philosophy of inward-looking development, based on import-substituting industrialization, despite its acknowledged economic inefficiencies and social costs? A succinct answer is provided by Angus Maddison when he states that the industrial strategy 'won support from the bureaucratic establishment because it added to their power, it was supported by politicians because it encouraged their patronage, it met no opposition from established industry because it did not interfere with vested interests and it was supported by intellectuals who generally identified capitalism with colonialism. . . . It aroused no opposition because it conflicted with no vested interests.'[12]

It is this constellation of political and economic factors which explains India's continued adherence to an inward-looking strategy of development. The extensive system of industrial licensing and import controls has enjoyed considerable support from entrenched private firms and official circles: from private firms because it limits both internal and external competition; from official circles because it satisfies their socially motivated desire to control big business. Capping all this is the self-reliance syndrome referred to earlier. Self-reliance in the Indian context is equated with self-sufficiency in the sense that the country's requirements of goods and services must be met from internal sources. Hence the need to replace imports with domestic production. The desire for self-sufficiency is also motivated by nationalistic considerations – by the need to avoid foreign domination of the economy. Thus foreign private enterprise participation in the Indian economy, though not altogether shunned, is fettered by various restrictions and regulations. Much of it is confined to technology collaboration agreements and joint ventures between Indian and foreign firms.

India possesses considerable resources of land, manpower, industrial enterprise and administrative expertise. From a long-term perspective, the successful use of these resources for development depends on her willingness to open up an economy which for far too long has been protected against competitive pressures. This requires a mustering of the political will to change long-conditioned attitudes towards market forces, private enterprise and competition. Although recent developments such as the liberalization of imports suggest a relaxation of attitudes, India has a long way to go before she can aspire to the status of a fully fledged NIC. In the meantime she is saddled with the problems that are common to NICs – mounting import bills on account of oil and inflation.

8.5   Recent developments

In recent years, several changes have occurred in India. The comfortable foreign exchange position she now enjoys, the upward trend in food production and the acceleration of domestic savings rates were referred to earlier. At the same time there has been the liberalization of imports and the provision of various export incentives. But all this has been a result of fortuitous circumstances and may be transient. The inflow of remittances from abroad, the spurt in exports of manufactures and exceptionally good harvests in the late 1970s account for the relatively high savings rates and foreign exchange position.

Successive crop failures and a decline in the inflow of remittances could abruptly end the increase in savings and reserves. This may also put an end to liberalization of imports. In fact, in 1979 a severe and damaging drought hit most parts of the country bringing to an end the spell of good harvests that India had enjoyed in the four previous years. Because of the drought and rising world prices of imported goods, especially of oil, the stocks of food and foreign exchange have been declining.

Mainly because of the increase in prices of oil and imported food grains, India has experienced an annual rate of inflation of around 20 per cent since 1972/73, compared with a rate of 7 per cent during the 1960s. India's consumption of oil, at around 30 million tonnes a year, is much lower than that of most other developing countries. Of this, nearly a third is supplied from domestic sources. The country also possesses considerable reserves of crude oil, natural gas and coal. But the exploitation of these reserves requires heavy investment and India's dependence on external sources for her requirements of oil is unlikely to decline in the near future. Oil has accounted for around 25 per cent of the total value of imports in recent years, and in 1979/80 oil imports are expected to equal a massive 45 per cent of total export earnings. The trade deficit, which was estimated at around $1.6 billion in 1978/79, is expected to increase to $2.5 billion by the end of the fiscal year 1979/80; some estimates put it even higher at around $3.75 billion[13]. The inflows of remittances from abroad, foreign aid and earnings from tourism may not cover this deficit and India may have to draw heavily on her reserves.

All this points to the imperative need to promote exports. The point made earlier in this paper bears repeating; although India's exports of manufactured goods have shown an upward trend in the 1970s, this export performance compares poorly with that of the other NICs. Again, it is internal factors – such as domestic demand pressures, lack of imported inputs, shortage of power in recent years and the absence of a sustained marketing effort – rather than external demand factors, which have constrained India's exports. Mitigation of these internal constraints requires an all-out commitment to exports. Despite official policy pronouncements favouring export promotion, there is little by way of an orchestrated programme. The cumbersome and complicated nature of India's export incentive schemes, subject to frequent changes and alterations, has often been noted. And the debate on the relative costs and benefits of export-led growth continues, despite the demonstrable success of the NICs with this strategy, and the compelling need to increase exports if only to finance the mounting oil bill.

Another key constraint on India's development effort is the performance of the agricultural sector. Admittedly weather conditions have been an important factor influencing India's agricultural performance. However, agricultural development is also dependent on infrastructural investments in land improvement and irrigation, and on institutional factors such as land reform. Indian economic planning has frequently been criticized for the low priority accorded to agriculture. There are various strains in this criticism, including the charges that not enough resources have been devoted to agriculture, that agricultural prices have been deliberately kept too low and that institutional reforms have been neglected. Whether or not the total resources devoted to agriculture have been inadequate is debatable. This depends on whether one includes private sector investments in agriculture and on whether account is taken of the indirect positive effects of some industrial investments on agriculture[14]. It cannot, however, be denied that in the context of an overall economic strategy which emphasized import-substituting industrialization, agriculture was accorded a low priority. Especially glaring is the neglect of institutional changes such as land reform and asset redistribution. John P. Lewis's comment in the 1960s that 'Indians are better talkers than doers, better planners than executors'. is nowhere as evident as in the domain of land reform[15].

The effects of asset redistribution and land reform on agricultural productivity and income distribution need no elaboration. It is not only the 'outward-looking' strategies of development followed by South Korea and Taiwan, but also their successful land reforms, which account for the relatively small income inequalities that prevail in these countries[16]. India presents a glaring contrast. An impressive amount of legislation has been enacted but little of it has been implemented. Pranab Bardhan sums up the situation: 'Laws setting ceilings on private ownership of land with provision for redistribution of surplus land adorn the statute books of all states in India. Yet by the end of 1970, for the country as a whole, the "declared surplus" has only been 2.4 million acres and the "area distributed" just half of that, or 0.3 per cent of the total cultivated land.'[17] Equally dismal has been the fate of tenancy legislation designed to provide security of tenure to tenant cultivators and that of legislation relating to rent ceilings.

It is, however, to be noted that the draft five-year plan for 1978–1983 formulated by the Janata government had placed a major emphasis on the development of agriculture. The plan had provision for redirecting public investment towards agriculture, irrigation and infrastructure development. Promotion of appropriate labour intensive technologies, land reform, special programmes for the assistance of backward areas, rural development and promotion of small-scale industries all figured prominently in this plan. Investment in agriculture, irrigation and small-scale industries were to account for 30.1 per cent of a total planned investment of Rs 693 billion. This figure represents a sizeable increase over that of the previous five-year plans (*Table 8.8*). The draft plan also set a growth rate target of 4.7 per cent a year, which (though slower than projected in the earlier five-year plans) is faster than the 3.5 per cent achieved so far.

This plan, however, has been shelved by the new Congress government headed by Mrs Gandhi, which came to power at the beginning of 1980. In any case it is doubtful whether a plan of this size could have been executed. Because of continuing inflation and increases in oil prices it would soon have come up against resource constraints. Although the domestic savings rate has increased appreciably, and currently exceeds the rate of domestic investment,

Table 8.8 India's actual outlays under plans, by sectors (Rs billion, percentages in brackets)

Plan period	Agriculture and allied programmes	Irrigation and flood control	Industry and minerals	Power	Transport and Communications	Social Services	Others	Total
1951–56	2.35 (11.99)	3.78 (19.28)	0.97 (4.95)	2.60 (13.26)	5.18 (26.43)	4.12 (21.02)	0.60 (3.06)	19.60 (100.00)
1956–61	4.55 (9.74)	5.24 (11.22)	11.25 (24.08)	4.52 (0.67)	12.61 (26.99)	7.58 (16.22)	0.97 (2.08)	46.72 (100.00)
1961–66	8.55 (9.97)	9.34 (10.89)	19.67 (22.93)	12.52 (14.60)	21.12 (24.62)	12.96 (15.11)	1.61 (1.88)	85.77 (100.00)
1969–74	16.83 (10.67)	18.67 (11.83)	31.07 (19.69)	29.32 (18.58)	30.80 (19.52)	24.37 (15.44)	6.73 (4.26)	157.79 (100.00)
1974–78 (estimates)	29.76 (10.26)	34.61 (11.94)	73.59 (25.38)	54.22 (18.70)	52.26 (18.03)	38.12 (13.15)	7.35 (2.53)	289.91 (100.00)
1978–83 (draft plan projections)	86.00 (12.40)	96.50 (13.91)	146.90 (21.17)	157.50 (22.70)	105.78 (15.25)	89.75 (12.94)	11.37 (1.64)	693.80 (100.00)

Data are for fiscal years beginning 1 April

Source: Planning Commission, Government of India

the upward trend in savings is unlikely to be sustained. Furthermore, the projected rate of growth of domestic investment of around 10.7 per cent a year would have required a substantial increase in the savings rate.

The new Government has yet to enunciate its economic policy. At the moment its main concern is with containing the rate of inflation. The indications are that the new Government is more favourably inclined to the private sector, but whether this also implies opening up the economy to competition is yet to be seen. Although the Congress party in its election manifesto indicated its hostility to the multinationals, press statements by Mrs Indira Gandhi suggest that the Government is likely to extend at least a lukewarm welcome to foreign private enterprise. Indeed, India has always vacillated between hostility and lukewarm welcome to foreign private investment. India is likely to maintain her preference for technology licensing agreements and joint ventures, while resisting wholly-owned foreign subsidiaries. However, without increased participation of foreign enterprises, India may find it hard to increase her competitiveness in the exports of engineering goods. Even the developing countries are getting increasingly conscious of the quality of imported goods and in future they will increasingly require technologically sophisticated products. It is significant that it is the Indian firms with foreign technology licensing agreements which account for a high proportion of India's exports of engineering goods. It is also to be noted that the Asian NICs owe much of their export success to foreign enterprise participation in their economies.

Further, the growth prospects for India – even the relatively modest growth rate of 4.5 per cent set as a target by the Janata government – may depend heavily on ability to attract foreign capital and technology. As suggested earlier, the country may not be able to sustain a high enough rate of domestic savings. And although in recent years foreign aid flows to India have been rising (*Table 8.9*), whether this momentum will be kept up depends both on the growth prospects of aid donors and on political factors. In favourable

Table 8.9 *Gross aid disbursements to India (Rs billion)*

	1960/61	1965/66	1970/71	1975/76	1976/77	1977/78
Net national product at factor cost (1970/71 prices)	241.83	270.49	344.12	398.49	403.95	433.95
Gross aid disbursements	4.20	7.94	8.82	20.26	17.58	14.28
Aid as percentage of NNP	1.74	2.93	2.56	5.08	4.35	3.29

Data are for fiscal years beginning 1 April

Sources: Ministry of Finance, Government of India
Central Statistical Organization, Government of India, *National Accounts Statistics*

circumstances, foreign private investment may prove to be a main source of capital and technology for the country. But if the political opposition to foreign private capital prevails, India is unlikely to import it on a major scale.

Thus recent developments do not suggest sanguine prospects for India attaining a growth rate of 4.5 per cent over the medium term. In fact, press reports suggest that in 1980 the growth rate may be negative. Whether India will rise to the challenge by opening up her economy to competition, promoting exports and liberalizing the restrictions on foreign private investment is a matter for speculation.

One other recent development which has attracted attention is India's *exports* of technology and consultancy services, principally to the OPEC countries. For several reasons India is well placed to emerge as a significant exporter of technology to the developing countries. With the growth in the size and complexity of her manufacturing sector, there has been a steady increase in the need for modern technology. India has acquired these capabilities through both imports of technology and her own efforts. Indian technology now is an amalgam of indigenous and imported technology and is particularly well suited to the needs of other developing countries. India now has several large and medium-sized consultancy houses. These have been active in the Middle East, providing a range of consultancy services including plant design, basic engineering, construction management and start-up services. Many of these consultancy contracts have been won against stiff competition from the developed countries.

India has also entered into a number of joint-ventures with firms in other developing countries. Most of these joint-ventures are in Southeast Asia and Africa. Firms from developing countries, such as India, possess distinct advantages over the established multinational enterprises from the developed countries in pursuing operations in other developing countries. They are willing to form joint-ventures with local entrepreneurs and are less concerned about the possible erosion of their technological information. They have an expertise in the production of unsophisticated, low technology goods. Their technology is more appropriate to local factor costs. It is reported in a case study on foreign direct investment in Thailand that developing country firms, especially Indian firms, used fully efficient technology with costs of production often below the theoretical minimum cost[18].

Indeed, there are good grounds to argue that it is the import-substituting industrialization strategy of India which has given Indian firms an incentive to engage in adaptive research. The 'in principle' principle requires locally owned firms to use indigenous inputs. This creates a need to adapt their technology to the use of these inputs. Much of the research and deveopment in Indian industry may have been directed at adaptation of materials and imported technology to suit local needs. It is also to be noted that research and development expenditure in India, though not high, is steadily increasing. It rose from 0.23 per cent of GNP in 1958/59 to 0.54 per cent in 1971/72 (the latest data readily available). Further, private sector expenditure on research and development has also steadily increased as a percentage of the total from 0.5 per cent in 1958/59 to 8 per cent in 1971/72[19]. For these reasons India may emerge as a significant exporter of technology to other developing countries. This may be an area where Indian firms and foreign firms from developed countries could collaborate. Foreign firms could complement the low level technology and labour skills of Indian firms with their managerial and marketing expertise.

8.6 Conclusions

This paper has attempted a brief survey of India's recent development experience and future prospects. The main issue addressed is the prospects for India's exports. This has necessarily involved an analysis of India's development strategy, especially in view of her pursuit of an "inward-looking" strategy of development. One of the main conclusions is that domestic constraints resulting from the strategy of import-substituting industrialization have been a major factor in deterring India's exports. It is also argued that though India's manufacturing exports have shown a buoyant trend in recent years, there is little reason to expect India to match the performance of other newly industrializing countires such as South Korea and Taiwan. It is, however, likely that India's exports will continue to expand in clothing, leather manufactures and handicrafts in which she has a comparative advantage. But these are just the goods in which India is likely to face external constraints in the form of quota restrictions. It is in this sphere that developed countries can make a contribution to India's development effort – by removing quantitative restrictions on imports.

In engineering goods, the other fast-growing item in India's exports, external constraints may not be a major problem. As yet India has an insignificant share in world exports of engineering goods and much of India's trade in this category is with the OPEC countries, the Southeast Asian countries and the East European countries. The major factors influencing India's exports of engineering goods are her productive capacity and her ability to maintain and improve the quality of these exports. India possesses considerable technological skills, but her export competitiveness in engineering goods may depend on continued access to modern technology which could be provided only by the multinational enterprises from the developed countries.

In general, although the absolute value of non-traditional exports may continue to grow at the rate recently achieved, India is unlikely to emerge as a major exporter, matching the performance of the other Asian NICs, in the foreseeable future. Supply constraints are likely to continue to bedevil India's export performance. As yet there are no indications that India is willing to depart in a major way from her inward-looking policies of development. Furthermore, the gestation lag involved in switching from an import-substituting strategy to a successful export-oriented one could be considerable. The entrepreneurial expertise required to serve a protected and secure domestic market is not the same as that required to cater to a highly competitive and uncertain export market. Indian entrepreneurs, conditioned to operating in a protected domestic market environment, may find it hard to make the transition to operating in export markets. India's attitude towards foreign private enterprise participation is also a factor inhibiting her export performance. She has not had the widespread sub-contracting and production sharing agreements of the type that the Asian NICs have used to build up their export markets. The one institutional arrangement enabling India to increase exports of manufactures in recent years is the bilateral trading agreements with the Eastern European countries. The present Government, which is favourably inclined towards forging stronger links with the USSR, may continue these trading arrangements, and India's exports to Eastern Europe may continue to grow.

It is also argued in the paper that India's future prospects, not only for exports, but also for growth in general, may hinge on her willingness to adopt outward-looking strategies of development. It could, however, be countered that for a country of India's size and diversity there could be no single effective macroeconomic policy. This may be so. But the advocacy of an outward-looking strategy does not necessarily imply an export-led growth strategy. The need is to open the economy to forces of competition and for resource allocation to be based on comparative advantage. This does *not* also imply that India should depart from her philosophy of fostering a mixed economy. It is just that the efficiency of public sector enterprises should also be measured by considerations of profitability, cost effectiveness and their ability to withstand competition.

Recent trends, however, suggest that an all-out export effort may prove an imperative necessity for India. In the face of a mounting import bill, mainly because of the increase in oil prices, India's ability to maintain even the modest rate of growth of 3–4 per cent achieved in the recent past may depend on her ability to increase her export earnings. Whether India will do so appears to be largely a question of ability to muster the political will to make a break from the inward-looking strategies of development hitherto pursued.

In sum, India has the potential and the necessary prerequisites to achieve a major expansion in her exports. She is well placed to do so because of her endowment of natural resources, the industrial structure she has in place and the administrative expertise she possesses. Whether she will in fact emerge as a major exporter is largely a matter for speculation. This paper has argued that she is unlikely to do so in the foreseeable future.

References

1 India's rank among the nations of the world in terms of manufacturing output is variously put as tenth, fifteenth and twentieth. She is probably the world's twentieth manufacturing nation, or fifteenth in the non-communist world.

2 J. N. Bhagwati and T. N. Srinivasan, *Foreign Trade Regimes and Economic Development; India. National Bureau of Economic Research, Conference Series on Foreign Trade Regimes and Economic Development* 6, *India*, New York, 1975, p. 16.

3 'Indian Economy through National Income Statistics'. *Reserve Bank of India Bulletin*, July 1979.

4 J. N. Bhagwati, and P. Desai, *India Planning for Industrialization*. Oxford University Press, London, 1970.

5 For a detailed analysis of these policies see J. N. Bhagwati and P. Desai, *India Planning for Industrialization*. Oxford University Press, London, 1970.

6 See also ch. 1.

7 For a detailed review of India's export performance see D. Nayyar, *India's Exports and Export Policies in the 1960s*. Cambridge University Press, London, 1976 and World Bank, *India: Export Performance, Problems and Policies*. May 1977.

8 See ch. 5.

9 M. Lipton and J. Firn, *The Erosion of a Relationship: India and Britain Since 1960*. Oxford University Press, London, 1975, p. 219.

10 See J. N. Bhagwati and P. Desai, *India Planning for Industrialization*. Oxford University Press, London, 1970 and J. N. Bhagwati and T. N. Srinivasan, *National Bureau of Economic Research, Conference Series on Foreign Trade Regimes and Economic Development*. 6, *India*, New York, 1975.

11 World Bank, *India: Export Performance, Problems and Policies*. May 1977.

12 A. Maddison, *Class Structure and Economic Growth*. Allen and Unwin, London, 1971, pp. 89–90.

13 *The Financial Times*, Special Supplement on India. 17 March 1980.

14 For a discussion of these issues see P. Chaudhuri, 'India: Objectives, Achievements and Constraints'. In P. Chadhuri (ed.), *Aspects of Indian Economic Development*. Allen and Unwin, London, 1971.

15 J. P. Lewis, *Quiet Crisis in India*. Anchor Books, New York, 1964, p. 5.

16 See country studies by J. Adelman on Korea and by G. Ranis on Taiwan. In H. B. Chenery *et al.* (ed.), *Redistribution with Growth*. Oxford University Press, London, 1974.

17 P. K. Bardhan on India. In H. B. Chenery *et al.* (eds.), *Redistribution with Growth*. Oxford University Press, London, 1974.

18 D. Lecraw, 'Direct Investment by Firms from Less Developed Countries'. *Oxford Economic Papers* 29 (3), 1977, p. 42.

19 J. N. Bhagwati and T. N. Srinivasan, *National Bureau of Economic Research, Conference Series on Foreign Trade Regimes and Economic Development* 6, *India*, New York, 1975.

9

Brazil

Ambassador Roberto de Oliveira Campos and
Dr Raphael Valentino

Henry William Spiegel begins his famous book on Brazil by writing, 'There is no other tropical country in the world where Western civilization has flowered more richly than in Brazil[1]. This fact alone, with all the qualifications it requires, is sufficient to make the country one of the most interesting cases in the study of development theory.

W. W. Rostow locates the Brazilian national take-off in the period 1933–1950, whereas São Paulo's regional take-off is described as having occurred from 1900 to 1928[2]. Although these landmarks may be debatable in the light of recent research, the most challenging question in this matter is related to the leading forces behind Brazil's neo-capitalism, which has been late and successful, despite great obstacles from the outside world and far from negligible contradictions in its internal process.

9.1   The three stages of industrialization

For brevity, we distinguish three main stages in Brazilian industrialization: the first industrialization of São Paulo, the import-substituting industrialization which started in the mid-1950s, and the second-generation import-substituting industrialization, which has been the Brazilian anti-recession response to the present world economic troubles. At least since the mid-1960s, however, there has also been a growing stress on export expansion. With such a selective emphasis, we do not intend to ignore the fact that a sizeable degree of industrialization had been achieved before World War I: the 1890s, and the six to eight years preceding the war (incidentally, both periods coincided with booming export activity in Brazilian primary production).

The industrialization of São Paulo: an entrepreneurial export-led growth

The industrialization of São Paulo depended from the beginning upon the demand generated by the growing overseas market for coffee. 'For fifty years', Warren Dean writes, 'the trade gained ground in Europe and stimulated the establishment of new plantings further and further to the west. . . . Demand in the United States and Europe was growing as industrialization increased productivity; Brazil's coffee was suitable for consumption for the masses.'[3]

Agricultural exports and industrial investment were closely related and immigrant entrepreneurs as well as immigrant firms played a decisive role in a movement away from the monocultural export dependency. Although both of them were originally established to service the foreign trade sector, they came to mobilize local savings along with foreign capital and thus became an important factor as purveyors of financial services to the economy generally[4]. Coffee and the linked development of railways, agricultural exports such as raw cotton, and industrial investment, were successively the major components of the first alliances which provided the bases for the Brazilian industrialization in its initial stage.

The import-substituting industrialization actually started in the mid-1950s. Incidentally, in Latin America as a whole, the phase of export-propelled growth (*crecimiento hacia afuera*) based on primary products lasted roughly from the middle of the nineteenth century until the Great Depression. As Hirschman points out, it took another 20 years, from 1929 to the Prebisch manifesto of 1949, before export-propelled growth ceased to be the official Latin American doctrine. Then came the next phase of Latin American growth, *crecimento hacia adentro*, i.e. growth by means of the domestic market. As Hirschman himself summarizes, this second stage of Latin American growth gathered strength during the Great Depression and World War II, flourished briefly in both theory and practice during the 1950s and was pronounced either dead or a dud in the 1960s[5]. But this death was not to be the last one; many revivals were to follow.

The inward-looking strategies: industrialization in the 1950s

It is useful to have in mind these distinct origins of import-substituting industrialization: *wars, balance-of-payments difficulties, growth of the domestic market* (as a result of export growth) and *official development policy*. Hirschman rightly stresses that industrialization as a result of export growth has a wholly different *Gestalt* from one that feeds on foreign exchange deprivation. In the latter situation it seems much more likely that inflationary developments will accompany the industrialization process.

Despite the wide variety of its national strategies, Latin American import-substituting industrialization has emerged from common theoretical and ideological roots. The Prebisch manifesto of 1949 opened with a description of the plight of the 'periphery' – this peripheral description being applicable to Latin America – and fervently preached a policy of deliberate industrialization for the Continent. It over-emphasized the asymmetry in the relations between the 'centre' and the 'periphery', an asymmetry which traditional theory was accused of having overlooked.

As Baer and Kerstenetzky point out[6], both critics and defenders of the Brazilian import-substituting policies of the 1950s would probably agree that they left a legacy of problems with which policy-makers in the 1960s would have to come to grips in order to assure continued economic growth. First, agriculture had been neglected, despite some investment in marketing facilities and extension services at various periods of time. It is generally accepted that although agriculture expanded satisfactorily when compared with the growth of population, this was more a result of extensive agriculture than increased productivity in older agricultural areas. Second, inflation was rising at rates that eliminated its possible contribution to growth through a forced savings mechanism. Finally, there were increasing balance-of-payments pressures, stemming from the fact that a subsantial part of the growth in the 1950s, especially the second half of the 1950s, was financed not by local savings but through a substantial influx of foreign capital, both in the form of direct investment and loans. By the beginning of the 1960s, Brazil's foreign debt had already reached more than $2 billion.

Among several interpretations of the slowing down of the growth rates in Brazil in the early and mid-1960s, one deserves particular emphasis – the import constraint explanation: Brazil paid little attention to exports whereas prime emphasis was placed on domestic production of formerly imported goods. As a consequence, the import coefficient was brought down, but an incompressible part remained, which could not be replaced at all or only in the very long term. As these imported inputs were of crucial importance in the short and medium term for continued growth, a decline of such imports because of balance-of-payments pressures forced a contraction in the rate of growth of industrial production.

It goes without saying that the 'import constraint' is not an exhaustive explanation of the deceleration of growth in Brazil in the early and mid-1960s. The phenomenon was far more complex, involving run-away inflation, a breakdown of social discipline and a political impasse. An exercise in 'reinvented realism' was needed after years of 'psychedelic developmentalism', which caused Brazil to experience stagflation in 1963/64, well before this hybrid creature made its appearance on the European scene.

Re-invented realism

One of the recipes of 're-invented realism' was the restoration of the country's external competitiveness which culminated in the adoption of a 'trotting peg' system for the determination of the foreign exchange price of cruzeiro. As a consequence of 're-invented realism', in addition to achieving high rates of overall export growth since the late 1960s, Brazil significantly diversified the commodity structure of her exports. Over the 20 years from 1957 to 1977, coffee declined from over 60 per cent to little more than 20 per cent of

Table 9.1 *Brazil: commodity structure of exports and imports*

SITC	Exports 1957 (%)	Exports 1967 (%)	Exports 1977 (%)	Imports 1957 (%)	Imports 1967 (%)	Imports 1977 (%)
Primary products						
0,1 *Food, beverages and tobacco, of which*	76.5	63.7	51.9	12.1	18.9	6.4
071 Coffee	60.8	42.6	21.7			
061 Sugar and products	3.3	5.1	4.3	..	..	..
072 Cocoa	6.6	5.1	5.0	..	..	..
2,4 *Crude materials, oils and fats, of which*	21.3	25.8	20.2	5.2	4.5	3.4
263 Raw cotton	4.6	5.6	0.4	..	..	..
24 Wood and cork	3.4	3.8	0.7	..	..	..
281.3 Iron ore	3.5	6.2	7.1	..	..	..
421.2 Soya bean oil	..	..	2.3	..	..	..
3 *Mineral fuels, of which*	0.2	0.1	1.8	19.5	15.6	34.0
331,332 Petroleum and products	..	..	..	17.9	13.2	31.8
Manufactures etc.						
5–9 *Total manufactures, of which*	2.0	10.5	26.1	63.3	60.9	56.2
5 Chemicals	0.5	1.8	1.5	9.7	13.8	14.7
67 Iron and steel	0.3	2.9	2.2	8.5	4.2	4.5
7 less 732 Machinery and transport equipment[a]	0.1	2.6	8.5	28.3	26.0	24.8
732 Road motor vehicles	..	..	3.0	7.0	2.5	1.1
65 Textile yarns and fabrics	..	..	3.2	0.5	0.2	0.6
841 Clothing	..	..	0.8	..	..	..
Total all commodities	100	100	100	100	100	100
Total in $ million	1392	1654	12 120	1488	1667	13 254

[a] Excluding road motor vehicles

Source: United Nations *Yearbooks of International Trade Statistics*

Brazilian exports. This is in contrast to the growth of non-traditional primary exports such as soybeans and iron ore; and the share of manufactured exports increased from 2 per cent in 1957 to 26 per cent in 1977 (*Table 9.1*). The main feature in the structure of imports was the great increase in petroleum imports which, by 1977, represented nearly one-third of total imports. The oil crisis drove home the point that the pattern of the Brazilian development was oil-intensive and unleashed a search for alternative energy sources.

For manufacturing, we can look at the phase 1967–1974 as one of 'growth-generating' imports, in the sense that a substantial growth of domestic production was fostered by an even more substantial increase of manufactured imports (*Table 9.2*). The relative share of imports in the total

Table 9.2 *Manufacturing sector: production, exports, imports and the important coefficient: 1965–1975 (in 1970 cruzeiros billion)*

Year	Production P	Exports X	Imports M	Total domestic supply $M + P - X$	Imports as % of domestic supply $\dfrac{M}{M + P - X}$	Exports as % of production X/P
1965	57.4	1.2	4.1	60.3	6.9	2.1
1966	64.5	1.3	5.7	68.9	8.3	2.0
1967	65.5	1.4	6.5	70.6	9.2	2.1
1968	76.6	1.5	8.8	83.9	10.5	2.0
1969	84.6	1.9	9.4	92.1	10.2	2.2
1970	95.5	2.2	11.9	105.2	11.3	2.3
1971	109.1	2.2	15.6	122.5	12.8	2.0
1972	128.9	3.4	19.1	144.6	13.2	2.6
1973	149.3	5.2	22.8	166.9	13.7	3.5
1974	160.6	5.4	32.3	187.5	17.2	3.4
1975	165.6	5.9	28.8	188.5	15.3	3.6

Source: P. S. Malan and R. Bonelli, 'The Brazilian Economy in the Seventies: Old and New Developments'. *World Development* 5 (5), nos. 1/2, January–February 1977, p. 31

domestic supply of manufactures grew from 6.9 per cent in 1965 to 17.2 per cent in 1974, a figure comparable to the levels reached in the mid-1950s. Malan and Bonelli argue that this seems to imply that decades of import substitution industrialization have come to naught; Baer and Von Doellinger modify this judgement, saying that Brazil's import substituting strategy of development was both a success and a failure. 'It resulted in the industrialization of the country. It did not, however, reduce the external dependency; it only changed the nature of this dependency. . . . The strategy made the country more dependent on inputs to run its industrial park[7]'.

In fact, we could distinguish, in our selective industrialization chronology, a second-generation import-substituting strategy, which started after the oil crisis in 1974, with great emphasis on capital goods and intermediate inputs.

Some qualitative keynotes characterize the three stages we discuss in this section.

Henri Pirenne has stressed that for each stage of economic history, there is a distinct and separate class of capitalists[8]. The industrialization of São Paulo as discussed above was particularly fertile in 'entrepreneurial-mindedness creation'. 'The industrialists of São Paulo emerged', says Warren Dean, 'during the 30 years following the establishment of the Republic, as a large and distinct economic group, nearly as important as the plantation and mercantile elites from which they evolved.'[9]

The first generation import-substitution was largely marked by an economic coalition between the state sponsorship and the foreign investor, national entrepreneurs being more visible in traditional industries or as suppliers and sub-contractors for the new industries.

Lately, new organizational forms have emerged. In the new petrochemical and metal processing industries there is often a tripartite formula, in which state companies, foreign entrepreneurs (providing the technology) and national private entrepreneurs work together. Sometimes this formula becomes quadripartite, through the participation of international or governmental financial agencies such as the International Finance Corporation, acting largely as catalytic agents for project implementation.

9.2   An assessment of import-substitution policies

A critical assessment of the Brazilian policies in their different stages, as described above, may now be attempted. To the historical phasing, we could add a functional classification of import-substituting policies to assess the distortions to which such policies have led. In this connection, three main biases could be distinguished:

(1) Import restrictions against non-essentials, unaccompanied by demand-curbing consumption taxes, tend to stimulate domestic substitutes. Accordingly, the pattern of industrialization was distorted in response to the higher profitability of the sheltered sectors.
(2) Import-substitution has placed prime emphasis upon final goods and neglected incentives to domestic production of basic inputs.
(3) Exaggerated emphasis was placed on capital goods import–substitution, especially from 1974 to 1979, with a number of drawbacks: it made it more difficult to incorporate continuous tehnological changes in rapidly evolving industries and it precluded processing industries from access to imported capital goods at cheaper prices and more comfortable delivery terms and payment conditions, thus hindering their export competitiveness.

The main distortion of import-substituting policies as a whole was, however, the one-sided view which prevailed for many years, stressing the potential domestic virtues of import-substitution, and without adequate attention to export promotion. Brazil's lack of interest in exporting was only reversed in the mid-1960s. As is well known, a sound export policy must encompass inducements to industry to attain competitive costs and must remove the various barriers in the way of those who make the effort. As Joel Bergsman put it, for many years policies in Brazil lessened the inducement to become competitive, while the overvalued export exchange rate meant that Brazilian manufacturers had to be more than competitive in order to compete, and even then saw export profit margins which were only a fraction of domestic ones[10]. One of the prevailing fears before the mid-1960s about primary exports was that increased exports of food products would probably imply higher domestic prices, a result which need not occur if the availability of foreign markets encourages additional production. Likewise, attention was not paid to the fact that increased inducements to exports of manufactures could mean greater productivity, faster innovation, better quality control and greater economies of scale for Brazilian industrial products.

The shift towards a more export-promoting stance in the mid-1960s meant, as stated above, a significant structural change in economic performance and entrepreneurial mentality. Bela Balassa points out that among 11 semi-industrial developing countries[11], Brazil's export performance in non-traditional primary products (an increase of 27 per cent in 1966–1973) was exceeded solely by South Korea (35 per cent), and her rate of growth of manufactured exports of 38 per cent was surpassed only by South Korea (51 per cent), Taiwan (47 per cent), and Singapore (42 per cent). At the same time, Brazil exceeded the average rate of growth of exports for the 11 countries (18 per cent for non-traditional primary products and 27 per cent for manufactured goods, between 1966 and 1973)[12]. All the same, the proportion of manufacturing output exported, although increasing, remains very small (*Table 9.2*).

Bela Balassa also underlines some particular features of the second generation Brazilian import-substituting policy, which are worth noting. In the capital goods industry, domestic production has been promoted by means of import protection and production subsidies. In the case of intermediate products the Government itself has promoted, or undertaken, investments within the framework of the Second National Development Plan (1975–1980). We would not entirely subscribe to Balassa's criticism of such investments, but it is fair to recognize that in many cases these investments were not subject to rigorous economic project appraisal and seem to have reflected the worn-out philosophy of import-substitution 'at any cost'.

In a broad assessment, Brazil's second and third-generation industrial spurts were quite impressive, in spite of the distortions already pointed out. By the early 1970s, Brazil's industrial establishment was already large enough to preclude considering her as merely a peripheral pre-industrial country. The point can be made quite simply by comparing Brazilian outputs of a few industrial commodities with the outputs of her former major supplier of manufactures, Great Britain (see *Table 9.3*). In 1960, Brazilian outputs were still only a small proportion of British. By the late 1970s, output in Brazil of these products had rapidly approached that in Britain. At these rates of relative advance, Brazilian output in a number of basic products will soon surpass the British level[13].

Table 9.3 *Brazilian and United Kingdom outputs of some industrial commodities (Brazilian output as a percentage of UK)*

	1960 (%)	1970 (%)	1978 (%)
Pig iron	11	24	88
Crude steel ingots	9	19	60
Cement	33	52	146
Passenger cars	4	16	44
Tyres	19	26	65
Television receivers	9	33	78

Source: United Nations *Statistical Yearbook*, 1977, and *Monthly Bulletin of Statistics*, various issues

The role of foreign capital in Brazilian industrialization has been often misconstrued both by unjustified laudatory appraisals and by xenophobic rejections. It would be tempting to argue that import-substituting industrialization was mainly carried out by foreign direct investment, because of the simultaneity of both phenomena. The four industries in which most foreign investment was concentrated in 1973 (chemicals, transport equipment, electrical equipment and metallurgy) accounted for 62 per cent of Brazil's imports of manufactured goods in 1949. On the other hand, the five (light) industries that had the smallest amounts of foreign investment in 1973 accounted for only 1 per cent of manufactured imports in 1949.

In the light of the recent measures adopted by the Brazilian government (described below) it is urgent to re-assess the role of the foreign sector at the present stage of the Brazilian development. The mutual interplay of direct investment, foreign indebtedness and export-promotion must be analysed in order to achieve their joint optimization. In his already cited article, Bela Balassa stresses that Brazil has comparative advantages in the production of some products such as pulp and paper, where world supply has the tendency to rise at a lower rate than demand. Brazil may also be capable of producing steel competitively. These are among the sectors in which import-substituting industrialization should proceed along the lines defined in the mid-1970s, if necessary in association with foreign capital mainly for absorption of technology.

9.3   Brazil as an NIC – problems and prospects

Contemporary Brazil can be described much more as a threshold country than as a purely semi-industrialized country. In fact, as an exporter of primary products, she shares the frustrations of developing countries at price instability and protectionist trade barriers imposed by industrialized countries against primary imports. As a semi-industrialized country and a very hungry capital importer, she has acquired a good understanding of the problems of trade, investment and transfer of technology.

Before the 1973/74 oil crisis, Brazil had managed to reconcile three desirable objectives:

(1)   acceleration of the rate of economic growth, which topped 10 per cent a year in real terms between 1968 and 1973;
(2)   deceleration of inflation, which had declined by 1973 to a yearly rate of about 15 per cent (from nearly 100 per cent in 1964); and
(3)   accumulation of foreign exchange reserves, which exceeded $6 billion by the end of 1976. The increase of 158 per cent in GNP and the doubling of the per capita real income in 12 years (1964–1976) were indeed an extraordinary performance which lent credence to its description as the 'Brazilian miracle'.

After the oil crisis, Brazil had to choose between two paths of adjustment, one rapid and the other gradualist – cathartic recession or structural transformation. The choice between the two reflected different evaluations of priorities. Most of the industrialized countries which make up the OECD group have given priority to price stability and the correction of balance-of-payments deficits, goals for which they inaugurated policies of monetary and fiscal restraint.

Some developing countries, among them Brazil, chose a different and more gradualist path of adjustment. Their priorities were growth of output and employment rather than price stability or external balance. This was the *strategy of structural transformation*, which aimed at a gradual absorption of balance-of-payments deficits by a combined effort of import restraint, import-substitution and export-diversification. This strategy involves, of course, accepting additional inflationary pressures during the adjustment period, as well as increases in foreign indebtedness in order to finance continuous economic expansion.

Brazil in the last five years since the energy crisis has experienced both the favourable and the unfavourable effects of the strategy of structural transformation. The first advantage was the avoidance of a major employment crisis which would be politically explosive in a country of rapid population growth. The second was an expansion and diversification of output. Between 1974 and 1978, the economy grew by over 7 per cent a year. The unfavourable results, predictably enough, were a sharp upturn of inflation and an excessive dependence on foreign finance for coverage of current account deficits.

The second wave of oil price increases in 1979 aggravated the unfavourable effects, by pushing both the rate of inflation and of growth of foreign indebtedness to unacceptable levels.

In December 1979 a new economic package was presented by the Government, encompassing measures of acute economic realism in the face of the double plague that the national economy is experiencing – inflation and external disequilibrium. On the anti-inflationary front, government investments are to be cut, taxes increased, subsidized rates for utilities and fuel discontinued and a new statutory wage policy put into effect. There will be greater emphasis placed on hitherto neglected agricultural development and curbs are to be imposed on the proliferation of government enterprises beyond the normal confines of governmental action. The package includes a maxi-devaluation of about 30 per cent, superimposed on the system of periodical mini-devaluations, and elimination of export subsidies and import deposits.

In fact, the periodical mini-devaluations, especially after 1973, had consistently lagged behind the domestic inflation rate, even if we subtract the inflation rate of the country's main trade partners; domestic inflation started to increase again after the constant decline of the period 1967–1973. Initially, the export incentive programme provided a compensation which was more than adequate to offset the negative effects of an overvalued cruzeiro. In the mid-1970s, the reluctance to devalue grew, for fear that devaluation might considerably increase inflationary pressures; but the result was a system of export subsidies which in itself became inflationary.

The promotion of manufactured exports is one wing of the strategy for the 1980s and is based on Brazil's export performance during the 'miracle years'. Efforts are being made to concentrate the attention of industry and business on the improvement of marketing strategies rather than on claims for government subsidies and incentives; to suggest selected areas for aggressive export campaigns, stressing particularly the relative advantages of Brazilian industry in less sophisticatd machinery and in civil engineering projects and engineering services; and to bring the private sector into closer cooperation with government in the formulation of foreign trade policy than has happened in the past.

A second wing of the programme is a new stress on the improvement of agriculture: some positive measures were introduced in 1979 – increasing credit facilities to farmers and raising support prices to encourage increased cultivation, notably of soya beans and rice, and expanding the transport system. A project of particular interest is a great extension of sugar planting and refineries for the production of alcohol as an alternative – and, at present oil prices, cost-effective – source of motor fuel. There are hopes that this project, if fully realized, may save by the mid-1980s something like 15 per cent of current oil imports. With the present vehicle fleet, alcohol can be used only in mixture with petroleum, but production is already beginning of vehicles specially designed to run exclusively on alcohol fuel, and it is expected that in about three to four years about 15 per cent of the vehicle fleet will be running on alcohol (such vehicles could also become a significant export). The sugar/alcohol programme should not only bring substantial relief to the balance of payments but should also spread the benefits of development to the northeast of the country and bring about an important de-centralization of the energy network.

Radical improvements in agriculture, including the alcohol project, are an obvious way of releasing the vast unexploited natural resources of the nation and, in the long run, of relaxing the constraints on fast growth created by present balance-of-payment difficulties. It is, however, recognized that these improvements require very substantial investments which are likely to mean a continuing strain on the balance-of-payments until the investments pay off.

Brazil's so-called 'economic miracle' was not an achievement of economic loneliness, as has been made clear in the preceding sections. We believe that Brazil has provided a stimulating example of the feasibility of economic development under a mixed economy and a modern capitalist system.

References

1 H. W. Spiegel, *The Brazilian Economy*. Blakiston, Philadelphia, 1949, p. 1.
2 W. W. Rostow, *The World Economy, History and Prospect*. Macmillan, London, 1978, p. 486.
3 W. Dean, *The Industrialization of São Paulo, 1880–1945*. University of Texas at Austin, Austin, 1969, p. 3.
4 On this point, see W. P. Glade, *The Latin American Economies*. American Book, New York, 1969, p. 175.
5 A. O. Hirschman, *A Bias for Hope; Essays on Development and Latin America*. Yale University Press, New Haven and London, 1971, p. 88.
6 See W. Baer and I. Kerstenetzky, 'The Brazilian Economy'. In R. Roett (ed.) *Brazil in the sixties*, Vanderbilt University Press, Nashville, 1972, pp. 105–145.
7 W. Baer and C. Von Doellinger, 'Determinants of Brazil's Foreign Economic policy'. In J. Grunwald (ed.), *Latin America and World Economy*. Sage, Beverly Hills, California, 1978, p. 159.
8 H. Pirenne, 'The Stages in the Social History of Capitalism'. *American Historical Review*, X1X (3) Winter 1914, p. 494.
9 W. Dean, *The Industrialization of São Paulo, 1880–1945*. University of Texas at Austin, Austin, p. 67.
10 J. Bergsman, *Brazil, Industrialization and Trade Policies*. Oxford University Press for OECD, London, New York, 1970, p. 184.
11 Argentina, Brazil, Chile, Colombia, India, Israel, Korea, Mexico, Singapore, Taiwan and Yugoslavia.
12 B. Balassa, 'Incentive Policies in Brazil'. *World Development 7* (11/12), November — December 1979, p. 1026.
13 P. Evans in *Dependent Development*. Princeton University Press, Princeton, New Jersey, 1979, p. 74, makes this point.

PART IV

Policy responses in the old industrial countries

Western Europe

N. Plessz*

10.1 Introduction

Western Europe's response to the challenge of the newly industrializing countries is an ill-defined subject. In the first place, we must decide whether we are concerned with the attitudes of some 19 governments (or of the Commission of the European Communities if we include only nine of them) or with the reactions and strategies of European enterprises. Secondly, the subject raises the danger of pushing the geo-political approach too far. The current revival of geo-politics is more akin to journalism than to detached economic analysis. It becomes particularly questionable when one deals with a region in which sovereign countries, despite economic integration, have strongly conflicting interests and attitudes. But even when it comes to individual countries, the excessive emphasis on nation-states, engaged as such in economic competition on the international scene, appears to be an oversimplification. Economic competition is increasing between corporate entities which cut across national or even regional borders.

Finally, we are bound to have misgivings about the pseudo-Toynbeean dialectics between the 'challenge' from the NICs and the 'responses' from Western Europe. This makes a good title for a chapter but it disregards the complexities of economic life. It is difficult to see how the setting-up of a subsidiary in Singapore by a German company can be construed as a 'challenge' from an NIC or, for that matter, why Taiwan 'challenges' the United States when Sears and Roebuck enter into sub-contracting arrangements with Taiwanese clothing manufacturers. More fundamentally, when the South Korean government embarked, against the best advice of most Western experts, in its ambitious development programme, this constituted a response à la Toynbee to the 'challenge' of remaining permanently an underdog and not the other way round. Hence the following presentation will address itself to corporate strategies and government policies in Western Europe and in the NICs, disregarding the concepts of challenge and response which are hopelessly intermingled on both sides.

* Counsellor for Special Studies, Organization for Economic Cooperation and Development, Paris. The opinions expressed are my own and not necessarily those of the OECD.

There are some factual reasons for which European attitudes towards the newly industrializing countries differ from those observed in North America and in Japan. One reason is simply geographical distance and the absence of close political and economic links. During the 1960s and early 1970s, the success of European economic integration has tended to reinforce the existing strong tendency towards 'Euro-centrism', making our small appendix of the Euro–Asian continent into the navel of the world. 'Looking outwards' consisted essentially in casting an apprehensive eye on the United States, flirting with Eastern Europe and patronizing Africa. This attitude was partly related to the fact that relatively few big multinationals were European-based and even those that were failed to realize the impending changes in the industrial structure of the world. Evidently these generalizations hold more or less true for individual Western European countries. Large differences in these countries' involvement in the NICs and hence in their attitudes towards them make it of course even more difficult to speak about Western Europe as a unit. The institutional set-up of the European Communities has hampered rather than facilitated close contacts with countries that were not associated with it. Indeed, the move towards common policies in the European Communities, notably as regards trade policies, resulted in a search for the lowest common denominator.

10.2   The NICs in the world trade pattern

As a first step towards assessing quantitatively the importance of NICs to Western Europe (and to individual Western European countries), *Tables 10.1* and *10.2* provide statistics about trade in manufactures. The figures show that, in 1977, the share of Western European imports originating from the Far Eastern NICs – Hong Kong, South Korea, Singapore and Taiwan – and Brazil and Mexico reached 2.7 per cent, as compared with 17.9 per cent for Japan and 12.7 per cent for North America. Even this represented a relatively new development: in 1963 and 1973 the overseas NICs were quite negligible as suppliers to Western Europe. The average for Western Europe hides considerable divergencies between individual countries. Thus the corresponding shares in 1977 were 4.3 per cent for Germany, and 4.2 for the UK[1] but only 2.2 per cent for Italy and 1.5 per cent for France. They have been also below 2 per cent, on average, for the smaller Western European countries.

Looking at it from the point of view of the overseas NICs, Western Europe accounted in 1977 only for less than one-third of their exports of manufactures to industrial areas, as compared with nearly three-fifths for North America and one-tenth for Japan. In other words, the trade figures suggest that, in terms of import market shares, the 'challenge' of the overseas NICs in Western Europe has been much more potential than actual.

Table 10.1(a) *Imports of manufactures by industrial countries ($ billion)*

Destination → Origin ↓	Western Europe	of which — France	Federal Republic of Germany	Italy	UK	Europe NICs	Other	Japan	North America	Total
1963										
North America	4.23	0.60	0.65	0.54	0.92	0.34	1.18	0.79	4.57	9.59
Japan	0.47	0.02	0.10	0.06	0.07	0.06	0.16	—	1.42	1.90
Western Europe (excluding NICs)	25.96	2.99	3.90	2.56	2.06	1.78	12.67	0.56	3.97	30.49
European NICs	0.26	0.03	0.05	0.02	0.07	0.03	0.07	0.01	0.09	0.36
Brazil and Mexico	0.03	0.00	0.01	0.00	0.01			0.01	0.10	0.14
Far Eastern NICs	0.29	0.00	0.05	0.01	0.19	0.14	0.57	0.02	0.23	0.54
Eastern trading area	0.72	0.04	0.07	0.09	0.14			0.06	0.04	0.82
Other developing countries and rest of world	0.87	0.09	0.17	0.06	0.28			0.07	0.58	1.51
Total	32.83	3.77	4.99	3.34	3.73	2.35	14.65	1.51	11.00	45.34
1973										
North America	15.95	2.32	2.44	1.16	3.29	1.27	5.46	3.54	24.30	43.78
Japan	6.90	0.51	1.27	0.32	1.00	0.64	3.16	—	10.07	16.97
Western Europe (excluding NICs)	124.88	17.79	21.72	10.00	11.40	8.04	55.92	3.46	17.05	145.39
European NICs	3.16	0.57	0.77	0.21	0.48	0.19	0.94	0.05	0.76	3.96
Brazil and Mexico	0.44	0.04	0.15	0.04	0.06			0.12	1.42	1.97
Far Eastern NICs	2.77	0.14	0.74	0.12	0.90	0.70	3.96	1.52	4.70	8.98
Eastern trading area	3.95	0.41	0.92	0.34	0.41			0.51	0.38	4.85
Other developing countries and rest of world	6.82	0.54	1.34	0.48	2.70			0.65	2.11	9.58
Total	164.85	22.31	29.35	12.67	20.24	10.84	69.44	9.84	60.79	235.48

Table 10.1(a) contd. *Imports of manufactures by industrial countries ($ billion)*

Destination / Origin	Western Europe	France	Federal Republic of Germany	Italy	UK	Europe NICs	Other	Japan	North America	Total
		of which								
1977										
North America	23.59	3.65	4.29	1.74	5.26	1.41	7.25	4.75	40.94	69.29
Japan	12.88	1.35	2.70	0.58	1.78	1.88	4.59	—	19.90	32.78
Western Europe (excluding NICs)	206.68	29.23	38.90	14.91	22.47	10.91	90.26	4.53	24.19	235.39
European NICs	6.65	1.67	1.76	0.58	0.72	0.39	1.54	0.07	0.94	7.66
Brazil and Mexico	0.97	0.09	0.36	0.11	0.11	0.07	0.24	0.14	2.82	3.92
Far Eastern NICs	6.34	0.51	1.98	0.32	1.38	0.16	2.00	2.19	10.49	19.02
Eastern trading area	7.57	0.93	1.98	0.64	1.14	0.34	2.52	0.47	0.74	8.77
Other developing countries and rest of world	9.56	1.27	2.43	0.80	2.32	0.25	2.50	0.79	4.62	14.96
Total	274.25	38.70	54.39	19.68	35.17	15.42	110.90	12.92	104.62	391.79

221

Origin / Destination	Western Europe	France	Federal Republic of Germany	Italy	UK	Europe NICs	Other	Japan	North America	Total
1977										
North America	8.6	9.4	7.9	8.8	15.0	9.1	6.5	36.8	39.2	17.7
Japan	4.7	3.5	5.0	2.9	5.1	12.2	4.1	—	19.0	8.4
Western Europe (excluding NICs)	75.3	75.6	71.5	75.7	63.9	70.8	81.4	35.1	23.1	60.0
European NICs	2.4	4.3	3.2	3.0	2.0	2.5	1.4	0.5	0.9	2.0
Brazil and Mexico	0.4	0.2	0.7	0.6	0.3	0.4	0.2	1.0	2.7	1.0
Far Eastern NICs	2.3	1.3	3.6	1.6	3.9	1.1	1.8	16.9	10.0	4.9
Eastern trading area	2.8	2.4	3.6	3.3	3.2	2.3	2.3	3.6	0.7	2.2
Other developing countries and rest of world	3.5	3.3	4.5	4.1	6.6	1.6	2.3	6.1	4.4	3.8
Total	100.0	100.0	100.0	100.0	100.0	100.0	100.0	100.0	100.0	100.0
1977										
North America	34.0	5.3	6.2	2.5	7.6	2.0	10.4	6.9	59.1	100.0
Japan	39.3	4.1	8.2	1.8	5.5	5.7	14.0	—	60.7	100.0
Western Europe (excluding NICs)	87.8	12.4	16.5	6.3	9.6	4.6	38.4	1.9	10.3	100.0
European NICs	86.9	21.8	23.0	7.6	9.3	5.1	20.1	0.9	12.2	100.0
Brazil and Mexico	24.8	2.2	9.3	2.8	2.8	1.7	6.0	3.4	71.8	100.0
Far Eastern NICs	33.4	2.6	10.4	1.7	7.3	0.9	10.5	11.5	55.1	100.0
Eastern trading area	86.3	10.6	22.5	7.3	13.0	4.1	28.8	5.3	8.4	100.0
Other developing countries and rest of world	63.9	8.5	16.2	5.3	15.5	1.7	16.7	5.3	30.8	100.0
Total	70.0	9.9	13.9	5.0	9.0	3.9	28.3	3.3	26.7	100.0

'Manufactures are SITC 5–8 less 68 and 667.
'European NICs' comprise Greece, Portugal, Spain and Yugoslavia; 'Far Eastern NICs' are Hong Kong, South Korea, Singapore and Taiwan; and the 'Eastern trading area' includes all Communist countries in Europe and Asia.

Table 10.2(a) *Exports of manufactures to industrial countries ($ billion)*

Origin \ Destination	Western Europe	of which					Other	Japan	North America	Total
		France	Federal Republic of Germany	Italy	UK	Europe NICs				
1963										
North America	4.08	0.35	1.08	0.44	1.07	0.08	1.05	1.47	4.33	9.87
Japan	0.50	0.04	0.19	0.04	0.10	—	0.13	—	0.57	1.07
Western Europe (excluding NICs)	26.03	2.94	8.15	1.98	3.97	0.21	8.79	0.64	3.85	30.52
European NICs	1.80	0.30	0.56	0.19	0.35	0.02	0.39	0.09	0.35	2.24
Brazil and Mexico	0.63	0.10	0.20	0.07	0.09	0.01	0.16	0.08	0.88	1.58
Far Eastern NICs	0.83	0.07	0.18	0.15	0.24	0.01	0.19	0.47	0.27	1.57
Eastern trading area	1.61	0.16	0.39	0.23	0.32	0.01	0.50	0.23	0.02	1.86
Other developing countries and rest of world	9.06	1.75	1.90	0.76	2.95	0.17	1.53	1.90	5.91	16.87
Total	44.54	5.70	12.65	3.85	9.08	0.50	12.75	4.87	16.17	65.58
1973										
North America	18.41	1.61	5.93	1.78	3.75	0.75	4.60	9.90	22.24	50.56
Japan	3.08	0.32	0.97	0.26	0.47	0.04	1.02	—	3.02	6.10
Western Europe (excluding NICs)	121.42	15.19	36.64	10.72	11.71	2.72	44.44	6.64	13.52	141.58
European NICs	8.79	1.41	2.74	1.18	1.07	0.17	2.23	0.92	1.16	10.87
Brazil and Mexico	2.90	0.32	1.08	0.25	0.32	0.12	0.81	0.78	3.64	7.32
Far Eastern NICs	5.29	0.44	1.79	0.69	0.85	0.14	1.38	4.89	2.25	12.43
Eastern trading area	9.45	1.13	3.61	0.98	0.74	0.11	2.87	1.85	0.47	11.76
Other developing countries and rest of world	26.12	4.79	6.21	2.56	5.41	1.12	6.02	9.44	9.42	44.97
Total	195.46	25.22	58.96	18.42	24.32	5.18	63.36	34.43	55.71	285.61

Table 10.2(a) contd.

Origin	Destination	of which							North America	Total
	Western Europe	France	Federal Republic of Germany	Italy	UK	Europe NICs	Other	Japan		
1977										
North America	26.08	3.11	8.14	2.82	5.12	0.94	5.96	20.91	37.71	84.71
Japan	3.55	0.37	1.17	0.34	0.61	0.05	1.01	—	3.77	7.32
Western Europe (excluding NICs)	205.68	25.39	60.35	20.43	22.50	5.19	71.82	13.36	22.13	241.17
European NICs	13.86	2.35	4.28	2.00	1.75	0.37	3.12	1.93	1.62	17.41
Brazil and Mexico	3.88	0.52	1.22	0.41	0.52	0.16	1.06	1.27	5.74	10.88
Far Eastern NICs	9.46	1.03	3.19	1.06	1.52	0.22	2.44	9.85	4.12	23.42
Eastern trading area	19.51	2.59	6.69	2.19	1.36	0.35	6.33	4.62	0.99	25.12
Other developing countries and rest of world	66.56	12.60	17.09	8.38	11.95	2.83	13.71	24.90	24.25	115.71
Total	348.58	47.95	102.12	37.62	45.33	10.11	105.45	76.83	100.33	525.74

Table 10.2(b) *Percentage distribution of exports of manufactures to industrial countries*

Origin \ Destination	Western Europe	of which						Japan	North America	Total
		France	Federal Republic of Germany	Italy	UK	Europe NICs	Other			
1977										
North America	7.5	6.5	8.0	7.5	11.3	9.2	5.6	27.3	37.6	16.1
Japan	1.0	0.8	1.1	0.9	1.3	0.5	1.0	—	3.8	1.4
Western Europe (excluding NICs)	59.0	52.9	59.1	54.3	49.6	51.3	68.1	17.4	22.0	45.8
European NICs	4.0	4.9	4.2	5.3	3.9	3.7	3.0	2.5	1.6	3.3
Brazil and Mexico	1.1	1.1	1.2	1.1	1.1	1.6	1.0	1.6	5.7	2.1
Far Eastern NICs	2.7	2.1	3.1	2.8	3.4	2.2	2.3	12.8	4.1	4.5
Eastern trading area	5.6	5.4	6.6	5.8	3.0	3.5	6.0	6.0	1.0	4.8
Other developing countries and rest of world	19.1	26.3	16.7	22.3	26.4	28.0	13.0	32.4	24.2	22.0
Total	100.0	100.0	100.0	100.0	100.0	100.0	100.0	100.0	100.0	100.0
1977										
North America	30.8	3.7	9.6	3.3	6.1	1.1	7.0	24.7	44.5	100.0
Japan	48.5	5.0	16.0	4.6	8.4	0.7	13.8	—	51.5	100.0
Western Europe (excluding NICs)	85.3	10.5	25.0	8.5	9.3	2.2	29.8	5.5	9.2	100.0
European NICs	79.6	13.5	24.6	11.5	10.0	2.1	17.9	11.1	9.3	100.0
Brazil and Mexico	35.6	4.8	11.2	3.7	4.7	1.5	9.7	11.6	52.8	100.0
Far Eastern NICs	40.4	4.4	13.6	4.5	6.5	0.9	10.5	42.0	17.6	100.0
Eastern trading area	77.7	10.3	26.7	8.7	5.4	1.4	25.2	18.4	3.9	100.0
Other developing countries and rest of world	57.5	10.9	14.8	7.2	10.3	2.4	11.9	21.5	21.0	100.0
Total	66.3	9.1	19.4	7.2	8.6	1.9	20.1	14.6	19.1	100.0

Manufactures are SITC 5–8 less 68 and 667.
'European NICs' comprise Greece, Portugal, Spain and Yugoslavia; 'Far Eastern NICs' are Hong Kong, South Korea, Singapore and Taiwan; and the 'Eastern trading area' includes all Communist countries in Europe and Asia.

It should be noted that the limited share of overseas NICs in Western European imports reflected, to some extent, Western Europe's closer links with the 'European NICs' (Greece, Portugal, Spain and Yugoslavia). These countries had many similarities with the overseas NICs as regards their comparative advantage and, in 1977 they accounted for 2.4 per cent of Western European imports but only for 0.5 per cent of those of Japan and 0.9 per cent of those of North America[2].

The performance of NIC exporters on Western European markets should not be construed as being merely a reflection of the 'challenge'. These figures reflect a variety of factors apart from the operation of comparative advantage and the development of an export potential.

First and foremost, the figures are already affected by trade policies, actual or threatened. Without them, the share of the NICs might have been considerably higher, notably in the UK, Italy, France and several smaller European countries.

Second, marketing strategies of the NICs have played an important role in concentrating export drives on the largest markets (the United States and the Federal Republic of Germany) where the initial investment in gaining access was likely to be most rewarding and the risk of protectionist reactions less evident.

Third, through various mechanisms, the expansion of NIC exports to individual markets was not unrelated to imports from them. In the case of offshore processing and assembling, the link between the two flows is mechanical[3]. In a more tenuous fashion, direct investment leads to exports of machinery and equipment one way, and to a reverse flow of the goods produced. Finally, there is inevitably a tendency towards some degree of bilateralism, in the sense that NICs prefer to purchase their imports from countries that take a more liberal attitude towards their exports.

Consequently, it is of equal relevance to examine the role played by NICs as markets for exports of manufactures from industrial areas (see *Table 10.2*). By so doing, one should, however, not attach an undue importance to the resulting bilateral balances, because we still live in an essentially multilateral trading system.

By and large, the pattern of exports mirrors that of imports. Overseas NICs have a small share of Western European exports of manufactures (3.8 per cent in 1977 compared with 18.8 and 9.8 per cent of Japanese and North American exports, respectively). This share is thus greater than for imports, but it varies less within Western Europe: 4.5 and 4.3 per cent in the UK[4] and Germany, but only 3.2 per cent for France and 3.3 per cent for the smaller Western European countries on average. Again, dependence on European NIC markets is more pronounced in Western Europe (4.0 per cent) than in North America (1.6 per cent) or Japan (2.5 per cent) but in this respect differences among individual Western European countries are also less marked.

More important, in 1977, Western Europe accounted only for somewhat less than two-fifths of industrial areas' total exports of manufactures to overseas NICs, contrasting with a share of two-thirds of the same exports to all destinations.

The figures given do not show *total* NIC imports of manufactures (i.e. they do not include their imports from other developing countries, from the Eastern Trading Area or their mutual trade). But there are indications that between 1973 and 1977 (or, for that matter, 1978) the overseas NICs have been the most dynamic market for exports of manufactures, second only to the OPEC countries.

In view of these figures, it is somewhat surprising that, around 1976–1977, benign neglect suddenly changed into excessive concern about the 'NIC challenge'. The NICs became the bogeyman of advanced industrial countries in Western Europe, giving rise to emotional pronouncements but also to some good fact-finding work and analysis. This turnaround deserves explanation. An important factor has been the perception of the loss of economic dynamism in Western Europe, in contrast to the success stories of the NICs, notably the Far Eastern ones. Depending much more heavily on the very slowly growing European markets than their North American or Japanese competitors, Western European exporters suddenly realized that they were, on the whole, not very well placed to benefit from the dynamism of the overseas NIC markets. In addition, on the OPEC markets, they felt the pinch not only of North American and Japanese competition but of NIC competition as well. At the same time, competition has become much stronger on Western European markets. In these circumstances it was not so surprising that Euro-centrism was suddenly giving way to Euro-defeatism.

These defeatist attitudes were reinforced by a number of features of the 1975–1978 situation which had little to do with the NICs. The first was the seemingly intractable trade and current account surplus of Japan. With the benefit of hindsight, this surplus appears to be the combined result of fast productivity growth not matched by the expansion of domestic demand, of unduly delayed currency appreciation leading to excessive export orientation and, last but not least, of a period of declining real prices of oil and industrial raw materials. In view of this surplus, the European outcry about the NICs was in reality often aimed at, without specifically naming, Japan.

Another factor was a misunderstanding about the nature of the NICs. Many analysts in Western Europe, notably in the UK, included in the NICs such countries as Iran, Saudi Arabia or India. The line taken by the OECD Secretariat has been that, to become an NIC, a country needs, at least, a large urban labour force, a class of local entrepreneurs, political stability and, most important, outward-looking or export-oriented growth policies. Impressed as they were by the oil wealth of the rich OPEC countries, European analysts were stunned by their ambitious plans in petrochemicals, steel, engineering, etc. Even if political stability had prevailed in the area, it is most unlikely that most of those plants would have become competitive or would even have produced at all in an environment so uncongenial to industrial effort. To put it bluntly, in order to become an NIC, a country needs a genuine challenge. Large windfall profits from oil are most unlikely to provide it. As regards India, the issue, besides political stability, is whether it is able and willing to shift wholeheartedly towards outward-looking policies. Low wages, combined with purely import-substituting policies, do not make an NIC. Countries such as India, or more immediately, Argentina and Chile, may seek to shift towards outward-looking policies but, even if they do so, it takes time to carry them out and to make them effective. In any case, the undue extension of the geographical scope of NICs[5] unnecessarily added to the worries of Western European policy-makers.

There has also been an inadequate perception of the general orientation of NIC marketing strategies, by governments though not by private business. In Western Europe, NIC competition was represented essentially as a threat to domestic markets, whereas in fact NIC exporters have tried, as far as possible, to open up new markets in third countries. This 'third market' approach is most clearly shown in the case of shipbuilding, where sales to flags of convenience represent in a sense inroads into a completely free market on the open sea[6]. Efforts to get into OPEC and other developing markets were also important for meeting competition from the advanced industrial countries on equal terms. But, inspired by those vested interests which had long lost any hope of being competitive on export markets, many Western European governments continued to be concerned for quite some time by rising import penetration.

The general economic context of slow growth, high unemployment, protracted inflation and lingering fears about oil and raw material supplies have also played an important – and mostly negative – role in determining attitudes towards the NICs. NICs were accused of adding to the economic difficulties of Western Europe, through their dynamism, price competitiveness and thrift. Evidently, NICs appeared to be a convenient scapegoat for the failure of government policies – a failure not confined to Western Europe and not felt to the same extent in each country – to ensure sustained non-inflationary growth. And the emphasis on this particular excuse was growing so long as real oil prices declined, i.e. until late 1978. Since then, OPEC recaptured its position as the most convincing scapegoat.

10.3   Western European responses

It would be a dangerous oversimplification to try to identify a single European 'response' to the NIC 'challenge'. Each government reacted differently and the response varied from one economic sector to another, reflecting a wide variety of economic interests and corporate strategies.

Nevertheless, the dominant feature of the response has been defensive, oriented to the status quo and protectionist. There have also been other responses such as 'moving up-market', displacing labour-intensive processes to NICs and other low-cost producers, specializing in exports of technology and know-how together with machinery and equipment, moving out from production into distribution and the organization of production on an international scale, etc. The real question is why these more 'positive' responses have played a lesser role in Western Europe than in North America or, for that matter, Japan, and why their importance varied so much from one country to another.

Part of the answer lies in the production and, more important, export patterns of various countries by commodity groups. The statistical demonstration of this point would require a considerable amount of data processing and space. It is enough to point out here that countries best placed for, and most attracted by, the 'positive' responses have been those where industries specializing in exports of know-how and technology loom particularly large.

In this respect, admittedly very difficult to quantify, Western Europe was situated in 1973, on average, well behind Japan and North America (*Table 10.3*). The figures for exports of investment goods, of course, display very different country positions: the Federal Republic of Germany, the United Kingdom and Sweden being about at par with Japan, and Switzerland with the United States. At the same time France, Italy and most smaller European countries have an export structure dominated by semi-finished and consumer goods. What is true for the structure of exports is even more striking for that of output and employment where enterprises mainly interested in the growing NIC markets account for a relatively low proportion of industry in most European countries.

To this feature one must add the contradictory nature of social and political pressures for employment. For one reason or another declining industries tend to be clustered in relatively small areas. Hence the related vested interests can enrol strong political support from unions and communities. Expanding industries, on the other hand, are much more scattered geographically and hence their power base tends to be weaker. This oversimplified statement evidently holds for France and the United Kingdom (and to some extent the United States) as well as for several other European countries. It is certainly much less relevant for the Federal Republic of Germany, Switzerland or Japan.

Another part of the explanation lies in the corporate structure of European industry. Generalizations are particularly dangerous here. Because of a lack of any easily presentable evidence, the following remarks are based on *Fortune* magazine's list which includes characteristics of the 300 largest industrial corporations outside the US in 1974.

Table 10.3 *Exports of investment goods^a by OECD countries, 1973–1977*

	Value of exports of investment goods ($ billion)		Share of investment goods in total exports of manufactures^b (%)	
	1973	1977	1973	1977
Canada	3.4	5.4	28.3	25.6
United States	24.7	44.9	56.4	56.5
Japan	15.8	36.7	45.9	47.7
Australia	0.6	0.7	32.6	25.6
Austria	1.4	2.9	34.5	36.2
Belgium	3.4	6.2	20.4	22.5
Denmark	1.8	3.0	54.1	53.7
Finland	0.7	2.1	24.9	36.9
France	9.1	19.2	36.3	40.0
Germany	26.5	47.2	45.0	46.2
Greece	0.0	0.2	8.1	14.1
Ireland	0.3	0.9	32.7	40.7
Italy	6.8	13.9	36.7	36.9
Netherlands	5.0	9.0	37.5	39.4
Norway	1.5	2.7	55.0	58.6
Portugal	0.3	0.4	23.0	25.5
Spain	1.0	2.2	32.1	30.7
Sweden	4.3	7.4	46.9	48.5
Switzerland	4.6	8.2	55.1	52.6
Turkey	0.0	0.0	5.4	5.8
United Kingdom	10.7	20.0	43.9	44.1
OECD Total	122.0	233.2	42.7	43.9
North America	28.1	50.2	50.4	50.1
Western Europe	77.5	145.6	40.0	41.4

^a SITC 69, 86, and 7 less 732
^b SITC 5–8 less 68
The Norwegian figure is inflated by 'exports' of ships, while in Denmark it is influenced by the relatively small share of all manufactures in total exports.

The corporate structure of British and French industry seems to be dominated by companies whose main line of activity lies in petroleum, metals, chemicals, other industrial inputs, textiles, food products and motor vehicles. This is less the case for Japan and the Federal Republic of Germany. The *Fortune* list characteristically does not include any West German company with a heavy involvement in textiles or food products while containing scores of them in the UK and France.

Recognizing these differences does not imply any value judgement: a company mainly engaged in textiles is not intrinsically 'inferior' to one producing computers. Also, the textile company can diversify into computers and a computer company can become a lame duck relying on protection and subsidies. The fact remains that there is a complex relationship among corporate structures and strategies. A large company engaged in the production of synthetic fibres and vertically integrated into the mass production of textiles will tend to be much more 'inward-looking' than a company specializing in turnkey factories.

The evidence does not allow for any quantitative assessment. But it does substantiate the impression that in most countries of Western Europe the corporate structure inherited from the past has been biased towards activities geared to national (or European) markets. Because of the natural tendency of corporations to protect their balance-sheets, it would have been rather surprising if they had not used their power and resources to avoid the capital losses usually associated with rapid structural change. This is not at all in contradiction to simultaneous efforts to diversify the pattern and geographical distribution of output and to move into upstream and downstream activities outside manufacturing.

Except for Christopher Saunders's recent book[7], I know of no attempt to quantify structural features of an industry at the microeconomic level. The material presented by Saunders, backed up by various qualitative indicators, strongly suggests that the differences, as amongst countries, in the role of investment goods industries in the corporate structure were matched by differences *within* these industries. Other evidence suggests that many British and, to a somewhat lesser extent, French producers of engineering products were affiliates of US multinationals and/or specialized in the production of mature products (cars, lorries, standardized ships, household appliances, etc.) and/or in industrial inputs (car parts, small electrical motors, etc.). Also, these enterprises tended to be more oriented towards the domestic and West European market than their West German, Japanese or US equivalents.

Employment protection

One can legitimately ask why the above presentation of the determinants of the Western European responses made hardly any reference to employment. After all, manufacturing employment has declined sharply in Western Europe after 1975, and this decline coincided with a marked worsening of the overall employment situation. Almost invariably, defensive policies have been justified by the desire to protect employment. The issue is too complicated to be dealt with here. But it is worth recalling some aspects, relevant to the assessment of the Western European situation.

First, the net effect of trade with the NICs on employment has been quite minimal in global terms[8]. Other influences, such as slow growth of demand and changes in its pattern, together with the continued rise in labour productivity, have played by far a more important role[9]. At the same time, it is true that while labour-shedding continued, or sometimes accelerated, in the 'declining' industries, the absorption of labour by 'growth' industries has slowed down dramatically[10]. In other words, the adjustment mechanism was blocked, at least within the manufacturing sector[11].

This bleak picture has to be put into a proper perspective. Until the early 1970s most Western European countries experienced a persistent shortage of industrial labour, as evidenced by the huge inflow of foreign workers. This reflected, at least partly, the fact that manufacturers found it profitable to maintain in operation large chunks of obsolete but also fully amortized equipment.

Labour shortage led to labour-hoarding, which aggravated the shortage and helped push up real wages at the lower end of the spectrum[12]. In any event, in most Western European countries, industry accounted for at least two-fifths of the total employment around 1973, a rather high share for a 'post-industrial' society[13].

These pressures, together with the threat of foreign competition, led European manufacturers to an all-out effort to modernize and rationalize, notably in the highly labour-intensive industries, and this effort continued unabated after 1973. As a result, the slackening of the labour-market as a result of weak overall demand was aggravated by the reaping of productivity gains in declining industries and, last but not least, a dishoarding of labour. In countries in a position to diminish reliance on migrant labour, the inevitable reduction in manufacturing employment did not encounter strong social and political resistance[14].

It is frequently claimed that in many communities and areas declining industries are the only providers of employment. This is true; and one of the main reasons for the absence of other industries is very simply the old tradition, notably in 'company-towns', of resisting the entry of alternative employers so as to avoid competition for low-cost labour and bidding-up wages[15]. Sometimes this attitude went so far as to make a monopoly position as local industrial employer a condition for setting up a plant, or to block the creation of industrial estates. This is not a value-loaded criticism: trying to establish and preserve control over the main input in labour-intensive industries is a perfectly rational attitude. But the consequence is that unions and local economic interests can be more easily mobilized to support campaigns for protection and government assistance. In North America, where such campaigns have been mainly directed to obtain import restrictions, their effect was confined to individual industries or even products. In some countries of Western Europe, it has also influenced the general attitude of governments with respect to employment subsidies and lame duck policies.

Another focal point of the interaction between employment concerns and policy responses to foreign competition has been the exceptionally high degree of occupational and geographical rigidity of manpower in most

Western European countries. Nearly all the institutional arrangements combine to add to the socio-psychological restraints on mobility. This applies to housing where, for example, moving frequently means losing the benefit of subsidized housing or a low rent, or requires engaging in too heavily penalized real estate transactions. Seniority rules and company-specific fringe benefits based on seniority involve a heavy penalty for changing jobs after more than a few years' employment. Paradoxically, the *threat* of unemployment further reduces mobility, because long tenure provides the best guarantee for job security and determines compensation in case of closures.

Until 1973, the lack of mobility was overcome partly by immigration and by the reliance on new entrants to the workforce (young people and women, notably from the countryside) and partly by the efforts of companies to promote the internal mobility of their own workforce. The first option is closed in a stagnating employment situation and the second tends to be considered as too costly and too risky.

It is easy to understand why enterprises facing high demand refrain from hiring new labour and from covering, if necessary, the high cost of mobility. First, there is uncertainty about the permanence of strong demand. Second, labour has become increasingly a fixed cost (with a high mobility component). Hence, it is less risky (and costly) to meet a surge in demand by stepping up overtime, installing labour-saving equipment and calling on temporary labour. If these solutions are not adequate, enterprises frequently prefer to forgo the increase of output.

It still remains true that huge corporations (in particular conglomerates), with a large and varied internal labour market, are in principle in a better position to adjust[16]. In Europe, however, such companies tend to be relatively less important employers than in Japan or the US and their attitudes towards local employment problems are rather ambiguous.

To sum up these observations on the employment aspect, it appears that the adjustment problem raised by NIC competition was neither new nor large. However, the broader adjustment problems created by technological change, shifts in relative prices and in the pattern of demand and other developments, have proved well beyond the capacity of most Western European countries under the post-1973 conditions. Instead of providing a coherent and rational response, governments have been pushed by strong vested interests into a negative stance, the concern for employment being the main justification and the NICs a convenient scapegoat.

One way to describe Western European responses is to go through the whole range of 'sub-macro' policies – industrial policy, social and man-power policy, regional policy, trade policy, agricultural policy, to quote the main ones – to clarify the purpose, nature and effects of the measures taken. This has been largely done by the Organization for Economic Cooperation and Development[17].

10.4   Examples: textiles and steel

In the context of this paper, it appears preferable to illustrate European responses by reference to two concrete examples, namely textiles and steel. Both of these industries have been exposed to NIC competition (though not to the same extent), have suffered from weak demand and have been subject to rapid technological change. They are also characterized by structural weaknesses and a reduced capacity to adjust in many European countries, and in both instances the European Communities played a special role in devising policies.

Textiles and clothing

In textiles and clothing, growing competition from low wage-cost countries in general, and from NICs in particular, has always been a fact of life[18]. Protectionism, practised by means of high tariffs and non-tariff barriers, even in the heyday of trade liberalization, has failed to counteract the overwhelming strength of comparative advantage. As import-substitution developed in the rest of the world, European industry was faced with the risk of losing not only its export markets but large chunks of the domestic market as well.

Industry strategies varied considerably from country to country as well as within countries. Some producers, following the Japanese and US lead, have tried to concentrate on some highly capital, skill and technology-intensive lines of production and processes (e.g. synthetic fibres and yarn, some categories of cloth and knitwear, fashion goods and textile machinery), while dispatching labour-intensive processes and products to low-cost locations. This strategy led to huge export flows to overseas countries and an even larger flow, notably of clothing products, in the opposite direction, frequently marketed by the same companies. Another strategy consisted of developing highly capital-intensive mass production in vertically-integrated corporations. This production was mainly destined for the domestic (or European) market where it was supposed to be competitive because of the high level of protection.

Needless to say that the distinction between the two strategies was far from being so clear-cut: even for the same corporation, they were not mutually exclusive and within each country they coincided to some extent. Nevertheless, it is possible to identify, quite broadly, the West German and Swiss textile industry as moving rather in the first direction and the British and French in the second. A further complicating factor comes from the fact that Italy and other low labour-cost producers in Europe have been in direct competition with NICs and other low-cost producers on the European market.

The outcome of these strategies, in the mid-1970s, has been to increase dramatically the pressure of the NICs and other non-Western European low labour-cost producers (frequently linked to Japanese, US, German and some Western European corporations) on those segments of the market where labour cost played a major role and where protection was not prohibitive. This is how the share of LDCs and of the Eastern Trading Area in the total clothing imports of the nine countries of the EEC (including intra-trade) increased from 19 per cent in 1963 to 27 per cent in 1973 and 34 per cent in 1976[19]. For the remaining EFTA countries the figures were 12, 16 and 24 per cent respectively, as compared with 28, 70 and 83 per cent for the US and 0, 83 and 80 per cent for Japan.

The response of Europe came mainly in the framework of the renewal of the Multi Fibre Arrangement. The facts are well-known and need not be recalled in detail. An elaborate system of bilateral agreements was forced upon low-cost suppliers and the most efficient among them, i.e. the NICs, had to face drastic reductions in their export quotas, sometimes by as much as 25 per cent below the level actually reached in 1976. Controls were reinforced, harassment intensified and uncertainty about market access has become prevalent.

At first glance, the new MFA appears to have achieved its immediate purpose. The share of LDC and Eastern trading area suppliers in EEC imports of clothing fell below 32 per cent whereas in the EFTA the drop was to less than 21 per cent[20]. In reality, the effects have been much more complex. In terms of sales, the main beneficiaries have been low-cost producers in Western Europe. Italy's surplus in clothing (and also in textiles) nearly trebled between 1973 and 1978, more than half of the increase taking place between 1976 and 1978. The increases in the surpluses of Spain, Greece, Portugal, Finland and Ireland have been equally impressive. At the same time, the fall in the Belgian export surplus was nearly stopped and France avoided sliding into a deficit.

In other words, as the most efficient suppliers have been neutralized, their place has been taken by other relatively low cost suppliers inside the tariff barriers (or at least not hit by non-tariff barriers). The gain, in terms of market shares, of West German, UK, Dutch and Swiss producers has been small if any[21].

The change in trade flows at current dollar prices is just the tip of the iceberg. The main consequence of the tightening of the MFA has been a general rise in prices, despite weak demand and relatively low prices for inputs (until the new oil crisis). Continuing the previous trend, NIC exporters tried to make the best use of their quotas by raising prices, 'moving up-market' and generally pushing towards higher sales per physical unit[22]. Relieved from the pressure of price competition, European producers raised their prices in turn, particularly at the lower end of the price range. Indeed it is not an exaggeration to say that in order to 'save the jobs' of workers in the low-pay occupations in textiles and clothing, consumers buying cheap clothing, i.e. essentially households with lower incomes, have been subjected to a special tax.

The jobs were not saved. Following an upsurge in 1976, textile and clothing output declined in Europe in both 1977 and 1978. The substantial windfall profits derived from increased protection accrued to a few efficient and well-placed European producers, while for others they meant at best a short respite. Consequently, concentration and closures continued relentlessly and so did the productivity drive of those who could afford the necessary investment. One could even venture a paradox: it might well be that, by concentrating its large windfall gains on a few dynamic producers, the MFA has on balance accelerated the displacement of labour.

Steel

In 1977, the NICs (including those of Europe) accounted for 4.8 per cent of the value of total OECD imports of steel, as compared with 1.3 per cent in 1963. The rise might look impressive but actually the NICs had, in value terms, a sizeable deficit in steel trade and even in terms of tonnage none of them appears to be moving towards a net export position[23].

The recent difficulties of the steel industry and the practical details of government action to solve them are again well documented and need not be recalled here. In a competitive market, persistent slack demand combined with wide differences in costs in various plants within and among countries would have resulted in falling prices and the closing of the least efficient production units. Most of these units were actually located in the United States and in Western Europe, notably the United Kingdom and France.

The process had actually started, at least as far as international prices were concerned. However, strong social and political pressures have interfered with the streamlining of production units. While waiting for the long-drawn process of rationalization to run its course, governments acted promptly to stop price competition and to shift the burden of adjustment to the most efficient suppliers, in this particular case very largely the Japanese steel producers[24]. In addition, several European governments have continued to inject huge resources into their ailing steel industries to sustain the hopeless rat-race of modernization.

During the surprisingly strong but short-lived recovery of 1978/79, these measures (essentially the US trigger price and the Community's Davignon Plan) succeeded beyond any expectation. Net trade moved in inverse relation to the efficiency of national steel industries. US net imports fell from 20 million tons in 1977 to about 16 million in 1979, EEC net exports rose from 22 to 29 million tons, while Japanese net exports fell from 44 to 36 million tons[25] and total OECD net exports to the rest of the world increased from 43 to 50 million tons.

By March 1979, dollar export prices for Community products increased by 50–60 per cent from the depressed level reached at the end of 1977, and the upsurge continued fairly strongly throughout the year. The rise in Japanese export prices and in the domestic price levels in North America and Western Europe followed this trend, albeit more slowly. Paradoxically the anticipation of price increases, notably after the oil price rise, led to a complete change in attitudes towards stockbuilding to which the surprising strength of apparent demand in 1979, notably in Western Europe, owed much. This rendered the position of the market even more unstable.

To sum up, the policies followed by Western Europe (and the US) in steel have succeeded in adding considerably to cost-push inflation, in postponing the pressure for domestic adjustment, although without much help to the employment situation, and in shifting the burden of adjustment to users of steel (and ultimately consumers), as well as to more efficient outside producers.

Although the policy measures in textiles and steel described above fairly well represent the main lines of European response, thinking about adjustment policies has evolved, on the whole, in a less negative direction over the last two or three years. This can be followed from the activities undertaken in the framework of the OECD on Positive Adjustment Policies, starting from the adoption by the Council at Ministerial Level of some general orientations and eventually leading to the establishment of a two-year work programme and a special group in the Economic Policy Committee[26].

Several important factors explain this perceptible shift in principle if not yet always in practice. In the first place, given the constraints on trade policies[27] and the growing importance of competition in third markets, defensive policies were bound to take the form of heavy subsidies, either to ailing industries or directly linked to employment maintenance. These implied very heavy budgetary costs, leading to higher taxation and larger public sector deficits which incurred growing unpopularity in public opinion and parliaments. The increases in public expenditure can be related to a political shift to the centre right, less favourable to interventionist policies in many countries. At the same time, the major employers' associations, and in some countries central trade union leaderships, have become more hostile (or less sympathetic) to policies penalizing efficient and dynamic enterprises and branches in order to avoid or at least slow down the process of structural change.

The renewal of inflationary pressures, even before the second oil crisis, has already led to a reappraisal of the rationale for defensive policies. Macroeconomists and government officials have increasingly realized that these policies have added significantly to losses in efficiency and productivity and hence to cost-push inflation.

Finally, the new oil crisis brought home the evident need to increase the flexibility and adaptability of the economic system so as to make it possible to reallocate substantial resources to energy-saving and energy producing investment.

In a highly schematic way, the opponents of defensive policies fall into two categories, The first advocates reliance on market forces, enhanced by the use of broad macroeconomic policy instruments such as investment incentives, tax reforms and general measures increasing mobility. This is the dominant view in West Germany, Switzerland and, more recently, the United Kingdom. The second attitude calls for government intervention in favour of dynamic industries in general, and more particularly the promotion of R and D and of regional policies on a fairly selective basis. This line is taken in the Netherlands and still to some extent in France. It rests on the idea, strongly disputed by many economists and businessmen, that governments are in a good position to 'pick the winners', i.e. to anticipate in detail the desirable directions of structural change.

The vague and extremely confusing discussion on adjustment policies was by necessity geared to the broad area of structural change, in which the competitive pressures from NICs are only a small, and not easily distinguishable, part. It is therefore hardly surprising that the endorsement of a less negative stance did not imply a move towards more liberal attitudes in concrete matters of concern to the new industrializing countries. On the contrary the Multilateral Trade Negotiations have not, by and large, resulted in any important benefits to developing countries in general, or to NICs in particular – although the latter may reap some windfall benefits from tariff reductions extended multilaterally on products where they have started to develop new exportable supplies[28]. Furthermore, depending on the way in which it is actually applied, a new safeguard clause could be positively detrimental to the most efficient suppliers. Hence there is a distinct danger that NICs might be compelled to turn their backs on outward-looking policies, and, even more, that other developing countries would be positively discouraged from adopting them.

10.5   Conclusions

The emergence of the newly industrializing countries is essentially a test of the dynamism of Western capitalism. For the second time (after Japan), countries with a non-European social and cultural background have reached a level of economic, and notably, industrial development comparable to that of the old industrial countries a couple of decades ago.

The question is whether capitalism will prove able gradually to integrate the newcomers into the kind of mutual relationship existing among major industrial countries. If so – and the example of Japan does not yet provide any conclusive evidence one way or the other – then the door will be open for other prospective NICs and the economic and political dynamism of the system will be preserved. If not, then the advanced industrial countries will demonstrate that they form a closed club (whether or not including Japan) following policies of 'helping' developing countries only so far as they remain dependent and underdeveloped.

Confronted with this choice, Western European countries – depending on their national circumstances and the power balance of internal lobbies – have so far reacted in an essentially defensive way. Moreover, concerted attitudes within the European Community appear to have reflected the lowest common denominator – as demonstrated by the Multi Fibre Arrangement and by the steel negotiations. It is not claimed here that attitudes were systematically negative and defensive: there have been a number of constructive moves and some countries did in fact shift towards more adjustment-oriented policies. However, in essential decisions, notably in trade policy, 'new mercantilism' most frequently carried the day.

Looking to the future, we might visualize, as usual, a whole range of scenarios. Under one, two semi-autonomous 'growth poles' could emerge in the world. The first, more dynamic, would include the Far Eastern NICs plus a few other countries in the area, leaning on the technological potential of Japan, as well as on markets of the OPEC countries in the Middle East, and possibly participating in the opening of the Chinese economy. The other pole would comprise Brazil, Mexico and possibly Venezuela. This scenario would require, in addition to a reasonable degree of political stability in the areas concerned, forthcoming and dynamic attitudes from North American and Japanese economic interests. If it materializes, and if Western Europe persists in a more inward-looking attitude (or falls back on the much less dynamic African market), this would simply accelerate the loss of momentum of the Western European economy.

Hence the basic question for Western European countries is whether they will be able to control the pressures of broadly-based vested interests favouring status quo policies and to overcome the rapidly spreading mood of self-fulfilling growth pessimism.

References

1 This high figure reflects largely the special links with Hong Kong. However, the share of overseas NICs in UK imports was much higher in 1963 and 1973.

2 The European NICs, however, failed to increase their market shares between 1973 and 1977 by much.

3 This is not necessarily the case. Thus Japanese companies have used offshore processing in neighbouring countries to produce goods for exports to third countries. This explains partly the huge Japanese trade surplus with NICs.

4 The UK figures are somewhat inflated by the inclusion of exports for re-export to Hong Kong and Singapore.

5 The OECD sample included Mexico among the NICs. Given its huge oil and gas resources, Mexico is unlikely to be able and willing to maintain outward-looking policies (which have anyhow been rather timid). Other NICs could also turn away from outward-looking policies. Hence the list of NICs might prove to be even shorter in the next few years than suggested by the OECD.

6 *Table 10.1* does not include such exports from Japan and several NICs (e.g. Korea, Yugoslavia, Brazil) because they are recorded as going to Nigeria, Panama, etc.

7 C. Saunders, *Engineering in Britain, West Germany and France: Some statistical comparisons of structure and competitiveness.* Sussex European Research Centre, University of Sussex, 1978.

8 See Organization for Economic Cooperation and Development (OECD), *The Impact of Newly Industrializing Countries.* Paris, 1979, pp. 45–46 and 83–94.

9 Productivity also slowed down somewhat in Western Europe (though much less than in the US), thereby reducing open unemployment.

10 See Organization for Economic Cooperation and Development (OECD), *The Impact of Newly Industrializing Countries.* Paris, 1979, p. 42.

11 The same thing happened to some extent in the US, but it was more than offset by large rises in employment in services.

12 Egalitarian wage policies and equal pay for women have also played an important role.

13 The corresponding share was 32 per cent in the US in 1973.

14 Manufacturing employment in Switzerland declined by some 16 per cent between 1973 and 1976 without any increase in unemployment. In Germany the fall was only 8 per cent and in Belgium 10 per cent.

15 A variant of this attitude in the South of the United States is to keep out unions as well as unionized industries and corporations.

16 In Japan, corporations have moved part of the textile labour force into shops and restaurants owned by them, thus maintaining the tie with the corporation and with its union. Another way to reduce rigidities arising from the lifetime employment system is the practice of 'lending' workers from companies with slack demand to those needing labour.

17 See Organization for Economic Cooperation and Development (OECD), *The Case for Positive Adjustment Policies: A compendium of OECD documents 1978/79* and the Resolution of the Council establishing a special programme of work for the Organization on Positive Adjustment Policies (C(79)) 93 Final).

18 For textiles and clothing, see also ch. 6.

19 For detailed statistics see GATT (General Agreement on Tariffs and Trade) *International Trade 1978/79,* 1979.

20 Within these percentages the share of the NICs has declined much more, even in value terms. In volume terms, the fall was even more important.

21 However, thanks to an extremely restrictive position adopted in their trade policies, Sweden and Norway managed to stabilize their trade deficit.

22 It was noted in the UK that the quotas led to the quasi-disappearance of children's clothing imported from NICs, because of their lower price per physical unit. Consumers Association *The Price of Protection – A Which? Campaign Report.* London, 1979, p. 14.

23 Thus Korea has an overall balance in steel trade in tonnage. Highly efficient large plants developed export sales in some standard mass products, while imports are concentrated in special steels. If this ideal form of specialization was abandoned it would have a high economic cost for all concerned.

24 The EEC has flanked its minimum price system by voluntary export restraints imposed on third country suppliers, notably NICs.

25 Despite this fall, the profits of Japanese steel producers increased substantially as the rise in sales prices (and, until early 1979, the fall in the prices of inputs) more than offset the decline in volume. Profits of US and most European steel producers also increased beyond all expectations.

26 For a full documentation see Organization for Economic Cooperation and Development (OECD), *The Case for Positive Adjustment Policies; A compendium of OECD documents 1978/79* and The Resolution of the Council establishing a special programme of work for the Organization on Positive Adjustment Policies (C(79)93 Final).

27 Reliance on trade policies is ruled out by definition among members of the EEC. It is also difficult to apply trade restrictions to other industrial countries that can retaliate.

28 Even countries, such as the Netherlands, that had introduced the idea of planned adjustment with the explicit purpose of making room for imports from LDCs, appear to have de-emphasized it in recent years.

11

North America

Robert E. Baldwin* and Malcolm D. Bale†

Policy responses in the United States and Canada to increases in imports that cause, or threaten to cause, serious injury to domestic industries can be divided into three types. The first, which is usually characterized as the 'positive' adjustment approach, involves financial assistance by the government to firms and workers in such forms as special lending facilities, extended unemployment benefits, migration allowances, and retraining grants. Their purpose is either to improve the ability of import-impacted firms to compete within the same industry or to shift firms and workers into alternative productive lines. A second way in which North American governments respond to disruptive import competition is to provide temporary import protection to an industry. Usually, gradually declining sets of tariffs or rising quotas are introduced with the objective of giving firms sufficient time to adjust on their own to the greater import competition.

The last type of government reaction to injurious imports to a particular industry is to manage the import flow on a long-run basis in the manner which is followed under the Multi Fibre Arrangement. This approach seems to be used when policy-makers believe that potential market disruption from imports is too significant to be handled either by the typical positive adjustment measures or by temporary protection. Consequently, a system of import quotas is established which permits the level of import penetration to grow only at a relatively moderate rate or perhaps that places an upper limit on the import penetration ratio.

This paper first outlines the overall dimensions of trade with the new industrial countries and discusses the types of industries in the United States that are likely to be subject to growing import pressures from these countries. Since the particular forms of positive adjustment measures in North America are much less well known than measures adopted to implement either the temporary protection or managed approach to import problems, section 11.2 will briefly describe the positive policies employed in the United States and Canada. Section 11.3 deals with the political problem of fashioning responses to import problems that satisfy those who are injured and also are consistent with the long-run growth and efficiency goals of the country facing such problems.

* Professor of Economics, University of Wisconsin, Madison, USA
† World Bank, Economic Analysis and Projections Department

11.1   Imports from the New Industrial Countries

New Industrial Countries (hereafter NICs) have expanded their exports of manufactures to industrialized countries very rapidly over recent years. They are the growth sector in world trade. As Balassa notes: 'while the United Nations foresaw an increase of only 60 per cent (in industrialized countries' imports of manufactures from NICs) during the 1960s, these imports increased fivefold between 1960 and 1970'[1]. From a level of \$4.6 billion in 1965 their exports have increased more than tenfold, to \$55 billion in 1977. Real growth has been at 14 per cent per annum over the last decade and there are few indications that it will decline appreciably in the next few years. The US absorbs nearly half of NIC exports of manufactures to industrialized countries and over 30 per cent of their exports of manufactures. Over 20 per cent of US imports of manufactures now come from developing countries[2].

In comparison with the United States, Canada has relatively underdeveloped trade ties with the Third World. Lack of colonial links, a relatively isolated geographic position, and preponderant trade dependence on the United States are often cited as reasons. Recent analysis indicates, however, that Canada is moving very slowly on the new export opportunities that are opening up in NICs. But like the US, Canada has been absorbing rising levels of developing country imports, up over 100 per cent from 1973 to 1977. On a per capita basis, Canadian imports of Third World manufactures are close to the average of other industrialized countries, but this is primarily a reflection of Canada's high level of trade exposure overall. More significantly, the Third World's import share remains relatively small (as in the case of Canada–Third World exports) and its product composition is more heavily concentrated than the OECD average in traditional NIC labour-intensive consumer goods such as textiles, clothing, and footwear. This divergence in the Canadian pattern of NIC imports can largely be explained by the structure of the Canadian manufacturing sector and its historical development behind a high tariff wall. The high level of foreign control, of intra-firm trade, and of market penetration by US suppliers whose products embody significant amounts of Third World value-added as a result of the utilization of US offshore assembly provisions, undoubtedly masks the actual NIC content of import flows.

The growth of exports of manufactures from NICs and their commodity concentration presents North America with major adjustment problems. The issue is not whether the NICs will industrialize further and increase their penetration of this market. Both are occurring. The question is at what rate will their manufactured exports increase, how rapidly will comparative advantage change in their favour, and what will be the US and Canadian reaction to these changes? North American attention has been focused on imports from NICs rather than on total imports because the NICs are the dynamic element in trade and are responsible for a large share of recent and prospective increases in import penetration. Further, NIC manufactured exports are very commodity-specific. Exports tend to be concentrated on labour-intensive industries where North American workers are least able to compete or adjust because of age, skill levels, geographic immobility, etc.[3] Industries such as footwear, textiles, certain electronics and fabricated goods are examples. Finally, exports of manufactures from developing countries originate from a small number of suppliers with Hong Kong, Taiwan, and South Korea taking the biggest shares. Exports of manufactures to the US increased from less than $4 billion in 1970 to nearly $17 billion in 1977 – an average annual growth rate of 23 per cent. The US share of NIC exports of manufactures to industrial countries increased from 39 to 48 per cent over that period – the most dynamic industrial country market for NIC manufactures.

The regional concentration of NIC manufactured exports has increased over the last decade. In 1975, three Asian countries accounted for 40 per cent of NIC exports of manufactures and the top seven countries supplied 64 per cent of the total.

The key question for the future is: what industries are particularly vulnerable to import competition? A rough idea of the answer for the United States can be given by performing the following experiment. Suppose that as other countries continue to close the technological gap with the United States and to reap relatively greater benefits from 'learning by doing', all import supply curves (assumed to be perfectly elastic) facing the United States decline by 10 per cent relative to the supply curves of US industries (also assumed to be perfectly elastic) producing similar products. Suppose further that, although imports are imperfect substitutes with domestic output in the same industry, any increase in import spending is matched by a corresponding fall in spending on the domestic substitute. Then by finding the initial value of imports, the import elasticity of demand, the direct labour coefficient for the industry, and the initial employment level in the domestic industry, it is possible to estimate the percentage decrease in direct employment from a 10 per cent decline in the import supply curve. If such a decline occurs in all manufacturing lines, the exchange rate will depreciate to offset the deficit effect of the greater imports and the employment losses will tend to be offset by increases in exports and decreases in imports. However, the relative size of the initial impact effects gives a rough idea of which industries will suffer most.

With the use of 1970 import and employment data, and of import-demand elasticities classified by US input–output sectors, such an experiment was undertaken for 276 manufacturing sectors. (Textile sectors subject to quantitative import restrictions were excluded.) There are 8 industries indicating employment losses of 10 per cent or more; 14 with losses of more than 5 but less than 10 per cent; 15 with losses of more than 3 but less than 5 per cent; and 239 with employment losses of less than 3 per cent. The sectors indicated in the first three groups (with the percentage employment losses in parenthesis) are as follows (of course, one should interpret the percentages as rough orders of magnitude):

10 per cent or more – rubber footwear (38); food utensils (46); pottery (29); electrical equipment (11); motorcycles, bicycles and parts (85); athletic equipment (11); artifical flowers (65); miscellaneous manufactures (10).

5 to < 10 per cent – vegetable oil mills (7); nonrubber footwear (8); other leather products (8); cutlery (6); textile machinery (6); computing machines (7); sewing machines (9); household appliances (5); radio and television sets (8); X-ray apparatus (5); watches (6); jewellery (9); musical instruments (7); and games and toys (8).

3 to < 5 per cent – sugar (4); candy (4); veneer and plywood (4); tires (4); industrial leather tanning (4); ceramic wall tiles (4); porcelain electrical supplies (3); primary copper (3); primary zinc (3); hand tools (3); electric lamps (3); wiring devices (4); aircraft equipment (4); optical instruments (4); and buttons, needles and fasteners (5).

The list contains the familiar set of simply manufactured, labour-intensive products but it also includes several relatively high technology items, for example computers and aircraft equipment. Of course, these are products in which the United States is less likely to suffer a relative decline in competition costs. Nevertheless, one should not be surprised to see significant import penetration even in these lines within a few years. And what is taking place in the United States is only a prelude to what will occur in other industrial nations or is already occurring in some developed countries.

The prospects for future export growth depend on general economic growth and on trade policies used by trading countries. As more developing countries shift toward export-oriented policies, total export supply will increase, but with the high export base today it is unlikely that the historic growth rate will be maintained. The World Bank projects annual growth of developing country exports of manufactures at 12 per cent over the period 1975–1985, with their share of industrialized country imports increasing from 10 per cent in 1976 to nearly 14 per cent in 1985 and to 16 per cent in 1990 ('base case' scenario)[4]. If the United States maintains its present market share its imports will increase from $17 billion in 1977 to $42 billion (1977

Table 11.1 *Canadian trade in manufactures – issues and responses*

Issue area – Third World demand	Northern response	Canadian specifics
Tariffs		
• removal of discriminatory bias in tariff structure (tariff escalation) and provision of preferential access • deeper than formula cuts on products of Third World interest; accelerated phasing maintenance and improvement of the GSP; delayed phasing of cuts if preferences adversely affected • total removal of tariffs for 29 poorest countries	• MFN cuts are of longer-term benefit to the Third World than the GSP (binding and unconditional) • unnecessary erosion of preferences to be avoided but strong opposition (US particularly) to the preservation of preferences because of their negative effect on overall trade liberalization • likely partial exemptions or less than formula cuts on sensitive products (e.g. textiles and clothing)	Tariff structure – one of the highest average rates of duty on dutiable imports; wide dispersion from high to low tariffs reflecting strong tariff escalation; high percentage of duty-free imports (63 per cent of end products): discriminatory bias against labour intensive Third World exports. General Preferential Tariff – Canada slow to introduce GSP; tariff reductions ⅓ MFN or BPT) not duty free; key products excluded; concessional and subject to unilateral safeguard action; includes donor country content rules. MTNs – Canada committed to partial exemption or less-than-formula cuts for textiles and clothing; like other OECD countries, Canada has paid little attention to Third World concerns; unlike the United States, Canada did not demand reciprocal concessions for its tariff cuts in tropical products. Most studies indicate that Canada has tended to utilize non-tariff barriers to a far less extent than Japan, US, France, Germany, or the United Kingdom.
Non-tariff barriers (MTNs) *Technical barriers to trade* • special and differential treatment: measures to expand exports through transfer of technology, provision of information on operation and application of technical barriers, priority attention to barriers affecting Third World products (e.g. Latin American meat products), special consideration for the need to use indigenous technology	• draft code; the only special and differential measure is provision of technical assistance	

Quantitative restrictions and import licensing
- binding multilateral rules governing the use of quantitative restrictions
- special and differential treatment
- provision in any code on import licensing for the use of licensing as a tool for general economic development

- quantitative restrictions being dealt with on bilateral basis
- special and differential treatment unlikely to be incorporated in GATT code on import licensing

- Canada finds the proposed code to be acceptable and is particularly pleased that it will apply to a number of licensing requirements it has found 'unnecessarily restrictive and complex' in the Third World

Customs valuation
- special and differential treatment including a longer implementation period and some exemptions

- special and differential treatment likely to be incorporated into GATT code

- Canada has not participated fully and has steadfastly refused to change its value for duty from the selling price or 'fair market value' in the exporting country to the Brussels definition of value; Canada remains the only major trading nation not using the standard Brussels valuation; it is Canada's most serious NTB and it has a particularly adverse effect on the Third World

Government procurement
(initiated to a large extent by the Third World)
- special and differential treatment; considering the pervasiveness of public sector involvement in economic development, Third World countries should be allowed significant exemptions (piecemeal exclusions unacceptable)

- provision of special and differential treatment on a case by case, country by country basis

- despite involvement in the negotiation of an agreement on government procurement, the Canadian Government has recently expressed its intention to intensify domestic procurement practices

Subsidies and countervailing duties (CVD)
- right to use subsidies for purposes of economic development (particularly export subsidies)
- amendment of US CVD legislation
- object to concept of 'graduation'

- draft code indicates vague recognition of the Third World's right to use export subsidies

- Canada promulgated its own CVD legislation in April 1977 which is consistent with GATT provisions but considered to be protectionist in intent
- first Canadian CVD case currently underway involving baler twine from Brazil, Mexico and Tanzania

Table 11.1 (contd.) *Canadian trade in manufactures – issues and responses*

Issue area – Third World demand	Northern response	Canadian specifics
Safeguards(MTNs) • overwhelming objection to 'selectivity' • publicly determined proof of injury • clear definition of injury • limits on duration of safeguard action • international surveillance • mandatory link to adjustment measures • exemptions for small suppliers or new entrants • consideration of export injury in the Third World when safeguards used • possible proposal at UNCTAD V of a special new international code of conduct requiring the Northern economies to adjust to changing competitive conditions ('positive adjustment')	• agreement on clearer definition, criteria, procedures, rights • general acceptance of 'selectivity' (disagreement between EEC and Japan/US on conditions and procedures) • no mention of adjustment assistance in code	MTNs • Canada appears to support 'selectivity' under strict conditions; it has endeavoured to tighten up the use of safeguards in resource-based sectors; it does not favour the obligatory extension of adjustment assistance claiming that it is unnecessary if safeguards are of a temporary nature Usage • before 1976 Canada used Article XIX almost exclusively in cases of short-term, seasonal disruptions in agricultural and horticultural products; in 1966/77 Canada took safeguard actions six times on manufactured products, the most significant being the global import quota on clothing (November 1976) and the global import quota on footwear (December 1977)
Multi Fibre Arrangement (MFA) • preservation of MFA objectives: orderly expansion of Third World textile and clothing exports; adherence to its adjustment provisions	• nominal reaffirmation of original agreement (December 1977); inclusion of an all-important provision allowing 'reasonable departures' from MFA tenets; relegation of the MFA to an 'organ of conciliation'	Usage 1974–1979 • under its Textile Policy, the Canadian Government followed the spirit and the law of the agreement quite strictly. Restraint measures were negotiated selectively under Article 3, using narrow product categories. Adjustment plans were not scrutinized carefully and protection was often provided when competitive viability was tenuous. Canada negated its MFA commitments when it imposed its global import quota on clothing in November 1976.

Renegotiation
- Canada delayed accession to the MFA in order to ensure its right to invoke the 'reasonable departures' provision; sought more restrictive terms (lower growth rates and base levels); advocated faster growth rates for small and new exporters.

1978
- Canada has begun to make much wider use of bilateral restrictions, using broader product groupings and wider country coverage. For example, Canada has negotiated restraint measures on apparel items with 13 countries including small, new suppliers such as Sri Lanka, Malaysia, and Thailand. It has also instituted a computerized import licensing procedure designed to detect any new supply threats.

Source: North–South Institute, *A Balance Sheet of Third World/Canada Relations*, Issues Papers, Ottawa, April 1979

dollars) by 1985. Assuming further that US imports of manufactures from other suppliers grow at 5 per cent, the average over the past eight years, by 1985 the share of the developing countries in US imports of manufactures would increase from its 1977 level of 21 per cent to 31 per cent in 1985.

The growth of imports can be put into perspective by observing that, during the period from 1970 to 1977, US imports of manufactures from Japan increased from $6 billion to $18 billion; a nominal annual growth of 21 per cent per year and an estimated real growth of perhaps 13 per cent. During that period Japan increased its market share of US imports of manufactures from 17 to 24 per cent[5]. From this viewpoint, the adjustment burden from developing country exports to the US over the next decade may be somewhat greater than that of adjusting to imports from Japan over the past decade[6].

Despite early Canadian pronouncements for 'trade not aid' and the Canadian government's official recogition of the importance of non-aid development initiatives in its 1970 Foreign Policy Review and 1975 Strategy for International Development Cooperation, Canada's responsiveness to Third World demands for market access and industrial restructuring has been limited. *Table 11.1* details Canada's policy performance on key trade and adjustment issues in this area of North–South relations. The continued maintenance of tariff 'peaks' in sectors of export interest to NIC exporters and the slow, highly imperfect implementation of Canada's key non-aid development instrument, the General Preferential Tariff, are noteworthy. The listing of non-tariff barriers (NTBs) indicates that Canada has not been one of the worst NTB offenders, but it has been in the vanguard during the recent escalation of quantitative restrictions against competitive NIC manufactures. It has also begun utilizing a protectionist-oriented countervailing duty mechanism.

11.2   'Positive' adjustment policies in US

Both the United States and Canada have specific trade adjustment assistance policies designed to assist in the orderly restructuring of factors of production displaced or threatened with displacement by import competition. The US legislation was first introduced as part of the Trade Exansion Act of 1962 but because of the restrictive conditions for eligibility for assistance, few import-displaced workers or firms received assistance[7]. In 1975 both the criteria for assistance and the benefits payable were liberalized making the programme more accessible to factors injured by increased imports. The old and new criteria for worker eligibility to adjustment assistance benefits are

Table 11.2 *United States: worker eligibility criteria for trade-adjustment assistance*

Trade Expansion Act of 1962	Trade Act of 1974
Imports	
Articles like or directly competitive with those produced by the applicant are being imported in increased quantities.	Articles like or directly competitive with those produced by the applicant are being imported in greater absolute or proportional quantities.
Displacement	
Sales or production at the worker's firm must have declined. Workers concerned must be unemployed or underemployed, or threatened with either.	Sales or production at the worker's firm must have declined. A significant number or proportion of workers in a firm have been or are threatened with total or partial layoff.
Causation	
Increased imports must be the major factor causing unemployment or underemployment. Increased imports must be in major part the results of trade concessions granted under the trade agreement.	Imports must have contributed importantly to the separation of workers.

Source: Paraphrased from the statutory language of 19 U.S.C. Sec. 1901 and Sec. 221, P.L. 93–618

given in *Table 11.2* while *Table 11.3* presents the benefits payable under the old and the new schemes. Trade adjustment assistance is available regardless of the source of imports. It is not a specific reaction to increased imports from the NICs.

(a) Adjustment assistance for workers

Following certification by the administering agency (Department of Labour), workers apply for benefits at the local office of their State Employment Agency. To be determined eligible for benefits, workers must have been laid off after the date of the import impact and must have had earnings in import-affected employment of at least $30 a week for 26 of the last 52 weeks prior to layoff.

Certified workers who meet requirements are then eligible for weekly trade-readjustment allowances. In addition to trade readjustment allowances, workers may enrol in existing training programmes or new training programmes established for certified workers who cannot otherwise obtain suitable employment. Workers who enrol in training can receive, in addition to their trade readjustment allowances, up to $25 a day and 12 cents a mile to defray expenses incurred while receiving training outside their local commuting area.

Table 11.3 *United States: worker benefits under trade-adjustment assistance*

Trade Expansion Act of 1962	*Trade Act of 1974*
Adjustment allowance A weekly adjustment allowance of 65 per cent of the worker's average weekly wage, but not to exceed 65 per cent of the average weekly manufacturing wage, for up to 52 weeks with up to 26 weeks extension for workers in training or workers over 60 years old.	A weekly adjustment allowance of 70 per cent of the worker's average weekly wage, but not to exceed 70 per cent of the average weekly manufacturing wage, for up to 52 weeks with up to 26 weeks extension for workers in training.
Employment services Training, testing, counselling, and placement services provided under other federal laws.	Training, testing, counselling, placement services, and other services through cooperating state agencies.
Relocation allowance If a worker has a job offer in another area and the worker is a family head, then a relocation allowance covering family moving expenses plus a lump-sum payment of 2.5 times the average weekly manufacturing wage will be paid to the worker.	Workers who wish to move to another area may receive a relocation allowance of 80 per cent of the necessary relocation expenses plus a lump-sum payment of 3 times the worker's average weekly wage, up to $500.
Other allowance For travel to distant training centres grant 10 cents per mile plus a $5 per day subsistance allowance.	Job-search allowance of 80 per cent of a worker's job-search expenses up to $500.

Source: Trade Expansion Act of 1962, Secs. 321–330, and Trade Act of 1974, Secs. 231–238

By the end of 1977, petitions for adjustment assistance had been received by the Department of Labour covering 372 000 workers. By 1 January 1978 about 270 000 workers had received weekly trade-adjustment allowances totalling about $363 million averaging $54 a week per worker. The numbers of workers using the other benefits offered under the Trade Act have been very much smaller[8].

(b) Adjustment assistance for firms

The criteria for firm eligibility are similar to those for worker eligibility. Benefits received by firms are in the form of loan guarantees and technical and financial assistance in preparing a firm restructuring plan.

To obtain benefits, certified firms submit applications to the Department of Commerce. Applications must include a detailed adjustment plan as well as various data on financial status, operating costs and market share. To be approved, the firm's adjustment plan must give adequate consideration to the interests of the firm's workers and demonstrate that the firm will make all reasonable efforts to use its own resources for economic development. Individual firms may receive up to $1 million in direct loans and up to $3 million in loan guarantees for periods of up to 25 years.

Firms may also receive direct technical assistance or technical assistance grants to help them develop and implement their adjustment plan. Firms may receive grants for up to 75 per cent of the cost of these services.

The three industry groups that have received the bulk of adjustment assistance payments under the Trade Act are footwear, textiles and stainless steel flatware, industries where a large proportion of imports originate from NICs. Thus, although the original intent of the adjustment assistance programme was not to direct aid at firms and workers affected by increased NIC imports, the effect of the legislation has been partially to offset the protectionist pressure which might normally accompany such increases in imports.

(c) Special programme to aid shoe firms

In July 1977 the Department of Commerce initiated a special programme to provide assistance to the ailing shoe industry. The purpose of the programme is to revitalize those segments of the American shoe industry that have been injured by foreign competition. Firms selected for assistance are those that can be certified as eligible for assistance under the Trade Act.

Both monetary and non-monetary assistance are offered under the programme. Over a three-year period, approximately $40 million in loans and loan guarantees will be made available to firms for investment in new plant and equipment, new technology, acquisitions and mergers or other cooperative arrangements among industry members. In addition, teams of experts in the fields of management, production, marketing and finance are available to provide consultative services to the estimated 150 trade-impacted shoe firms.

The shoe industry programme is only a temporary mechanism designed to help the troubled shoe industry. It is planned as a one-time experimental programme to concentrate resources on a single trade-impacted industry.

(d) General firm and community assistance

Firms and communities needing adjustment assistance can get help from a variety of sources for restructuring. These programmes are not trade-specific ones but any firm or community is eligible. The Small Business Administration and the Department of Commerce are the main agencies. Since the programmes are not trade-specific and certainly not NIC specific, they are of little further interest here.

In summary, US adjustment policies have been modest and of marginal assistance to trade ajustment. With the exception of multilateral efforts such as the GSP, US trade policies have not been directed at the specific problems of NICs. This is, of course, entirely consistent with the predominant American belief in the primacy of the market mechanism.

11.3   Canadian assistance programmes[9]

The Canadian assistance programmes differ from the US adjustment assistance programme in that the Canadian programmes generally encourage the industries that are most capable of competing with foreign imports rather than assist those firms that are adversely affected by imports. Canadian programmes also target special worker benefits to the specific portions of the workforce that are likely to encounter the most difficulty in adjusting to new employment rather than providing the same general assistance benefits for all trade-displaced workers. Like the US programmes they are not specifically tailored to assist in adjustment to imports from NICs. Examples of Canadian assistance programmes follow.

(a) General Adjustment Assistance Programme

The General Adjustment Assistance Programme (GAAP) was introduced in December 1967 to assist Canadian manufacturers affected by the 1962 Kennedy Round trade negotiations. As initially conceived, the programme was directed at assisting manufacturers injured, or threatened with injury, by increased import competition resulting from tariff reductions and at encouraging manufacturers to take advantage of expanding market opportunities resulting from tariff concessions.

In 1973, GAAP regulations were modified in an effort to liberalize programme eligibility. The requirement that a causal link be established with Kennedy Round concessions was eliminated. Now firms may apply for assistance if they need a loan in order to improve their international trade position, take advantage of new production opportunities on goods which will face significant international trade competition, or adapt efficiently to competition from goods imported at such prices, in such quantities, or under such conditions as would cause or threaten to cause serious injury.

When firms cannot obtain a Government-insured loan from a private lending institution, the Board may make a direct loan of up to Can$250 000 for a term of up to 20 years.

Firms requiring the services of qualified consultants to develop proposals for loans or guarantees may apply for consulting grants of up to 80 per cent of the cost of the service, depending on the size of the firm.

As a result of the change in 1973, GAAP has not assisted Canadian firms that are adversely affected by increased import competition. Rather, it has developed into a programme to assist Canadian firms to take advantage of expanding market opportunities.

(b) Automotive Adjustment Assistance Programme

In 1965 the US and Canada entered into an agreement to integrate the North American auto market by removing duties on US–Canadian trade in motor vehicles and original equipment parts. This permitted manufacturers to schedule production in either country without considering tariff restraints. The agreement resulted in increased competition among parts manufacturers, and many of the less competitive producers either closed or were absorbed by larger manufacturers. Since this programme was a bilateral one, not involving NICs, it will be treated briefly.

An Automotive Adjustment Assistance Programme was implemented in Canada in 1965 to provide financial assistance to Canadian auto parts manufacturers and workers affected by the US–Canadian Automotive Agreement. Direct loans were offered to parts manufacturers experiencing overall declines in production as well as those wanting to take advantage of the expanding parts market. The programme also provided benefits to workers having to change their jobs as a result of concessions made under the automotive agreement. In addition to regular unemployed benefits, assistance benefits were available to workers for up to 52 weeks in an amount that raised total benefits to a range of 62–75 per cent of previous average weekly wages. The programme expired in June 1973 and according to an auto parts spokesman, it was one of the most successful government assistance programmes.

(c) Textile and Clothing Industry Adjustment Assistance Programme

In May 1971 the Textile and Clothing Industry Board was established to implement a special programme to assist Canadian firms and workers in the industry that were being affected by increased imports. The programme was established at a time when imports were claiming a larger share of the Canadian clothing and textile market.

To qualify for assistance, textiles and clothing manufacturers must submit plans describing the operational changes which will lead to an improvement of their international competitive position. Following a Board inquiry to determine whether textile and clothing goods are being imported at such prices, in such quantities, and under such conditions as to cause, or threaten to cause, serious injury, the Board may recommend that special import restrictions or other temporary measures of protection be implemented. The programme does not provide financial assistance to firms; firm assistance must be obtained through other programmes.

In addition to assisting textile and clothing firms through tariffs and quotas, the programme provides financial benefits to laid-off workers in the form of supplementary benefits and pre-retirement benefits. For employees to be eligible, the Board must certify that they are being injured as a result of

- a reduction in tariffs on any textile and clothing goods imported into Canada;
- any conditions set by the Government for special protection; and/or
- serious injury or threat of injury to the production of any textile or clothing goods caused by import competition in circumstances where special measures of protection have not been recommended or deemed practical.

Lay-offs must have occurred after 18 December 1979, reduced the firm's workforce by 10 per cent, or 50 employees, and lasted for at least four months.

All certified workers receiving unemployment insurance benefits are entitled to a supplementary benefit, where combined benefits equal two-thirds of average weekly earnings, to a maximum of Can$100 a week, for up to 52 weeks of lay-off. This supplementary benefit was discontinued in July 1972, when Canada's regular unemployment insurance benefits were increased to the same combined rate.

Textile and clothing workers between 54 and 65 years of age at the time of lay-off, who are certified by the Department of Manpower and Immigration as having no prospect of re-employment, are eligible to receive pre-retirement benefits provided they were employed in the industry for at least 10 of the last 15 years, working at least 1000 hours a year. The pre-retirement benefit is equal to two-thirds of the worker's average weekly earnings payable after regular unemployment benefits have expired, and continuing until the recipient reaches age 65.

There are mixed opinions as to just how successful this programme is in helping workers and firms in the clothing and textile industry. An industry-association spokesman characterizes the programme as being responsive to industry needs. Conversely, labour union representatives characterize it as providing little assistance to laid-off workers. Within the textile industry, for example, there were an estimated 103 000 workers in 1973; in three years that number dropped to 89 000 – a decline of about 14 000 workers. However, during the same period, programme benefits were provided to only 132 individuals.

The limited programme activity is attributable to the worker and seniority –lay-off structure. Those eligible for programme benefits – workers who are 54 and over – are generally those with the highest seniority and therefore are the last to be laid off. Most of the workers who are laid off first have low seniority, are generally under age 54, and must therefore rely on general manpower programmes for employment assistance.

(d) Canada Manpower Adjustment Programme

The Canada Manpower Adjustment Programme was established in June 1963 to encourage management and labour to assume responsibility for manpower adjustments necessitated by production cut-backs, plant relocation, technological advances or increased imports. The manpower adjustment necessitated by such changes generally takes the form of either a contraction or a restructuring of the workforce.

The programme provides funds to pay for up to 50 per cent of the costs of research, planning and consultations undertaken by management and labour to identify mutually acceptable solutions to adjustment needs. Further, the programme provides funds to pay 50 per cent of the costs of relocating workers to another of the company's plants or to another job. In addition, the programme aims at coordinating the delivery of training, counselling and job referral services which are available through Canada Manpower Centres. Firms are required to notify provincial governments of pending lay-offs from two to four months in advance, depending on the number of workers to be furloughed.

If the employer and union agree to accept assistance, an assessment agreement is developed where a joint firm, worker and government committee is established to assess the firm's problem, develop solutions, evaluate the effect of solutions on the workers, and recommend action to allow workers to adapt to the solution.

The firm is not obligated to implement the committee's recommendations. The agreement simply requires that the principal parties to the agreement assess its recommendations and implement them as they deem advisable in order to facilitate the adjustment of affected workers.

In addition to identifying problems, the Administrator (Ministry of Manpower and Immigration) is also directly involved in implementing the solutions to worker-adjustment problems. For example, if training or counselling is required, it is obtained through the Canada Manpower Centres. However, when relocation is required the Ministry can provide direct assistance, usually paying 50 per cent of the cost involved in relocating employees.

From the start of the programme in February 1965 until January 1977, an estimated 1.3 million workers were assisted under 1106 agreements, at a cost to the federal government of Can$4.2 million. During the same period about 200 mobility agreements were negotiated relocating nearly 2000 workers at a cost of Can$1.4 million.

The number of firm-assessment agreements formed because of the increased import problem is not available. However, approximately 172 agreements are in industries where trade-related programmes have been enacted.

Federal, provincial, industry and union officials involved with the pro-gramme are unanimous that it is a workable approach for dealing with structural adjustment. According to a textile official, this is particularly true for the textile industry, which is characterized by many small plants and a substantial number of plant closings[10]. Features of the programme which contribute to its success are that it goes into effect before the lay-offs occur, and union participation in the development of solutions helps make the programme appealing to workers.

In addition to these specific programmes there are numerous general employment insurance, manpower and firm programmes operated by both the federal and state governments.

11.4 The political economy of responses to import competition

There are few economic policies that have received more widespread support over the years within the economics profession than trade liberalization. Yet a look at the history of international economic policy leads to the conclusion that economists have not been very successful in convincing the electorate of the merits of reducing the host of tariffs and non-tariff measures which impede international commerce. The immediate post-World War II period is sometimes cited as a time when the viewpoint of economists on trade matters prevailed, but it seems clear in retrospect that this trade liberaliza-tion was related much more to political than economic factors. As attitudes in the industrial market economies towards Soviet expansion changed, and the dominance of the United States in the world economy disappeared, international trade policy reverted to a more inward-looking form.

Economists have usually explained the failure of their views on trade issues to be implemented by the existence of various market imperfections coupled with the highly skewed manner in which the benefits and injury from imports are distributed within the economy. One key market im-perfection is the fact that economic knowledge is not perfect but involves costs to acquire and disseminate. The existence of costs of voting, and of compensating those who are injured by import increases, also act as impediments to the 'perfect' operation of economic and political markets. Moreover, as has often been pointed out, the benefits of trade liberalization tend to be spread thinly among many consumers of imports whereas the harm is concentrated among a small group of suppliers whose products compete with imports. This distributional pattern, coupled with the various costs cited above, tends – so it is argued – to rule out political action by individual consumers backing liberalization. They are either unaware of the benefits of this policy or find the costs of such action greater than the benefits. Moreover, because consumers are so numerous, the 'free rider' problem prevents them from organizing into effective pressure groups. When protectionism is piecemeal, exporters also do not organize to resist trade restrictions, since the likelihood is small for each industry that it will be hurt by foreign retaliation. Individual import-competing producers, on the other hand, suffer much more from imports than individual consumers gain, and consequently it is in their interests to oppose liberalization in a vigorous manner. Their smaller numbers and better communications with each other also make it easier to improve the effectiveness of this opposition by organizing into lobbying groups.

As a result of these various factors, so that usual argument goes, producing interests harmed by imports dominate the decision-making process and thwart the type of trade liberalization favoured by most economists. The implications of this reasoning, with respect to correcting the outcome, are, of course, that more information should be provided to consumers about the benefits of expanded trade, that less expensive channels are needed to enable consumers to register their views on such matters, that consumers should be urged to organize into political action groups on trade issues, etc. In short, the answer to achieving the results favoured by economists is to make economic and political markets more perfect.

We would like to suggest that the above explanation of the limited degree of trade liberalization, and of the weakness of the opposition to trade restrictionist pressures, is not adequate to explain the manner in which trade policy is determined. In modern industrial democracies, when a political decision is made to provide import relief or some other form of government assistance to an important industry facing economic difficulties, the pros and cons of such an action are usually well publicized prior to the decision. Elected officials not only are informed immediately by many voters employed outside the industry directly concerned about their views on the matter, but these officials know that they will be judged on the issue by all the voters when they next stand for election. Consequently, elected representatives must be very sensitive to the perception that they favour a special interest group at the expense of the general electorate. If this is so, then why in fact is special assistance given to particular industries, though economists often regard this as contrary to the public interest? The answer, we think, is that in reaching a decision about the merits of the particular action, voters do not consider just its short-run consumption effects but also both the redistributive effect of the assistance and its long-run implications as a social insurance measure that has the effect of improving their own long-run income prospects.

Expressed more formally, the imposition of a tariff or quota in response to a sudden surge of imports that causes injury to an industry has both private and collective implications. The private effect is that the prices of import goods rise and reduce the 'own' utility of consumers. The collective implication is that incomes in the injured industry are prevented from falling at all or as much as they would do in the absence of any import restriction. Economists typically assume that an individual's utility level depends only upon the quantity of goods and services he consumes. While all agree that interpersonal effects are a real phenomenon (as the existence of private charitable contributions verifies), the usual rationale for not making an individual's utility depend on the economic welfare of others, as well as on the goods he consumes himself, is that either these interpersonal effects are small compared to 'own' consumption effects (and thus can be ignored) or that the utility from interpersonal and 'own' consumption effects are independent of each other. While such assumptions seem plausible when analysing most private markets, they do not seem justified when analysing economic decisions made in political markets where there is a large 'collective good' element in the decision.

When an industry is seriously injured by a sudden surge of imports, some consumers are likely to be concerned about the loss of jobs and resulting economic hardships faced by workers in the affected industry. One way to model this is to think of there being a certain disutility associated with the knowledge of these economic hardships to others. The typical consumer may be prepared to pay a little more for domestic goods than for imports in order to eliminate these hardships, but he knows that this action by himself alone will have no effect on the situation. However, he may support a tariff that does in fact eliminate the injury by raising the price of imports to all consumers on the grounds that the interpersonal disutility associated with a slight rise in prices to other consumers, plus his own utility loss resulting from these higher prices, are less than the interpersonal utility gained from the knowledge that workers in other industries will not suffer injury. In other words, knowing that free trade, coupled with some ideal, costless redistribution mechanism to compensate fully those who are injured, is not a feasible alternative in the actual world, the consumer may be prepared to vote for temporary import-protection to an industry. This kind of explanation of why protectionist measures are introduced is, we think, more realistic than the model that relies heavily on the existence of ignorance among voters.

A somewhat different approach from the interpersonal utility framework is to confine an individual's utility function to the goods consumed by the individual even though he has knowledge of the utility that other individuals gain. However, the individual also has his own social welfare function in which he makes judgements about the distribution of welfare to himself and others. If he votes for a policy where his own welfare is less than would be possible under alternative policies, this is regarded as being a result not of any overall personal and interpersonal utility evaluation on his part but a set of distributive values that are not related to the notion of utility. However, to state that one's judgements concerning interpersonal comparisons of utility are determined in a utility framework, or in a quite different fashion, seems largely a question of semantics. The important matter is that either under the interpersonal utility framework, or under a model that specifies an individual's social welfare function by unexplained value judgements, one can conclude that individual voters may very well favour temporary protection for an industry even though they are not employed in the industry (or closely related ones); whereas under the usual personal utility framework, which generally ignores an individual's social welfare function, this conclusion does not emerge.

Another way to account for the support of protectionism on the part of the general voter, and still maintain that this voter is motivated only by self-interest, is to assume that he is risk-adverse. He supports laws providing for protection in cases of sudden surges in imports and thus accepts reductions in his real income when protection is granted to others in these circumstances, in order to insure against the possibility that his own income may fall sharply in the future as a consequence of rapid import increases. The voter prefers an income stream with a lower average level to one with a higher average level if the variations in the former are less than in the latter.

If the view is accepted that temporary trade assistance may reflect the wishes of the majority of voters rather than simply the machinations of a relatively small producer group, there are definite implications for developing a long-run trade policy that maintains enough efficiency to yield adequate economic growth. The approach must be based on the notion that acceptable means of preventing serious injury from import competition are the cornerstone of any trade policy rather than an 'afterthought' introduced to gain more support for trade liberalization. Furthermore, it is essential that the major industrial and labour groups in a country should be deeply involved in the formulation of such policies. Unfortunately, most of the adjustment policies implemented in the United States, Canada, and many other industrial countries have been fashioned largely in response to liberalization efforts, and they consist primarily of allowing continued or increased protection by means of tariffs or quotas and by temporary income-maintenance arrangements. Their effect has been to delay adjustment more than to aid it. Moreover, social scientists, with their characteristically long-run view of society, have been rightly concerned about the adverse effect on the long-run vitality of the economy of the measures adopted to prevent injury. It is, of course, also in the interests of labour and industry that adequate growth and rising income levels should be maintained. Given the political realities of the modern industrial society, unless a positive adjustment strategy is devised that can meet the short-run concerns of the major labour and industry groups adversely affected by greater imports, and that is also attractive to these groups from a longer-term point of view, the prospects for satisfying the long-run concerns of economists and other social scientists in the trade area do not seem very favourable.

References

1 B. Balassa, *World Trade and the International Economy: Trends, Prospects and Policies.* World Bank Staff Working Paper No. 282, Washington, D. C., May 1978.

2 General Agreement on Tariffs and Trade (GATT), *International Trade 1978/79* appendix Table B. While the terms 'new industrial countries' and 'developing countries' are not synonyms, we have, for convenience, often used developing country data on manufactured exports rather than using NIC data. Because most LDC exports of manufactured goods come from the NICs, developing country data does not distort the results.

3 M. D. Bale, 'Worker Adjustment to Import Competition: the United States Experience'. *International Journal of Social Economics* **5**, 1978, pp. 71–80.

4 World Bank, *World Development Reports 1978*, Table 27 and 1979, Table 19.

5 General Agreement on Tariffs and Trade (GATT). *International Trade 1978/79.* Appendix Table B.

6 C. Pearson, 'Adjusting to Imports of Manufactures from Developing Countries'. US Congress, Joint Economic Committee, special study on Economic Change, 1981.

7 See M. D. Bale, 'Adjustment Assistance under the Trade Expansion Act'. *The Journal of International Law and Economics* **9**, 1974 pp. 49–79, for a discussion of the 1962 criteria and of the problems met by workers and firms petitioning for assistance.

8 US Department of Labour, *Cumulative Summary of Trade Adjustment Assistance Cases*, ILAB/TA, 1978.

9 Data on Canadian programmes largely derived from:
   C. R. Frank (with S. Levinson), *Foreign Trade and Domestic Aid.* Brookings Institution, Washington D.C., 1978;
   General Accounting Office, *Considerations for Adjustment Assistance under the 1974 Trade Act: A Summary of Techniques used in other Countries.* JD–78–43, Washington, D.C., 18 January 1979;
   S. Mukherjee (with C. Feller), *Restructuring of Industrial Economies and Trade with Developing Countries.* International Labour Office, Geneva, 1978.

10 General Accounting Office, *Considerations for Adjustment Assistance under the 1974 Trade Act: A Summary of Techniques used in other Countries..* JD–78–43, Washington, D.C., 1978, p. 48.

12

Japan and East Asia

Ariyoshi Okumura*

Some features of the Japanese response to the widening circle of industrializing nations, in particular the rapid structural change in the pattern of her manufacturing production and exports, are often taken as models of the adjustment process. This chapter is concerned with this process of adjustment in Japan, with special reference to the interactions between Japan's structural adjustment and the industrial development of her four industrializing neighbours: Hong Kong, South Korea, Singapore and Taiwan – the East Asian NICs. These economies resemble Japan in lack of natural resources and in the important part played in their development by manufactured exports. The question arises: how can Japan manage the 'challenge' from the Asian NICs?

12.1   Japan's trade with the East Asian NICS

The dramatic growth of the total exports of the four East Asian NICs (described in other chapters) is summarized in *Table 12.1*. Their rate of increase in value in 1970–1977 ranged from over 40 per cent a year for South Korea to 20 per cent a year for Hong Kong; and the increase was mainly an increase in volume (e.g. over 30 per cent a year for South Korea and nearly 20 per cent a year for Taiwan). These rapid growth rates were accompanied by some diversification both of markets and of products. Diversification by markets is particularly notable in South Korea – a switch from the United States and Japan to Western Europe, the Middle East oil producers and other developing countries. Changes in the market patterns were less striking for the other three exporters.

Diversification by products is marked chiefly by the increasing importance of electrical machinery and appliances, which by 1976 accounted for 13 per cent of the total exports of the four Asian NICs. But light industry products still represented half their total exports in 1976 as in 1970 (*Table 12.2*).

* Mr Okumura is General Manager of the Industrial Research Department, The Industrial Bank of Japan, Tokyo.

Table 12.1 *Exports of East Asian NICs by destination*

	USA	Japan	Asia	West Europe	Oil producing countries in Middle East	Others	Total
		Annual average growth rate (%, 1970–77) to each market					
South Korea	33.8	35.5	37.6	53.9	93.2	68.8	42.7
Taiwan	30.5	26.7	23.6	35.0	56.1	43.1	30.8
Hong Kong	19.4	18.6	25.0	21.3	29.7	20.6	21.1
Singapore	33.2	31.1	24.2	25.5	37.2	26.1	26.9
Total East Asian NICs	27.4	29.2	25.2	28.4	46.5	33.3	28.8

Source: Bank of Japan, *Monthly Survey*, June 1978

Japanese – NIC competition in third markets

How has Japan been affected by this emergence of the East Asian NICs as exporters, either in third markets or in the Japanese home market?

In third markets the net effect on total Japanese exports does not appear to have been very substantial. Indeed, taking total imports into OECD countries, Japan has kept pace with the growth of the East Asian NICs. Over the twelve years 1965–1977, imports from the four NICs rose from 1 to 3 per cent of total OECD imports (excluding Japan) while Japan's market share rose from 3 to 5 per cent (*Table 12.3*). More significant is the complementary shift in the product pattern of OECD manufactured imports (*Table 12.4*). A fall in the Japanese market share in textiles, clothing and other consumer goods has been much more than offset by Japan's growing market shares in metals and machinery, particularly in electrical goods and motor vehicles. By contrast, the East Asian NICs have gained a very substantial market share in clothing (approaching one-third of total OECD imports of clothing) and considerable gains in leather and travel goods – but not in the tightly restricted market for textiles; and in electrical goods the East Asian NICs have increased their import share in the OECD markets but still fall behind Japan. In non-electrical machinery, iron and steel, and vehicles, penetration of OECD markets by NICs is only beginning. Thus, developments during the past decade or two indicate a kind of international division of labour between Japan and the East Asian NICs in their penetration of OECD markets.

These changes in the commodity structure of Japanese exports to OECD reflect the same kind of movement in Japan's exports to the world as a

Table 12.1 (contd.)

								Oil producing countries in Middle			
USA		Japan		Asia		West Europe		East		Others	
1970	*1977*	*1970*	*1977*	*1970*	*1977*	*1970*	*1977*	*1970*	*1977*	*1970*	*1977*
47.3	29.9	29.1	19.5	7.9	7.1	8.7	14.7	0.8	5.3	6.2	23.5
39.8	39.1	15.1	12.1	24.2	16.2	10.3	12.8	1.2	4.6	9.4	15.2
35.7	32.2	7.1	6.1	14.9	17.9	25.2	25.4	1.4	3.3	15.7	15.1
11.1	15.5	7.6	9.5	43.1	36.1	16.4	15.1	1.0	3.9	20.8	19.9
32.1	29.6	11.9	12.0	23.0	18.6	17.5	17.1	1.2	4.3	14.3	18.4

Per cent of total exports to each market

whole: between 1960 and 1976, textiles and clothing have fallen from 28 to 6 per cent of Japan's total exports, while machinery and vehicles have risen from 23 to 53 per cent.

Japan and the East Asian NICs as trading partners

The next question is the direct influence of the emergence of the East Asian NICs on the Japanese domestic economy. The expanding trade between Japan and the East Asian NICs has been one element, but only one, in the structural transformation of Japanese trade and industry. But it has played an important part in the growth of Japan's overall trading surplus.

In 1978, Japan's overall trading surplus was $18 billions, of which the surplus with the four East Asian NICs accounted for $9 billions; these NICs accounted for 15 per cent of Japan's total exports against only 7 per cent of her total imports (*Table 12.5*). It must be noted that the Japanese domestic demand structures is less favourable to the pattern of NICs' exports than is domestic demand in the NICs to the pattern of Japan's exports. However, the expansion of trade in both directions has been remarkable – Japan's exports growing by 24 per cent a year from 1966 to 1978 while imports increased by 28 per cent a year. Over this period as a whole, the Japanese surplus with these four NICs has been somewhat reduced as a proportion of trade turnover (the surplus falling from 58 per cent of imports plus exports in 1966 to 45 per cent in 1978).

Moreover, Japan's imports from the East Asian NICs, which in the 1960s consisted largely of food and raw materials, are now predominantly

Table 12.2 *Exports of East Asian NICs*[a] *by commodities*

	Value ($ million)		Per cent of total exports		Average annual growth rate (%)	Contribution to increase (%)
	1970	1976	1970	1976	1970–1976	1970–1976
Textile products	1 671	9 489	28.1	30.6	33.6	31.2
Plywood	170	618	2.9	2.0	24.0	1.8
Footwear	90	1 013	1.5	3.3	49.7	3.7
Light industry goods total[b]	3 153	15 475	51.3	49.9	31.0	49.5
Electrical machinery and appliances	451	3 951	7.6	12.7	43.6	14.0
Iron and steel	60	566	1.0	1.8	45.4	2.0
Ships	30	730	0.5	2.4	70.2	2.8
Heavy industry goods total[b]	1 125	9 115	18.9	29.4	41.7	31.9
Total[b]	5 953	30 989	100.0	100.0	31.6	100.0

[a] South Korea, Taiwan, Hong Kong and Singapore
[b] Including other items

Source: Bank of Japan, *Research Monthly* (June, 1978), *Yearbook of International Trade Statistics*, Official Statistics (for Taiwan)

Table 12.3 *Imports of OECD countries from East Asian NICs and Japan*

	1965		1971		1975		1977	
	(%)	($ million)	(%)	($ million)	(%)	($ million)	(%)	($ million)
East Asian NICs of which	(1.0)	1 207	(1.9)	4 712	(2.4)	13 754	(3.1)	23 668
South Korea	(0.0)	118	(0.4)	875	(0.7)	3 846	(1.0)	7 305
Taiwan	(0.2)	306	(0.6)	1 409	(0.7)	3 901	(0.9)	6 704
Hong Kong	(0.6)	782	(0.8)	2 040	(0.7)	4 306	(0.9)	6 736
Singapore	—	—	(0.1)	416	(0.3)	1 701	(0.4)	2 923
Japan	(2.9)	3 645	(4.6)	11 267	(4.0)	23 151	(4.8)	37 065
Total all sources	100	124 633	100	245 714	100	584 725	100	767 531
NICs' share								
Japan's share	0.34		0.41		0.60		0.65	

Source: OECD, *Statistics of Foreign Trade, Series C*, trade by commodities

Table 12.4 *OECD Imports of manufactures from Japan and East Asian NICs, 1970–1977 (% of total OECD, excluding Japan, imports)*

		From Japan			From East Asian NICs		
		1960	1970	1977	1960	1970	1977
SITC							
65	Textiles	7	7	3	2	4	5
84	Clothing	7	6	2	13	20	30
61, 83	Leather, travel						
85	goods and footwear	10	8	6	—	8	18
63, 64	Wood and paper products	4	2	1	—	4	5
67	Iron and steel	7	13	14	—	—	1
69	Metal manufactures	6	9	9	—	2	5
71	Non-electrical machinery	1	3	6	—	—	1
72	Electrical machinery,						
	appliances, etc.	5	11	14	—	3	9
73	Transport equipment	2	7	15	—	—	1
5	Chemicals	2	3	2	—	—	1
5–8	Total	4	7	8	1	2	5

Source: Organization for Economic Cooperation and Development (OECD), *The Impact of the Newly Industrializing Countries.* Paris, 1979, Annex Table I (the percentages are only approximate, being derived from rounded data in the source)

manufactured goods (apart from recorded imports of mineral fuels from the Singapore refinery; see *Figure 12.1*). Of the imports of manufactures, 70 per cent consist of light industry products such as textiles, leather products and wood products from which Japan is withdrawing. At the same time, Japan's imports of more sophisticated goods from the East Asian NICs have been increasing fast, although the amounts are still small. For example, imports of industrial machinery have risen between 1970 and 1977, in $ million, from 0.4 to 16.6, of electrical machinery from 8.3 to 88.4, and of precision machinery from 0.9 to 14.4 (figures for imports from Korea, Taiwan and Singapore); yet these three categories made up in 1977 only 2 per cent of total Japanese imports from the countries concerned. The expansion of Japanese imports of these items has been mainly in consumer-type products, such as office equipment, domestic applicances, simple radios, standard calculators with elementary functions, 'disposable' watches, small cameras and monochromatic televisions. Thus a division of labour is developing under which lower-priced and less differentiated goods of these general categories are being produced in the East Asian NICs while Japanese producers move into the higher and more differentiated items. (To some extent the growth of such imports into Japan is attributable to imports from overseas subsidiaries – a matter discussed below.) A similar specialization could occur also in basic industrial materials. An example is the steep

Table 12.5 *Japan's trade balance with East Asian NICs*

		1966 ($ million)	1966 (%)	1970 ($ million)	1970 (%)	1974 ($ million)	1974 (%)	1978 ($ million)	1978 (%)
South Korea	Exports	335	(3)	818	(4)	2 656	(5)	6 003	(6)
	Imports	72	(0.9)	229	(1)	1 568	(3)	2 591	(3)
	Balance	263		589		1 088		3 412	
Taiwan	Exports	255	(3)	700	(4)	2 009	(4)	3 585	(4)
	Imports	147	(2)	251	(1)	955	(2)	1 750	(2)
	Balance	108		449		1 054		1 835	
Hong Kong	Exports	370	(4)	700	(4)	1 360	(2)	3 088	(3)
	Imports	47	(0.6)	92	(0.3)	273	(0.4)	498	(0.6)
	Balance	323		608		1 087		2 590	
Singapore	Exports	143	(2)	423	(2)	1 388	(3)	2 325	(2)
	Imports	30	(0.4)	87	(0.5)	619	(1)	869	(1)
	Balance	113		336		769		1 456	
Total with Asian NICs	Exports	1 103	(11)	2 641	(14)	7 413	(13)	15 001	(15)
	Imports	296	(4)	659	(4)	3 415	(6)	5 708	(7)
	Balance	807		1 982		3 998		9 293	
Total with all countries	Exports	9 793	(100)	19 318	(100)	55 536	(100)	97 543	(100)
	Imports	7 738	(100)	18 881	(100)	62 111	(100)	79 343	(100)
	Balance	2 055		437		−6 575		18 200	

Source: Ministry of International Trade and Industry, *White Paper on International Trade and Industry*

increase in Japan's imports of galvanized products and castings; although the second largest producer of iron and steel in the world, Japan is now withdrawing from these low value-added categories.

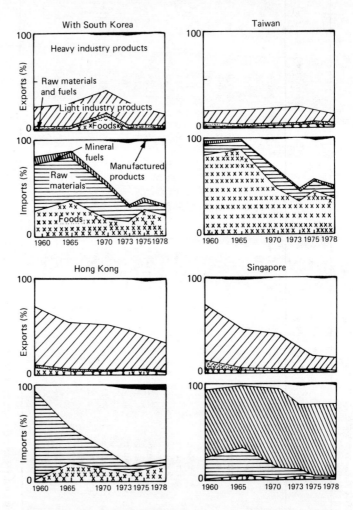

Figure 12.1   *Japan's trade with East Asian NICs. (Source: MITI, White Paper on International Trade and Industry*

Meanwhile, the commodity composition of Japanese exports to the East Asian NICs displays the other side of the interdependent relationship. As examples, we may take the four to sixford growth (as measured in $ million) of the following Japanese exports to the East Asian NICs (in this case South

Korea, Taiwan and Singapore) between 1970 and 1977 – items indispensable
to industrialization and in some cases associated with technology transfer
from Japan:

	1970	1977
Iron and steel primary products	81	321
Non-metallic primary products	13	76
Synthetic resins	14	60
Industrial machinery	36	156
Telecommunications equipment	38	217

Source:Ministry of Finance, *Japan's Exports and Imports* (n.b. during this period the Japanese
export price index for all manufactured goods approximately doubled)

Labour cost disparities

Despite Japan's productivity advantage, there are industries in which her
competitiveness is directly affected by the lower wage levels in the East
Asian NICs. The East Asian NICs wage levels, expressed in dollars, are
one-quarter or less of those in Japan. Further, the gap has widened in recent
years (see *Table 12.6*). Even when productivity changes are taken into
account, labour costs in dollars per unit of output increased, between 1970
and 1977, by 13 per cent in Japan compared with 6 per cent in South Korea
(but 12 per cent in Taiwan). It is understandable that Japan should lose
cost-competitiveness in labour-intensive light industries where differentiation in the products is insufficient to absorb the difference in labour costs.

12.2   Complementary changes in productive capacity

The complementary nature of the trade relations between Japan and East
Asian economies is reflected, too, in the trends in production capacity in the
two areas. Some examples are given in *Table 12.7*. In the labour-intensive
industries, of which textiles is typical, the number of spindles in South
Korea, Taiwan and Hong Kong doubled from 1970 to 1977, reaching 7.4
million by 1977 – over half the Japanese capacity. As will be shown below
(section 12.3) efforts have been made in Japan to cut down spinning
capacity.

In domestic appliances, Japan's production of television sets increased
only minimally in the 1970s, and of radios was almost halved; by 1977 South
Korea and Taiwan were together producing almost as many radios as Japan
and half as many television sets (although, as noted above, mostly with
limited functions). In many of these domestic electrical products, Japanese

Table 12.6 *Labour costs, Japan and East Asian NICs, 1970–1977*

	Percentage increase in wages		Percentage increase in labour productivity	Percentage increase in wages per unit of output		Wage level, 1977 (in $)
	(in domestic currency)	(in $)		(in domestic currency)	(in $)	
South Korea	24.9	17.6	10.5	13.0	6.4	143
Taiwan	17.1	17.8	5.4	11.1	11.8	142
Hong Kong	10.9	15.2	..	..	..	189
Singapore[a]	9.2	13.5	..	..	..	124
Japan	15.9	20.8	6.9	8.4	13.0	748

[a] 1970–1976
[b] Wages are monthly wages per person

Source: Bank of Japan, *Research Monthly*, June 1978

Table 12.7 *Production capacities of Japan and East Asian NICs*

	Year	Japan	South Korea	Taiwan	Hong Kong
No. of spindles	1970	14 159	1 271	1 551	964
(thousands)	1977	13 745	3 116	3 400	925
No. of looms	1970	727	51	42	26
(thousands)	1977	658	142	80	31
No. of sewing machines	1970	173	60	30	80
(thousands)	1977	229	130	70[c]	90[c]
Actual output of television	1970	12 488	114	1 254	n.a.
sets (thousands)	1977	14 339	2 990	4 926	
Actual output of radios	1970	32 618	1 088	6 248	n.a.
(thousands)	1977	17 310	6 404	7 427	
Plywood [a] (converted into	1970	2 400[d]	3 988	n.a.	n.a.
million square metres 4 mm thick)	1977	2 400	6 831[c]	6 862[e]	
Crude steel	1970	114 630	910[f]	n.a.	n.a.
(thousand tons/year)	1977	161 310[c]	5 890	1 000[c]	
Shipbuilding	1970	10 710	190	220[b]	n.a.
(thousand gross tons)	1977	19 000	2 600[c]	700[b]	
Ethylene	1970	3 954	100	54[g]	n.a.
(thousand tons/year)	1977	5 602	150	345	

[a] Japan includes ordinary plywood only
[b] Actual ships built
[c] 1976
[d] 1974
[e] 1973
[f] 1971
[g] 1968

Source: Bank of Japan, *Research Monthly*, June 1978

production is becoming increasingly unprofitable and is being gradually shifted overseas, a fact which reflects Japan's programme of direct investment abroad.

Asian NICs have also established the production of basic materials including iron and steel and petrochemicals – capital-intensive industries in which large-scale production is necessary. (For example, an ethylene plant of 100 000 tons a year capacity first appeared in South Korea in 1972.) In Japan, these basic material industries were mainly established in the 1960s – backed by fast growth in both domestic and world demand and by an increasingly cheap (in real terms) and stable supply of energy.

Shipbuilding presents a rather different story. A producing capacity of about 19 million gross tons a year – almost fully used in 1975 when Japan produced half the world's tonnage – represents vast overcapacity when related to the 10 million tons launched in 1977. The reason lies in the general world recession in shipbuilding. The growth of the shipbuilding industries in the East Asian NICs has played only a minor part but is not to be overlooked (South Korea plans for output of over 1 million tons in 1981); other industrializing countries (such as Poland and Brazil) have also increased their share of world output. Hence a programme for the 'freezing' of as much as 35 per cent of Japan's shipbuilding capacity is now under way. Shipbuilding is fundamentally an assembly industry and fairly labour-intensive, not necessarily involving a particularly sophisticated technology: because of higher wages than in the NICs, it is probable that Japan will gradually lose her competitiveness at least for the more unsophisticated types of ships. However, for Japanese shipbuilding there is some ground for optimism: the Japanese domestic market has not yet been penetrated by the NICs, and much of the NIC production depends on imports from Japan of such essential components as engines and control systems.

12.3   Textiles – a special case of adjustment

Textiles is probably the Japanese industry most seriously affected by the 'challenge' of the East Asian NICs both in third markets and in increasing penetration of the domestic market. Yet although almost constantly embarrassed by excess capacity, Japan remains among the world's largest producers of cotton textiles and is the world's second largest producer (second only to the United States) of synthetic fibres (polyester, nylon and acrylic combined). The coming of age of the East Asian NICs in an industry distinguished by unskilled labour intensiveness has made it basically impossible for most Japanese producers to compete with them in relatively standardized products. The Japan Spinners' Association has reckoned that in such cotton products, production costs in South Korea are about three-quarters, and in Thailand and Indonesia about one-half, of Japanese costs.

As well as losing markets in the East Asian NICs and in third markets from NIC competition, Japan's textile industry is now suffering from the sharp increase in imports, half of the total coming in 1978 from the East Asian NICs (and another 11 per cent from the People's Republic of China) (*Tables 12.8 and 12.9*). In 1974/75 imports accounted for over 5 per cent of total Japanese consumption of textiles and for 14 per cent of that of clothing[1]. With the normally slow growth of the domestic market, intensified by the prolonged recession since the mid-1970s, and continued fast increases in imports not effectively controlled by official restrictions, especially from the East Asian NICs, import penetration must have increased further.

Recently imports appear to have exceeded the limits imposed for preferential customs duties. For example, imports of synthetic staple fibres amounted to Yen 966 million in fiscal 1977 and Yen 3211 million in 1978 against the ceiling of Yen 475 million fixed for both years. Similarly imports of polyester filament were Yen 1705 million in 1977 and Yen 2532 million in 1978 against a limit of Yen 1153 million. (The disparities appear to be attributable in part to an officially recognized attitude of 'benign neglect' at the Customs.)

Table 12.8 Japanese imports of textile manufactures, 1970–1978

	($ million)
1970	309
1971	377
1972	538
1973	1715
1974	1829
1975	1310
1976	1699
1977	1732
1978	2732

Table 12.9 *Japanese imports of textile manufactures by source, 1978*

	($US million)	*(%)*
South Korea	1035	38
Taiwan	282	10
Hong Kong	144	5
China (Peoples Republic)	307	11
EEC	510	19
Other countries	453	17
Total all sources	2732	100

The increases in textile imports, notably those from the East Asian NICs, have become a source of growing bewilderment to Japan's textile producers. However – from either the international or the domestic point of view – it is unlikely that the Japanese government will resort in the foreseeable future to drastic measures for the effective restriction of textile imports. Basically, the Government's attitude can again be described as 'benign neglect'.

The recent adjustment process in the Japanese textile industry began with the 'Law on temporary measures for the stabilization of specific depressed industries' – a law enacted in mid-1978 to cover several 'structurally

depressed' industries in the depression following the oil crisis and authoriz-
ing, for cotton and manmade fibre spinning, the disposal of as much as 16
per cent of spinning capacity (over 2 million spindles).

The Act was not the first to encourage the closures or scrapping of excess
capacity. Earlier examples include:

(1) the 'law for temporary disposal of capacity in the textile industry'
    (called the 'old textile law') of 1956;
(2) the 'new textile law' (similarly titled) of 1964, aimed at the closure of
    about 2 million spindles (15 per cent) while allowing the new installa-
    tion of 1 million (the '2–1 scrap and build system'). But by April 1965
    only 700 000 spindles had been scrapped and later that year the industry
    was forced into an anti-depression cartel.
(3) the 'law on temporary measures for the improvement of the structure
    of the textile industry' of 1967; the excess capacity to be scrapped was
    reckoned at around 3 million spindles. But considerable price increases
    occurred in the textile market (especially in cotton) after 1967 and no
    significant scrapping was realized.

The rather modest results of these earlier efforts at reducing surplus
capacity illustrate the difficulties of such schemes. It is only recently that the
need has been agreed for a long-term policy of capacity reduction, as distinct
from measures for replacing old plant by new. It is recognized, however,
that the new measures are a consequence not only of domestic circumstances
in Japan but also of the new challenge of increasing capacity in the Asian
NICs – to which the reduction of inefficient excess capacity in Japan is one
method of response. However, the reduction of excess capcity is not the
only form of Japanese response. The 1978 'law on temporary measures'
described above provided a wide variety of other forms of assistance. Thus
small and medium enterprises are encouraged to 'restructure' – i.e. to quit or
to convert to other activities – by long-term (16 years) loans at low interest,
and a government guarantee system was introduced for such loans. Some big
producers have established joint sales companies and unified their marketing
departments (e.g. Toyo Boseki and Mitsubishi Rayon in 1977; Asahi
Chemical Industry and Kanebo in 1978). This strategy aims at adjusting the
product mix, item by item, by reducing each partner's excess capacity. For
this kind of collective strategy, the generally rigid anti-trust rulings have
been temporarily waived.

At the same time, Japanese producers have moved towards further
rationalization and cost reductions – introducing the newest automatic
high-speed equipment to reap larger economies of scale – in order to
compete directly with the lower labour costs in the Asian NICs. Some
producers have been able to expand downstream into higher value-added
goods (e.g. fashion clothing) or have developed textile-related products (e.g.

sophisticated 'georgettes' and artificial leather). Others have entered non-textile sectors: cosmetics, foodstuffs, building materials, etc. These are highly profitable compared with textiles. Kanebo (one of the 'Big 10' textile producers) gains more than half its profits from non-textile products.

It is not easy to predict the future direction of the Japanese textile industry. Thus in synthetic fibres the challenge comes less from the East Asian NICs than from the United States. In the NICs, synthetic production is based mainly on oil and is thus more vulnerable and uncertain in the current situation than in the United States where low-priced natural gas cheapens production costs. Thus, in addition to benefiting from the anti-depression cartel and the down-floating of the yen, Japan's synthetic fibre producers can enjoy fair profitability. Moreover, these producers are also moving into non-textile areas. The Toray and Asahi Chemical Industry – recognized as the foremost in technological capability – is developing the anti-virus drug Interferon and also the uranium concentration method by ion exchange. These are reckoned to be useful, strategic areas to follow textiles.

But for the textile industry as a whole, essentially difficult conditions must be expected to continue, especially in standard textiles such as cotton based on natural fibres. In 1977 the Japanese textile and clothing industries employed nearly 1.7 million people. Although employment in the industries has been falling (a 13 per cent overall reduction from 1970 to 1977, employment falling heavily in textiles but rising in clothing), it remains a very large industry. Its structure, from production to distribution, is complicated, and it includes inefficient and small enterprises which present problems not soluble by economic logic alone. Even in cotton, the recent relative stability of the industry may continue temporarily. But this in part is a result of the operation of the anti-depression cartel which operated, although with interruptions, during half the period from April 1975 to June 1978. In view of rising imports, the Japanese industry is increasingly demanding restrictive measures. As observed above, the government's present attitude is opposed to protection and imports will probably continue to rise. But if rising imports undermine an appropriate restructuring of employment, the government will be forced to adopt some kind of strategy to buy time – such as 'voluntary' restraint measures on a substantial scale. A rational coordination of policies among the parties concerned is needed.

12.4 Direct investment abroad as a dynamic response

One Japanese response to the new circumstances has thus been adjustment of the industrial structure. The other response has taken the form of direct investment abroad, in the East Asian NICs and elsewhere.

276

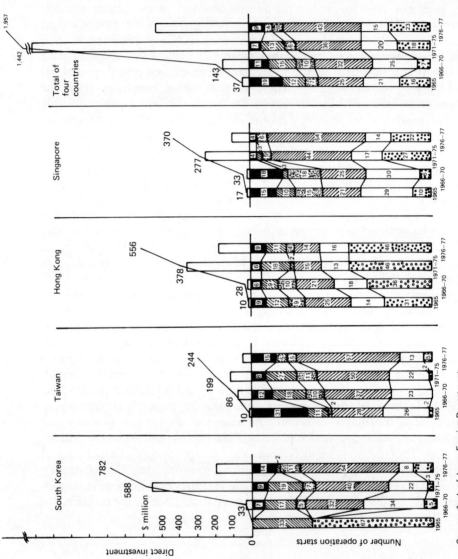

Source: Bank of Japan Foreign Department

Figure 12.2 Japan's direct investment in East Asian NICs. The bars give the direct investment permissions, the solid line

In the East Asian NICs, Japanese investment has been mostly small-scale: average investment in manufacturing projects is estimated at $970 000 in Singapore, $660 000 in South Korea and $330 000 in Taiwan – while the average for Japan's total overseas investment is $1 430 000 per project. Thus the East Asian NICs account for 20 per cent of the number of overseas investment projects, but for only 10 per cent of their value. Japan's investment in the East Asian NICs started mainly in light industries, in small urban factories, with a view to securing markets and making use of wage differentials: this in turn offered employment opportunities and contributed to the development of local communities. Investment in light industries reached a peak in the early 1970s, and there has been a gradual move towards the manufacture of machinery and electrical goods accompanying the general diversification of industry in the host countries. These shifts in the emphasis of the structure of Japanese direct investment in the Asian NICs are illustrated by *Figure 12.2*.

The development of overseas investment in machinery production, particularly in electrical goods and appliances, is of special interest to Japan. It represents an evolution in the pattern of Japanese overseas investment and in the division of labour between Japan and the East Asian NICs. In electrical goods, the process started in the early 1960s, mainly with the establishment of sales networks for exports from Japan; producers of household electrical appliances were particularly active, not only in exporting directly but also in establishing overseas selling affiliates as joint ventures with Japanese trading companies. As sales increased in the early 1970s, direct exports from Japan became large enough to create favourable conditions for production in the NICs (stimulated in part by relatively high Japanese labour costs). Thus the purpose of overseas investment shifted from sales to direct production abroad on a substantial scale.

A certain differentiation in the pattern of Japanese investment can be observed among the East Asian NICs. In *South Korea*, the shift from textiles to machinery started in the late 1960s. In recent years more than half of the Japanese investment has been in the machine-making industry – corresponding to the changing stress of Korean development policy. Moreover, while in earlier years the main activity was in end-products, producers of parts and components are increasingly entering the field. A similar shift away from light industry appears in *Taiwan* – again with increasing emphasis on parts makers. In *Singapore*, because of the scarcity of industrial sites, a good supply of qualified workers and high capital accumulation, direct investment in machinery production, especially electrical, has long been appropriate; there has never been any important entry into Singapore of Japanese textile producers. The pattern of investment in *Hong Kong* has been rather different from that in the other Asian NICs. There has been Japanese investment in light industry; but the emphasis has now shifted to banking and insurance for which Hong Kong offers special advantages: a liberal policy on foreign exchange transactions, including freedom to remit profits, and freedom for foreigners to establish enterprises. This change in the pattern of Japanese investment may be associated with a loss of Hong Kong's manufacturing advantages in view of the rise of land prices in the small territory.

There are important common features in the evolution of the pattern of Japanese investment in the machinery industry in the East Asian NICs (apart from Hong Kong). In the early years, the object was to make use both of skilled but low-paid labour and of the incentives offered to foreign investors by most governments. It involved very often the import of parts and components from Japan. As the market expanded, production of parts in the host country became profitable and was also encouraged by regulations insisting on local procurement – sometimes backed by political nationalism. Makers of parts and components entered into direct production in the NICs, sometimes in cooperation with producers of the end-products. For example, several Japanese producers of electronic components recently set up a joint undertaking to supply local producers of end-products in Singapore – a new pattern not seen before.

In end-products, an international division of labour is proceeding: many Japanese firms divide their activities between plants at home and abroad in a clear pattern of specialization. Thus they produce colour television sets in Japan and monochromatic sets abroad; high-class tape recorders equipped with radios in Japan and standard tape recorders abroad. Further, the modus of Japanese capital exports is changing. Earlier, the motives were profits from the sale of end-products and from the exports of parts and the dividends arising from these activities. Now there is more emphasis on the effective re-investment of profits. In these ways, Japan is maturing as a capital exporter.

12.5   The trading activities of Japanese overseas subsidiaries

The fear is often expressed in Japan that the increase of low-priced imports from overseas subsidiaries may seriously damage domestic industry, and that a similar 'boomerang' effect from overseas investment may also arise from the export to developing countries of Japanese equipment, technology and know-how. From a different point of view, it is also sometimes argued that Japanese resistance to imports from Asian NICs is weak because so large a proportion of the imports comes from overseas subsidiaries. Such arguments apply particularly to the effects of Japanese investment abroad in textiles and other light industries. How much ground is there for these anxieties?

Japanese companies do not as a rule provide data in their annual financial reports about their transactions with their overseas subsidiaries (nor do most

Table 12.10 *Sales and purchases of Japanese overseas subsidiaries*

	Agriculture and fisheries	Mining	Foodstuffs	Textiles	Wood, pulp and paper	Chemicals	Iron and steel	Non-ferrous metals	General machinery	Electric machinery	Transportation equipment	Precision machinery	Other manufactures	Commerce	Total
Destination of sales															
Percentage of sales by subsidiaries in Asia															
To domestic market	12.1	0.7	65.0	58.4	91.8	90.0	95.4	86.9	78.3	56.3	82.3	54.5	58.3	53.7	60.7
To third countries	3.6	0.0	21.9	31.2	0.0	7.8	3.9	5.1	21.7	29.7	13.6	3.1	29.9	18.5	20.8
To Japan	84.3	99.3	13.2	10.4	8.2	2.2	0.7	8.0	0.0	14.0	4.2	42.4	11.8	27.8	18.4
Percentage of sales by subsidiaries in all areas															
To domestic market	47.8	3.9	67.2	68.7	16.7	84.9	92.3	51.2	84.6	74.9	88.6	60.0	59.5	47.0	53.1
To third countries	6.5	17.7	18.8	24.1	30.1	11.8	6.4	24.7	15.4	17.5	8.9	4.0	20.6	15.6	15.7
To Japan	45.8	78.4	14.0	7.2	53.3	3.3	1.3	24.1	0.0	7.5	2.4	36.1	19.9	37.4	31.2
Origin of purchases															
Percentage of purchases by subsidiaries in Asia															
From domestic market	96.0	0.0	88.3	40.3	35.1	31.3	13.3	35.0	59.5	41.2	34.1	29.7	42.6	33.9	36.3
From third countries	0.2	100.0	6.1	35.7	6.5	18.6	10.5	18.5	0.3	4.1	0.7	3.8	8.5	25.9	19.2
From Japan	3.8	0.0	5.5	24.1	58.5	50.1	76.3	46.5	40.3	54.6	65.2	66.5	48.9	40.3	44.5
Percentage of purchases by subsidiaries in all areas															
From domestic market	85.8	0.2	85.7	51.2	97.1	37.3	31.4	27.2	63.7	35.3	24.5	32.3	53.6	34.5	35.4
From third countries	6.4	99.7	3.3	27.9	0.3	17.0	32.0	33.1	0.1	4.9	1.0	5.8	6.8	26.3	24.4
From Japan	7.8	0.1	11.0	20.9	2.6	45.8	36.5	37.7	36.2	59.8	74.5	61.9	39.6	39.3	40.2

Source: Ministry of International Trade and Industry, *Overseas Business Activity of Japanese Enterprises, 1978*, Tokyo (in Japanese)

Western companies). But a survey by the Ministry of International Trade and Industry of the sales and purchases of overseas subsidiaries in 1978 provides evidence (*Table 12.10*)[2]. This suggests that the 'boomerang' effects from the trading activities of subsidiaries are not very large, and that they are less important for the Asian subsidiaries than for subsidiaries in other areas of the world. Thus, taking subsidiaries in all industries together, the bulk (61 per cent) of sales by the Asian subsidiaries goes to the domestic market in the host country; only 18 per cent of the sales go to Japan and 21 per cent to third countries. The proportion of sales exported to Japan is low in nearly all industries (e.g. in textiles only 10 per cent) except for agriculture and fisheries and mining – where the purpose of investment is to meet Japan's need for natural resources – and precision instruments. Sales to third markets, however, are larger than sales to Japan in most other industries – e.g. 20 to 30 per cent in foodstuffs, textiles, general and electrical machinery and miscellaneous manufactures.

Comparison of these sales proportions for Asian subsidiaries with their purchases illustrates the structure of Japanese investment. The Asian subsidiaries buy 45 per cent of their total purchases from Japan (against the 18 per cent of their output sold to Japan); the purchases are mainly necessary imports, particularly parts and components, for final production in the host country. In the precision instruments industry, the Asian overseas subsidiaries buy two-thirds of their inputs from Japan and, rather exceptionally, sell back to Japan as much as 42 per cent of their output.

The pattern of subsidiaries' activities in other parts of the world (as shown by the data in *Table 12.10* for subsidiaries in all areas) differs in some respects. The subsidiaries outside Asia sell less of their output in their domestic markets than the Asian subsidiaries, more back to Japan, and less to third countries; but the patterns for subsidiaries' purchases are not dissimilar in the two areas.

Finally, it may be noted that on balance the activities of the overseas subsidiaries contribute positively to the trade balances of the host countries.

12.6   Future issues

In basic industries, Asian NICs, particularly South Korea and Taiwan, are aiming at a further rapid expansion of capacity; targets for some basic products based on construction plans are set out in *Table 12.11*. Thus a capacity of 8.5 million tons of crude steel a year is planned for South Korea in 1981, and over 4 million tons in Taiwan. Similarly, in petrochemicals, South Korea, after completing a capacity of 500 000 tons a year for ethylene in 1981, has recently announced a further expansion of 350 000 tons; and Taiwan plans capacity by 1983 of nearly 900 000 tons. These expansions, aimed principally at meeting domestic demand, are not in themselves

Table 12.11 *Sector targets for Japan and East Asian NICs*

Sector		Japan 1977	South Korea Target 1981	South Korea 1981 as multiple of 1975	Taiwan Target 1981	Taiwan 1981 as multiple of 1975
Basic industries						
Crude steel (1000 tons)	Production	102 405	8 000	3.5	4 150	2.9
	Production capacity	161 308	8 500	3.0		
Ethylene (1000 tons)	Production	3 979	500	5.2	..	..
	Production capacity	5 602	500	5.0	568	1.7
Chemical fertilizer (1000 tons)	Production	1 193	1 546	1.8	500	2.1
	Production capacity	2 600	3 131	1.7	..	..
Assembly and Processing Industries						
Electronic equipment ($ million)	Production	19 700	4 127	4.4	1 010	2.2
Colour TV (1000 units)	Production	9 631	n.a.	..	1 200	4.6
Monochromatic TV (1000 units)	Production	4 708	n.a.	..	5 300	2.0
Automobiles (1000 cars)	Production	8 505	160	..	68	2.3
Shipbuilding (1000 gross tons)	Production	10 070	1 389	2.8	1 225ª	4.4
	Production capacity	19 000	4 250	1.8		

ª It is understood that the production plan for 1981 has now been reduced to about 400 000 tons.

Source: Bank of Japan, *Research Monthly*, June 1978

thought likely to affect very directly the Japanese industries concerned. The amounts are small by comparison with those of Japan; the advantages of low labour costs are not very marked; and Japan's comparative advantages in reliability and efficiency remain.

In basic industries, however, Japan's competitive position in the international market – and the possibility of excess capacity in the world as a whole – is more likely to be affected by developments elsewhere. Thus in petrochemicals, big new projects are in progress in Saudi Arabia and the new revolutionary government in Iran is believed to be anxious for the completion of a petrochemical complex. Because of the limited domestic market in these countries, and also because of Japanese participation in some projects, the Japanese home market might be affected in future unless new supplies can be absorbed by sustained economic growth. Also construction of new petrochemical plants is proceeding fast in resource-rich countries such as Canada, Mexico and Australia – based on gas, oil and coal respectively. And, within Asia, Indonesia, the Philippines and China are all potential petrochemical producers.

In other basic products, too, resource-rich countries in particular are moving from raw materials towards higher value-added products – e.g. from metal ores to metal products, from sawn logs to wood products. This process of extending activities 'downstream' is inevitably pursued by developing countries; it goes slowly, partly because competitiveness in the processing stages demands both technological skills and large-scale production[3]. Because of their dependence on imported primary products and energy, basic industries in Japan, as in other industrial countries, face not only a certain excess capacity in the present world situation and a threat to prices (even from marginal producers such as the East Asian NICs), but also, in the long run, some loss of comparative advantage.

The shift of parts of Japanese manufacturing – particularly of textiles, light industry, some basic chemicals, simple engineering assembly and shipbuilding – to East Asian and other NICs, as described above, and perhaps in future to China, has been much faster than the shift in basic industries and is bound to continue. In the longer run, but before the end of the century, industrial development in China is very likely to bring a quite new dimension into the whole structure of the East Asian (or Pacific) economy and to create new and major problems of adjustment.

It is clear that Japan's response and continued expansion lies in further development on the 'frontiers of technology'. A recent survey of the views of Japanese experts in techno-economics suggests that Japan is expected to maintain or improve her competitiveness, even with other advanced industrial countries, in such products as computers, telecommunication equipment, integrated circuits; it has been said that information-oriented industries such as computer–communication systems will be at the centre of the development of Japan over the next decade. At the same time, it is expected that Japan can at least maintain competitiveness in automobiles and much of engineering, and in some basic materials, such as cold-rolled sheet steel, special steels and fine chemicals. These are the ways in which Japan, as an economy emerging into maturity, can and must, respond to the changing pattern of international development.

It is in our view highly desirable that the inevitable structural transformation in both industrialized and industrializing countries should be as smooth as possible. A rational synchronization of structural change requires at least a full exchange of detailed information, between industrial policy-makers in both groups of countries, about the realities and expectations of supply and demand. Such an exchange is an essential step in smoothing the process of mutual adjustment of the policies – especially of the large-scale investment policies – of both governments and enterprises.

Such exchanges on a global level may be slow to develop. But there could be advantages in making a beginning on a regional scale. Thus, the Pacific area may well hold the best hope of fast expansion in the world economy in the 1980s. If so, Japan must cooperate with other industrial and industrializing nations in the formation of a Pan-Pacific consensus on the future pattern of economic progress in the Pacific area.

References

1 UNCTAD (United Nations Conference on Trade and Development), *Handbook of International Trade and Development Statistics, 1979*. Table 7.1.
2 This is a preliminary analysis based on a sample inquiry.
3 For an excellent detailed review, see UNIDO, *World Industry since 1960*. New York 1979, ch. VI, 'The industrial processing of natural resources'.

PART V

Can the old system work?
Is a new one possible?

13

The strains on the international system

Wolfgang Hager[*]

A wide gap seems to exist between scholarly and expert analysis of the NIC phenomenon and the perceptions, pronouncements and actions of many bureaucrats, politicians, trade unionists and industrialists directly concerned with the issue. For most economists, including those of the GATT and OECD[1], the NICs are too marginal a part of the world economy to warrant the – by implication – irrational fears they provoke. They are, by contrast, important symbols of success: examples of 'the right approach' to development; symbols and tests for the advanced countries torn between the high road of growth and the low road of complacent stagnation. They are a challenge but not a problem: a challenge to seize the opportunities for an evolution of mature industrial societies towards a state which in material and other terms is one of dynamism, and where drudgery gives way to a new division of labour between men and machines, domestically and internationally.

Spelling out the policy implications of this last view – which is implicit in most of the papers of this volume – would require a few pages rather than a chapter.

The NICs are considered to be a *faux problème*. They are a major addition to world welfare, of which a share can be captured by those who seize the opportunity in the advanced countries. A reduction of trade barriers at the border, and adjustment of capital and labour markets within borders, are the keys to opening up new avenues for growth and wealth. Paradoxically, the papers hint at a general pessimism concerning the likely adoption of this course. The discussion at Sussex revealed a universal conviction that protectionism would increase, if not in Japan, then in the European Community and in the United States.

Even at this simple level, policy recommendations face a fundamental dilemma. Should the academic analyst restrict himself to propagating the economically rational cause, or should he consider second-best solutions which *de facto* imply an accommodation to fundamentally wrong approaches? The dilemma is a familiar one from fields as far apart as drug control, abortion or the regulation of prostitution. In such cases, the fight to uphold a principle is half lost when breaches of principle are legalized. The

* *European University Institute*, Florence

motive for doing precisely this is to avoid uncontrolled breaches which remain totally outside social control. Proponents of one view are seen to be virtuous; those of the other soft. Each appears to be dangerous to the other.

The gulf between the upholders of strict principles and those willing to accommodate and channel socially deviant behaviour becomes even wider when the latter, in making their argument, play down the enormity of the crime at issue. Pragmatism then shades over into heresy. To make the case for 'second-best solutions' in international trade, it is not necessary to go this far – only to take as given the folly or ignorance of short-term maximizers and accommodators of special interests (as described in ch. 11). Without second-best solutions, the rapid increase in trade between old and new industrial countries would seem to have, in political terms, all the qualities of an unstable equilibrium, with high economic costs likely to accrue especially to the NICs when this equilibrium breaks down.

The most significant innovation in modern trade policy has been achieved by Japan, which manages virtually all its overseas trade in such a way as to avoid costly breakdowns (sudden denial of access) in the wake of socio-political backlashes. The NICs – a heterogenous group of countries without sharp boundaries – cannot, by themselves, conduct a trade strategy of this kind. With the existing institutional structure, they are condemned to probe and try – as Japan did two decades ago – to discover the socio-political tolerance limits of the advanced countries the hard way. The sudden cut-back by the US of South Korean colour television imports in 1979, which left that purely export-oriented industry working at 20 per cent of capacity[2], is a warning. The difficulty of achieving an alternative institutional framework is demonstrated by the Multi Fibre Arrangement which is a far cry from the elegance of Japan's commercial diplomacy.

Posing the policy dilemma in these preliminary and practical terms is broadly compatible with the other contributions to this volume, although it violates the spirit of most. However, before returning to what is in fact a fairly conventional set of policy proposals, it is perhaps necessary to question the easy optimism with which such recommendations are usually advanced.

13.1   Threat or challenge?

One single finding contained in the OECD report on the NICs should remove it from the agenda of discussions among serious men: their share in the apparent consumption of manufactures in the OECD countries was slightly above 1 per cent in 1976/77[3]. Roughly the same figure applies if the rather misplaced European NICs are taken out of the sample and all the rest of the developing countries are added instead. How can such a small economic magnitude have attracted all this attention?

The first and obvious point to make is the highly uneven distribution of this share as among different product groups. The OECD report shows the NICs supplying large shares of OECD imports only in three product groups: clothing (38.5 per cent), leather products (32 per cent), and wood manufactures (23 per cent). Even for the much talked-about textiles, the NICs only achieved about 11 per cent of imports, manufactures of metal 7 per cent, and so on. The breakdown, however, is given at the two-digit level (separating only 14 groups of manufactured products[4]) which only rarely corresponds to firms, much less plants. A possible justification is the generally recognized fact that so-called intra-industry adjustment – dropping a product line and expanding the production of another – is generally easier than adjusting whole industries. Yet it is a major shortcoming of the OECD report that it fails to give a differentiated picture, if only by way of illustration, of the speed and magnitude of import penetration for individual product groups, at say four- or seven-digit level. The exception is a footnote which reveals for example NIC shares of up to 80 per cent in certain items of the two-digit group electrical machinery for which the overall average is only 12 per cent 1974[5].

There are good reasons why this should be so: only volume sales of a narrow range of products can be profitably undertaken across large distances, and industrial development cannot proceed if the available capital is allocated to a large number of plants, each of inadequate size. Japan, equally, chose to concentrate initial development and (modern) production on a narrow range of goods (somewhat more broadly on the three-digit level). Nevertheless, this alone gives trade with NICs (other than formerly import-substituting ones) a pattern quite different from that of European and North American trade. One can state this point in different ways.

One is to stress the strong possibility that the choice of products is governed, not merely by the logic of comparative advantage, but by strategic considerations internal to the industrializing country. Japan's ultra-modern steel industry did not just happen, but was the result of a deliberate choice and of exceptional commitment of national resources, laying the basis for eventual exports not only of steel but of ships and cars as well. Contemporary South Korea exhibits close parallels. Once the 'voluntarist' nature of the emerging industrial pattern is admitted, i.e. that it is the result of will rather than just of market forces, the reciprocal adjustment to this pattern by others becomes, by implication, a matter of choice rather than equity. This point will be elaborated and enlarged below.

A second consequence of the 'voluntarist' nature of NIC development is the uncertainty which it creates for the investment decisions in the advanced countries. Simple considerations of comparative advantage are not enough. It may be quite safe to produce a labour-intensive item for another decade because none of the NICs bothers to choose it for initial consideration. Equally well, it could arrive in large numbers three years later, initially depressing profit levels in the advanced country, and later forcing total adjustment. In many non-labour intensive industries the uncertainty is, if anything, greater. What European shipyard, planning its investment in 1970, could have foreseen the South Korean development?

Something like this realization must be behind the now near-universal practice of industrialists in *all* sectors to cast anxious backward glances in the direction of the NICs. One result may well be to push rationalization beyond the point warranted, say, by relative prices of capital and labour in the advanced countries, so as to be better prepared, just in case. Such a mechanism is hard to demonstrate empirically, although a great deal of anecdotal evidence points in this direction.

The irrational fears provoked by the NICs may thus rest as much on extrapolation as on actual experience. One crucial assumption of those who eagerly seek an expansion of North–South trade is that of an automatic, stochastic equilibrium in trade, growth and employment between North and South, irrespective of the level of this trade.

The assumption that increased trade with the industrializing South is going to produce an equilibrium – or, rather, will not increase the existing disequilibrium in world labour markets – rests on assumptions which on closer considerations must be qualified as hopes. The most solid argument is the balance-of-payments argument: any additional earnings by the new industrial countries will be spent on imports – indeed, to go by recent experience, rather more than that. The deficit in manufactured trade of the NICs cited in the OECD report – some $18 billion in 1977 – gives support to this claim.

The first objection to this – one generally admitted by free trade advocates – is not important: that the labour content of a dollar's worth of exports to NICs is less than that of imports, and hence that, with balanced trade expansion, there is a net loss of employment in the advanced countries. The effect is swamped by the surplus. Anyway, these 'losses' are the gains from trade, provided there is full employment.

A more serious objection to an argument based on the balance of payments is the unequal geographical distribution of the advanced countries' aggregate surplus. In theory, given a multilateral payments system, this is a non-problem. In a world where the OPEC group gains an unavoidable current account surplus of some $100 billion, the problem changes its character. A surplus by Japan in manufacturing trade with the NICs, which allows it to finance its deficit with OPEC, does nothing to compensate for the deficit of the EEC with the East Asian NICs of some $2 billion. Japan has the employment gain *and* the means to pay cash for its oil. The Community has an employment loss, and a proportionally greater need to finance its current oil bill.

The OECD report on the NICs understates this problem, and its future dimensions, by including three semi-developed European Mediterranean countries in its sample. Even then, Japan managed to have more than half of the OECD surplus in manufactures with the NICs (10.6 out of 18.2 billion dollars in 1977) having had only a third of this surplus in 1973[6]. The rest of the surplus accrues to OECD-Europe, but this is wholly accounted for by the Mediterranean NICs, who can be considered quite atypical, and Brazil. The days of super-competitivity of the European Mediterranean countries were over when they joined the social democratic mainstream of European politics. The OECD report, typically, criticized this as 'overadjustment', but still manages to suggest that trade unions and the spread of accumulated wealth are part of a typical progression for underdeveloped countries (discussed below)! Morover, the Mediterranean countries will continue to earn substantial surpluses on the tourist and transfer accounts, assuring a continued deficit in manufacturing trade with the EEC. The EEC balance with the East Asian NICs, as early as 1977, was sharply in deficit: imports of $4.5 billion against exports of $2.8 billiion[7], recalling the early days of Euro-Japanese trade. For every dollar's worth of textile machinary sold by the EEC to Hong Kong, a hundred dollars' worth of textiles are imported. For Western Europe, the direct link between export of capital goods and imports of products exists in trade with Eastern Europe. Thanks to the dominant position of Japan, it does not exist in trade with Asia. Trade policy, when it comes to the crunch, will almost certainly take account of this circumstance.

Balance-of-trade considerations allow an assessment of the distribution of employment opportunities in essentially static terms. The more important fears are, of course, associated with dynamic considerations, including adjustment. The present NIC share in OECD imports of manufactures is broadly equivalent to that of Japan. For some observers this implies a manageable trade problem. Others may remember that the introduction of Japan into the Western trading system was accompanied by a host of protective innovations, from the first Cotton Textile Arrangement to the voluntary restriction deals imposed by the US in the 1960s. The fact that Japan was boxed in, and continues to operate more or less voluntarily in a system of restraints and self-restraints, rather suggests that the adjustment problems posed even by this now mature and high-cost economy are anything but routine. As Professor Baldwin points out in ch. 11, the adjustment problem posed by the NICs to the United States in the 1980s will be somewhat greater than that posed earlier by Japan. European observers will also recall that part of the US solution to the problem posed by Japan was to deflect that country's export drive to Europe.

Japan keeps cropping up in these pages. Its relevance to the subject is in fact considerable. First, it was the original NIC. Secondly, it is a country whose unbroken dynamism continues to provide adjustment problems to the slow-adjusting majority of its fellow OECD members. There is, in other words, an accumulation of adjustment problems, covering the entire range of industrial production (not, of course, all products). Thirdly, and perhaps more important, the NICs that really worry people, i.e. those of East Asia, are in themselves in part offshoots of the Japanese dynamism. And they in turn are ridding themselves of some of the initial LDC-export industries, with their low value-added and vulnerability to protectionism, passing these on to their Asian hinterland (including export enclaves on the Indian sub-continent).

This is a dream of development planners come true. There are, however, questions. The process by which the East Asian NICs sub-contract work to their regional periphery seems unlikely to result in anything like the increasingly broadly-based development which is finally being achieved, say, in Taiwan. Already the present NICs feel that their development is controlled by the Japanese, both as provider of capital and through trading companies. Nevertheless, these countries possess a strong indigenous business elite, and a political and administration infrastructure quite able to impose its own pattern of development, within certain constraints. The countries now accepting the crumbs from the industrial table of the richer NICs are likely to remain for a long time in a dependent role, as suppliers of a basic labour input. Moreover, they are getting nothing but 'footloose' industries, attracted by tax-holidays and free infrastructural incentives, and likely to leave as quickly as they came. This third generation of would-be industrializing countries effectively competes on a world-wide labour market which is in strong potential surplus.

13.2   The NICs: models for the Third World?

Thus a crucial question to be answered when devising a 'common response' to the NICs relates to their contemporary significance for the Third World as a whole. If they are the first of many, there is a very strong normative case for facilitating such a promising route of escape for poor countries out of the twin traps of poverty and unemployment. By the same token, the problem of adjustment then looks much more formidable.

In terms of contemporary thinking on development issues in both the North and the South, the NICs seem to belong to an earlier and less complicated world. Thus the key transformation of the last decade towards emphasizing basic human needs is irrelevant for countries such as South Korea who are already achieving much more than that modest aim. What, then, has happened to that traditional North–South trade paradigm according to which poor countries overcame the deficiencies of effective demand in early stages of industralization by exporting manufactures to rich countries? For the time being, the NICs with their 80 per cent share of the import markets for LDC manufactures, seem to have pre-empted this route. It is often asserted that the NICs will provide regional growth opportunities for less advanced LDCs. The poor import performance of Japan until very recently, and the $6.8 billion surplus of NICs in trade in manufactures with all LDCs (1976)[8], suggest that this is one of these 'in the long run' situations which are of such scant comfort to policy-makers.

Some of the large NICs such as Brazil and Mexico, with their dualistic economies, have a particularly long way to go before they will need to accept less sophisticated manufactured imports because of internal labour-market constraints. For those development economists who consider world-market oriented development the wrong approach for the truly underdeveloped, the pre-emption of the advanced countries' market for manufactures by a handful of countries presumably constitutes one more argument in favour of individual and collective self-reliance and for abandoning at least for the time being the export-led growth strategy. For others, the NICs show what can be done if appropriate policies are pursued. Most of them would presumably admit that large areas of the globe will not, in fact, be able to emulate the NICs: most of Africa, most countries of Latin America other than the big three (Argentina, Brazil, Mexico) and Indonesia for example.

The Indian sub-continent and China are both the most important in terms of population and the most ambiguous of cases. Their combined population is more than 10 times that of either Japan or the East Asian NICs. Even a (relatively) modest step in the direction of emulating existing NICs (Sri Lanka, India and Bangladesh are all setting up offshore processing industrial parks) would magnify adjustment problems elsewhere, not least in the existing NICs. In the short term, a problem of potential over-capacity in the labour-intensive manufactures typical of the first stages of development could perhaps be solved by further contraction in the industrial countries. In the long term, a total abandonment even of textiles, for example, by advanced countries would provide employment for an additional 5 million people elsewhere, or 1 per cent of the relevant labour force.

Whatever the merits of these particular figures, the orders of magnitude raise a number of troubling questions about the significance of the NIC phenomenon for the most pressing problem, next to food, of the last quarter of the century in development economics: the provision of (industrial) employment for the growing labour capacities of the Third World. The NICs may be able to escape the trap of over-capacity by rapid adjustment out of LDC-type production (although it took Japan two decades to get out of exporting textiles). At the very least, the problem of 'footloose' industries will become an issue of Third World industrial policy. In addition, latecomers to the NIC-stakes may find themselves engaged in potentially loss-making competition: offering foreign firms cheap infrastructure, capital and services without reaping the eventual benefits.

The significance of the NICs for the larger problem of Third World development is thus ambiguous. They may provide a false model (one more in the long series of such models offered by the West), whose inappropriateness stems not least from the established presence of the NICs themselves. In devising responses to the NICs, therefore, it may be wrong to accept without question the view that a liberal policy towards them is automatically a contribution towards the welfare of the Third World in general and of the majority of under-achievers in particular.

The relatively modest employment opportunities offered to a vast untapped labour-pool by a partial spread of the NIC phenomenon may look quite different when seen from the point of view of the 74 million people at present employed in manufacturing in the industrial market economies.

The notion of an automatic equilibrium so confidently explained in the OECD study rests, like all trade theory, on classical assumptions. One in particular seems to have survived in this branch of economics long after it has been discredited in macroeconomic analysis: Say's law which states that there cannot be unemployment, except very temporarily, and that everything produced will find a buyer.

The unemployment point deserves special attention. In classical thinking, unemployment will disappear if wages fall enough. The publication of Keynes's General Theory put this notion to rest as a general proposition, although in its modern version it may apply to particular industries: high wages may lead to labour-substituting investment, and hence to sectoral unemployment, if the increased productivity is not matched by increased demand. The renaissance of classical theory which we can observe, both macro (parts of 'monetarism') and microeconomic thinking, fits in rather well with trade theory which has never ceased to be classical.

As in the post-World War I era, there is a growing conviction among politicians and some of their economic advisers that wages are too high. Probably more by instinct than by theoretical reflection, trade is seen as a useful corrective device. More formally, trade theory offers the factor-price equalization theorem, according to which trade causes a tendency for, *inter alia*, (productivity) wages to equalize[9].

The OECD study, characteristically, assumes that (productivity) wages in the NICs (and their successors?) will rise:

> 'In countries with large excess labour supply, real wages may lag behind productivity, but this will generate very high profits, which will attract the attention of governments and wage-earners alike, leading over time to social and political pressures, higher wages or higher taxation.'[10]

The short-term evidence available is inconclusive. Brazil's unit labour costs fell at an annual rate of 5.2 per cent in 1963–1970; so did South Korea's, by 4.4 per cent in 1970–1973, to rise roughly in line with OECD's (9.8 per cent) in 1973–1976; Hong Kong's costs rose by only 3.4 per cent in

1973–1976. Because of the large initial gap, and the very considerable reductions which must have been realized in capital costs and other overheads as a result of learning and economies of scale, labour's ability to capture profits must be judged slight. Only in Taiwan (19 per cent in 1973–1976) did unit labour costs rise twice as fast as in major OECD countries[11].

As a general proposition, and seen from the standpoint of labour in the advanced countries, the factor price equalization theorem could imply, with equal plausibility, a reduction in their wages. The confident free trader would deny this. All that is required of the worker is to give up the, by implication, small part of economic activity where his wages would have to fall in line with international (i.e. 'Southern') factor prices, and transfer to activities where his skill, and the capital put at his disposal, allow wages to be maintained and raised. The unanswered question in this context, however, is why there should be a match, in terms of employment, between activities rendered uneconomical by international market forces, and the new high value-added activities.

At the very least we can expect a lag between the disappearance and creation of industries, as lead-times differ significantly in the two categories. The technical problem is compound by differences in the ability to respond to market signals between established and 'green-field' economies, and their very different socio-economic adjustment possibilities. Thus, in addition to a permanent high level of frictional or search unemployment in the short term, there may well be frictional or search unemployment for capital in the medium term. Indeed, the simultaneous presence in our labour and goods markets of surplus and scarcity is a familiar phenomenon. Transition is not a transitory but a permanent state. It depends, among other things, on the level, or rate of change, whether the related under-utilization/destruction of capacity, combined with inflationary bottlenecks, is an engine for growth or not. Moreover, at present, the advanced sectors form a small part of our economies. This share could only be larger if *consumption* patterns shift radically in the developed countries, or if vast new markets for these advanced sectors are opened up outside. Both of these are happening, but surely at a pace which is much slower than the potential displacement of the old labour-intensive or mature capital-intensive jobs. Thus a strong argument against an automatic, stochastic equilibrium being maintained between routine and advanced products is the composition of demand, which in a reasonably short-term perspective puts a ceiling on the total size of productive activity which can be considered safe – for how long? – from lower cost competition.

History abounds with examples of civilizations which decline because they lose a monopoly position: Venice and the Netherlands as traders, Florence as banker and advanced textile producer, etc. The most telling parallel with today's situation is the fate of late medieval cities in Europe, with their guild-administered restrictive (monopoly) practices, which were wiped out, overnight, when early capitalism discovered the possibilities of rural cottage production – the offshore enterprises of its day. This may have been for the greater good of Europe as a whole (the rapidity of the decline is responsible for the perfect conservation of many of these cities), but this argument is less than convincing for those who lose from the shift. And the period of 'adjustment' was characterized by political conflicts which were (with apologies to Hobbes), nasty, brutish, and long.

13.3 Social democracy and labour oligopoly

There is a more fundamental reason to doubt whether an extensive North–South division of labour in manufactures will automatically provide full employment conditions in the North. The starting point of this doubt is the admission that labour markets in advanced countries, taken collectively, are not characterized by market pricing (of wages) but by oligopoly pricing. This fact is only revealed when the *accidental* external protection of this oligopoly of high-priced labour is removed, or replaced by deliberate protection.

Instead of distinguishing between old and new industrial countries, we can divide the world into two parts: the unionized; and the non-unionized or weakly unionized (including, of course, Eastern Europe). As it happens, the unionized part of the world has produced most of the technology on which world economic development is based. For the term 'unionized', one could just as well use the term 'democratic', with its implications, among other things of (re-)distributive politics. The term 'unionized', however, is linked more precisely to a particular factor cost. A major purpose of unions is to capture the gains derived from technological progress and capital accumulation, i.e. increased productivity, in higher wages and shorter working hours. Clever unions always leave enough margin for profits to be made, so that they become co-proprietors of increasing wealth.

One condition for the smooth working of unionized economies was the *de facto* oligopoly held by democratic labour over the right to make use of technology. This oligopoly was protected, *inter alia*, by the gap in educational levels separating them from the South, and by the inability of the managerial systems of Eastern Europe to make full use either of their educated populations or of the fruits of technological advance. The price workers set on their labour, although strictly speaking not a market price, did not seem artificial in a general high wage environment whose different constituents were linked by intensive trade. The unit-labour cost of the most efficient country set a market limit to all others, but this could as well have been a country with high nominal wages such as the US and, later, Germany, as a relatively low-wage producer such as Italy.

This then was a harmonious world where marginal differences in comparative advantage leading rarely to rapid and upsetting shifts in trade patterns. One of the few exceptions, easily handled in a period of rapid growth, was the disturbance caused by the competitive successes of Italian electric applicances in the early years of the EEC.

The ability of the workers of advanced industrialized states to capture a fair proportion of the 'rent' provided by technology and productivity advances rested, apart from the systemic need to maintain effective demand, on a monopoly hold over the exploitation of technology. The story of the erosion of that monopoly, first and most sharply experienced in the United States (where it was accelerated by an overvalued dollar), is usually told with reference to the investment activities of multinational companies. These removed at least three barriers to the diffusion of technology: shortage of indigenous capital resources, shortage of managerial and engineering capacity to utilize complex production processes, and Third World difficulties of access to distant and sophisticated markets. In the 1970s, and perhaps even more in the 1980s, a transformation of the nature of production technology itself is helping to overcome the most difficult of barriers, that of education, specifically the lack of skilled and craft labour.

Automation through numerically controlled machine tools, or in certain production processes, not only saves labour, but depresses the skill levels needed in the labour force. The most difficult educational qualities to impart to a labour force – reliable and sophisticated monitoring of production processes, and precision in the application of tools – are precisely the qualities in which the new industrial robots excel. In many industries, the simplification of production, and the degrading of skill levels required, facilitates the transfer of certain industries to the Third World, provided there is a substantial amount of manual work left in the process.

For other products, thanks to the micro-chip and to the introduction of veritable production robots, neither the First World nor the Third World worker is needed. Thus Japan is regaining its comparative advantage in the most mass-produced and basic processes of cloth manufacture which it formerly left to the Third World. The machines give employment to those who make them, and to a few engineers with oil cans, or more precisely with electronic monitoring devices.

Decisions on whether to place these robots in the old or the new industrial countries will depend not only on wage differentials, but also on the cost of capital and transport and, above all, on secure access to markets. Another factor may be trade union resistance to their introduction, or to their regular, round-the-clock operation. Both the initial capital cost, and the capital-utilization considerations favour the NICs.

It is true that the substitution of capital for labour has been frightening people since the 1920s (or since the Luddites, for that matter) and has proved, with more or less of a lag, to be compatible with full employment at higher real wages. So it is not impossible that the ultimate in production rationalization ushered in by cheap micro-chips will turn out to have similar benign effects.

But clearly, the effect of the new production techniques on the quality and quantity of the demand for labour pose important questions. Have the NICs, by accelerating defensive rationalization in the advanced countries, stimulated the production of an antibody in the economic bloodstream of the latter which may eventually carry off both the patient and his affliction?

Opportunities for capital-deepening and automation, pushed to extremes where they replace the ordinary factory worker altogether, will vary greatly from sector to sector. The unmanned halls of robots assembling cars for Nissan and Volkswagen are, however, a contemporary reality. Capital-deepening has allowed both the United States and Switzerland to increase their exports of textiles. Capital-intensive agriculture in the rich countries has long been producing many commodities more cheaply than LDCs paying subsistence wages.

This constellation has of course implications for one of the core-areas of domestic politics in Western democracies – the wages and employment of industrial workers. The workers' ability to increase real wages – capturing the rent offered by increased productivity – is now limited by the competition both of capital at home, *and* of cheap labour abroad. Any attempt to resist the competition of capital (resisting rationalization) is made futile by the loss of export markets, and hence of employment, even when the home market is protected. Any attempt to raise real wages is answered by a combination of rationalization and transfer of investment to low-wage countries. This process will presumably be accelerated when capital goods themselves can be bought cheaply from NICs, and slowed down as the wage gap between NICs and advanced countries narrows.

By a rather long detour, we arrive at the conclusion that there is little alternative to trying the optimist approach, for all that it is worth, until trade reaches higher levels and the doubts expressed earlier are settled one way or another. Recent examples, notably in Italian industry, have shown the tremendous reserves of adjustment capacity which remain even in European economies seemingly in the grip of socio-political sclerosis. In the short term, the 'cold shower hypothesis' implicit in the ready – as opposed to reluctant – embrace of the new trading partners may very well work. Note that most of the doubts expressed earlier rested on extrapolation. Trade, in short, is conceived as a medicine: useful in homeopathic doses, but potentially debilitating if administered too generously.

Embracing the optimist approach implies a basic readiness to allow, and even deliberately to facilitate, adjustment. Within this broad commitment, however, there are alternative strategies. To some extent, these strategies are dictated by political forces over which no democratic government has absolute control. Here we return to the idea of the 'second-best', or damage limitation, alluded to at the beginning of this paper. To some extent, however, strategies can and must be worked out at international levels to minimize the clash of interests. Such strategies are not necessarily in conflict with a commitment to the market where they address the 'voluntarist' aspects of industrial policies and seek to forestall the emergence of incompatible patterns.

The urgency of the need for the international community to be seen to tackle potential trade problems in a constructive rather than haphazard manner (as past GATT rounds have been used to keep protectionism at bay) derives from the rather unpropitious situation which provides the short-term setting for NIC integration into the world economy. To this setting we therefore turn before considering some policy steps.

13.4 The world economy in the 1980s: growth, inflation and energy

The first crucial element in the setting for NIC integration in the world economy is the growth performance of the old industrial countries. Perhaps more subtly, if we consider employment as the crucial variable in the political economy of trade, the key relationship is between productivity growth on the one hand and final demand on the other. It is at least possible – and to this possibility recent US experience of stagnating or even falling productivity adds some realism – to picture the West matching production to consumption by reducing potential productivity through work-sharing, thus allowing full employment to be maintained. The work-sharing assumption is crucial if we assume that, even without some net addition to the value of capital stock, replacement investment will improve productivity per man-hour in the manufacturing sector, the sector most relevant to trade.

Two mechanisms making for slow growth deserve to be considered separately, as they influence the way in which 'the problem' may present itself. The first mechanism is inflation. Whatever its origins, on which whole libraries have been produced since 1965 – the rigidities of goods or labour markets, government attempts to disguise distributional choices in its own spending, complicity in disguising non-market behaviour by labour, loss of money illusion by labour without a compensating gain in money sense, cost-push introduced by government regulation, etc. – all these will not disappear despite partial successes in most OECD countries. With direct methods such as prices and incomes policies out of favour, and with the world too impatient or sceptical to await the results of supply-oriented approaches to the problem, the ultimate weapon, deflation, is being used. This is, in fact, the second time that this method has been resorted to on a world-wide scale. As in 1974, the nations of the OECD ignore the deflationary impact of the oil price rise. The coming recession, again accompanied (and deepened) by huge balance-of-payments deficits (the counterpart of the oil producers' renewed surpluses), will form the backdrop to the attempts during the early 1980s to keep the world trading system on an even keel.

The point of this detour from our main subject is this: low growth is merely a statistical aggregate, which may or may not have deeper causes. Its actual manifestation, in the crucial half-decade, may turn out not as a steady state that one can learn to live with, but as a short-term deterioration of some violence. This in turn may generate expectations of stop–go cycles, implying an increasingly sluggish response to 'go' policies.

Oil is the second major element making for growth pessimism. It now seems that we shall be forced to live, for at least half a decade, in a situation in which, at best, the oil market is delicately balanced, with at worst, 'unscheduled' production cut-backs, say, by Saudi Arabia. Leaving aside the worst case, a balanced market is one where production is matched to demand in the downswing but cannot satisfy demand in any substantial upswing (there is no new Alaska and North Sea on the horizon to disguise this fact in the next recession). So we cannot count, this time round, on terms-of-trade gains, increased imports by oil producers, and anti-inflationary effects of lower oil prices to shorten the coming recession; and any modest upswing will be killed in its tracks by a tight oil market.

As an optimist I would hope that 'something will turn up' to save us in the late 1980s from a third repetition of the oil-cum-inflation boom and bust cycle. By 1990 the world may have regained enough confidence, and may have been sufficiently chastened by past failures, to take a new look at the international trading system. But a lot of temporary or emergency measures will, by then, have hardened into established insitutions. Like the Multi Fibre Arrangement, *c'est le provisoire qui dure*.

The oil constraint, besides its macroeconomic effects of deepening and prolonging the next recession, also has microeconomic and industrial policy implications which change the setting for NIC trade. At the most general level, a shift in relative prices of the magnitude we are now experiencing leads to an increased rate of adjustment. Some products will be more expensive to make, others more expensive to use (e.g. cars). Other products, such as home insulation materials and perhaps body insulation (textiles), will be in greater demand. Adjustment and the resultant 'frictional' unemployment would worsen the climate for NICs. The car industry is the most likely sector to suffer from the shift in energy prices. Although the potential protectionism in this sector would not touch the classical NICs (except possibly Brazil and South Korea), and would be directed mainly against Japan and the US, the climate for liberal trade would deteriorate considerably.

Much more speculative would be the effects of deliberate government measures to ensure energy efficiency in industry. It is not inconceivable that governments, by a combination of regulation and incentives, will accelerate the shift away from energy-inefficient production technologies, notably in metal treatment, chemicals and especially textile treatment, towards known and better alternatives. Indeed the shift might even help a number of countries by bringing about a reversion of demand to, for example, natural fibres and natural rubber. During such a period of accelerated write-off of existing capital stock, industries could legitimately ask for protection.

There are two further jokers in the new pack of cards dealt to the world economy by the energy situation. We are living with a dual oil market. The OPEC-controlled market has the lower prices and is rationed by a combination of producer country and oil company control. The spot market is dear. Rationing is biased towards the status quo. The NICs, with steeply rising import needs, and with fewer established links with the multinationals, are liable to find themselves at a cost disadvantage. The prospect of Brazil being forced onto the spot market for 40 per cent of its needs in 1980 is a case in point. This mechanism could reduce the competitiveness of NICs while at the same time reducing their capital spending, as their international borrowing capacity for current balance-of-payment purposes becomes exhausted.

The oil-related balance-of-payments pressures, besides the constraints on growth and on ability to import which they put on most participants in the world economy, contain a special uncertainty about the NICs: the extent to which the United States will want to pay cash for its oil rather than finance it on credit. To the extent that the US wants to pay cash, i.e. aim for a healthy current account balance, the competition in world export markets will be severe. Already, by comparison with parts of Europe, the US is a cheap labour country. Indeed, some areas of the country still offer investors a non-union environment not very different from that of Singapore. Many sectors, as different as textiles and motor cars, are adapting to world market conditions and are poised to capture increasing market shares. It is thus in the West European market battlefield that the contending armies – the Japanese, the Americans and the NICs – will meet (joined by the Eastern Europeans, forced onto the international oil market by the Soviet Union, and desperate for hard currency earnings). Oil-induced neo-mercantilism may give the *coup de grâce* to Western Europe's faltering commitment to free trade.

These, then, are some of the medium-term developments which provide the setting for the integration into the world economy of the industrial newcomers. While the picture may seem unduly gloomy, it may be a useful corrective to a facile, and potentially dangerous, rhetoric of 'business as usual' seducing the NICs into basing their growth strategies on rather shifty foundations. Sri Lanka, a would-be NIC, has installed capacity to produce 670 million items of clothing, while the export markets in the rich countries open to it under the various quota restraints amount to 16.7 million units[12]. This seems the road to disappointment and waste.

13.5   A 'common response'?

From the standpoint of 'systems management', the single most important change brought about by the heterogeneity of the participants is the internationalization of production and the spread of trade in manufactures. To apply a single standard to a diverse group is attractive from the point of view of simplicity and predictability, and it satisfies basic criteria of equity. In practice, for most purposes, voluntary agreements among the participants in the world economy, undertaken within a general framework of cooperation and orderly dispute settlement, seem to be the most that can be expected of a global order.

This does not imply that all trade, for instance, must be of the 'organized' variety. On the contrary, trade amongst most participants and in most products will continue to be conducted within the traditional GATT framework. At the margins of tolerance, however, adherence to that framework is a convenience rather than a commitment, and one which can be suspended in individual cases.

However, only rarely will such suspension be wholly unilateral. Nations prefer to have the agreement, however grudgingly given, of those whom they confront with a change in the rules of the game. The reasons lie, first in a concern for the system of cooperation as such; secondly, they stem from a nation's genuine concern for the welfare of the party about to be damaged, even if the nation's own interests take preference. At the very least this allows discussions about the least costly ways of achieving a desired effect. Voluntary restriction agreements are the most obvious example; the European preference for a trigger-price based system of steel protectionism in the United States is another. Thirdly, all trading nations, including those of Eastern Europe, are at the same time partners in a global pattern of political cooperation. However, the political emphasis which countries or groups of countries attach to their respective relationships varies. This is one of the reasons for trade discrimination and its counterpart, preferences.

A common response defined as the conditional adherence to free trade, supplemented by bargains within the constraints of interdependence and a shared concern for order which is ultimately political, can only be valid as a prediction (or description of contemporary reality), not as a normative prescription. For the latter the free trade doctrine has to serve.

La Rochefoucauld knew of the social usefulness of such a fiction when he defined hypocrisy as the compliment which vice pays to virtue. Until we have an economic theory (preferably an internationally shared one) ascribing positive sum values to departures from free trade, such departures will be made within a zero-sum frame of thinking and the rest on the exercise of power, tempered by the constraints of interdependence.

For trade in raw materials, we have the beginnings of such a theory. For trade in other goods, we have partial theories serving the perceived interests of particular groups, such as the infant industry–import-substitution paradigm still popular in the Third World and sanctioned by international agreement (e.g. article XVIII of GATT). Among the OECD countries, the notion of rationalization cartels which maintain profits in time of oversupply and thus preserve the vitality of industry, and which has been such a successful and routine feature of Japanese industrial policy, is being extended to the international level by arrangements in the steel and shipbuilding sectors. Revisionism in all these cases explicitly takes account of the diseconomies of instability, a point made by Galbraith and the neo-Keynesians in the US in more general terms.

In Great Britain, the Cambridge school has developed theories which at least contain some of the elements of a realistic welfare theory of trade, incorporating dynamic elements derived from macroeconomic thinking. Although its parochial British bias precludes an easy extension to the global level, some of the 'Cambridge' thinking could interestingly be extended to Europe and the Atlantic area, probably with much more moderate results. These might even have validity in global welfare terms: one may refer, in particular, to the contradiction between de-industrialization occurring in Northern countries (as a result of near-zero growth of output and trade) while those same countries are meant to make up the deficiencies of the new industrial countries as regards *both* effective demand and capital formation. Until such a theory is developed, however, the normative implications of free trade theory, with all its unrealistic assumptions, will have to serve as the standard for international behaviour.

The more interesting policy questions concern, however, the departures from the norm which are generally expected, and which have to be both minimized and structured. Again it is easier to predict than to prescribe. One particularly thorny problem is that of discrimination. Postwar economic history is rich in examples of both positive and negative discrimination. We can think of positive discrimination in much the same terms as we think of the 'affirmative action' by which the US 'unfairly' favours minority groups in the job market and education. The dual trade standard operated in the Atlantic community until the lifting of exchange controls in the late 1950s can serve as an early example of positive discrimination (by the strong against himself); so can the dual standard in North–South trade which hardened from the denial of reciprocity to the adoption of the Generalized System of Preferences. Japan, incidentally, was granted a dispensation from reciprocity for twice as long as was Europe. Japan, too, suffered the first major case of negative discrimination, i.e. the early Cotton Agreements which were almost wholly directed against this first NIC. The present, restrictionist Multi Fibre Arrangement, and the generally high level of protection against imports from the Third World are in the same tradition.

Discrimination is also implicit in the many, if mostly unsuccessful, attempts to form regional blocs in the Third World, and in the rhetoric about collective self-reliance. Two features of LDC regional groupings, whether in Latin America, Africa or Asia, are noteworthy in a discussion of principles. First, discrimination against the strongest member(s) is usually agreed within the group, rather in the spirit of the early postwar Atlantic System. Where rules (e.g. liberalization *à deux vitesses*) are insufficient to produce perceived equality of opportunity and risk, industrial planning, in the sense of a negotiated regional division of labour, is attempted. Secondly, the rationale for the whole group's discrimination against the outside world is the perception that liberalization of trade is safe only if competition is confined to economies with similar conditions, and if it takes place within a political context which allows for correction of remaining equalities.

Specific regimes, tailor-made to fit particular economic and political conditions, are also found among advanced countries. The US – Canadian Automotive Agreement, with its allocation of investment, local production and export opportunities, has its counterpart in less formal arrangements between Australia and Japan. Nascent regimes to organize not only trade, but also investment and prices in certain crisis sectors – shipbuilding, steel, fibres – in the OECD and EEC frameworks, can also be cited. Within the EEC, moves towards a negotiated division of labour in fields of high technology such as aircraft and lately telecommunications provide a close parallel to general industrialization schemes in LDC regional groupings[13].

To put the question of the 'response to the NICs' into this broader context of an evolving system of managed international trade avoids the misleadingly simplified view of a bilateral North–South relation, seen in isolation, requiring essentially a yes–no answer with regard to protectionism. As global interdependence in industry has deepened and extended outside the Atlantic area, the very diversity of countries, which has offered such opportunities to trade, has tended to pose novel problems. There is more involved than the mutual, and mutually beneficial, adjustment of markets with different cost structures or the mutual accommodation of different ways of doing business, producing and trading. There is a similarity between the problems posed by the NICs setting up processing zones with special incentives on the one hand, and, on the other, the US achieving sudden market penetration in the petrochemical products as a result of artificially low energy prices, the EEC doing the same with subsidized steel, Japan achieving another export conquest because of a careful concentration of capital and scientific resources, or, again, Comecon countries pursuing industrialization strategies based on more or less explicit buy-back provisions. The world is a highly mixed economy, where 'natural' economic forces are modified to suit the choices and priorities of different societies.

13.6   Opportunities for accommodation

With this kind of approach we move on to dangerous ground. If trade adjustment is not merely a matter of accommodating market forces, but the economic strategies of others, it clearly becomes legitimate for those who are to supply the markets to choose whether they want to profit from the new and cheaper sources of supply, or whether they want to implement their own industrial strategies, which in practice may mean the maintenance of the status quo. Alternatively, industrialization strategies which depend heavily on the cooperation of importing countries can arguably be made the subject of *ex ante* consultation. In practice, this may simply introduce protectionism at an earlier stage. The discouragement by the European Community of industrial projects of virtually all kinds in the (partially state-dominated, 'voluntarist') economies of Spain and Portugal in the early stages of enlargement negotiations, may point in this direction. The ultimate sanctions which the Community can apply differ significantly. In the Mediterranean case, competition rules of the Common Market can be dusted off and applied once membership is completed. For the non-member NICs, *ex post* protectionism remains an option. In the latter case, there is the risk of waste as installed (export) capacity is suddenly idled. The South Korean television example (the sudden imposition of US quotas already cited) is one of many during the 1970s. In the slow growth environment of the 1980s, much more extensive recourse to such practices seems likely.

The aim must be to minimize such instances. Free-trade rhetoric, while useful as a device for resisting domestic pressures, is dangerous when it creates illusions in the new exporting countries. In the broadest sense, consultations about their industrialization strategies must serve to introduce a sense of realism. The Multi Fibre Arrangement, for all its shortcomings, has given clear signals as to the likely market growth in the old industrial countries – signals which are clearly being heeded in the more sophisticated NICs (but apparently not in Sri Lanka). For other products, especially those needing even more costly and long-term capital investment, some consultative process which confronts individual investment plans and brings out their potential incompatibilities may be useful. The kind of naive ruthlessness which led Japan to build up a shipbuilding capacity in the early 1970s – even on the basis of falsely optimistic demand projections implying a decimation of European industry – could succeed only for a time in this particular non-national market. The experiment proved costly, both to the Europeans who first subsidized and then cut production and to the Japanese who are 'freezing' about one-third of their capacity. The episode illustrates both the limited effectiveness of the kind of early warning system proposed – after all there were global demand forecasts, and there was an OECD shipbuilding committee – but also its potential usefulness. It would be unduly pessimistic to argue that the international community is unable to learn, or is condemned to continue to accommodate conflicting industrial strategies by pure trial and error.

Some consultation may also be useful on more general economic policies which affect the nature of the adjustment challenge. The most controversial element here is the trade-off chosen by the NICs between capital accumulation and redistributive policies. The latter not only influence the degree of competitiveness, but also the size and nature of import demand; most important, policies which create a broadly-based home demand lead to a more diversified industrial structure, which in turn allows a diversification of exports. Concern for the welfare of Third World workers as expressed by trade unions in the old countries rests in part on hypocritical motives. But the willingness of trade unions to cooperate, in a statesmanlike way, in the elimination of their members' jobs, is not eased by the conviction that they are playing the game of the capitalists. If insistence on ILO (International Labour Office) standards as a condition for allowing imports is interference in the affairs of others, so are, in an interdependent world, investment strategies which imply rapid adjustment. Moreover, the concern is not only hypocritical. So long as workers have no effective advocates in autocratic countries, defence of their social and human rights is arguably as important – not least because of the number of human beings affected – as the concern for the human rights of a politically active minority.

In economic terms, this amounts to a prescription that the NICs join, as soon as possible, the high-wage cartel of the advanced countries as a condition for peaceful coexistence. Other suggestions that would increase the chances of harmony equally imply raising costs (and thus reducing competitive advantage), but are based on market considerations. While labour cannot be said to be exploited, or underpaid, in strictly economic terms, the subsidies given to capital in most NICs can legitimately be made the subject of consultation if efficient factor allocation is to be the normative basis for trade. Preferential loans, tax holidays, the free or subsidized provision of infrastructure, power, etc. fall under this heading. The main motive for these practices, which effectively amount to self-exploitation, is competition among the NICs and other LDCs. Attempts to form at least regional 'condition cartels' – the Andean Group provides an early example – should be encouraged rather than hindered by Western champions of multinational enterprises[15].

Some experts in the World Bank appear to be emerging almost as champions of export subsidies for Third World countries. While a reasonable economic case can be made for this practice for any single country, for the developing world as a whole it seems a self-defeating strategy: self-exploitation only shortens the time until the protectionist backlash occurs. This is in fact the heart of the argument advanced here: any economic strategy in a developing country which looks reasonable if the environment is treated as exogenous may look quite different when policies of different countries are aggregated and when the notion is introduced of an (ultimately fixed) ceiling on the adjustment capacity of the old industrial centres.

The Japanese, as stated earlier, have become masters in designing their export strategies in such a way as to stay just below the backlash threshold. But MITI holds little sway over the extra-territorial offshoots of Japanese industry in the NICs, or over the Japanese trading companies which conduct a good deal of the trade of these countries. The secondary effects of Japanese exports of capital and trading techniques threaten to undermine the open trading system on which direct exports from Japan depend. Of course, firms from Europe and the United States are also heavily present in the NICs. But their activities are aimed at their home markets, and thus form part of integrated investment strategies with built-in adjustment. The Japanese are also, of course, importers of offshore products, but much of the Japanese-derived investment in the NICs is destined for third markets[16].

It can be argued that the NICs which really worry people are those in East Asia (including export zones outside the NICs but part of the same economic network). The short-term problem can thus be reduced to one of accommodation between a dynamic East Asia and a stagnating Atlantic area. Japan can reasonably be expected to take a role in managing this accommodation – to export also its politico-economic management skill to the area. The opportunity for doing so may arise, if plans to institute a Pacific Community are realized. Already, the main countries likely to be part of such a community – the US, Australia, Japan and the ASEAN group – have developed a unique system of organized free trade amongst themselves. Any attempt to formulate this multi-bilateral system into a coherent whole would necessitate a serious look at the respective industrial strategies: it is precisely this *vue d'ensemble* which seems to be required. But as the history of bilateral US–Japanese trade accommodations has shown, Western Europe tends to be affected by such deals. Nevertheless, with its strong negotiating position, derived from a negative trade balance with all partners of a prospective Pacific community, the European Community should be able to insert itself into the process of implicit bargaining envisaged.

The fact that, in an international economic system composed of 'voluntarist' actors, trade requires not simply an adjustment to different cost patterns, but an accommodation to the economic strategies of others has not so far been greatly stressed with regard to the NICs, but is clear enough within the OECD world of mixed economies. As the advanced countries increase government intervention at the industrial level, subsidies are becoming a contentious issue among them. The inefficiency introduced by this form of 'financial protectionism' – arguably a multiple of the misallocation effect measured in pure trade terms – makes it highly desirable to remove incentives for engaging in the practice. In some important cases where all, not just some, countries are the sinners, and are clearly engaged in a negative-sum game, the OECD and the EEC have attempted to arrive at an

MBSR, a mutually balanced subsidy reduction. Ships, steel and export credits are well-known examples. The New General Agreement on Tariffs and Trade (GATT) code on subsidies, and the OECD campaign against subsidies launched under the term 'positive adjustment', provide for a broad attack on the problem. To some extent the issue *is* much more important in the Atlantic area: the countries concerned have large interventionist budgets and trade heavily with each other. On the other hand, precisely because these countries trade such a wide variety of goods with each other and thus have to remain competitive over the whole range, resources can normally not be concentrated too narrowly. Basically, operating in a vast 'free' trade area for industrial goods requires an even, but necessarily thin, spread of capital resources. Neither Japan (until recently) nor the NICs face this problem.

In the old industrialized countries, subsidies of the protectionist variety are usually granted in spectacular and visible cases. One circumstance which makes for visibility is the sudden advent of a new competitor on the market. The NICs have an interest in achieving a market penetration which can be handled without recourse to industrial policy: again the notion of a threshold of tolerance must be respected if the openness is to be maintained. If the NICs conduct their own industrial policies with this in mind – e.g. by diversifying, producing for home demand, and at true cost – the chances of staying within the threshold are improved.

The OECD countries, in their turn, can introduce policy measures to extend their threshold of tolerance. Successful macroeconomic policies would be the most helpful but seem the least likely. Labour market policies, including wage differentials which improve mobility, are an essential ingredient. Work-sharing, judiciously applied to categories, sectors, and regions where it would not produce bottlenecks of labour in expanding sectors, seems near to inevitable in the 1980s. None of these measures would be sufficient to cope with sudden market penetration of the kind that triggers protectionist responses. The worst possible solution would be to pretend that the problem does not exist and will not get worse in future. Everything that can be done to provide to developing countries a realistic picture of future market opportunities and to confront these opportunities, in time, with their perhaps mutually incompatible investment and export plans, may help to avoid waste and a sharp deterioration of the international trading climate.

References

1 See e.g.: R. Blackhurst, N. Marian and J. Tumlir, *Trade Liberalization, Protectionism and Interdependence*. General Agreement on Tariffs and Trade (GATT) Studies in International Trade, No. 5, Geneva, 1977; OECD, *The Impact of the Newly Industrializing Countries on Production and Trade in Manufactures*, Paris, 1979.

2 *Financial Times*, 24 September 1979.

3 Organization for Economic Cooperation and Development (OECD), *The Impact of the Newly Industrializing Countries on Production and Trade in Manufactures*, Paris, 1979, para 99.

4 Organization for Economic Cooperation and Development (OECD), *The Impact of the Newly Industrializing Countries on Production and Trade in Manufactures*, Table 5.

5 Organization for Economic Cooperation and Development (OECD), *The Impact of the Newly Industrializing Countries on Production and Trade in Manufactures*, para 107, footnote 24.

6 Organization for Economic Cooperation and Development (OECD), *The Impact of the Newly Industrializing Countries on Production and Trade in Manufactures*, Table 10.

7 M. Noelke, *Europe – Third World Interdependence: Facts and Figures. EEC Commission Development Series, 1978, p. 82*.

8 *Organization for Economic Cooperation and Development (OECD), The Impact of the Newly Industrializing Countries on Production and Trade in Manufactures*, Table 33.

9 Complete equalization, first posited by Heckscher ('The Effect of Foreign Trade on the Distribution of Income', *Ekonomisk Tidskrift*, 1919) and elaborated by B. Ohlin, has since been shown to be a special case. Such equalization would of course eliminate commodity trade. See on this B. Ohlin *et al.* (eds.), *The International Allocation of Economic Activity*, Macmillan, London, 1977, esp. pp. 28–30.

10 Organization for Economic Cooperation and Development (OECD), *The Impact of the Newly Industrializing Countries on Production and Trade in Manufactures*, para 34.

11 Organization for Economic Cooperation and Development (OECD), *The Impact of the Newly Industrializing Countries on Production and Trade in Manufactures*, Table 22.

12 Hans Maull is thanked for this telling information.

13 Other examples of moves towards a negotiated international division of labour – leaving aside the obvious case of the Multi Fibre Arrangement – are the successful attempts by ASEAN to discourage synthetic rubber production in Japan in order to increase market opportunities for the natural product, attempts by the Third World to achieve a similar result on a broader range of synthetic products in the North–South context, and discussions within the Euro–Arab dialogue on future investment and market patterns in petrochemicals.

14 See ch. 12, section 12.2.

15 The Andean Pact's famous 'Decision 24' of 1971 was an attempt to restrain competition for foreign investment by the adoption of common standards for taxation, repatriation of profits, terms for technology transfers, etc. See D. Morawetz *The Andean Group: a case study in Economic Integration among Developing Countries*. MIT Press, Cambridge, Massachusetts, 1974, pp. 46–47.

16 For data on the activities of Japanese subsidiaries abroad, see ch. 12, section 12.5.

Appendix

Notes on conference discussion

In the course of preparing this book, the authors presented draft versions of their papers to a conference organized at the University of Sussex by the Sussex European Research Centre in January 1980. Over 30 people, known for their active roles in the discussion of development problems, took part in the conference – a list of participants follows – and have influenced the final presentations.

More issues were raised in the conference than can be summarized here. Only a few selected points will be mentioned.

In the discussion of the concepts of diffusion and dependency the question of the role of transnational corporations gave rise, as might be expected, to considerable differences of opinion. The rather negative view of their function in development, expressed by **Kreye** in ch. 4, was criticized by several participants who could not agree that transnational enterprises have played so large a part as Kreye argues; indeed it was suggested that their importance is diminishing. On the question whether industrialization has succeeded in alleviating the living conditions of the poor in developing countries, it was pointed out that massive poverty and malnutrition are most conspicuous in those parts of the Third World not so far much penetrated by industrialization.

Discussion of future prospects for the world economy turned in part on whether the optimistic or the pessimistic scenario for the future outlined in ch. 5 (by **Hughes**) is in fact the more likely to be realized. Most participants inclined towards pessimistic views, expressing little confidence in the political will or ability to overcome the obstacles to carrying through the policies needed for a full use of potential resources, either in developed or developing economies.

In discussing the special case of relatively slow growth of the Indian economy (as analysed by **Balasubramanyan** in ch. 8), emphasis was put on the variegated character of the different regions of the huge country – some parts exhibiting a much more successful economic performance than others; the great difficulties of formulating common policies for so large and diverse a territory were also stressed. It was suggested, however, that even if the prospects for faster growth in the 1980s are slim, it should nevertheless be possible by appropriate policies to lay foundations for a more successful economic performance in later years.

On the response of the older industrial economies to the new trends, some participants took a more hopeful view than is sometimes expressed (e.g. in **Plessz's** comments on 'self-fulfilling growth pessimism' in Western Europe in ch. 10). It was maintained that the extent to which structural adjustment has already been achieved, despite recent but limited backslidings into protectionism, is more encouraging for the future than it is often represented to be. In the same vein, the ability of the United States to use its human capacity for speedier adjustment was felt to be under-rated.

The analysis of Japanese development by **Okumura** (ch. 12) was complemented. The relative ease of industrial adjustment in Japan, it was said, rested on historical, political and social factors promoting a strong general consensus on the need for continuous structural change. This consensus was evident before the special issue of NIC competition arose (it emerged, in part, from the perception of industrial overcrowding and environmental damage). Thus successful adjustment appears possible – as in Japan – when a clear idea prevails in industry and government of the necessary pattern of future development. Such clear strategies are less evident elsewhere.

The question was also raised, as might be expected, of the reasons underlying the low level of import penetration by NICs of the Japanese market. One suggested factor was the control of much of Japanese trade by the large trading houses; against this, it was maintained that would-be exporters to Japan lacked adequate marketing systems and sufficiently competitive prices. The issue, as could also be expected, was not resolved.

The final chapter, 13, by **Hager**, gave participants the opportunity for a general appreciation of the policy conclusions that might be drawn and particularly of how the dilemma could be resolved between the rationality which economic theory finds in liberalization of trade and the existence of strong resistances to its application. While some accepted the need to accommodate policies to those resistances – at least as a holding operation to avert collapse of the international system – others were highly sceptical of the concept of a modified system of 'management' of international trade. The limitations of the existing intergovernmental agreements on the conduct of international trade were also stressed. It was pointed out firstly that the effective actors in the international trading system are not only governments; the actual flow of trade can be dominated by the actions and reactions of great enterprises, of groupings of nations, of banking systems, all of which immensely complicates the devising of workable schemes for any form of international trade policies. Moreover, the existing international trade policies, as agreed in the GATT, are much too limited; it is desirable to recreate in some form the institutional arrangements originally contemplated when the postwar system was erected: in particular, there is a need for an institution (like the aborted International Trade Organization) concerned not only with trade but also with commodity stabilization schemes and with capital flows.

The acuteness of the present problems facing international policy-makers, it was suggested, derived from two outstanding and unprecedented features of the present world economy. First, there is no longer a hegemonic power in a position – as the United States was, to a great extent, in earlier postwar years – to take strong and persuasive initiatives in constructing the world trading system, and also to lubricate its operation. Second, the accelerating potential for new nations to 'catch up' by entering the industrial trading system is accompanied in established industrial nations by increasing reluctance, aggravated by recession, to face the problems of adjustment. These two, largely conflicting, impulses may explain the policy uncertainties. Every possible effort must be made to find acceptable solutions which can bring about a smoother integration between the new and old industrial sectors of the world economy than seems likely to occur under the conflict of power groups and policies now prevailing.

International Conference on
'New and Old Industrial Countries in the 1980s'
held at University of Sussex, Brighton, England

6 – 8 January 1980

List of Authors and Participants

List of Authors (marked*) and Participants

* *Professor Henri Aujac*
Director of Studies
Ecole des Hautes Etudes en Sciences Sociales
Paris

* *Dr V. N. Balasubramanyan*
Senior Lecturer in Economics
University of Lancaster
Lancaster, UK

* *Professor R. Baldwin*
Professor of Economics
University of Wisconsin
Madison, Wisconsin, USA

Professor Tibor Barna
Professor of Economics
University of Sussex

Dr Manfred Bienefeld
Fellow
Institute of Development Studies
University of Sussex

* *Ambassador Roberto Campos*
Brazilian Embassy
London

Mrs Miriam Camps
Senior Fellow
Council on Foreign Relations
New York

Dr P. L. Cook
Reader in Economics
University of Sussex

Professor Ronald Dore
Professorial Fellow
Institute of Development Studies
University of Sussex

Mr G. Dosi
Research Student
University of Sussex

Professor François Duchêne, Chairman
Director
Sussex European Research Centre
University of Sussex

* *Dr Wolfgang Hager*
Professor in International Economics
European University Institute
Florence

* *Mrs Helen Hughes*
Economic Analysis and Projections Department
The World Bank
Washington, D.C.

Mr Bimal Jalam
Director
Economic Affairs
Commonwealth Secretariat
London

Mr D. Jones
Senior Research Fellow
Sussex European Research Centre
University of Sussex

Mr N. Kagami
General Manager
Nomura Research Institute
London

Mr M. Kikkawa
Visiting Fellow
Sussex European Research Centre
University of Sussex

* Dr K. W. Kim
  Director of Research
  Korean International Economic Institute
  Seoul, South Korea

* Dr Otto Kreye
  Research Fellow
  Max-Planck Institute
  Starnberg, Federal Republic of Germany

Mr William U. Lawrence
Acting Public Affairs Counsellor
US Mission to the EEC
Brussels

Professor P. Malan
Department of Economics
Pontificia Universidade Catolica do Rio de Janeiro

Mr David Marsden
Research Fellow
Sussex European Research Centre
University of Sussex

Dr Hans Maull
Former European Secretary of the Trilateral Commission
Journalist on Bavarian Radio
Munich, Federal Republic of Germany

Dr J. Müller
Research Fellow
Sussex European Research Centre
University of Sussex

Mr Paul Murphy
Industrial Affairs Officer
US Mission to EEC
Brussels

* Mr A. Okumura
  General Manager
  Industrial Research Department
  The Industrial Bank of Japan
  Tokyo

Mr K. Pavitt
Senior Research Fellow
Science Policy Research Unit
University of Sussex

* *Dr N. Plessz*
Counsellor for Special Studies
Organization for Economic Cooperation and Development
Paris

* *Professor Christopher Saunders*
Professorial Fellow
Sussex European Research Centre
University of Sussex

* *Dr G. Shepherd*
Deputy Director
Sussex European Research Centre
University of Sussex

Professor Hans Singer
Professorial Fellow
Institute of Development Studies
University of Sussex

* *Dr B. Stecher*
Research Fellow
Institut für Weltwirtschaft
University of Kiel, Federal Republic of Germany

Dr C. Stoffaes
Director, Research and Planning
Chef du Centre d'Etudes et de Prévision
Paris

Dr Louis Turner
Senior Research Fellow
Royal Institute of International Affairs
London

* *Dr Raphael Valentino*
Brazilian Embassy
London

Mr M. Wolf
The World Bank
Washington, D.C.

Index

319